S0-AJJ-628

This Wired Home

THIRD EDITION

The Microsoft Guide to Home Networking

Alan Neibauer

PUBLISHED BY
Microsoft Press
A Division of Microsoft Corporation
One Microsoft Way
Redmond, Washington 98052-6399

Copyright © 2002 by Alan R. Neibauer

All rights reserved. No part of the contents of this book may be reproduced or transmitted in any form or by any means without the written permission of the publisher.

Library of Congress Cataloging-in-Publication Data
Neibauer, Alan R.
    This Wired Home : The Microsoft Guide to Home Networking.--3rd ed.
       p. cm.
    Includes index.
    ISBN 0-7356-1494-6
    1. Home computer networks--Amateur's manuals.   2. Home automation--Amateur's manuals. I. Title.

TK5105.75 .N45   2002
004.6'8--dc21   2001059091

Printed and bound in the United States of America.

1 2 3 4 5 6 7 8 9   QWT   7 6 5 4 3 2

Distributed in Canada by Penguin Books Canada Limited.

A CIP catalogue record for this book is available from the British Library.

Microsoft Press books are available through booksellers and distributors worldwide. For further information about international editions, contact your local Microsoft Corporation office or contact Microsoft Press International directly at fax (425) 936-7329. Visit our Web site at www.microsoft.com/mspress. Send comments to *mspinput@microsoft.com*.

Microsoft, Microsoft Press, Midtown Madness, MSN, NetMeeting, and Windows are either registered trademarks or trademarks of Microsoft Corporation in the United States and/or other countries. Other product and company names mentioned herein may be the trademarks of their respective owners.

The example companies, organizations, products, domain names, e-mail addresses, logos, people, places, and events depicted herein are fictitious. No association with any real company, organization, product, domain name, e-mail address, logo, person, place, or event is intended or should be inferred.

Acquisitions Editor: Alex Blanton
Project Editor: Aileen Wrothwell
Technical Editor: Don Lessing

Body Part No. X08-41928

Contents

Part 1

Getting Started

Chapter 2

Getting Connected Without a Network   **21**

Chapter 3

Planning a Network   **59**

Chapter 6
Connecting Your Network

Part 3

Setting Up the Software

Part 4

Running the Network

Chapter 10
Printing Across the Network   **297**

Chapter 11

Going Online Through the Network

Chapter 12

Playing Games

Acknowledgments

Many people deserve my thanks and appreciation for making this book a reality. My thanks to Aileen Wrothwell who served as project editor, coordinating everyone's efforts and keeping the entire process on track, and to Sue McClung, of nSight, who served as project manager.

I also want to thank Don Lesser and his team at Pioneer Training for their careful attention to detail in technical editing, and copyeditor Chrisa Hotchkiss for checking and rechecking this book for accuracy. Because of them, you can be sure that every step and instruction does exactly what it's supposed to do.

Thanks also to Heather Galioto, Tom Fout, Matthew McGinnis, and Andrew Sinclair at Microsoft for their input, and to Chris Kaminski at www.HomeNetHelp.com for his suggestions about troubleshooting information.

Thanks also to Joel Panchot at Microsoft, who redesigned the graphics for the book; Joanna Zito and Mary Beth McDaniel, the production specialists who laid out the text and graphics on the pages; and proofreaders Darla Bruno, Rebecca Merz, and Peter Tietjen.

My thanks also to Alex Blanton, acquisitions editor, and to Claudette Moore, my agent.

Thanks also to James Mustarde at Allied Telesyn for use of the excellent AT-FS716E 16-port Ethernet switch, and to Intel Corporation, WatchGuard, Netopia, ZyXEL, D-Link, U. S. Robotics, SMC, 2-Wire, ORiNOCO, Asanté, and Netgear for their support.

I'd like to thank Barbara Lichtman-Tayar for introducing me to her beautiful and bright children, Gabriel Chai Tayar and Estey Yehudit Tayar.

Finally, my thanks, love, and devotion to Barbara, the woman I am blessed to call my wife and best friend. We had our first date more than 38 years ago, walked down the aisle in marriage three years later, and have never ended the honeymoon.

Introduction

Asking yourself if it pays to connect your home computers in a network? The question really should be "Can I afford NOT to network my computers?"

By creating a home network, you can share printers and files, and even share one Internet connection among all the members of your family. Whether you're at home or somewhere around the world, you can see and talk to other members of your family on a video display without getting out of your chair or making an expensive phone call. You can play games with your family and help with homework even when you're away on business.

Connecting your home computers on a network is neither difficult nor expensive. Anyone can do it, and it costs relatively little. In fact, you can get some of the benefits of setting up a network just by purchasing a single cable that costs less than $20. You can get almost all the benefits of networking for less than $100. And if you have Microsoft Windows, you already have the necessary software, and the networking capability is free. (What a nice word!)

In the old days—maybe as far back as 10 years ago—networking was indeed expensive and difficult. You had to know a lot and spend a good deal of money to set up a network. But that was then. Today, if you hear someone say that setting up a network is too complicated, point out that it's the new millennium and things have changed.

In this book, you'll learn all about connecting your home computers on a network, from simple file-sharing solutions involving a single cable to more advanced systems that hook up your entire home. You'll learn about networks that run with cables and without wires, and you'll learn how to harness the free networking capabilities of Windows. You'll be able to choose the networking solution that's best suited to your own home and needs, even if you have both Windows and Apple Macintosh computers that you'd like to connect on a network. You'll also learn how a home network can include audio and video—letting you share your stereo, television, VCR, DVD player, and other equipment to create an entertainment system for your entire house, as well as home automation.

Microsoft Windows comes in various flavors. Several versions of Windows are designed for home and small-office computing. These include Microsoft Windows 95, Windows 98, Windows Millennium Edition (Me), and Windows XP Home Edition.

Other versions of Windows are designed for business computing. These include Windows XP Professional and its older relatives, Windows NT Server, Windows NT Workstation, and Windows 2000.

Windows 2000 comes in a couple of versions itself—Windows 2000 Professional and Windows 2000 Server. Windows XP Professional, Windows 2000 Server,

Windows NT Server, and Windows NT Workstation are aimed at medium and large corporate networks and they're beyond the scope of this book. Windows 2000 Professional, however, can be used as a desktop operating system in the home as well as business, so I'll discuss its use in home networking in this book. Unless otherwise indicated, "Windows 2000" refers to Windows 2000 Professional, and "Windows XP" refers to Windows XP Home Edition.

Chapter 1 shows you why it pays to connect your home computers on a network, and it describes the main benefits of networking, such as sharing printers and files, sending and receiving e-mail, playing family games, and home automation. In Chapter 2, you'll discover some quick and inexpensive ways to share printers and files even without a network. (This is where the $20 cable comes in.)

In Chapter 3, you'll find out about the different types of networks and the different ways that you can connect your computers: with and without cables. Using this information, you'll be able to start making some initial decisions about your future home network.

Chapter 4 covers the types of network hardware that you can choose among—wired Ethernet, wireless, phone-line, USB, and power-line—and how they can be combined. You'll also learn about the components of a home automation system.

In Chapter 5, you'll learn how to select and install an important piece of equipment called the *network interface card* (NIC). If you don't feel comfortable opening the case of your computer to install a new card, you'll find out about adapters that connect to the USB port, and how to choose a card and then have someone install it for you.

In Chapter 6, you'll see how to connect your computers to create all types of networks. Here, you'll learn more about the types of networking cable and how to run wire from room to room within your home. You'll learn how to create a wireless network, and how to set up phone-line, USB, and power-line hardware. You'll also learn how to create hybrid networks combining wired and wireless hardware, and about wiring for a future home automation system. Chapter 7 guides you through the process of installing the software you need to get your network up and running, and how to troubleshoot network problems.

Sharing a computer and its resources with other members of the family is the subject of Chapters 8, 9, and 10. In Chapter 8, you'll learn how to create and use profiles that let each family member maintain his or her own custom settings on the same computer. In Chapter 9, you'll find out how to share documents, graphics, programs, and other files with the members of your family over the network—one of the best reasons to set up a network. You'll also learn how to back up files for safekeeping and how to manage your network. Sharing printers is covered in detail in Chapter 10. Thanks to your network, you'll be able to use any printer in your home across the network, without having to move disks or printers from room to room.

In Chapter 11, you'll discover the ultimate in sharing: how to set up your network so that every member of the family can surf the Internet at the same time through a single telephone line and modem, or by sharing a high-speed cable or digital subscriber line (DSL) connection. In Chapter 12, the accent is on entertainment, showing you how to play computer games on your network that encourage communication and competition and can also be just great fun.

In Chapter 13, you'll learn how to connect Windows and Apple Macintosh computers on one network so that you'll be able to share files, printers, and even an Internet account.

If you travel for business or pleasure, you'll certainly want to read Chapter 14. There, you'll learn how to stay in touch with the family and access your home computer and network while you're on the road.

Finally, in Chapter 15, you'll explore the exciting future of networking. You'll find out what's happening in home automation, and discover what the future might hold for your home network. You'll learn, for example, about Universal Plug and Play, mobile Internet devices, and universal connectivity. There's also a glossary of networking terms at the back of this book.

Use this book as your personal guide to creating and using a family network. And have some fun while doing it! If you have any questions about setting up your network, you can contact me at alan@neibauer.net.

Part 1

Getting Started

Chapter 1

Why Set Up a Network?

It just makes sense!

You're spending good money on your Internet account, especially if you have a high-speed digital subscriber line (DSL) or cable. So why limit your connection to one person at a time? Wouldn't it be great if everyone in the family could be online at the same time? It can be done if you network.

Say you have a laser printer in your home office while the kids have a color printer. Wouldn't you like to access that color printer from your desktop or laptop, or let the kids print their papers on your laser printer without kicking you off your computer? It can be done if you network.

Need to get to a file you stored on another computer? Want to send a message to the kids that dinner is ready? Tired of searching the house for that CD-ROM or Iomega Zip disk that contains the files you need? Need to back up an important file that's too big to fit on a floppy disk?

All of this (and a lot more) can be done if you network!

See Also

In Chapter 15, "Your Future Home Network," you'll look into the future and see how networking will change the way you live and work.

Sharing an Internet Connection

If you have only one phone line and one Internet account, you know what it's like when several people in the house are competing for the same dial tone. Try to access the Internet while someone else is on the phone, and you won't be able to connect.

It's even worse with a single high-speed DSL or cable Internet account. That expensive DSL or cable modem is connected to one computer, so users of other computers with their old analog modems are just out of luck.

Even if you have two phone lines, you still have a problem. Most *Internet service providers* (ISPs)—the companies through which you connect to the World Wide Web—let only one person per account log on at a time, regardless of the number of screen names or e-mail accounts you have. To add another user, you'd need to set up a second ISP account as well, and that would start to get expensive: two phone bills each month and two ISP charges.

Note

Sharing an Internet account is subject to the terms of the ISP agreement. You should check your membership agreement before sharing an account; some ISPs will allow you to share your account for a small fee. But if the membership agreement forbids account sharing, you shouldn't do it.

When you connect your home computers to a network, everyone in the house can share a single phone line and a single ISP account—or a single DSL or cable modem. You can have everyone chatting online, browsing the Web, and even downloading software, all at the same time. Unfortunately, such sharing also has some drawbacks:

- With a dial-up modem and Internet account, browsing and downloading might be a little slower when someone else is connected. However, at least you're online, and you don't have to wait all night for the phone to be free.

- Sharing an Internet connection might not work with some ISPs. Some require their own special software and won't let you connect using the Windows Dial-Up Networking feature.

See Also

Windows Dial-Up Networking is explained in Chapter 11, "Going Online Through the Network."

- Networking costs more, but the same hardware you need to set up your network will let you share a dial-up account, and the software comes free with all versions of

Windows except Windows 95. You might need to purchase some additional hardware to share a DSL or cable modem, or pay your broadband provider a few extra bucks per month to share an account.

Note

Microsoft Windows 98, Second Edition, Windows Millennium Edition (Me), Windows 2000, and Windows XP all have modem-sharing features built in. With these programs, you don't have to buy any additional software or hardware to share a phone line and an Internet account.

Don't Worry If the Line Is Busy

Nearly all computers come with built-in modems, so you'll probably have a separate modem for each computer in your home. But to avoid dueling over a dial tone, you can connect your home computers in a network and designate a modem on one of them to be *shared*—that is, used by family members on other computers connected to the network. If one modem is faster than the others, such as an ultra-fast cable modem, it makes sense to share the fastest connection. You'll learn how to share modems and Internet accounts in Chapter 11, "Going Online Through the Network," but for now, let's see how sharing a modem on a network can help.

Suppose your computer has the modem that's being shared. Here's what can happen. Another family member working on a computer connected to the network opens a Web browser or uses an e-mail program. The browser or e-mail program goes online using your modem. If your modem isn't connected to the Internet, it dials in and becomes connected. It's as though the other family member reached into your room and dialed the phone with your modem.

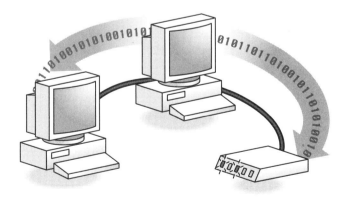

If you're already using the shared modem, other family members on the network just share the ride. They don't have to dial in because the connection to the phone company is already made. When they go online, they won't hear a phone dialing; they just connect.

What if your computer isn't turned on? No problem. Other family members can still go online using their own modems, so long as the line is free.

Getting Your Money's Worth from Your ISP

Because of the way sharing works, a second or third person connecting to the Internet doesn't even have to log on to the ISP. The person wouldn't have to enter a user name or password and wouldn't have to wait until a connection is made. The browser or e-mail program just slips in line with others that are already connected.

As far as the ISP is concerned, you're using only one account, so you pay for only one account. If your ISP offers unlimited use, you don't have to worry. But if your ISP gives you only so many hours for free and charges for additional time, sharing is an even better idea. If two people are on at the same time for one hour, their use counts as only one hour, not two.

Getting the Most from Broadband

If you connect to the Internet through a DSL or cable modem, you might not have to worry about dialing in to the Internet at all, because some DSL and cable connections are always connected. Other broadband connections use a process called Point to Point Protocol over Ethernet (PPPoE), which requires the logon/logoff process each time you connect, but which does not have problems with missing dial tones and busy signals.

Note

PPPoE requires software to manage the initiation of Internet connections and authentication of Internet accounts. Windows XP includes PPPoE software; for other versions of Windows, this software is provided by any ISP that uses PPPoE connections.

If you network your home computers, you can share the broadband connection, which is a tremendous money- and time-saver. Typically, DSL and cable Internet services cost more than dial-up accounts—sometimes twice as much. The modems used to connect to a DSL or cable ISP don't come cheap, either. Most computers come with an analog modem already installed, and you can purchase 56-kilobyte (KB) analog modems for as little as $10 these days; DSL and cable modems, on the other hand, can cost several hundred dollars. In fact, you usually have to lease or purchase the DSL or cable modem from your ISP to make certain it's compatible with their system. Still, DSL and cable modems are perfect for more than one user to share.

With a network, you can share that expensive DSL or cable modem and that costly DSL or cable Internet account. Everyone on the network can access the high-speed account at the same time, with little or no decrease in performance. You don't need to lease or purchase a separate modem for each computer, and you won't need to pay your ISP to set up each computer in the house.

DSL and cable modems connect to a computer through a network Ethernet port, so they are already network-savvy. You or the ISP technician must configure the computer attached to the modem to communicate over something called an Internet Protocol (IP) address. If you have the ISP connect their modem directly to the network, you'll have to pay a monthly charge for each IP address that they set up. By connecting the modem to a network yourself, as you'll learn how to do in this book, you can save these extra charges and make the high-speed account available to everyone.

The Bottom Line

The easiest way to share a phone line and modem is to get a free or inexpensive program and install it on your computer. You'll learn how to get and use such programs in Chapter 11, "Going Online Through the Network." With Windows 98, Second Edition, Windows Me, Windows 2000, and Windows XP, the software is built in.

Sharing Printers

Suppose you have a laser printer connected to your PC, but the kids have a color printer on theirs. If you weren't on a network and wanted to print in color, you'd have to take the following steps:

1. Put the file on a disk.

2. Take the disk to the kids' computer.

3. Print the document on their machine—assuming, that is, that their computer has the program needed to print.

The other option would be to do this:

1. Unplug the color printer from the kids' machine.

2. Carry the printer over to your computer.

3. Unplug your printer and plug in the kids' printer.

4. Install the necessary printer driver on your computer if it's the first time you've used the kids' printer.

5. Print the document.

6. Reverse the procedure to return the printer.

There must be a better way!

When you've set up a network, anyone on the network can connect to any printer, even if the printer is attached to another computer. You don't need to transfer files or printers from computer to computer. These are some of the advantages of using printers on a network:

• If you have only one printer, everyone on the network can use it.

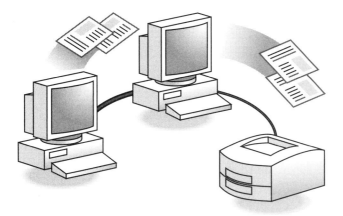

See Also

You'll learn how to share printers in Chapter 2, "Getting Connected Without a Network," and Chapter 10, "Printing Across the Network."

• If you have more than one printer, you can just pick the one you want to use.

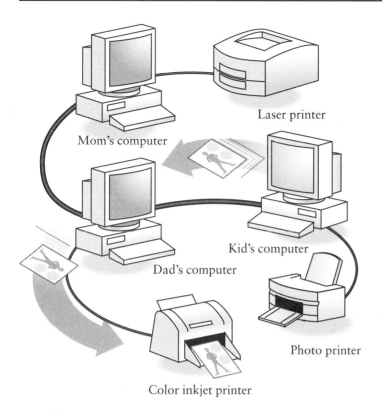

Laser printer

Mom's computer

Kid's computer

Dad's computer

Photo printer

Color inkjet printer

When your computers are on a network, you can print a document on your kids' color printer by following these simple steps:

1. Select Print from the File menu.

2. Choose the printer you want to use.

3. Click OK.

If your printer is in use, the document just waits in line until the printer is free.

Putting the Printer Online

Normally, a printer is connected to a computer through its printer port. When you share a printer that is connected to only one computer, that computer must be turned on before anyone else on the network can use the printer.

But with a home network, you can connect a printer directly to the network, rather than to an individual computer. That way, anyone on the network can use the printer as long as it's turned on.

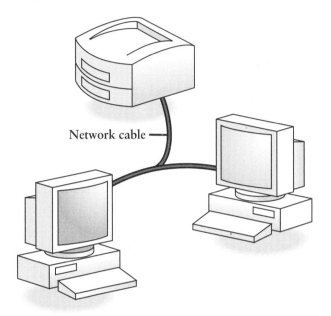

Network cable

Connecting a printer to the network also saves you from the potential problems that can occur when you use your computer's printer port for more than one device. In addition to a printer, you might have a Zip drive, scanner, and other hardware connected to the printer port, which is also called the *parallel port*. Usually, everything works fine. But if you try to use two devices at the same time, you're asking for trouble. If you were to print a document while accessing your Zip drive, for example, your system might freeze. By connecting the printer directly to the network, you avoid this problem by not having to attach it to the parallel port.

The Bottom Line

Networking can save you the expense of buying another printer and the trouble of shuffling disks and printers between computers. You can use any printer that is attached to a computer on the network, getting the most from your investment.

Sharing Files and Folders

If you have more than one computer in the house, sooner or later, you'll need to share files between them. Your spouse might be using your computer to write a letter, for instance, when you'd like to work on a document that you've saved on your hard disk.

If you're not on a network, here's what you have to do before you can begin working:

1. Ask your spouse to stop working for a moment.

2. Copy the file to a floppy disk—assuming it fits on one.

3. Go to another computer in the house, and copy the file from the floppy disk.

Avoiding the Floppy Shuffle

When your computers are on a network, though, you can give other network users permission to access files and folders located on your machine. If others have given you access, you can get to files on their hard disks, too. You just access the files as though they were on your own system. You can copy or move a file from one system to another, and you can even delete a file. Not only do you avoid shuffling floppies, but also you can easily move files around that are too large to fit on a floppy.

Does this mean that all your personal files are available for everyone to read? Not at all. You can control who has access to your files and whether others can just read them or also change and delete them.

Making Files Easy to Find

Because files don't have to be moved from one machine to another, you can designate set locations for certain documents. For example, you can store all the household budget information on the computer in the family room, save investment information on the computer in the spare bedroom, and put miscellaneous files on the kids' machine.

When you need a certain type of document, you'll know exactly where to find it. And if you can't remember which computer the file is stored on, you can search for it on the network by using the handy Find command on the Start menu. (In Windows Me, Windows 2000, and Windows XP, you perform this function using the Search command on the Start menu.)

Keeping Documents Current

"But it's no big deal to copy a file to a floppy," you might be thinking. Maybe not. But even if the inconvenience of copying the file doesn't bother you, you might end up with "version nightmare." Here's a scenario that might sound familiar.

You have your budget on the computer in the den and you want to work on it in the spare bedroom, so you copy it to a floppy and move it to the hard disk on the bedroom computer. You make some additions, a few changes, one or two deletions, and then save the budget on the bedroom computer's hard disk. As you're working, your spouse decides to make a few changes to the version of the file on the den computer. So now you have three versions of the budget: the one on the bedroom computer, the one on the floppy, and the one on the den computer. And of course, none of them match.

When your computers are on a network, you can just access the computer in the den from any other computer in the house, making changes to the budget in its original location. If someone else tries to access the file while you're working on it, that person gets a message saying that the file is in use. Once you're done with the file, you can be sure that anyone who uses it after you will be working with the most recent version.

Working Together

Because networking allows you to share files, you can collaborate with other family members. After you make changes to the budget, for example, your spouse can review what you've done. You can take a look at your child's homework, suggest some improvements, and then let your child make the corrections before printing it out.

Most word processing programs help you collaborate by tracking revisions. *Revision marks* in the document show the text you think should be deleted, rather than actually deleting it. They can also indicate—with a color and formatting—text you've added. Figure 1-1 shows a document in Microsoft Word 2002 that's been edited with revision marks: changes are easy to see, and they can quickly be incorporated into the final document. You can also add a *comment*, a short note that doesn't appear on the screen but is indicated by a color or an abbreviation. To display the comment, you simply point to the color or the abbreviation, and the text appears in a small pop-up box.

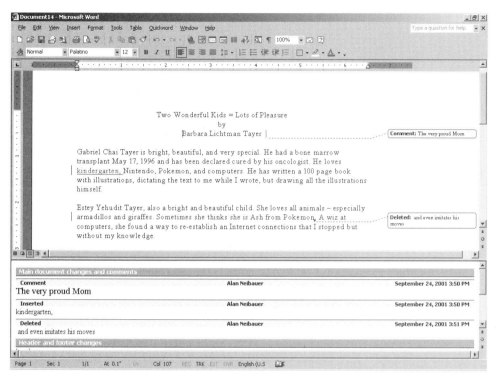

Figure 1-1.

Collaborating on a document on the network.

Safeguarding Important Documents

While you want only one *working* copy of a file, you can make *backup* copies on other machines. That way, if a hard disk goes berserk and the original file is corrupted or lost, you'll always have a safety net.

You should always back up important files. You can copy them to a Zip disk or, if they're small enough, to a floppy disk. If the original file gets damaged, all you have to do is retrieve the backup. When you're on a network, you can also back up files to another hard disk on the system, taking advantage of the larger disk drives found on newer computers. Moving a file from one networked computer to another is faster than making backups on a tape or a series of floppy disks. In addition, the backup version is available to everyone on the network.

The Bottom Line

When you set up a network, you save time and trouble by sharing files, while maintaining privacy and security. You can avoid multiple versions of the same file, locate files easily, and back up files for safekeeping. As your disk becomes full, you can avoid upgrading to a larger disk by storing your files on a computer that has extra room, a feature that saves you money and time.

See Also

You'll learn how to share documents in Chapter 9, "Learning to Share."

Sharing CD-ROMs and Removable Drives

CD-ROMs and removable drives, such as Zip drives and Superdisks, are a real boon to computer users. They store vast amounts of information, and they're fast, safe, and convenient. These days, most computers come with CD-ROM drives and many also come with removable disk drives.

Escaping the CD Shuffle

Many people keep an encyclopedia or some other reference CD in their CD-ROM drive at all times. Whenever they need to look up a word, find a map, or do some research, they can access the information quickly and easily.

Most computer programs, such as the Windows program itself, are supplied on CDs to save space. (Windows, for example, would fill hundreds of floppy disks.) When you're working with a program or doing some magic on the computer, you might need to access the CD. Take Microsoft Office XP, for example. When you install Office, just the main parts of the program are usually copied to your hard disk. When you want to use a feature that hasn't been installed, Office automatically checks the CD for the necessary information. If the CD isn't in the drive, you have to insert it. This would mean removing the encyclopedia or other CD from the drive and inserting the Office CD. When you finished installing the Office feature, you would once again have to swap CDs.

With a network, you can access any CD on any computer on the network. So that means you can leave the CD for your encyclopedia or other program in the drive of one machine and access it from any other one.

You can also use a network to create virtual CD drives. This means copying the contents of a CD to a special file on one of the networked computers. A virtual CD program, like those we'll discuss in Chapter 9, "Learning to Share," lets you treat the file as an actual CD drive.

Adding Zip to Your Life

A Zip drive is one of the greatest add-ons you can get for your computer. The newest Zip disks, the storage media used in Zip drives, can store up to 250 megabytes (MB) of information—all on a cartridge small enough to fit in a shirt pocket!

Of course, Zip disks aren't the only high-capacity disks available. Superdisks, for example, are popular with iMac computer users. Because the iMac computer doesn't include a built-in floppy disk, many users purchase a Superdisk drive that plugs into the iMac's universal serial bus (USB) port and that can store 240 MB of data on one easy-to-carry disk. In addition, Iomega Clik! drives can store 40 MB per disk, and Jaz drives can store up to 2 gigabytes (GB) of data on a removable cartridge.

You can also consider a rewriteable CD drive, called a *CD-RW*. A CD-RW lets you record information on a CD that can be used in almost any computer. You might not be able to directly record information on a CD-RW that's attached to another computer on the network, but you can easily transfer your files over the network so that they can be recorded on the CD. You can then use the CD on any computer that has a CD drive, which is far more common than Zip, Jaz, and Clik! drives, Superdisks, and other forms of removable media. Removable disks are great for backups and for transferring files that are too large to fit on a floppy. They're also terrific for storing those files you don't need often but still want to have around. Anyone on the network can access a removable drive that's attached to one of the computers. They can access files from the drive and save files to it.

Some removable drives are built into the computer. When the drive is attached to the computer's parallel port, though, you have to be careful. No one can access the drive while that machine is printing.

You can also use removable drives that plug into your computer's USB port. These drives are the easiest to connect. They don't interfere with printers and other devices connected to the parallel port, and they can be plugged in without restarting the computer. You can also use USB devices on both PCs and iMac computers, so you can share the drive with computers even if they aren't connected to a network.

See Also

You'll learn how to share disks in Chapter 9, "Learning to Share."

The Bottom Line

You can save money by buying one removable drive and sharing it with other members of the family, and you can access files on a CD without swapping CDs in your own machine.

Communicating with Others

With everyone on a separate computer and, perhaps, connected to the Internet, you might think that there would be less personal communication in the family. Although that is a possibility, people have complained about that sort of problem since the invention of record players (now CD players, of course), television, and video games.

Networking might not bring the family closer together physically, but it does foster its own brand of communication.

Using an Electronic Intercom

By using a system known as instant messaging (IM), you can find out whether a friend across town—or across the world—is online and send a message that pops up on that person's screen. You can also send pop-up messages within the family network, as a sort of electronic intercom. The software for this comes with Windows 95, Windows 98, and Windows Me, but not Windows 2000 and Windows XP. You can download pop-up messaging software from the Internet that can be used with Windows 2000 and Windows XP.

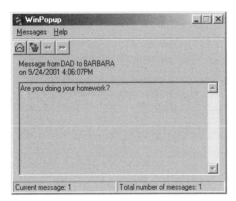

If your computer is equipped with microphones and speakers, you can also speak to each other through the network, and if your computers are equipped with cameras, you can even see each other.

Note

You can also send and receive messages to each other by using Internet instant messaging programs, such as those provided by MSN, Yahoo!, America Online (AOL), or the Windows Messenger program of Windows XP.

In addition, using software that you can download from the Internet, you can leave electronic "sticky notes" on other peoples' computers, as long as their computers are turned on. The notes appear on their desktop.

Note

Some sources for sticky-note software include Netnote from Alshare, which can be used with Windows 95 and Windows 98; Stickynote from Phord Software (*http://www.phord.com/stickynote.html*), which can be used only with Windows 95; and NoteWonder from Forty Software (*http://www.forty.com*), which works with Windows 2000.

Staying in Touch

It's never been easier for traveling family members to stay in touch. By using a laptop computer to dial in to the network at home, they can send and receive e-mail, transfer files, and even update their calendars. And once again, the software used to make the connection comes with Windows 95, Windows 98, Windows Me, Windows 2000, and Windows XP.

The Bottom Line

Networking opens all sorts of communication channels that might otherwise be closed. You can send quick notes that appear directly on the screen of other computers—just like Internet instant messaging. The family can share a calendar to keep track of important events, birthdays, and other family happenings. And when someone is on the road or away at school, the family connection can be maintained.

See Also

You'll learn how to communicate over the network in Chapter 9, "Learning to Share."

Playing Family Games

As the old saying goes, "The family that plays together stays together." And that's another strong case for networking. Play is a form of communication, and families can use computer games to enhance their quality time together. Kids love to play action games on their computers, while parents might enjoy more cerebral pastimes such as bridge, hearts, or chess.

Setting Up for Multiplayer Gaming

On a network, family members can go head-to-head in games of all sorts, many of them inexpensive or even free. Each member of your family can be sitting at a different computer but interacting in a virtual environment in which you can see each other, compete against each other, or even cooperate with each other against a common foe. You can all be racing on the same track or moving around some science fiction landscape trying to solve a puzzle together.

Games on the network can also keep score for you automatically, so there's no arguing over who's right or wrong, who shot first, or who's cheating. Many games will even remember the score, enabling you to pause and pick up later where you left off, or keep a running record for everyone to see.

The Bottom Line

Through interactive game playing, the entire family can share adventures without leaving the house. You'll draw the family closer together even when you're all playing in different rooms. You can compete individually or in teams, and you can have more than one game going if not everyone wants to play the same one.

See Also

You'll learn how to play games on the network in Chapter 12, "Playing Games."

Bridging PCs and Macs

Why can't we all just learn to live together and share? Because there are PCs and there are Macintoshes. These two types of computers use different operating systems and store information on disk in different ways. A Mac doesn't use Windows unless you add special hardware and software, and the programs you get with or purchase for your PC or Mac can't be run on the other machine.

Popping a floppy out of your Mac and into your PC, for example, doesn't mean you'll be able to use it in the PC. In fact, an entire new breed of Mac, the colorful iMac computer, doesn't even come with a floppy drive.

Note

Macintosh computers with floppy disks do have the ability to read and write to PC-formatted disks. But you can't read a Mac disk in a PC unless you get special software.

That doesn't mean that PCs and Macs can't live together in harmony. When your computers are connected on a network, your PCs and Macs can indeed talk to each other. You can share files and printers; you can even share an Internet account.

Although you can't use the same program with each type of computer, many programs come in two versions. You can get Office, for example, in both Windows and Mac versions. So if you write a document with Microsoft Word or a spreadsheet with Microsoft Excel on your PC, someone else in the house can read and edit the document or spreadsheet on her Mac.

See Also

In Chapter 13, "Networking PCs and Macs," you'll learn how to connect your PCs and Macs on the network.

Making It Educational

By connecting your computers on a network, you'll also learn more about computers and software. You'll become familiar with the role networks play in society because all networks, large and small, enjoy the same benefits, but just on different levels. If you have children who are old enough, let them share in the process of setting up the network. They can help make decisions, run wires, even help install software. The experience will give them an edge in school and maybe even point them toward a career.

Home Entertainment and Automation

While networking traditionally involves computers and their peripherals, advances in technology give the term a whole new meaning. A home network can incorporate home entertainment equipment to share audio and video with the entire family, and enable lighting and other appliances to automate many functions.

Imagine, for example, controlling all of your home's lights, your security system, your heating and cooling system—even the coffeepot and bread maker—from anywhere in the house. Imagine being able to control your audio system, television, DVD, or VCR from every room of the house.

Some of this technology is already available (as you will learn in Chapter 15, "Your Future Home Network"), so you could start incorporating home automation into your network now. But tremendous advances in home automation await just around the corner, bringing a network of home entertainment and control into everyone's budget.

The Bottom Line

For one reason or another, connecting your home computers on a network is a time-saver, a money-saver, and just a smart move. In the following chapters, you'll learn how to design, install, and use a home network, but first, you'll learn how to accomplish some basic networking tasks without having to set up a network.

Chapter 2

Getting Connected Without a Network

Now that you're all excited about networking, here's a small surprise: Sometimes you might not need a network at all. Perhaps you're interested in sharing a printer and occasionally transferring some files between computers, but you don't want to play games or send and receive e-mail among the family. Maybe you'd rather communicate in person, the old-fashioned way. While you'll be missing out on the many other benefits of using a network if you choose not to hook one up, you can still share printers and files, which is the subject of this chapter.

When Sharing a Printer Is Enough

If you're considering sharing a printer, take a look at the distance between the computers and the printer. If they're all located in the same room, sharing the printer will be a piece of cake. You won't need to purchase expensive devices that help you share printers and you won't need to run wires from room to room.

   If the computers and printers are in different rooms, your options will be a bit trickier and more costly. Printer cable is thick and not that easy to fish through walls or hide along the baseboard. In addition, because a standard printer cable shouldn't be more than 15 feet (4.5 meters) long (any longer and the signals fade on their way to the printer), you'll need to buy extra hardware if the devices you're linking are far apart. *If the computer and printer are far apart, see "Extending Your Reach," later in this chapter.*

Using Printer Switches

When two computers and a printer are near each other, the easiest way to share the printer is with a printer switch. The least expensive type is a manual switch box with a knob that you turn by hand. As shown in Figure 2-1, you connect a cable from one computer to the A side of the switch, and a second cable from the other computer to the B side. You then connect a printer cable from the printer to the printer connection on the switch. The printer connection is usually labeled *common* because it's connected to the device shared by the two computers.

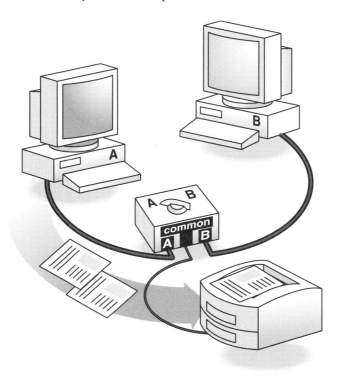

Figure 2-1.
You can connect two computers and a printer with a switch box.

When the knob is in the A position, the job you're printing flows from the A computer, through the box, and into the printer. When the knob is in the B position, the job flows from the B computer, through the switch, and into the printer. Some switch boxes can link three, four, or even more computers to the same printer.

Manual switches have a few drawbacks, however. You must position the switch so that users at both computers can reach it easily, preferably from their chairs. In addition, if either person forgets to turn the switch before trying to print a document, assumes the document has gone through to the printer, and then exits the word processor without saving the file, the document might be lost. Although all versions of Microsoft Windows will display a printer error message, it might be too late to retrieve the document by then.

Similarly, if you turn the switch while someone else is printing, you can cut off a print job in the middle. This unexpected interruption can cause another error message and generate some glares. Wait until the printer has stopped printing completely before turning the switch.

Some people used to believe that turning a manual switch while the printer was powered on could damage some printers. This might have been true in the early days of computers and printers, but it's no longer a concern with newer, more robust printers and switch boxes. Of course, if you worry about such problems, just shut off the printer before turning the switch, and then turn the printer back on.

Finally, as printers become more sophisticated and complex, you must make sure of the quality of the electrical signals going to them. Printer cables should be labeled "bidirectional" and "IEEE 1284–compliant." *Bidirectional* means that the cable is capable of carrying signals both to and from the printer, thus allowing the printer to keep the computer informed about its printing status. *IEEE 1284–compliant* means that the cable meets industry standards for quality.

When you connect the cable, make sure that all connections are tight and that they can't slip off. Switch boxes not only extend the path that the signals must travel to get to the printer, but they also introduce additional connections that have to be checked. Make sure to check them regularly.

On the positive side, a switch box for two computers and one printer (called a *2-to-1 switch*) can cost less than $15. Use the existing printer cable to connect the switch box to the printer, and buy two additional cables (costing approximately $15 each) to run from the printer ports of the computers to the switch box. These cables have 25-pin male connectors at both ends, as shown here, to fit the female connectors at the back of the computer and at the switch. So for around $50, you can share a printer between two computers.

To link your computers to a printer via a switch box, follow these simple steps:

1. Make sure the computers and printer are turned off.

2. Disconnect the printer cable from the computer, and plug it into the "C" or "common" connection on the switch.

3. Connect either end of one of the new cables to the printer port on the back of one of the computers.

4. Connect the other end of the cable to the A connector on the back of the switch.

5. Connect one end of the other new cable to the printer port of the second computer.

6. Connect the other end of that cable to the B connector on the back of the switch.

Figure 2-2 illustrates the process described above.

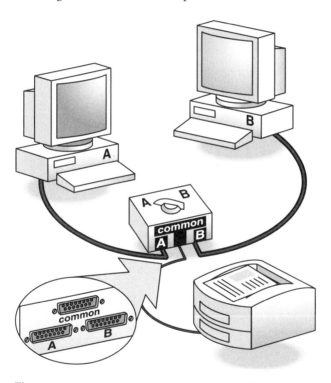

Figure 2-2.

Connecting two computers and one printer to a switch box.

You can use the same type of switch, by the way, to connect two printers (a laser printer and a color inkjet printer, for example) to one computer. To install both printers, use the Add Printer Wizard in the Print dialog box. (Click Start, choose Settings, and then click Printers.) Make sure to select the same printer port for both printers. Then hook up the switch box as shown in Figure 2-3.

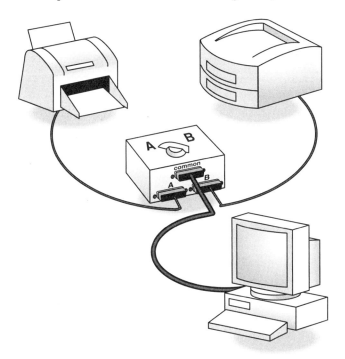

Figure 2-3.
A switch box can connect two printers to one computer.

With the computer and printers turned off, connect the printers to the A and B connectors on the switch box and the computer to the common connector. It's that simple. Before you print a document, select the correct printer in the application's Print dialog box and turn the switch to that printer. There is usually a Name field with a drop-down list of printers in every application's Print dialog box. Select the list and choose the printer you want before clicking the Print button in the dialog box.

Putting It on Automatic

Automatic switches hook up like manual switches, but there's no switch to turn. An automatic switch is like a traffic officer in the middle of the intersection, managing the flow of print jobs to the printer. The switch electronically watches the incoming cables for a document that needs to be printed. If the printer is busy and a document comes in from another computer, the switch holds up its hand and says, "Wait." When the printer is free, it says, "OK, it's your turn," and sends the next print job through.

Costing between $50 and $100, automatic switches are more expensive than manual switches. Some models can handle just two computers and one printer; others can link several computers and several printers. The JetDirect auto switch from Hewlett-Packard, for example, can accommodate four computers sharing a single printer. To install it, you connect a cable from each computer to one of the four ports on the switch, and then connect the common port to the printer.

You can place the switch in manual or automatic mode. In manual mode, you have to press a button on the device to change printers. In automatic mode, the switch constantly scans the incoming lines for activity to the printer. It then sends the documents to the printer in the order they are received.

You can use the same switch to connect up to four different devices, such as a printer, a scanner, and a Zip drive, to one computer's printer port. In this configuration, you connect a device to each of the four ports on the switch, and then connect your computer to the common port on the switch.

When you use a switch to connect several devices to one computer, it's useful to be able to specify which device you want to use from within Windows. The JetDirect auto switch comes with its own software. A screen from this software is shown below.

With this software, you can specify whether you're sharing one device among multiple computers or several devices on one computer. If you select One PC Sharing Multiple Devices, you can click Advanced and specify the device that is connected to each port, as shown below.

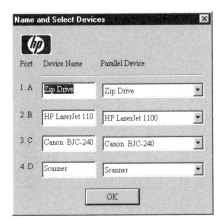

To use a device, select it by clicking the JetDirect icon on the Windows taskbar.

Note

When you add a Zip drive to the switch, you must connect it to port A so that Windows will be able to detect it properly.

We Need a Buffer Here

Not all automatic switches are created equal. Some of the inexpensive models lack a key feature that can prevent traffic tie-ups. Let's say that Tom sends a document to the printer first. While it's being transmitted and printed, you try to print a document from your computer. Because the printer is busy, your job is held up, waiting in line until the printer is free. Until Tom's job is printed and yours begins, you might not be able to exit the application you're using. You'll have the same trouble if you use a switch to connect several devices to one computer. While a job is being printed, you won't be able to access the Zip drive, for example, or scan a document by using other devices connected to the switch.

The solution is a *buffer*, a device that contains memory and is installed between the computer and the printer. Now, as Tom's job prints, your document is fed directly into the buffer's memory. As far as your computer is concerned, the document is off and printed, so you can go on to other work. When Tom's job is done, your document is printed from the buffer's memory.

Some automatic switches come with their own built-in buffers, or you can purchase separate buffer devices that connect between the switch and the printer, as shown below.

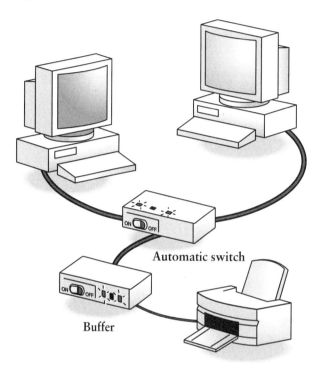

Automatic switch

Buffer

Extending Your Reach

No one wants to get up and walk into another room to flick a manual switch. Fortunately, there's a special type of automatic switch designed for use with computers that are far apart or in separate rooms. The most common model employs transmitters that are plugged into the printer port of each computer and a receiver that plugs into the printer's parallel port. The transmitters and receiver are connected with regular telephone cable. Such devices can link up to 30 computers, with a total distance between them of 2000 feet. The Extended Systems ShareLink product is one example of these systems. Some of these systems also let you print from a computer's serial port to a parallel printer.

If you need to extend the distance between just a single computer and a printer, install a transmitter on the computer's printer port and connect a receiver to the printer or to one side of a switch, as shown in Figure 2-4. The printer signals can go a lot farther on the telephone cable used to connect the transmitter and receiver than they can on a regular printer cable. To add another computer to the configuration, just buy another transmitter.

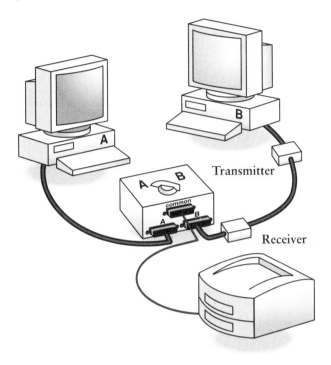

Figure 2-4.
Extending the distance to a switch.

Devices also exist that enhance the signals from your computer so that you can link it to a printer up to 50 feet (15 meters) away, using standard printer cable. Most of these devices plug into the computer's printer port to amplify the signal before it's transmitted down the printer cable.

Making a Direct Connection

One great benefit of networking is the capability it gives you to transfer files between two computers. But if you need to do this only occasionally and the two computers are close to each other, there's another way to hook up your computers and save some money in the process. Microsoft Windows 95, Windows 98, Windows Millennium Edition (Me),

Windows 2000, and Windows XP let you connect two computers with one simple cable. That's why it's called a *direct cable connection*. With this system, you can transfer files between two non-networked computers or between a networked and a non-networked computer. The direct cable connection can be between any two Windows machines—both machines do not have to be using the same version of Windows.

Note

You can connect two computers directly and get all the benefits of a network at low cost by using a special universal serial bus (USB) cable and software. See the section "Working Without Cards," in Chapter 5, "Installing Network Cards and Adapters," on page 100.

One Simple Cable Is All It Takes

To set up a direct cable connection you need a cable, of course. With all versions of Windows, including Windows XP, you can use any of four types of cables:

- A null modem serial cable

- An Extended Capabilities Port (ECP) parallel cable

- A Universal Cable Module (UCM) parallel cable

- A Standard (also known as Basic) 4-bit parallel cable

Of these four options, the ECP parallel cable is probably your best bet. Information flows faster through parallel cables than through serial cables, and the ECP cable is cheaper and easier to find than the UCM cable. The Standard 4-bit parallel cable was popular in the past, but it's no longer easily available, and it's slower than the ECP cable anyway.

Cables used for a direct cable connection have the same type of connection on both ends because they're going into the same plug on both computers. If there's a cable connecting your parallel port to a switch box, you could try that cable for a direct cable connection, but it probably won't work. The cable might look like the one you need, but it won't be able to handle file transfers. You're better off getting a separate cable.

When you buy the cable at the computer store, ask for "a parallel cable to use with a direct cable connection in Windows." You'll probably be given LapLink cables, named after the program that's a popular alternative to a direct cable connection.

Note

If the store doesn't have a cable for a direct cable connection and you have to transfer files right away, consider buying a file transfer program, such as LapLink, which comes with its own cable. We'll look at such options in the section "Another Way to Share Files and Printers," later in this chapter.

Installing the Software

Once you have the cable, the software you need is free and built into all versions of Windows, including Windows XP. Follow these steps to make sure that the software has been installed.

Note

The instructions in the following three sections apply to Windows 95, Windows 98, and Windows Me. To set up a direct cable connection with Windows 2000 or Windows XP, refer to the section "Using a Direct Connection with Windows 2000 or Windows XP," later in this chapter.

1. Click Start on the Windows taskbar.

2. Point to Programs, and then point to Accessories on the Programs submenu.

3. In Windows 95, look for Direct Cable Connection on the Accessories menu. In Windows 98 and Windows Me, you may have to point to Communications on the Accessories submenu.

Do you see Direct Cable Connection on the menu that appears? If you do, skip ahead to the section "Choosing a Protocol." If you don't see Direct Cable Connection, you'll have to add it. You might need your Windows CD to do this, so make sure you know where it is, and then follow these steps:

1. Click Start, point to Settings, and then click Control Panel on the Settings submenu.

2. In Control Panel, double-click Add/Remove Programs.

3. Click the Windows Setup tab in the Add/Remove Programs Properties dialog box.

4. On the Windows Setup tab, shown in Figure 2-5, click the word "Communications," but don't click the check box next to Communications or you'll remove the check mark.

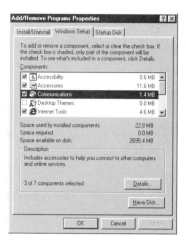

Figure 2-5.

Add Direct Cable Connection by using the Add/Remove Programs Properties dialog box.

5. Click the Details button.

6. Click to select the check box next to Direct Cable Connection, as shown here.

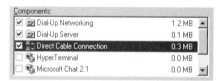

7. Click OK to close the Communications dialog box.

8. Click OK to close the Add/Remove Programs Properties dialog box.

Here's where you might need your Windows CD. On some computers, the files that Windows needs to add more components are stored on the hard disk. If so, Direct Cable Connection will be installed and you're ready for the next stage. If the files aren't on your hard disk, you'll be asked to insert the Windows CD. Put the CD in the drive and click OK. The Direct Cable Connection feature will then be installed. You might be asked to restart your computer.

Choosing a Protocol

For two people to communicate, they must know the same language, or be awfully good at charades. The same goes for computers, but with computers, we call the shared language a *protocol*. The two computers use the same protocol to be able to understand what the other is saying.

A lot of different protocols exist, but for home networking, only three are important: Transmission Control Protocol/Internet Protocol (TCP/IP), Internetwork Packet Exchange/Sequenced Packet Exchange (IPX/SPX), and NetBIOS Enhanced User Interface (NetBEUI, pronounced *net-buoy*). IPX/SPX is the one you need for a direct cable connection, but it's best to make sure that all three protocols are installed in Windows, just in case you need them.

If you're running Windows 95, Windows 98, or Windows Me, here's how to see whether the protocols are on your computer and how to install them if you need to:

1. Click Start, point to Settings, and then click Control Panel on the Settings submenu.

2. In Control Panel, double-click Network. The Network dialog box, shown in Figure 2-6, appears.

Figure 2-6.

The network components list shows the protocols that are installed.

On the Configuration tab of the Network dialog box, look for the big three—TCP/IP, IPX/SPX, and NetBEUI. If any of them aren't listed, you'll have to add them. Follow these steps to add a protocol:

1. In the Network dialog box, click Add to see the Select Network Component Type dialog box, shown below.

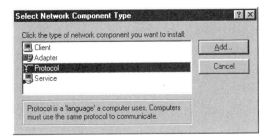

2. Click Protocol, and then click Add.

3. Click Microsoft in the list of manufacturers to see the options shown in Figure 2-7.

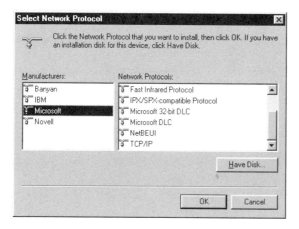

Figure 2-7.
Select a protocol to install.

4. In the Network Protocols list, select the protocol you want to add, and then click OK.

5. Repeat steps 1 through 4 to add the other two protocols, if necessary.

6. When you're done, click OK to close the Network dialog box. A message tells you that you must restart your computer for these new additions to work.

7. Click OK to restart the computer.

Setting Up a Direct Cable Connection

Now that the protocols you need are installed, you're ready to set up a direct cable connection. With the two computers turned off, plug in the connecting cable. If you're using a parallel cable, make sure the printer is off, remove the printer cable, and then plug the new cable into the printer port. If your cable is a serial cable, plug it into the computer's serial or COM port.

Now that the hardware is set up, you need to deal with the software end of things. First, you have to choose one computer to be the host and the other to be the client. The *host* machine contains the information you want to get to. The *client* is the computer you will use to access the information.

After you've chosen a host computer, you need to allow its files and folders to be shared. *Sharing* means that other users can view and work with them over a network and over the cable connection.

You can provide access to your entire hard drive or just to selected folders. Sharing your entire drive in one step makes it easy for other users to get to the files they need. If you're worried about security, you can limit another user's access to just reading and copying files but not changing or deleting them. If you want to keep another user from even seeing certain folders on your drive, it's possible to share only those folders you want to make available.

To allow access to the entire drive on the host, follow these steps:

1. Double-click My Computer on the desktop.

2. Right-click the C: drive.

3. Click Sharing on the shortcut menu to open the Properties dialog box shown in Figure 2-8.

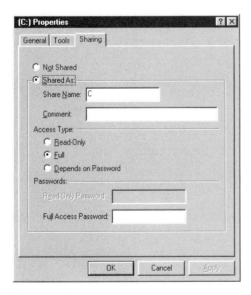

Figure 2-8.
You can change how drives and folders are shared on the Sharing tab of the Properties dialog box.

4. If Sharing doesn't appear on the Quick menu, you'll have to enable File Sharing. In Control Panel, select Network, and click the File And Print Sharing button. Select I Want To Be Able To Give Others Access To My Files, and click OK. Click OK to close the Network dialog box. You'll have to restart your computer to enable File Sharing.

5. On the Sharing tab of the Properties dialog box, click Shared As.

6. You can leave the Share Name field as is, or replace it with another name that others connecting to your computer will see. You should use a descriptive name, such as "Dad's C: Drive," to help others identify the computer and hard drive that are being shared.

7. In the Access Type section of the dialog box, choose the type of access you want to offer to others:

   • **Read-Only** means that the person on the guest computer can copy and look at information on the host but not delete or change the information. The person on the guest computer can't, for example, add a file to the host computer.

   • **Full** means that the person on the guest computer can do anything at all to the information on the host, including adding, deleting, or editing files.

   • **Depends On Password** determines the level of access according to the password the guest enters, either a read-only or a full access password.

8. Depending on the type of access you've chosen, you can enter a password in either the Read-Only Password field, in the Full Access Password field, or in both fields. If you don't want to require a password, you can leave these fields blank.

9. Click OK.

10. If you entered a password, a dialog box opens asking you to confirm it. Reenter the password, and then click OK.

   A small hand attached to the drive icon, shown below, indicates that the drive is shared.

Note

You also can choose to share only specific folders. Right-click a folder in My Computer, choose Sharing, and then set the folder's sharing properties in the Properties dialog box.

Now start the direct cable connection on the host computer by following these steps:

1. Click Start, point to Programs, and then point to Accessories on the Program submenu.

2. In Windows 95, click Direct Cable Connection. In Windows 98 or Windows Me, point to Communications and then click Direct Cable Connection on the Communications submenu.

If this is the first time you're running a direct cable connection, you'll see the dialog box in Figure 2-9.

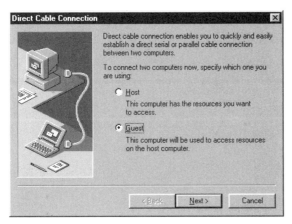

Figure 2-9.
Choose whether the computer you're using is a host or a guest.

3. Click Host and then click Next.

4. In the Direct Cable Connection dialog box, shown in Figure 2-10, select the port you're using, and then click Next.

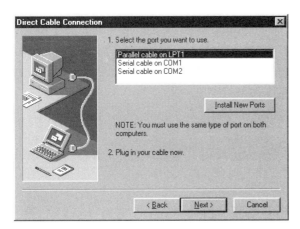

Figure 2-10.
Select the port you're using.

5. If you want to require the person using the guest computer to enter a password, select the check box labeled Use Password Protection, and then click Set Password. In the next dialog box, enter the password in both fields and click OK.

6. Click Finish.

A message reports that the host computer is waiting for the guest computer to connect, as shown below.

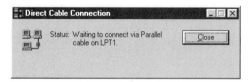

7. Now follow the same procedure on the guest computer, but select Guest in the first dialog box rather than Host.

When you click Finish, the machines connect. On both machines, you see messages that they're verifying the user name and password. Then the guest computer reports that it's looking for shared folders. Finally, the host computer shows a message, such as this one, to indicate that both computers are connected:

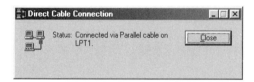

The next time you start a direct cable connection on the host computer, you'll see the dialog box shown in Figure 2-11. Click Listen if you are the host. To change from being the host to being the guest, click Change. (If you are the guest computer, click Connect after starting a direct cable connection.)

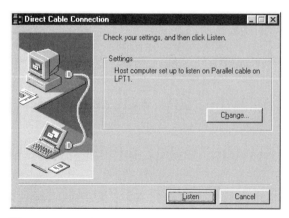

Figure 2-11.

Starting Direct Cable Connection on the host computer after the first time.

Using a Direct Cable Connection

After you connect the host and guest computers, the guest computer displays a dialog box showing the shared resources on the host, as shown in Figure 2-12. The person using the guest computer can then open any shared folder to access its files and move or copy files between the two computers using the drag-and-drop method.

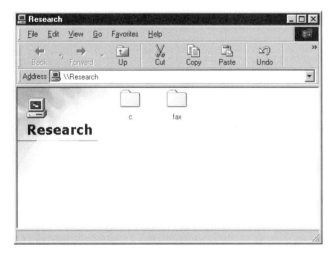

Figure 2-12.
The shared resources on the host computer are visible on the guest computer.

Note

If the guest computer cannot locate the shared folders, a message might appear asking for the name of the host computer. Enter the host computer name and click OK.

See Also

To learn the name of the host computer, ask the person who set up the computer. For instructions on finding a computer's name, refer to the section "Identifying Your Computer on the Network," in Chapter 7, "Installing the Software," on page 176.

The host computer must leave the Direct Cable Connection dialog box open on the screen. Closing this dialog box stops the connection and causes the guest to receive a message that the connection has been closed. With the Direct Cable Connection dialog box open, you can always click View Host to display the shared folders on the host computer.

Using a Direct Connection with Windows 2000 or Windows XP

Setting up and running a direct connection between Windows 2000 or Windows XP computers is slightly different than for Windows 95, Windows 98, and Windows Me. The software for a direct connection is installed by default when you install Windows 2000 or Windows XP. You do, however, have to set your computer to act as a host or guest, and you must make sure the proper protocols are installed.

First, see whether your computer is already set up as a guest or as a host. Remember, the host computer makes its resources available to the guest computer. The guest computer will be initiating the connection.

Note

Two computers running Windows XP that have FireWire adapters installed can network directly through these adapters. Windows XP automatically configures a network for the FireWire adapter, and the network runs just as though two Ethernet network cards were installed and connected.

To find out the status of your computer if you're using Windows 2000, perform the following steps:

1. Double-click My Computer on your Windows desktop.
2. Click Network And Dial-Up Connections.

If you see an icon for Direct Connection, your computer is set up to act as the guest by connecting to another computer. If you see the icon for Incoming Connections, your computer is set up as the host. The Make New Connections icon allows you to create a new connection. These icons are shown below.

Make New   Direct   Incoming
Connection   Connection   Connections

To find out the status of your computer if you are using Windows XP, click Start, point to Connect To, and click Show All Connections to open the Network Connections window. If you see an icon for a direct connection, your computer is set up to act as the guest by connecting to another computer. If you see an icon for incoming connections, your computer is set up as the host. These icons are shown on the next page.

Direct

Valinor
Disconnected
Direct Parallel

Incoming

Incoming Connections
No clients connected

Note

The Connect To option only appears once you've set up a direct connection or an Internet account in Windows XP Home Edition, and it doesn't appear at all in Windows XP Professional. If Connect To is not an option on your Start menu, click Start, point to My Network Places, and then click View Network Connections.

Setting Up a Direct Connection

If one or neither of the icons appears, you have to set up your computer before you make a direct connection. This involves selecting the option of acting as a host or guest for the connection and selecting the connection device to be used. The connection device options in both Windows 2000 and Windows XP include

- Infrared Port (IRDA0-0)
- Direct Parallel (LPT1)
- Communications Port (COM2)
- Communications Port (COM1)

An infrared port is normally found on laptop computers, but it might also be on or added to a desktop computer. The direct parallel port is the printer port on your computer, and the communications ports are the serial ports.

Setting Up a Direct Connection with Windows 2000   To set up your computer as a host from the Network and Dial-Up Connections window of Windows 2000, follow these steps:

1. Double-click Make New Connection to open the Network Connection Wizard.

2. Click Next to open the Network Connection Type dialog box to see the options in Figure 2-13.

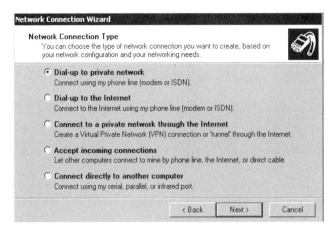

Figure 2-13.

Selecting a connection type in Windows 2000.

3. Click Connect Directly To Another Computer.

4. Click Next to see the choices: Host or Guest.

5. Click Host and then click Next to see the Connection Device box with a drop-down list of options.

6. Select the port you want to use and then click Next to open the Allowed Users dialog box, shown in Figure 2-14. The two types of users that automatically appear are Administrator and Guest. Select the check boxes for both options.

7. If you want to add the names of specific users, click Add. Enter the person's user name, full name, and password, and then click OK.

Figure 2-14.

Choosing who can allow direct connections.

8. Click Next to see that Incoming Connections has been set as the default name for the connection.

9. Click Finish.

The procedure to set up your computer as a guest is similar to the one used to designate your computer as a host. Just follow these steps:

1. Double-click Make New Connection and click Next.

2. Select Connect Directly To Another Computer and click Next.

3. Click Guest, and then click Next to see Connection Device options.

4. Select the port you want to use—it must match the port on the host computer—and then click Next to open the Connection Availability box with the options For All Users and Only For Myself. Select the option that determines which users you want to give permission to access your computer as a guest.

5. Click Next, and then click Finish.

Your computer will now be able to connect to the host computer.

Setting Up a Direct Connection with Windows XP   To set up your computer as a host from the New Connections window of Windows XP, follow these steps:

1. If My Network Places is not already visible, Click Start and select My Network Places.

2. In the Network Tasks section, select View Network Connections, click Create A New Connection to start the New Connection Wizard, and finally click Next.

3. Select Set Up An Advanced Connection, and then click Next.

4. Select Connect Directly To Another Computer, and click Next to see the choices: Host or Guest.

5. Click Host and then click Next to see the Connection Device options.

6. From the Device For This Connection list, select the port you want to use, and then click Next to display the User Permissions options, shown in Figure 2-15. The two types of users that automatically appear are Guest and the name used to install Windows XP. Select the check boxes for both options.

Figure 2-15.
Choosing who can allow direct connections in Windows XP.

7. If you want to add the names of specific users, click Add. Enter the person's user name, full name, and password, and then click OK.

8. Click Next to see that Incoming Connections has been set as the default name for the connection.

9. Click Finish.

Note

You must be signed on as an administrator to set up Windows XP as a host computer.

The procedure to set up your computer as a guest is similar to the one used to designate your computer as a host. Just follow these steps:

1. In the Network Tasks list, click Create A New Connection to start the New Connection Wizard, and then click Next.

2. Select Set Up An Advanced Connection, and then click Next.

3. Select Connect Directly To Another Computer, and click Next to see the choices: Host or Guest.

4. Click Guest, and then click Next.

5. Type the name of the computer serving as the host, and then click Next to see Connection Device options.

6. Select the port you want to use—it must match the port on the host computer.

7. Click Next to verify that the name of the other computer has been set as the default name for the connection.

8. Click Next, and then click Finish. If the Connect box opens and you aren't yet ready to make a direct connection, click Cancel.

   Your computer will now be able to connect to the host computer.

Selecting the Protocol

The next step is to make sure that the IPX/SPX protocol is installed to enable communications between computers. To do this in either Windows 2000 or Windows XP, follow these steps:

1. Right-click Incoming Connections and choose Properties.

2. Click the Networking tab. If the IPX/SPX option isn't listed, continue with these steps.

3. Click Install to see a list of the network components you can add to your computer.

4. Click Protocol.

5. Click Add.

6. Click NWLink IPX/SPX/NetBIOS Compatible Transport Protocol.

7. Click OK, and then click Close.

8. Right-click Direct Connection and choose Properties.

9. Click the Networking tab. If the IPX/SPX protocol isn't listed, repeat the previous steps to install it.

Turning on the Sharing Function

Before a guest can access files on a host computer, folders on the host must be made available for sharing. You can turn on the sharing function for the entire C: drive or just for selected folders within the drive. For security and safety, it's best to turn on sharing only for those folders that you want other people to access.

Sharing with Windows 2000   If you are using Windows 2000, enable sharing from My Computer. To turn on sharing for a specific folder, follow these steps:

1. Using My Computer, open the disk drive that contains the folder you want to share.

2. Right-click the folder and select Sharing from the shortcut menu.

3. Click Share This Folder.

4. Click Permissions. In the Permissions dialog box that appears, shown in Figure 2-16, you'll see the notation Everyone at the top and two columns at the bottom—Allow and Deny.

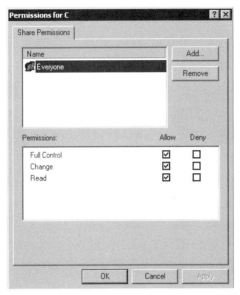

Figure 2-16.
Setting permissions for shared folders.

5. In the Allow column, select the type of permissions you want to grant users: Full Control, Change, or Read.

6. Click OK.

You can also turn on sharing for the entire disk drive so that all the folders within the drive are available for sharing. When you right-click the drive's icon and select Sharing, however, you might see that the drive is already being shared with the name C$. The dollar sign indicates that this is a special share that Windows 2000 requires. To also share the disk with guests over a direct cable, you have to create an additional new share name for the drive. To do so, click the New Share button. In the dialog box that appears, enter a name for the shared drive, and then click OK.

Sharing with Windows XP   To turn on sharing for a specific drive or folder using the Properties shortcut menu, follow these steps:

1. Click Start and then click My Computer.

2. Locate the drive or folder that you want to share.

3. Right-click the icon for the drive or folder and choose Sharing And Security.

4. If you selected a disk drive rather than a folder within a drive, click the message
   If You Understand The Risk But Still Want To Share The Root of The Drive,
   Click Here.

   If this is the first time you set a folder or drive to be shared, you have to enable
   network sharing. You'll see these options in the Network Sharing and Security section of the Properties dialog box, shown below.

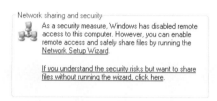

   The Network Setup Wizard can take you step-by-step through creating a
   home network. Since we're only using a direct cable connection, however, we'll skip
   the wizard for now and just turn on sharing.

5. Click If You Understand the Security Risks But Want to Share Files Without Running the Wizard, Click Here.

6. In the dialog box that appears, click the option Just Enable File Sharing, and then
   click OK. You'll see the options shown in Figure 2-17.

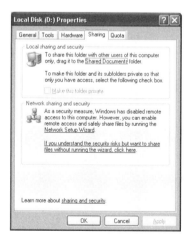

Figure 2-17.
Setting permissions for shared folders.

7. In the Network Sharing And Security section, click the check box labeled Share This Folder On The Network.

8. Enter a name that identifies the drive or folder in the Share Name field.

9. If you do not want the guest user to be able to change the contents of the drive or folder, clear the option Allow Network Users To Change My Files.

10. Click OK.

The last task you have to perform before making the connection is to check that the Guest user account is turned on. The Guest account allows others to have limited access to your host computer. To do this, follow these steps:

1. Click Start and then click Control Panel.

2. Double-click User Accounts. If the icon for Guest is labeled Guest Account On, just close the User Accounts window. Otherwise, continue with these steps.

3. Click Guest. A message appears asking if you want to turn the guest account on.

4. Click Turn On Guest Account, and then close the User Accounts window.

See Also

You'll learn more about user accounts in Windows XP in the section "Using Profiles in Windows XP," in Chapter 8, "Creating User Profiles," on page 227.

Making the Connection

You're now ready to make the actual connection. The process varies slightly between Windows 2000 and Windows XP.

Connecting with Windows 2000   When you want to connect as a guest to the host computer using Windows 2000, follow these steps:

1. Double-click My Computer.

2. Click Network And Dial-Up Connections.

3. Double-click Direct Connection.

4. Enter your user name if it doesn't appear in the box.

5. Enter your password.

6. Click Connect. You'll see an icon on the taskbar that indicates a connection has been made.

To access the shared files on the host computer, perform the following steps:

1. Click Start on the taskbar, and then click Run.

2. In the box that appears, type \\ followed by the name of the computer that is serving as the host, as in **\\john**, and click OK.

   A window appears showing the shared drives and folders. You can now access the files in a folder by double-clicking the folder.

Network Paths

You probably know about the convention used to designate the location of a file, called its *path*. For example, your hard drive is C:, the Windows folder is C:\Windows, and the System subfolder is C:\Windows\System.

The path to resources on a network or over a direct cable connection uses a different syntax called the Universal Naming Convention (UNC). Start the UNC with two backslashes (\\) followed by the name of the computer, as in \\Joe. To access a specific drive or folder on the remote computer, add the path to the UNC, as in \\Joe\C\Budget.

Connecting with Windows XP   If you are using Windows XP, connect as a guest to the host computer by following these steps:

1. Click Start and then point to Connect To.

Note

The Connect To option appears only when you've set up an Internet account or direct connection in Windows XP Home Edition, and it doesn't appear at all in Windows XP Professional. If Connect To is not an option on your Start menu, click Start, point to My Network Places, and then click View Network Connections. Right-click the Direct icon and click Connect.

2. Click the name of the host computer.

3. Enter your user name if it doesn't appear in the box.

4. Enter your password.

5. Click Connect. You'll see an icon on the taskbar that indicates a connection has been made.

To access the shared files on the host computer, perform the following steps:

1. Click Start on the taskbar, and then click Run.

2. In the box that appears, type \\ followed by the name of the computer that is serving as the host, as in **\\john**, and click OK.

   A window appears showing the shared drives and folders. You can now access the files in a folder by double-clicking the folder.

On the host computer, you'll see that the connection had been made in the Network Connections window, as shown below.

Incoming

Another Way to Share Files and Printers

So far in this chapter, you've learned how to share printers and transfer files without a network. Here's yet another way to accomplish these tasks without a network.

An entire class of programs lets you remotely control one computer from another. You connect the computers through a serial, parallel, or USB cable, or through a telephone line and modem. Once the connection is made, you can transfer files and print documents on a printer linked to either computer. Some of these programs also let you control another computer remotely by connecting to it via the Internet.

Note

Windows XP includes Remote Desktop, a built-in program that allows one computer to control another remotely. You can use Windows XP Home Edition, however, to remotely control only a Windows XP Professional computer. A computer running Windows XP Home Edition can't be controlled remotely with the Remote Desktop feature.

Using remote control means that you can sit at your system and actually operate another computer you're connected to. Your keyboard and mouse control the other computer, and you see on your screen what appears on the other computer's screen.

Several programs provide these capabilities, including the following:

- Carbon Copy
- Close-Up
- CoSession Remote
- LapLink
- PCAnywhere
- Rapid Remote
- ReachOut
- Remote Desktop
- Remotely Possible
- Timbuktu

As an example of a remote control program, let's take a look at LapLink Gold, shown in Figure 2-18. LapLink, like some of the other file transfer programs, comes complete with the appropriate cables for connecting computers. In fact, Laplink Gold includes parallel and serial cables, as well as a USB Network Cable for easily creating a network of two computers using their USB ports.

Note

The makers of Laplink Gold also offer PCSync, a similar program but with only serial and USB connectivity, and designed primarily for sharing files. PCSync does not include the printer redirection, remote control, and chat features of LapLink Gold. However, it does enable you to share files over the Internet with its SurfUp feature.

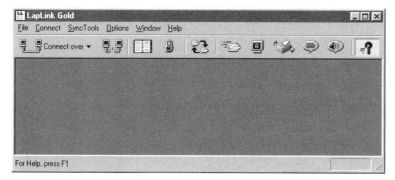

Figure 2-18.

LapLink Gold allows you to share files and printers remotely.

Your first task with LapLink, and similar programs, is to designate how the computers are to be connected. It's possible to enable more than one port so that you can connect to your computer from another computer in the home and dial in to your computer from the road with a laptop. In LapLink, you select Port Setup from the Options menu to open the Port Setup dialog box shown below.

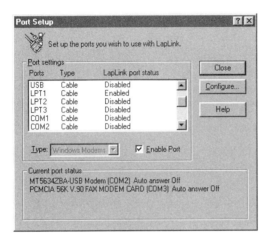

To enable the ports you want, select each one in the Port Settings list, and then select the Enable Port check box.

As with a direct cable connection, you must have the proper cable to make the link work. In the Port Setup dialog box, the entry in the Type field shows the type of LapLink cable required. To connect the parallel (printer) ports of two computers, for example, use the yellow cable that comes with LapLink. If you later have problems connecting through the port, you can open the Port Setup dialog box again, choose the port, and click the Configure button to fine-tune how the port works.

By default, each time LapLink makes a connection between two computers, it lets you copy files between them. You can choose other services from the following list by selecting Connect Options from the LapLink Options menu and then clicking the Connect tab in the Options dialog box.

- **Remote Control** lets you control the other computer from yours.

- **Print Redirection** lets you print a document from your computer to the printer attached to the remote machine and from the remote machine to the printer attached to your computer.

- **Text Chat** lets you exchange messages with the person using the remote computer, just as you would in a chat room online. In fact, a chat window pops up on your screen automatically whenever the remote user sends a message, as shown in Figure 2-19.

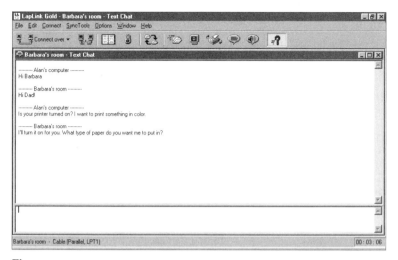

Figure 2-19.

LapLink's Text Chat feature lets you exchange typed messages between computers.

When you're ready to make the connection, start LapLink on both computers. The program automatically detects the connection you've established with the other computer and displays the disks, folders, and files of your computer and the remote computer side by side, as shown in Figure 2-20.

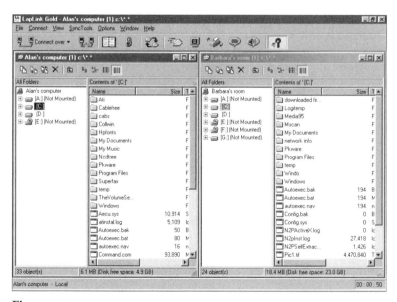

Figure 2-20.

LapLink displays the disks, folders, and files on both computers.

If LapLink is unable to detect the connection automatically, you might need to open the Connect menu and select Connect Over Cable. This opens the Connect Over Cable dialog box, shown below, in which you choose the remote computer to which you want to connect and the combination of services that you want available: File Transfer, Remote Control, Print Redirection, and Text Chat.

To transfer a file, open the folder on either computer containing the file as you would in Windows Explorer, and then drag the file to a folder on the other computer. In addition to moving and copying files, you can synchronize them by using a feature called Xchange Agent. This feature keeps track of changes to files and makes sure that both computers have the most recent version by automatically copying that version to both computers.

Going Wireless with Infrared

Another way to transfer files among laptops is to connect them through their infrared ports. This process is easy because laptops can be connected without wires, and the software you need is built into Windows.

In Windows 95, Windows 98, or Windows Me, follow these steps to make sure that infrared communication has been enabled on both computers:

1. Open Control Panel, and double-click the Infrared icon.

2. In the Infrared Monitor dialog box, click the Options tab, shown in Figure 2-21.

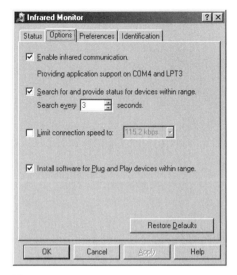

Figure 2-21.

Enabling infrared communication in Windows 95, Windows 98, and Windows Me.

3. If the Enable Infrared Communication check box isn't selected, click it now.

4. Click OK.

5. Repeat the procedure on the other laptop to enable infrared communication.

When you're ready to transfer a file between two computers connected by infrared, follow these steps:

1. Position the computers so that their infrared ports are facing each other.

2. On the computer containing the file you want to transfer, double-click My Computer on the Windows desktop and double-click the Infrared Recipient icon, shown below.

Infrared
Recipient ...

Windows opens the Infrared Transfer dialog box, shown in Figure 2-22.

Figure 2-22.

Transferring files by infrared.

3. If more than one computer is shown in the box, click the one to which you want to send the file.

4. Click the Send Files button, select the file you want to send, and then click Open. The file will be transferred to the other computer and saved in a folder named My Received Files.

On the other computer, you can click Received Files in the Infrared Transfer dialog box to see which files have been sent to that computer by infrared.

Note

In Windows 2000 or Windows XP, you can communicate over infrared ports by using the Direct Connection feature. When you set up the host and guest computers, select the Infrared Port (IRDA0-0) option as the connection device.

What to Do with an Old CPU

As your computer hardware ages, you might find yourself purchasing another computer but using your existing monitor, keyboard, and mouse. You'll have the old computer left over, and it'll just sit there in the closet or basement collecting dust—unless you want to put it to good use.

Although the older computer probably won't stack up to the new one in terms of speed and resources, you might still want to use it occasionally—say, for downloading software from the Internet. That way, you can test the software for viruses before using it on your new machine. Or there could be some files or programs on your older machine that you don't want on your new computer but that you're not quite ready to delete.

By purchasing some inexpensive hardware, you can set up both your old and new computer to use the same keyboard, monitor, and mouse. You can't use both at the same time, but you can then decide which computer to use before turning on either one. If you have a removable disk drive, such as a Zip drive that plugs into the computer's parallel port or USB port, you can then use the drive to transfer files from one computer to the next.

To share a keyboard, monitor, and mouse, you need to purchase a keyboard, video, and mouse (KVM) switch and two sets of cables. You hook up the switch as shown in Figure 2-23. The switch is similar to one used to share a printer but with three connections for each computer.

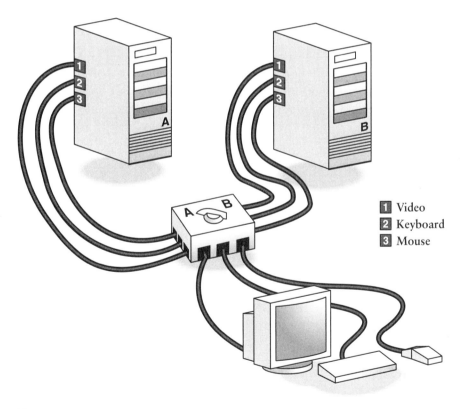

Figure 2-23.

Sharing a keyboard, monitor, and mouse between an old computer and a new one.

Your keyboard, monitor, and mouse plug into one set of connections on the switch. You then plug in a separate keyboard, monitor, and mouse extension cable between the switch and each of the computers. You then turn a switch or push a button on the front of the unit to determine which computer will be used.

The KVM switch and cables must match the type of hardware you have. Two types of connections exist for keyboards and mice: AT and PS/2. PS/2 uses small round connectors, and AT uses a large round connector for the keyboard and a D-shaped serial connection for the mouse. Although you can purchase adapters to convert one to the other, it's best to purchase the switch and cables that are ready to be connected.

The Bottom Line

In this chapter, you learned a number of ways to share files and printers, even when your computers aren't connected through a network. You can share printers with an inexpensive manual switch box or with an automatic switch. You can share files by using the software built into Windows, and with some additional software and hardware, you can share both printers and files at the same time.

In the next chapter, you'll learn how to get started when you want to do more than just share a printer and transfer an occasional file. You'll learn about the types of networks you can set up and the hardware and software you'll need to connect your home computers in a network.

Chapter 3

Planning a Network

You know it's time to set up a network when just sharing a printer or transferring an occasional file doesn't cut it anymore. Networking doesn't have to be complex or expensive; you won't have to learn the history of networking or study arcane subjects such as network layers. But before you run down to the computer store and part with your hard-earned cash, you should take the time to make some basic decisions about your networking needs.

This chapter will help you decide on the type of network you want and how best to connect your computers. You'll learn the difference between a peer-to-peer network and a client/server network, and you'll find out how to decide which type of network connection will work best for your situation. But first, here's a little network preamble.

A Little Network Preamble

Before we look at ways to connect computers, you need to know about an important piece of hardware called a *network interface card*, or NIC for short.

To connect to a network, a computer needs a NIC to handle the flow of information to and from the network. Some computers come with the NIC already built in, but most don't, so you'll have to order one when you buy your computer or add one afterward.

Some NICs fit inside a computer; others come on PC cards that plug into laptops. There are external devices that perform the same function as a NIC, but they connect to a computer's universal serial bus (USB), parallel port, or serial port, as shown in Figure 3-1. There are internal and external NICs for wired networks, as well as wireless networks and networks that use the telephone and electrical lines in your home to transfer information between computers.

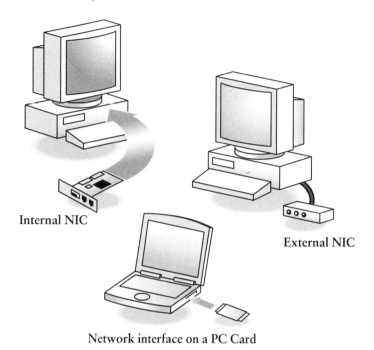

Internal NIC

External NIC

Network interface on a PC Card

Figure 3-1.
Network interfaces can be internal, external, or on a PC card.

Note

Microsoft Windows XP automatically configures a network for installed FireWire adapters. FireWire (also known as IEEE 1394) is a fast bus standard that supports data rates of up to 400 megabits per second (Mbps).

Network devices that plug into the USB port are perhaps the easiest to install because you don't need to physically open up your computer. To use your computer's USB port, you need to have Microsoft Windows 95 version 4.00.95B or any version of Windows 98, Windows Millennium Edition (Me), Windows 2000, or Windows XP. To see which version of Windows 95 you have, right-click My Computer on the desktop, click Properties, and then look under System on the General tab of the System Properties dialog box that appears.

Note

You can connect and disconnect many types of USB devices while your computer is turned on. And when using Windows XP (but not earlier versions of Windows), you can connect and disconnect a network USB device when the computer is on as well.

Because the type of NIC you'll need depends on how you want to connect your computers, read the rest of this chapter before you go out and buy one.

Deciding on Network Control

One of the first decisions you have to make when you're planning how to set up your network is whether to give someone control of it. In one type of setup, called the *client/server network*, a single computer controls access to the network and serves as a central storage area for files and information. But before you decide to go this route, consider these points:

- Putting someone in charge of your network means spending more money on additional computer resources and on software that isn't free.

- Putting someone in charge dramatically increases the complexity of creating a network and the likelihood that you'll run into trouble.

Because of the potential downside to this option, consider the alternative—a peer-to-peer network—carefully before choosing to let someone control your network.

We'll look at each of these options in more detail in a moment, but first, take a look at Table 3-1, which summarizes the features of peer-to-peer vs. client/server networks.

Table 3-1.   Peer-to-Peer vs. Client/Server Networks

Peer-to-Peer Network	Client/Server Network
Can share files, printers, and modems	Can share files, printers, and modems
Anyone can connect to the network (except for wireless networks, which use data encryption)	Only authorized users can connect to the network
No central file storage	Central file storage
Each user sets own security	Central security
Easy setup and maintenance	More complicated setup and maintenance
Low cost	Moderate to high cost
Limited expansion	Unlimited expansion

Setting Up a Level Playing Field

When no single computer acts as the controller, you have a *peer-to-peer network*. This means that everyone on the network is equal—all are *peers*. Any computer on the network can communicate with any other computer on an equal basis. It also means that information flows directly between two computers without being controlled by any other, as shown in Figure 3-2.

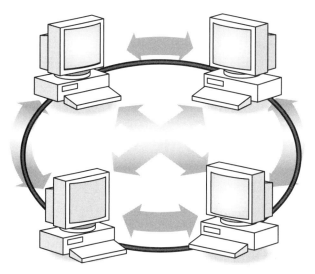

Figure 3-2.

Computers on a peer-to-peer network communicate with each other directly.

A peer-to-peer network doesn't eliminate all forms of control, however. Each person on the network can use a password to protect files and folders. You don't have to let people share your files or use your printer or modem. How other people can access your computer is entirely up to you.

See Also

For more information about using passwords, see the section "Accessing Resources with Passwords," in Chapter 9, "Learning to Share," on page 247.

For example, you can allow only certain folders to be shared. In fact, to protect critical Windows files, you always want to prevent the Windows folder from being shared. You can also grant *read-only rights* to a folder. This means that others on the network can look at a file in a shared folder on your computer and copy it to their computers, but they won't be able to change or delete it.

You can also grant *full access*, which means that everyone on the network can read, change, and delete files just as you can. Grant full access only to people you really trust and only to those folders that you want to be totally accessible.

In a peer-to-peer network, if any one computer is *down*—is turned off or not working—everyone else on the network can still communicate. In Figure 3-3, for example, even though two of the four networked computers are turned off, the other two computers can still share files and printers. The printers attached to computers that are off won't be available to others on the network, but you'll still be able to use the files and resources of those computers that are on.

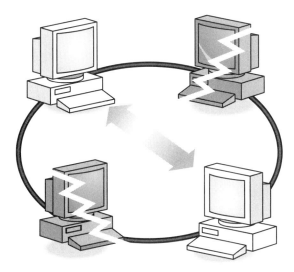

Figure 3-3.
Peer-to-peer networked computers can still communicate when other computers are turned off.

Of course, to use a printer connected to any computer on the network, the computer and printer must be turned on and working properly. Some computers, especially laptops, have a *suspend state*. After a certain period of inactivity, a computer that is in suspend state saves information about all open programs on its hard disk and turns off automatically. When you turn the computer back on later, the screen appears exactly as it was. If a computer on the network goes into suspend, its resources won't be available to the rest of the network.

Other computers have an energy-saving feature that turns off the display or the disk drive only after a period of inactivity. The resources of such computers might also be unavailable when they go into energy-saving mode. Because so many different kinds of computers exist, you'll have to experiment to see how a particular computer reacts on your network.

A peer-to-peer network has no central storage location for everyone's files. If you're looking for a file that's not on your machine, you'll need to know where it is on the network or search all the computers on the network to locate the file. And if the computer that has the file is turned off, you're out of luck. You'll have to wait until it's back on to get to the file.

Still, the advantages of peer-to-peer networks—they're inexpensive and easy to set up, run, and maintain—clearly outweigh the disadvantages, particularly for home computers.

Putting Someone in Charge

As you've seen, when you want tighter control over a network, the solution is to set up a client/server network. The *server* is a single computer equipped with special software that supervises everything on the network. The *clients* are the computers that connect to the server. Communication among the clients must go through the server, as shown in Figure 3-4.

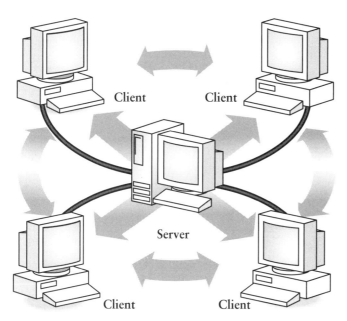

Figure 3-4.
Client computers connect through a server in a client/server network.

In most client/server networks in large offices, the server computer is usually dedicated to the task of being the server and isn't used as a regular workstation for everyday jobs. The tasks the server has to do, and the information stored in it, are just too important to take a chance on. If the server is down, the network goes down and none of the computers can communicate, as shown in Figure 3-5.

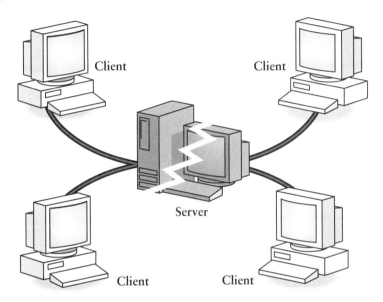

Figure 3-5.
When the server is down, the entire network goes down with it.

The server computer doesn't have to be dedicated, however, especially in a small home office network. You can still use it as a workstation for ordinary tasks, but it's not the best idea. Server software is much more complex than workstation software and requires more effort and patience to keep it running. The server software also might not include the software needed to run scanners and other devices. On the other hand, operating a Windows 95, Windows 98, Windows Me, Windows 2000, or Windows XP client computer on a client/server network is a piece of cake. You pretty much just turn on the computer and start working.

A client/server network offers a number of advantages in addition to control. For example, the server can act as a central storage location that everyone on the network can reach. Because the server is always on, you can use it to store graphics, downloaded files from the Internet, and other documents that you want everyone to share. The files are always available and accessible to everyone.

You can also load and run applications from the server instead of installing them on every computer. This way, you can be sure that everyone on the network is using the same programs and can easily share files. When you want to update a program from version 6 to version 7, for example, you need to install the update on only one machine.

And finally, the server can act as a central e-mail message center. Like with an Internet newsgroup or bulletin board, you can leave messages on the server for everyone else on the network to see and respond to.

Setting up a client/server network at home can be impractical, though. If you're using Windows 95, Windows 98, or Windows Me, you can't create a server for a client/server network, although you can connect to one. To create a client/server network, you'll need to run either Windows NT 4 Server, Windows 2000 Server, or Windows XP Server. All of these programs are expensive, however, and none are necessary for the average home network.

Note

You can set up Windows NT or Windows 2000 computers so that they also have Windows 95, Windows 98, or Windows Me in a dual-boot configuration. You can then decide which system to use when you start your server. If you start in Windows 95, Windows 98, or Windows Me, however, you lose the benefits of client/server computing because the server computer will be operating on a peer-to-peer basis. A dual-boot configuration is useful, however, if you have some hardware or software that runs under one version of Windows (such as Windows 98) but not under another (such as Windows XP).

A client/server network offers many advantages to the business user. But for the average home network, the two major disadvantages of the client/server setup—cost and complexity—usually outweigh the advantages. For this reason, we'll leave the client/server option to large businesses and concentrate in this book on peer-to-peer networks using Windows 95, Windows 98, Windows Me, Windows 2000, and Windows XP.

Note

Although in this book I've distinguished between peer-to-peer and client/server networks, in real life, many networks are a blend of the two. You can have a client/server network set up so that if the server goes down, the other computers on the network can still communicate on a peer-to-peer basis.

Deciding on the Connection

Your next decision is how to connect the computers so that information can flow between them. Your choice depends on several factors:

- The number of computers
- The distance between the computers
- The speed you want
- How much work you want to do
- How much money you want to spend

  Generally, there are five different types of network connections:

- Network cable (Ethernet)
- Wireless
- Home phone line
- USB direct connection
- Home power line

Note

You can also create a network by connecting two IEEE 1394 (FireWire) adapters together with a cable. Networking software over IEEE 1394 is built into Windows XP.

We'll be looking at each type of network in detail in later chapters. In the meantime, Table 3-2 summarizes the major differences among them.

Table 3-2.   Comparing Network Connections

Network Connection	The Good	The Bad
Network cable (Ethernet)	The fastest and most expandable type of network connection.	Requires running cable between computers. Might require running cable through walls, ceilings, and floors; extra jacks and special hardware might also be needed.
Wireless	Requires no cables; "broadcasts" network over the air.	Generally slower than network cable, although most are now equal to or better than the low end of Ethernet speed. Might be subject to interference from large electrical appliances.
Home phone line	Requires no cables; plugs into existing telephone wiring.	Requires a phone jack in rooms in which you want to connect to the network. Best used when there is less than about 500 feet (150 meters) of phone line throughout the house. Some home phone line systems are slower than network cable, although some are equal to the low end of Ethernet speed.
USB direct connection	Requires no internal cards to be installed; a special cable plugs into the USB ports of both computers.	Slower than network cable but faster than power line and many other types of connections. Limited to a maximum of 16.4 feet (5 meters) between any two computers, although computers can be farther apart with additional hardware.
Home power line	Requires no cables; plugs into a wall outlet.	Slower than network cable. Might be subject to electrical interference, which can break contact between network computers and result in data loss.

For most business networks, network cable is the preferred choice because of its speed and dependability using what's called an Ethernet network. *Ethernet* is a set of specifications that determine how information is communicated across a network. Because the specifications are universally accepted, you can mix Ethernet hardware from any manufacturer in the same network. If you later need to purchase another NIC, for example, you don't have to purchase the same model that you're using on other computers. You can also use internal NICs on some computers, devices that connect to the USB ports on others, and a NIC on a PC Card for a laptop.

USB Speed Limitations

USB Ethernet adapters are easy to install and let you connect to a wired Ethernet network without opening up your computer case. But even though a USB adapter might be labeled 10/100 Mbps, you might not be able to connect to wired Ethernet at the 100-Mbps speed.

The USB ports on all but the most recent computers adhere to the USB 1.1 standard that operates at a maximum of 12 Mbps. If your computer uses USB 1.1, actual speeds of about 5 to 6 Mbps are typical even when the rest of your network is 10 or 100 Mbps.

However, a new USB 2 standard is just emerging and can be used with newer computers. The USB 2 standard operates at a maximum of 480 Mbps. Look for computers and USB network adapters that adhere to this standard when shopping for new hardware.

The other types of networks are suitable when you don't want to or can't run cables between computers in various parts of the house. Although telephone and wireless networks are slower than the fastest Ethernet connections, newer systems are equal to or faster than the low end of Ethernet speeds. For home networks, however, the network speed usually isn't critical. USB direct connection networks are suitable when the computers are in the same room or no further than an adjoining room. Some non-Ethernet kits do allow easy migration to an Ethernet network. For example, some adapters for telephone networks also contain Ethernet ports.

The hardware you use with nonwired Ethernet alternatives, however, might not be compatible among manufacturers. To make sure your hardware is compatible, you should purchase it all from the same manufacturer. Otherwise, look for hardware that meets industrywide standards, such as the Wi-Fi (802.11b) standard for wireless networks or Home Phoneline Networking Alliance (HomePNA) for phone-line networks.

Hardware that meets the same standard should be able to communicate with each other. With HomePNA hardware, however, two levels of standards exist: HomePNA 1, which operates at 1 Mbps, and HomePNA 2, which runs at 10 Mbps. You might be able to mix the levels on the same network, but your performance will be at the slower rate.

As for price, you can find starter kits of each type of network connection that include the hardware and software to network two computers for less than $100, but the non-Ethernet alternatives are generally more expensive. Kits that contain Ethernet network cards that fit inside your computer are the least expensive, followed by internal telephone cards and internal wireless cards. Kits that contain adapters that plug into the USB port or that fit into the slot in a laptop computer can cost between $100 and $200 for each type of network connection. Wireless and telephone network adapters that operate at the low end of Ethernet speeds also cost between $100 and $200, but they are dropping in price. Depending on your situation, the extra cost of a telephone or wireless solution might be compensated by the convenience of not having to run Ethernet wires through the house.

Planning for Internet Sharing

If you're planning to use your network for Internet sharing, you should keep a few factors in mind.

If you connect to the Internet through a dial-up modem, any of the networking alternatives will be fast enough to keep up with the flow of information. In fact, all of the networking methods described would be suitable for all but the fastest digital subscriber line (DSL) or cable modems being used today.

However, if you plan to use your network for sharing an Internet connection, files, and printers at the same time, you should consider Ethernet, wireless, or telephone networks running at a speed of at least 10 Mbps. This would eliminate some of the older wireless and telephone network hardware that runs at considerably slower speeds. In addition, although wireless hardware might be possible for communicating at 10 Mbps, the actual speed depends on the distance between computers and the number and type of obstacles between them. The farther apart the computers are, and the greater the number of obstacles, the slower the actual speed. It might be possible, for example, to have a 10-Mbps wireless system that provides an actual speed of only 5 Mbps or even 2 Mbps.

High-speed DSL and cable modems require an Ethernet connection on your computer. So regardless of the type of hardware you choose for your network, you'll need at least one Ethernet connection to use high-speed Internet. You can install the Ethernet connection on one specific computer, or you can purchase hardware that lets you connect the modem directly to the network. Some hardware even combines a wireless or telephone local area network (for your computers) with one Ethernet connection for the Internet.

See Also

You'll learn more about these devices in Chapter 11, "Going Online Through the Network."

Planning for the Future

Sometime in the future, you might want your home network to include your home entertainment, security, and control equipment, thus creating an automated, or *smart*, home.

Even if you don't plan to do this now, you might want to design your network in a way that leaves the possibility open for the future.

If you wanted to set up a smart home, you would need to place computers or control panels in convenient locations, often even in places where you wouldn't want to have a computer for Internet access. For example, you would probably want a computer or control panel in the master bedroom so you could turn on the television, control lights throughout the house, or check a security camera at the front door.

Distributing video signals, such as from cable television or VCR/DVD players, requires cabling. So, you would need to run wires to each room where you wanted to broadcast or control home entertainment, watch films, or listen to your stereo system. While some home automation systems don't require any additional cabling because they run through your existing wiring, a comprehensive smart home system would require you to run wires somewhere in the house, even if you selected a wireless or telephone computer network.

Because you will need to use new wires one way or another, you might as well plan on using Ethernet as your primary network method. If you have a location that's difficult to wire up, you might also need to add some wireless capabilities and then combine the Ethernet and wireless networks into one.

See Also

We'll take a closer look at the types of wiring you might want to consider for the future in Chapter 4, "Types of Networks."

Understanding Networking Software

Once you decide on the type of network and connections you want, you'll need two basic types of software:

- Network drivers
- A network operating system

Network Drivers

Your NIC will come with a floppy disk or CD that contains *network drivers*, the special programs that Windows needs to access your specific NIC. The disk or CD might also include drivers for *MS-DOS* (the disk operating system that preceded Windows) and for other types of operating systems. Complete instructions for installing the drivers come with the interface card.

See Also

To learn more about installing drivers, see the section "Installing Network Drivers," in Chapter 7, "Installing the Software," on page 158.

An increasing number of NICs are *plug and play*, meaning that the software drivers are built into Windows. When you install a new card in a machine running any version of Windows, the system will recognize the card and load the drivers from the Windows CD. If the drivers aren't on the CD, you'll need the disk that came with your card, or you could download the latest driver from the manufacturer's site on the Internet.

Network Operating Systems

In addition to the network drivers, you'll also need a network operating system. This software contains the programs necessary to perform network tasks and to share files and printers. For home networks, the choice is easy. If you have most versions of Windows running, you have everything you need; you don't need to buy any other software. Windows 98, Windows Me, Windows 2000, and Windows XP even have software that lets you share a modem over a network.

Note

If you have Windows 95, and want to share an Internet account, you must first download free or inexpensive sharing software over the Internet, such as the programs Proxy from *http://www.analogx.com* and WinProxy from *http://www.ositis.com*.

The Bottom Line

In home networking, the best option is clearly a peer-to-peer network using Windows. You'll get the network drivers you need with the NIC, and Windows supplies a network operating system and other networking programs for free.

In terms of price and performance, your best choice for hooking up your network is wired Ethernet. If you can't run cable from one computer to the other in your home, and you want the speed of Ethernet, consider a home wireless network or a phone-line network that operates at Ethernet speeds. USB cable networks are great for connecting two computers in the same room, as long as both computers have USB ports.

In the next chapter, you'll learn about the different types of networks in detail.

Chapter 4

Types of Networks

Wired Ethernet has been the mainstay for networks for many years. The inconvenience of running the required cables, however, is a major disadvantage if you're networking an existing home. The alternatives to wired Ethernet are ideal when you don't want to cut holes in walls and otherwise run Ethernet cable.

Your network might also be a combination of types, so it pays to understand something about all of the network types that are available. For example, you might use Ethernet cables for connecting some computers and wireless or phone networking for computers in locations that are difficult to wire. You might want to add wireless capability to a wired network, for example, so you can roam the house and garden with a laptop computer while staying connected to the Internet or being able to share and print documents.

Wired Ethernet

The most common type of network today uses network cabling to communicate information, and Ethernet is the most popular network of this kind. *Ethernet*, developed by Xerox Corporation in 1976, is a set of specifications that determine how information is communicated across a network. As long as each computer has a working internal or external Ethernet adapter and the cables are connected, little can interfere with the flow of information in an Ethernet network. In home Ethernet networks, information can travel through the cables at speeds of 10 megabits per second (Mbps) to 100 Mbps, depending on the speed of the network interface card (NIC) and your cables.

These numbers might not mean much to you unless you've waited online for a file to download. The fastest telephone modems can download files at about 53 kilobits per second (Kbps) if you have a great phone line. A file that takes 10 minutes to download from the Internet takes only a few seconds to transfer from computer to computer on an Ethernet network.

Gigabit Ethernet (GbE)

Gigabit (1000 Mbps) speed networks are just emerging, but they are expensive. Gigabit Ethernet (GbE) requires special (and pricey) copper twisted-pair wire or fiberoptic cable. One type of GbE runs on coaxial cable, but up to lengths of only 82 feet (25 meters).

The problem with GbE is that many computers just can't keep up with the network, so you won't see the full benefit of gigabit speeds unless you have very high-end computers.

The problem with cable is that you have to run it physically to each computer. This problem is easily solved if the computers are in the same or adjacent rooms and you don't mind drilling a hole in the wall. But when your computers are spread throughout the house, running cable can be difficult unless one of the following conditions applies:

- You're lucky enough to find ways to run the cable without having to pass through too many walls.

- You're building a new house.

Types of Cable

The two most common types of cable are twisted pair, also known as 10BaseT cable, and 10Base2 thin Ethernet coaxial cable.

Note

The term 10BaseT is named for its original maximum speed of 10 Mbps on twisted-pair wire. The term 10Base2 is named because the maximum length of the coaxial cable is less than 656 feet (200 meters).

Twisted-pair cable looks like telephone cable on steroids, with plugs that look like pumped-up telephone connectors, as shown in Figure 4-1. Twisted-pair connectors, called RJ-45 connectors, and telephone connectors, called RJ-11 connectors, can't be used interchangeably.

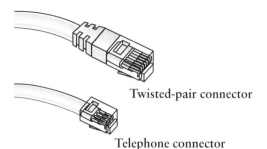

Twisted-pair connector

Telephone connector

Figure 4-1.
Network cable connectors resemble oversized phone connectors.

Twisted-pair cable comes in two types and several grades. The higher the grade, the better and the more reliable the cable, but quality comes at a price.

See Also

For more about wire grades, see the section "Making the Grade," in Chapter 6, "Connecting Your Network," on page 121.

The two types of twisted-pair cables are *unshielded twisted pair* (UTP) and *shielded twisted pair* (STP). As shown in Figure 4-2, UTP cable consists of eight insulated wires, twisted together in pairs within an insulating sheath.

Figure 4-2.
Twisted-pair cable contains four pairs of insulated wires that are twisted together.

STP cable is similar to UTP cable but has a layer of woven copper and foil around the wires within the plastic sheath to shield them from extraneous electrical signals. STP cable is more expensive than UTP and is more difficult to work with because it is heavier and less flexible. The advantage of STP, however, is its resistance to *crosstalk*—when signals from one cable mix with signals in another cable running adjacent to it.

In most cases, when you wire a network with either type of twisted-pair cable, all the cables must converge at a device called a *hub*, as shown in Figure 4-3. The hub acts like a traffic intersection, where all roads come together and traffic can flow in any direction. This means you have to run all the network cables to a central location in the house, and the hub has to be turned on for any of the computers to communicate. As you'll learn in Chapter 6, "Connecting Your Network," several types of hubs exist, and you can use other devices called *switches* as the converging point of the network cables.

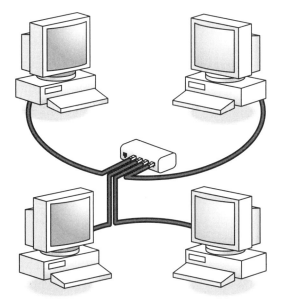

Figure 4-3.
The hub serves as a central data distribution point for a network wired with twisted-pair cable.

See Also

If you're networking only two computers, you don't need a hub. See the section "Hubless Networking," in Chapter 6, "Connecting Your Network," on page 122.

An alternative to twisted-pair cable is 10Base2 *thin Ethernet coaxial cable*. It looks like the cable from your VCR or cable box, only a little thinner, which is why it's called thin Ethernet, or just thinnet. As shown in Figure 4-4, thinnet is a round cable with a solid insulated wire at its core and a layer of braided metal under its external sheath. Although thinner than other coaxial cables, thinnet is thicker than twisted-pair cable, so it's slightly more difficult to fish through walls and lay along baseboards.

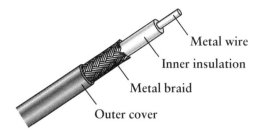

Figure 4-4.
A 10Base2 thin Ethernet coaxial cable consists of a central wire wrapped with insulation and an insulated metal conducting sheath.

A coaxial cable network doesn't require a hub. As shown in Figure 4-5, you simply run the cable from one NIC to another. The absence of a central hub reduces the amount of cable you need to run from room to room and between floors. You can join two lengths of coaxial cable to make a longer cable, and two lengths of coaxial cable joined with a coupler (a small device that connects the end of two cables) are more reliable than two lengths of twisted-pair cable coupled together.

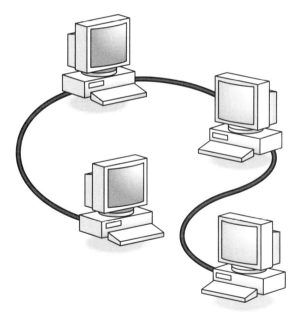

Figure 4-5.
Coaxial cable connects computers directly, without a hub.

Fiber Optics

Fiberoptic cable is growing in popularity for larger network installations and new homes. *Fiberoptic cable* consists of a thin glass wire through which light passes in pulses. The light pulses represent the digital information being carried over the network.

It has a lower error rate than coaxial or twisted pair and because it isn't made of metal, it isn't susceptible to electromagnetic interference. The cable can transmit signals in the tens of gigabits per second and can handle several different gigabits of channels simultaneously, each channel on a different wavelength of light.

However, fiberoptic cable costs more than twisted pair or coaxial, and it's more difficult to install. You shouldn't make any sharp bends when installing any type of cable, and fiberoptic cable is much less flexible than other types. If you need to install your own connector to the end of a fiberoptic cable, it must be attached with epoxy or by a heat process, although some connectors can be crimped on for emergency repairs.

As shown in Figure 4-6, fiberoptic cable contains five parts:

- A glass core that carries the light
- Glass cladding surrounding the core, which reflects the light back to the core so that it travels without loss of the signals
- A buffer layer that protects the core and cladding from damage
- A layer of material that strengthens the cable
- An outer jacket, such as polyvinyl chloride (PVC) plastic

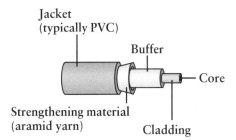

Figure 4-6.
Parts of a fiberoptic cable.

Two fiberoptic cables connect the computer's NIC to the network hub, as shown in Figure 4-7. One carries information to the computer, the other to the hub for distribution to the network. For that reason, the cable is usually purchased with two fibers together in the same outer jacket.

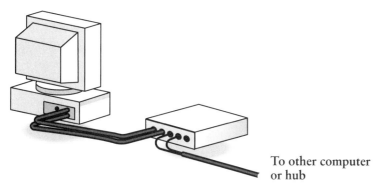

To other computer
or hub

Figure 4-7.
Connecting a fiberoptic cable.

Using some kind of cable—whether it is twisted pair, coaxial, or fiberoptic—is generally the preferred option as long as you can physically run wire between your computers. Wire is faster than the alternatives and can connect almost any distance in an office. But some environments are inhospitable to laying cable, so you might want to consider other options.

Note

You can mix twisted-pair, coaxial, and fiberoptic cables in the same network, but you'll need additional hardware. See the section "Expanding Your Ethernet Network," in Chapter 6, "Connecting Your Network," on page 136.

Wireless Networks

If you don't want to string cable throughout the house, consider a wireless network. Just like a wireless phone system, a *wireless network* transmits information via radio waves to other computers in the house. You can use a wireless system for any application for which you would use wired Ethernet, including sharing files, printers, and an Internet connection—either dial-up or broadband.

Wireless systems use a special interface device called a *transceiver* that takes the information you want to send to other computers and transmits it over the air. The transceiver also receives signals from other computers. In some wireless systems, the transceiver fits inside your computer on an interface card, with an antenna that sticks out the back that sends and picks up the signals. Other transceivers are external, connecting to your computer through the universal serial bus (USB) or printer port. The USB versions are the easiest to set up because you don't have to open the computer to install an internal NIC or share a parallel port with a printer.

Figure 4-8 shows computers communicating over a wireless network through transceivers.

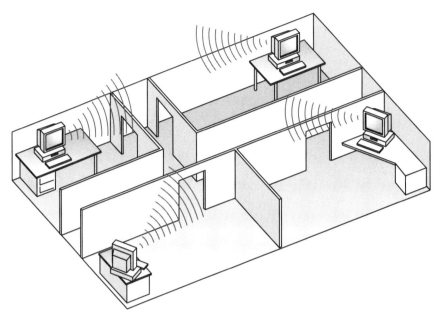

Figure 4-8.
Wireless network transceivers send and receive information on radio waves over the air.

Competing Protocols

Although many different types of wireless systems exist, they usually fall into two general categories: HomeRF and Wi-Fi:

- **HomeRF** (*RF* stands for radio frequency) was the original standard for small wireless networks suited for the home, communicating at 1.6 Mbps.

- **Wi-Fi** (wireless fidelity), also known as the 802.11b standard and wireless Ethernet, operates at 11 Mbps. Originally designed for the business environment, Wi-Fi hardware once cost much more than HomeRF networks, but prices have dropped, bringing Wi-Fi into the home networking market.

Note

When discussing wireless networks, placing the letter *b* at the end of 802.11b carries an important distinction. An older 802.11 standard, which operates at 2 Mbps, is not compatible with 802.11b hardware.

HomeRF and Wi-Fi systems are not compatible because each uses a different wireless standard of communication—frequency hopping and direct sequence, respectively. The technology that wireless systems use to create a secure network, called *spread spectrum*, divides the wireless signal into small pieces.

In a *frequency-hopping spread spectrum* (FHSS), used by HomeRF and the original 2-Mbps 802.11 systems, the system switches, or *hops*, between several different frequencies for a specific amount of time. Both the sending device and the receiving device know the pattern, so the signals are received intact.

In a *direct sequence spread spectrum* (DSSS), used by Wi-Fi 802.11b hardware, the signal is encoded with extra redundant bits of information that the receiving device can decode. The redundant bits help ensure that the information can be received successfully even if some bits are lost during the transmission.

Note

A new HomeRF standard, called HomeRF 2, is being developed to compete with the 11-Mbps speed of Wi-Fi, but it might not be supported by many manufactures. Similarly, a new Wi-Fi standard is being developed (called 802.11a) that supports data rates of up to 54 Mbps.

Bluetooth Wireless Technology

Bluetooth, an evolving wireless standard, is a high-speed, low-power microwave link that strives to enable mobile phones, computers, and other devices to communicate both voice and data. Bluetooth is built into a microchip that is installed in devices, and the software provides security to allow communications only between authorized devices. Bluetooth devices automatically connect when they are brought within range of each other. However, Bluetooth is intended to create a Personal Area Network (PAN) for devices within 33 feet (10 meters) of each other. It is ideal for replacing wires connecting computers, mice, and printers.

The Pros and Cons of Going Wireless

Wireless systems that operate at 11 Mbps cost more than an Ethernet starter kit, but they are easy to install because there are no network cables. Expect to pay about two or three times the average cost of an Ethernet two-computer startup kit for a two-system wireless network.

Wireless networks that are designed and priced for the home function only within a certain distance. Although most systems advertise a range of 150 to 250 feet (46 to 76 meters) or more between computers, the actual range and speed varies widely. A range of only 50 feet (15 meters) or so is common within a typical home, where more than two walls separate networked computers.

As the distance and obstacles between computers increase, the speed of a wireless system decreases dramatically. For example, even without any obstacles, you should expect the speed of an 11-Mbps network to drop by half over 100 feet (30.5 meters), and by half again over 150 feet (46 meters). Most wireless systems can accommodate the distances in an average-sized home, but check the documentation that came with your wireless network kit to find its range.

A more common problem with wireless networks is interference from walls and large metal objects. If a computer on the network is located on the floor under a metal desk, for example, the metal might block incoming and outgoing signals. A wall with metal pipes or studs can also interfere with signal transmission, and you can't have large metal objects or huge containers of water, such as fish tanks and water coolers, between computers.

Choosing a Wireless System

Most of the companies that sold HomeRF systems (such as SohoWare, Breezecom, and Lucent Technologies) have converted to Wi-Fi 802.11b. While you can still get HomeRF networking hardware from companies such as Intel and SohoWare, the popularity of Wi-Fi, as well as the decreasing prices of Wi-Fi products, make it a better choice. It is questionable how long companies will support their HomeRF products and whether additional HomeRF products will be available in the future if you want to expand your network.

With Wi-Fi 802.11b wireless systems, you have plenty of choices that are competitively priced, including the following:

- 2Wire (*http://www.2wire.com*)

- 3Com (*http://www.3com.com*)

- Buffalo Technology (*http://www.buffalotech.com*)

- Dlink (*http://www.dlink.com*)

- Intel (*http://www.intel.com*)

- Linksys (*http://www.linksys.com*)

- Netgear (*http://www.netgear.com*)

- ORiNOCO (*http://www.wavelan.com*)

- Proxim (*http://www.proxim.com*)

- SMC (*http://www.smc.com*)

- SohoWare (*http://www.sohoware.com*)

All of the systems named above adhere to the 802.11b standard. As a result, they should be *interoperable*—in other words, they work with each other so you don't have to purchase all of your hardware from the same manufacturer. The main differences between systems is the chipset on which they are based and their level of security.

Two main chipsets are used to create wireless hardware: the Lucent/WaveLAN chipset and the Intersil PRISM chipset. The two types of systems are compatible, so you can combine Lucent/WaveLAN-based and Intersil PRISM–based hardware on the same network. Each has its own way of setting up the drivers on your computer and for setting up security. Some users feel that the Lucent/WaveLAN systems have a greater range.

The Wi-Fi standard also supports the Wired Equivalent Privacy (WEP) feature. WEP lets you encrypt data to prevent an unauthorized person from gaining access to the wireless network. It's called WEP because it's similar to the type of data security available in wired Ethernet networks.

Using WEP, your data is encrypted when transmitted and decrypted when received using a password called a *key*. Wi-Fi systems use either a 64-bit key of up to 5 text characters (10 hexadecimal) or a 128-bit key of up to 13 text characters (26 hexadecimal). In theory, the longer the key, the higher the security. You can mix 64-bit and 128-bit systems on the same network as long as you can set the 128-bit devices for the lower encryption.

You might also see some systems advertised as using a 40-bit WEP key. Actually, this is the same as using a 64-bit key. The 64-bit key is composed of 40 bits that you designate (5 text or 10 hex characters) and 24 bits (called the Initialization Vector) that the system adds to the key. Some vendors choose to call this 40-bit WEP rather than 64-bit WEP.

Note

The 128-bit key actually contains a 104-bit code (13 text or 26 hexadecimal characters) plus a 24-bit Initialization Vector.

Phone-Line Networks

As you learned in Chapter 3, "Planning a Network," telephone networks operate on the principle that the phone lines running through your home can be shared. The technical term is *frequency-division multiplexing* (FDM), which means that the waves running through the phone line can be divided into separate frequencies, as shown in Figure 4-9.

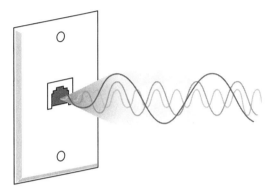

Figure 4-9.
Standard phone lines can carry three separate transmissions on different frequencies.

One frequency is used by voice and fax calls coming or going over the phone line. Your home network uses a totally different frequency, so the network signals can travel through the phone line while you're using your phone to talk to someone, send a fax, or surf the Internet. You can't talk on the phone and surf the Internet at the same time, but that's true with any type of network if you have only one phone line.

A group of companies and agencies joined together in June 1998 to form the Home Phoneline Networking Alliance (HomePNA) to create standards for phone-line networks. They started with the tried and true Ethernet standard and modified it when necessary to fit into the phone-line hardware.

The Pros and Cons of Phone-Line Networks

Phone-line networks are convenient for two main reasons:

- You don't need to run any special cable.

- You can connect a computer to the network in any room that has a phone jack.

Most homes have phone jacks in the places where you'll want to put a computer anyway. After all, you'll want to use the phone to connect your computer to the Internet. The phone jack can then serve a dual purpose by also letting you connect computers on a network.

Although the original telephone networks operated much more slowly than Ethernet, in the 1-Mbps to 2-Mbps range, they cost about the same as Ethernet starter kits. The newer systems that communicate at 10 Mbps cost slightly more, but you can still network two computers for between $100 and $200.

Note

Some HomePNA network cards include a 10/100BaseT port in case you want to convert from a phone-line network to Ethernet. Connecting a cable to the port disables the NIC's phone network capabilities.

Choosing a Phone-Line System

Several companies sell phone-line network kits. The AnyPoint Phoneline Home Network kit from Intel offers a choice of an internal NIC for a desktop computer, a PC Card for a laptop, and an external USB model, all of which operate at 10 Mbps. You can also purchase a less expensive 1-Mbps USB model.

The HomeLink Phoneline system from Linksys offers the same equipment options as the AnyPoint Phoneline Home Network kit. All of the adapters operate at 10 Mbps over the phone line. All of the Linksys systems also include an Ethernet port just in case you want to change to an Ethernet network later by installing twisted-pair cables and a hub.

Diamond Multimedia (*http://www.diamond-networks.com*) offers both a USB and an internal model that fits inside your computer and operates at 10 Mbps. The USB model includes software to let the device work with both PCs and Apple iMac computers, so you can use it to network both types of computers together. All the devices are compatible with each other.

USB Direct Cable Networks

If you want to connect two computers that are in the same room and they both have USB ports, you can get all the benefits of a full network but with the convenience of a direct connection. You can use your computer's USB ports to network computers by Ethernet, telephone, or wireless technology. When you use a USB Ethernet connection, for example, your computer has the same performance and benefits as one with an Ethernet network card installed internally. In this section, however, we'll look at special systems that network computers by connecting them directly by their USB ports.

See Also

For information on using USB devices to connect to an Ethernet network, see the section "Working Without Cards" in Chapter 5, "Installing Network Cards and Adapters," on page 100.

Because the USB port is external, you can connect USB devices without having to open your computer and install an internal card. Many desktop and laptop computers include two USB ports, so you can use one port for networking and the other for a USB printer, scanner, or other device.

Note

If you have an older computer without a USB port, you can install an add-in card to give your computer USB capabilities.

If you have more USB devices than you have ports, you can purchase a *USB hub*, a device that allows multiple USB devices to be connected to one computer, as shown in the following illustration. You might even be able to combine or stack hubs to connect additional USB devices.

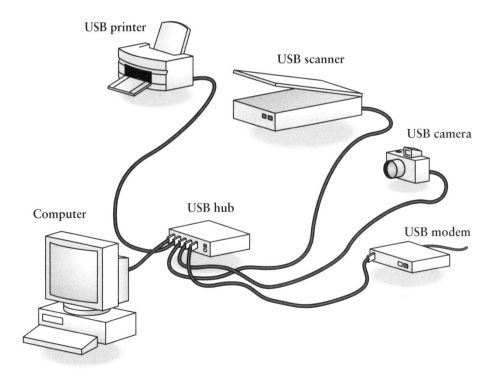

USB printer

USB scanner

USB camera

Computer

USB hub

USB modem

The disadvantage of connecting computers by USB cable is distance. Because USB cables can be no longer than 16.5 feet (5 meters), the two networked computers must usually be in the same room. You can extend the distance between computers, however, by connecting them to a hub. The hub acts as a signal booster, extending the distance another 16.5 feet (5 meters). Therefore, the two machines can be up to 33 feet (10 meters) apart if they have a hub between them, as shown here. However, that distance often still isn't long enough to connect computers in two rooms.

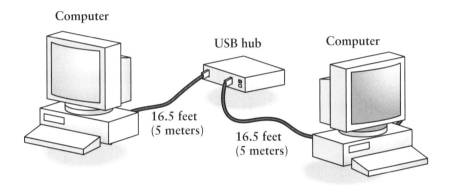

Choosing a USB Network System

Several companies sell kits that contain a special USB cable and software for creating a two-computer network. The kits cost less than $100 and they let you share and transfer files, share Internet access, play games over the network, and share printers. The following are some examples of these kits:

- USB Direct Connect (*http://www.belkin.com*)
- EZLink USB (*http://www.ezlinkusb.com*)
- PCSync (*http://www.laplink.com*)

USB Direct Connect

The USB Direct Connect system from Belkin includes a device with two USB connections. The device acts as a hub, so you can connect 16.5-foot (5-meter) USB cables to each port, separating the two computers by as much as 33 feet (10 meters).

You can also use multiple USB Direct Connect devices to network more than two computers through their USB ports, as shown in Figure 4-10. To determine how many devices you'll need, just subtract 1 from the number of computers you want to network. You'll need four devices to network five computers, for example.

Connecting two computers

Daisy chain

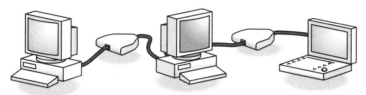

Figure 4-10.
You can create a multiple-computer network using USB cables and USB Direct Connect devices.

If the computers have two USB ports, you can either go from one computer to an-other in a row (called a daisy chain), or connect up to eight computers to one host that has multiple USB ports or is connected to a USB hub, as shown in Figure 4-11. When you daisy chain the devices, each computer in the chain except the first and the last must have two USB ports.

Host with multiple computers connected

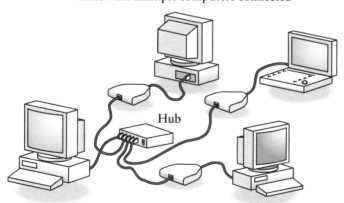

Figure 4-11.
The USB Direct Connect system can be used to network multiple computers.

You set up the system in two steps. First, you install the network drivers, and then you set up your computer to communicate over a network. The device uses the same types of protocols that must be set up for an Ethernet network, as described in Chapter 7, "Installing the Software," and the network must then be set up to share folders and files, as explained in Chapter 9, "Learning to Share."

EZLink

The EZLink system includes a hub-like device with a USB port and a built-in cable. You plug the built-in cable into the USB port of one computer, and then you run a 16.5-foot (5-meter) cable (supplied with the system) between the EZLink USB port and the USB port of the other computer to be networked. The EZLink software installs and configures your computer for the network using all the standard network protocols, although you'll have to specify which disks and folders will be shared, as described in Chapter 9, "Learning to Share."

You can also use multiple EZLink devices to daisy chain up to eight computers together, as long as each computer except the first and last have two USB ports. You can also connect up to eight computers through a series of USB hubs, with each computer connected through an EZLink device.

PCSync

PCSync, as well as the more comprehensive LapLink Gold program (which was discussed in Chapter 2, "Getting Connected Without a Network"), make setting up a two-computer network simple. Both programs include an 8-foot (2.4-meter) USB network cable and all of the software needed to create your network. In fact, you don't have to install the complete PCSync or LapLink programs, just the USB cable drivers that are offered as a choice on the installation menus.

Note

You can plug in the PCSync and LapLink USB network cable even when your computer is already running.

Your computer is set up to recognize the USB cable like it would any other type of NIC and communicate using common network protocols.

See Also

You'll learn how to work with network protocols in Chapter 7, "Installing the Software," and how to share files and folders in Chapter 9, "Learning to Share."

Power-Line Networks

A power-line network, called a Home Power Line Cable (HomePLC) network, sends and receives information directly through the power lines of your house, so your existing electrical wiring serves as the network cable. You don't have to run any special cable, and you can network a computer at any location that has an electrical outlet.

Here's how it works:

1. A device connects your computer to an electrical outlet, as shown below.

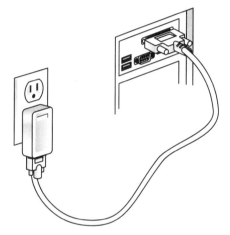

2. Your computer sends information through that device as a low-frequency radio wave. The frequency of the radio wave normally prevents it from interfering with or being interfered by the regular electric current running through the wires.

3. The radio wave travels throughout your entire house until it is picked up by another device connected to another networked computer.

The Pros and Cons of Power-Line Networks

Some potential problems exist with this technology, however, especially if you share an electrical transformer with a neighbor. A *transformer* is a device that reduces the huge amount of power running through the outside power lines to the voltage you need for your house. The radio waves from a power-line network travel throughout all the wiring from the electrical outlet to the transformer supplying current to your house. In some cases, the transformer serves more than one house, so your network signals actually travel through the wires of other houses or apartments served by the same transformer.

Theoretically, if the family in the apartment or house next door shares your transformer and has the same type of power-line network as you do, they could automatically (and inadvertently) be part of your family's network, and vice versa. To prevent this problem from occurring, power-line networks let you create a *secure network* that blocks unauthorized users from your computers. You can make a secure network by building what's called a *firewall*, which limits access to your network to only authorized persons.

The other problems with HomePLC networks are electrical interference and power-line fluctuations. Although the radio waves traveling through the power lines are separate from the electric current, some interference can come from other electronic equipment in the house, especially other power-line devices, such as those for the telephone and video equipment. Power-line fluctuations can occur when you turn on a large electrical appliance, such as an air conditioner. These fluctuations can temporarily interrupt your network connection. Power-line networks help overcome this problem by using devices that filter out the interference before it reaches the network. Like all Ethernet alternatives, power-line technologies are constantly becoming faster and more dependable.

Choosing a Power-Line System

Power-line networks that work with the new HomePlug standard are still under development. Linksys and Cayman, two network hardware manufacturers, plan on releasing HomePlug 1 power-line hardware in the near future. Phonex Broadband Corporation, a manufacturer of a wireless telephone system, has announced a 14-Mbps product called Neverwire 14. Neverwire is an interface that connects a computer's Ethernet or USB port to the home power line. It can also connect to a cable or digital subscriber line (DSL) modem for sharing an Internet connection, and it can connect to a network printer for printer sharing.

To learn more about power-line networking, check out these sites:

* *http://www.phonex.com*
* *http://www.homeplug.com/members/adopter.html*
* *http://www.plugtek.com/index.shtml*

Bridging Network Types

You can use two or more different types of network connections within the same network. For example, suppose you have several computers networked using Ethernet cable, but you also have another computer in the house located where network cable can't be extended. You can install a non-Ethernet device such as a wireless network adapter or telephone network adapter into that computer, and install a similar device into one or more of the networked computers.

Such a network is illustrated in Figure 4-12. Computer A has an external non-Ethernet adapter, while computer B has both Ethernet and non-Ethernet adapters.

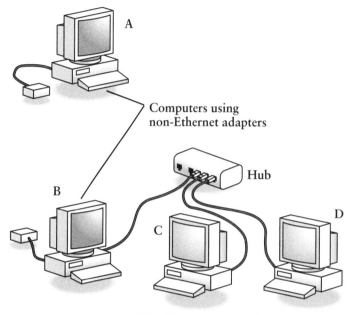

Figure 4-12.

Computers A and B can communicate with each other over the non-Ethernet network, but computer A can't communicate with computers C and D on the Ethernet network unless all of the computers are using Microsoft Windows XP.

In this configuration, computers A and B communicate and share files over the non-Ethernet network, and computers B, C, and D communicate and share files over Ethernet. However, unless you are using Microsoft Windows XP on all of the computers, computer A can't communicate or share files with computers C and D because they don't share a similar network interface.

With Windows XP, you can create a software bridge that links both network types. In fact, a Windows XP bridge can link any combination of network types, such as wired, wireless, and phone line, from two or more network adapters of any type, such as internal, USB, and PC Card. So if you are using Windows XP and have the setup shown in Figure 4-12, all of your computers can communicate because Windows XP bridges the two types of networks. The only problem with using a software bridge such as Windows XP is that both types of interfaces must be installed in one computer, and the bridging computer must be running for any Ethernet and non-Ethernet computers to communicate.

If you aren't using Windows XP, the solution is to connect the two different types of networks by using a device called an *access point*, as illustrated in Figure 4-13. In this illustration, computer A has an external non-Ethernet adapter, whereas the remaining computers have only internal Ethernet cards. A wireless access point has been connected to the network hub with an Ethernet cable. The access point acts as a transceiver that converts wireless signals into Ethernet. Now all the computers can communicate and share files.

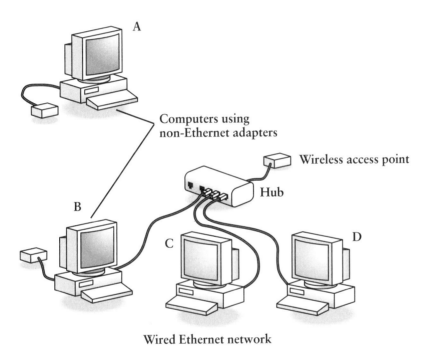

Figure 4-13.
A wireless access point connects the wireless and wired networks so that all of the computers can communicate with each other.

Access points are available for both wireless and phone networks, and some, such as the 2Wire Home Portal, can accommodate both.

The USB network cable drivers with PCSync and LapLink Gold also let you bridge networks. For example, suppose computers A and B in Figure 4-13 were connected using PCSync and a USB network cable. When you install the USB network cable drivers, you can choose to allow bridging, which would network computers A and C as well.

See Also

We'll look at some specific access points and residential gateways in Chapter 6, "Connecting Your Network."

Many access points act not only as a bridge to the wired Ethernet network, but they also serve as residential gateways to allow network users to share a high-speed DSL or cable modem. You can connect your DSL or cable modem either directly to the access point or to a network hub to which the access point is connected.

Home Automation Networks

If you're building a new house or remodeling your current home, you might want to create a complete home automation and entertainment network. In addition to a computer network, you can wire your home for the following functions:

Home Entertainment

In a completely networked home, audio and video would be integrated throughout the entire house. You could control your audio system from every room, selecting CDs or radio stations and TV channels independently of other users. You could be listening to a CD, for example, while another family member listens to the radio; and all of the audio can come from one central location.

You could have the same control over satellite and cable television, your VCR, and your DVD player, so every member of the family could watch exactly what he or she wants. In a completely networked home, family members could record their favorite TV shows, create their own programs on the family closed-circuit TV system, and even record video from their computer.

Telephone and Intercom

Every room of the home could be wired for telephone and faxing, with multiple lines in each room. The telephone could also serve as an intercom, allowing voice communication between rooms, and even broadcasting messages to the entire house and garden. You also could access your telephone answering machine from any phone in the house and access an online phone book to look up and dial numbers. In addition, you could install voice changers on each phone, which prevent callers from knowing if they are speaking with a man, woman, or child—a good safeguard for children who answer the phone.

Security

The network should accommodate an expandable and zoned security system, including front- and rear-door cameras. From any computer in the house, you could see who is at your door, walking up the steps, or pulling into the drive.

Motion detectors would report when someone approaches or enters your house, while pressure sensors indicate when someone is climbing the stairs. Your security system could also include audio and video baby monitors, so you could see and hear your children from any location, and you could speak to them through the system even though you are located somewhere else.

The system would be integrated with your phone line, so activities can trigger calls to the police or fire departments, or any other numbers that you specify. For instance, you could notify a friend or neighbor, or forward a warning message to your office.

In addition, using panic buttons, small key chain devices, and communications units built into jewelry, you could protect yourself both inside and outside your house.

Home Automation

You could control your home's lights and appliances from other locations around the house with an automation system. For example, before going to sleep, you could turn any light in the house on or off from your master bedroom, or you could set the coffee machine to brew a fresh pot for when you wake up in the morning.

You could install systems that will open and close windows, drapes, and blinds at the touch of a switch or by voice command, or perform tasks such as the following:

- Alert you when mail has been delivered to your mailbox or when packages have been dropped off at the doorstep

- Dispense food to a dog, cat, or fish

- Water your houseplants

- Control lawn sprinklers by sensing heat and dryness

- Monitor and report current weather conditions

Environmental Controls

A home network can control heating and air-conditioning systems that automate temperature and ventilation control and that compensate automatically for changing weather conditions. Smart thermostats and other devices can communicate with each other to balance the temperature and air flow throughout the entire house, saving money and making everyone comfortable at the same time. You could call into the system from the road on the way home, for instance, to turn on the heat or air conditioning so the house is comfortable when you arrive.

Connected to the security system, environmental controls could report if your heat goes off and your pipes are in danger of freezing, if your refrigerator or freezer stops working, or if a burst pipe or other plumbing problem is spilling water on the floor.

You could create parts of a home automation network yourself, such as audio and video distribution, but most complete home systems are designed and installed by professionals.

See Also

You'll learn more about connecting home networks in Chapter 6, "Connecting Your Network."

The Bottom Line

Once you've made some basic decisions about the type of network you want, you're ready to install network cards and other types of adaptors into your computers. In the next chapter, you'll learn how to install internal network cards and work with external networking adapters.

Part 2

Installing the Hardware

Chapter 5

Installing Network Cards and Adapters

The next step toward getting your home network going is to purchase and install the *networking hardware*—the network interface cards (NICs) or adapters, and perhaps a hub and cables. If you're lucky enough to have computers with built-in network cards, you can just skip this chapter. Unfortunately, most home computers don't come with a NIC built in, so you'll have to install one yourself or hire someone else to do it.

Note

All internal cards are installed in about the same way, so you can use this chapter to learn how to install an internal card for a telephone or wireless network as well as for Ethernet.

Are You Network-Ready?

Before going any further, you might want to check to see whether your computers are already equipped with NICs. Your machines have NICs if you purchased computers ready to be connected to a network, or if you inherited used computers that had NICs installed when you received them. Many laptop computers, for example, come with a built-in Ethernet port. If a computer is new, check its documentation or the specifications on the box the computer came in. Chances are, if your computer is network-ready, the box will say so prominently.

With a hand-me-down or used computer, check the case for an RJ-45 connector, which looks like an extra-large telephone jack, or look for a small metal barrel that sticks out. The large, telephone-like jack is for a twisted-pair Ethernet connection; the metal barrel is for 10Base2 Thin Ethernet coaxial cable. The following illustration shows the typical network connections on the back of a network card. Make sure not to confuse the large RJ-45 plug with the smaller RJ-11 plug, which is used by a modem. If you have an internal modem, there will be a separate set of connections for it, typically with two RJ-11 plugs—one for the line in and one for the line out.

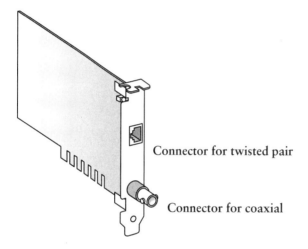

Connector for twisted pair

Connector for coaxial

If you see neither a twisted-pair connection nor a coaxial connection, your computer isn't network-ready. If you see both, you're in good shape. If you see only one type of connection, it must be the correct type for the cable you'll use. Let's say you've inherited an older computer that has a NIC with only a coaxial connection. You can't connect your computer to other computers that have twisted-pair connections without replacing the NIC.

Working Without Cards

Perhaps the one aspect of setting up for networking that might make you uncomfortable is installing the NIC. As you'll learn in the section, "Playing the Card Game," later in this chapter, installing a NIC inside your computer is easy. But if you'd rather not open your computer case, you can either pay someone to do it for you or consider using a network adapter that doesn't have to be installed in your computer. For example, some devices exist for Ethernet, wireless networking, and phone-line networking that easily plug into your computer's universal serial bus (USB) port.

A USB Ethernet device, for example, has a USB connection at one end and a twisted-pair connection at the other end. You plug the adapter into the USB connection on your computer and connect a cable from the adapter to the network hub, which joins all the cables from all the NICs. A USB phone-line device has both a USB connection and a telephone connection. You plug the adapter into the USB connection on your computer and connect a cable from the adapter to a telephone jack. A USB wireless device, on the other hand, has only a USB connection. The device itself is the transceiver that sends and receives wireless network signals.

Note

Your USB ports may be located in the back or front of your computer, or in both locations. In addition, be sure to check the instructions that came with your USB or other external network interface. Sometimes you must install the provided software before connecting the device to your computer.

To use a USB network device, you must be running Microsoft Windows 95 version 4.00950B or later, Windows 98, Windows Millennium Edition (Me), Windows 2000, or Windows XP, and you must have at least one USB connection on your computer.

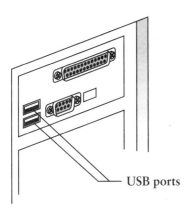

USB ports

You might also be able to find external network devices that plug into your computer's printer port or serial port. But printer port devices should be used only as a last resort—say, if your computer doesn't have a USB port or empty slot—because they are usually slower than Ethernet networks. As for serial port network interfaces, they are usually more expensive than other types, and they can be complicated to set up. Therefore, serial port devices are recommended for businesses with older computers but not for home networks.

Networking for Broadband Internet

If you connect or are planning to connect to a digital subscriber line (DSL) or cable modem for the Internet, you'll probably need an Ethernet connection for the modem, although some cable modems connect to a USB port. If you also want to connect the computer to a home network, you'll need a second Ethernet port. You use one port for the modem and the other for your network.

You can use USB Ethernet adapters for both a network and a high-speed modem. They're ideal when you already have an Ethernet card installed on your computer, and you either don't have another internal slot or you don't want to take up another internal slot.

Cook It Yourself or Order Out?

If you decide that the speed advantages of using networking hardware that includes an internal NIC are for you, consider installing the card yourself. There's nothing difficult or mysterious about the inside of a computer—it's just a collection of wires, circuit boards, and other paraphernalia. Lots of people insert network cards, sound cards, and other kinds of cards themselves. They save a little money and they get the satisfaction of having faced the computer monster and triumphed.

Others would never operate on their computer even if you paid them. They'd rather have a professional do it. They save themselves the frustration if something goes wrong, and they have the comforting feeling that they can just take the computer back to the professional who installed the hardware for them if problems arise later.

Installing a Network Card Yourself

You don't have to be an electronics expert to install a NIC in your computer. You just need some patience, common sense, and the ability to use a screwdriver, which is about the only tool you'll need.

Of course, whenever you open a computer, you're exposing a lot of sensitive and expensive equipment. Certainly, pulling or poking the wrong part can damage your computer, but if you're careful, nothing will go wrong. A lot of wires and cables are also running around inside your computer. You can safely move wires out of the way as long as you're careful not to disconnect them.

Caution

Keep in mind that you shouldn't open your computer with wet hands, when the computer is plugged in, or while the kids, the spouse, the television, or the telephone are distracting you.

If you have more than two computers to network, start with just two of them. Buy enough hardware for the two and no more. Setting up a network isn't difficult, but it takes some time, and it's best to get two computers communicating before you invest your whole bankroll. Starting with just two gives you time to concentrate on the basics.

Note

Purchasing hardware by mail order can be a money-saving alternative if you want to install it yourself. See the "Where to Shop?" section later in this chapter for more information.

If you're uncomfortable taking apart your computer to install the card yourself, however, you should consider having a professional install the hardware for you, as described in the next section.

Finding Someone Else to Do It

If you decide not to install the hardware yourself, you'll need to have someone do it for you. That person can also set up the software drivers for your network card and configure Microsoft Windows for the network. *Network drivers* are the programs needed for your computer to access the NIC.

See Also

If you install the card yourself, you can learn about drivers in the section "Installing Network Drivers" in Chapter 7, "Installing the Software," on page 158.

You might be able to find someone to come to your home to install the NIC, but the home visit will cost you extra. The less expensive alternative is to take your computer to a store that will insert the NIC; however, that solution has these drawbacks:

- You'll have to disconnect all of the cables connected to the computer and pack up your computer to carry it to the store—which can be a real hassle.

- You'll have to do without your computer for a while.

- You'll have to consider deleting any sensitive material you have on your hard disk before you take the computer to the shop.

- You'll have to carry the computer back from the store and reconnect everything after the shop is finished working on it.

- If you have a problem with the NIC later on, you'll have to take it to the store again.

If you decide to take the computer to the store, you won't need to include the keyboard, mouse, or monitor—just the computer case. The shop will connect a keyboard and monitor for the installation process.

Some stores might be able to install the NIC while you wait, but others will make you drop off the computer and come back another day. It doesn't take long to install the card, but some shops are quite busy, especially around the holidays. If you can't do without your computer for long, ask when the shop is least busy and try to schedule your visit for that time.

I also suggest that you go back to the same store where you bought the computer; you might get a price break on installation. When you purchase a computer at a computer superstore, for example, you can usually have a network card installed for a small flat rate. You'll save a little money and gain some peace of mind knowing that trained professionals are working on your computer.

Buying and Installing a Network Card

Now it's time to make some choices. You'll need to decide what to buy, where to buy it, and whether you should buy separate components or obtain everything in a kit.

It's All in the Cards

In Chapter 3, "Planning a Network," you learned about the various types of NICs and how to connect your computers. When you select hardware that includes an internal NIC, whether it works through Ethernet, a wireless network, or the telephone line, you'll have to make sure you get the correct NIC for your computer.

If you decide on an Ethernet network, the NIC you buy must be either twisted-pair cable or coaxial cable. Here's a recap of the choices:

- **Twisted-pair cable** looks like telephone cable on steroids, and it's by far the most popular type of cable. You'll need a hub to which cables from all the computers connect. The hub must be turned on for any computer to communicate with another.

- **Coaxial cable** (also known as thin Ethernet) looks like cable TV wire and doesn't require a hub. You run the wire from one computer to the next.

Note

You can use fiberoptic cable with the new Gigabit Ethernet (GbE) cards, and it's more expandable for the future. Because fiberoptic cable is expensive and harder to install, however, it isn't commonly used for home networks.

When you buy a network card, make sure it's designed for the type of cable you select. You can play it safe by purchasing *combo cards*: NICs that have connectors for both coaxial cables and twisted-pair cables.

Next, consider whether you'll be satisfied with the usual 10-megabit-per-second (Mbps) network speed of regular Ethernet or whether you'll want a 100-Mbps network (also called Fast Ethernet). For home networks, 10 Mbps is fast enough for now. But when the price of 100-Mbps hardware drops in the near future, slower cards and hubs might become obsolete.

Your network hub should be capable of handling the highest speed of network card. Older hubs, for example, can handle communications only at the 10-Mbps speed. The hubs generally available today, however, are dual-speed hubs that can accommodate network signals at both the 10-Mbps and 100-Mbps speeds. Using a dual-speed hub, you can mix 10-Mbps cards and 100-Mbps cards on the same network so you can always upgrade the parts of the network that you'd like to go faster.

If you are planning to set up a wireless network, review Chapter 4, "Types of Networks," to decide whether you want to use the Wi-Fi 802.11b standard, which runs at 11 Mbps, or consider a less expensive HomeRF system. Remember, HomeRF is now technologically outdated until the faster HomeRF 2 hardware becomes available. Also consider whether you want to create a peer-to-peer network of all wireless computers, or use an access point that allows the wireless devices to connect to a wired Ethernet network.

If you want to use your home's telephone wires for your network, you can choose between a newer 10-Mbps system and an older 1-Mbps system. An older system might cost a little less, but you'll have to contend with its decreased system performance and obsolescence of hardware if you want to expand your network later.

Catching the Right Bus

The *bus* is the part of the computer that moves information around among all the components. The signals flowing in and out of the NIC and other parts of the computer flow through the bus, like traffic on city streets.

The NIC plugs into an expansion slot on the bus that's not already occupied by a video card, modem, or other device. The metal contacts in the slot mesh with the contacts on the card so that electronic information can pass between them.

Most computers today have three types of slots (shown in the illustration below):

- **Industry Standard Architecture (ISA) slots** are the type used in older machines. Most new computers do not include ISA ports, but you might still find them in some machines. They're usually black and have a plastic divider across the slot about two-thirds of the way from the end. The card fits into the slot and has a space to accommodate the divider.

- **Peripheral Component Interconnect (PCI) slots** are usually white. They're shorter than ISA sockets and have a divider about three-quarters of the way along.

- **The Accelerated Graphics Port (AGP) slot** is shorter than the PCI slots. It also has a divider, and it's set back further than the other slots. The AGP slot is used for a high-speed graphics card, so you can't use it for a NIC.

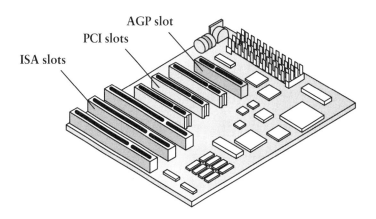

Note

Some older computers might have Extended ISA (EISA) sockets, which look like ISA sockets except that they're brown.

You must purchase the correct type of NIC for the type of slot that's open and available in your computer. You can often determine which slots are free by looking at a photograph or an illustration in your computer's manual that shows the inside of the computer. It should show you which slots are occupied, and by what.

If the manual doesn't help, you might be able to tell by looking at the back of the computer for unused slots. You'll see a series of metal plates covering openings. Some of these will have connections for items such as the monitor, modem, and sound card, and others will be empty. If the computer manual shows what each type of slot is for, match up the blank plate with the slot to determine the type of slot that's empty.

If you still can't tell, open the computer and look around inside to find an empty peripheral slot. If your computer doesn't have any empty slots, you'll need the type of NIC that connects to a USB port.

PCI cards are the easiest type of NIC to install inside a computer because they require the least software configuration. In most cases, they'll configure themselves when you plug them in and turn on the computer because they are *plug-and-play compatible*. This means that Windows senses that the card is installed and either installs the correct software by itself or prompts you to insert the disk that came with the NIC.

ISA cards are usually more complicated to install, even those that are plug and play. With ISA cards, you might have to worry about changing their settings to avoid conflicts with other cards in your computer.

Connecting Laptops

Although a few laptop computers have built-in NICs, laptops normally don't have internal slots into which you can plug a NIC. You can still connect a laptop to a network by using a network interface device on a PC Card or by using an external network interface device that connects to the laptop's USB port.

PC Cards are about the size of credit cards; they slide into a PC Card slot on your laptop and they work just like other NICs. The Ethernet or network phone-line cable connects directly to the end of the card sticking out of the computer or to a smaller cable that plugs into the card. Some Ethernet cards use only twisted-pair cable, but others have adapters that can accept either twisted-pair cable or coaxial cable. Wireless PC Cards have a section extending out of the computer that serves as an antenna.

Installing a PC Card is a piece of cake. The label on the card is on top, and the end of the card with the small holes fits into the PC Card slot, which is usually on the side of the computer. Figure 3-1, in Chapter 3, shows how a PC Card network interface fits into a laptop.

Most laptops have two PC Card slots: an upper and a lower slot. If one slot already has something in it, such as a modem, slide the NIC into the other slot. Then push the card in firmly. This action pushes out a small tab on the side of the slot that you can press in when you want to remove the card.

Getting to the Hub of the Matter

If you decide to use twisted-pair cables to connect computers to an Ethernet network, you'll need a twisted-pair cable for each computer, and you'll need a hub. As you learned in Chapter 4, "Types of Networks," the hub serves as a central connection through which all network signals flow. The least expensive hubs are probably all you'll need for a home network. They have ports for up to five computers. You can also get hubs that handle more than five computers, but they are more expensive.

A five-port hub might also have a sixth connector called an *uplink port,* which lets you connect hubs and link them in a chain. When you need to add a sixth or seventh computer to your network, you can purchase another hub and add it to the chain.

You can get 10-Mbps hubs, 100-Mbps (Fast Ethernet) hubs, and dual-speed 10/100-Mbps hubs. The dual-speed hubs are perfect for networks that have both 10-Mbps and 100-Mbps NICs attached because you'll get the maximum speed of each NIC.

Note

As an alternative to a hub, you can use a more expensive device called a *switch.* A switch gives each connection on the network its own path to travel for faster performance.

In Chapter 6, we'll look at installing and locating hubs in more detail. You'll also learn that you can avoid using a hub altogether if you want to connect only two computers.

Multifunction Hubs

Before purchasing a network hub, consider whether you'd like to share a modem with everyone on the network. As you'll learn in Chapter 11, "Going Online Through the Network," you can connect a modem, even a DSL or cable modem, so that it's available to everyone.

One way to share a modem is to connect it to one computer and let other users share it. This option is inexpensive, but it means that the computer to which the modem is attached must be turned on for other users to connect to the Internet.

The alternative is to connect the modem directly to the network hub. This way, only the hub must be turned on for anyone on the network to access the modem. This solution is more expensive because you'll need some extra hardware or software.

If you think you might want to connect a modem to a hub, you can purchase a special hub that either has a modem built in or that already contains the hardware needed to share a DSL or cable modem. These hubs cost more than a plain Ethernet hub but might be less expensive than purchasing separate modem-sharing hardware.

If you plan to add wireless systems or phone-line systems to your Ethernet network, consider a wireless or phone-line access point or residential gateway that has a built-in Ethernet hub.

You'll learn more about these types of hubs in Chapter 6, "Connecting Your Network."

The Whole Kit and Caboodle

Because of the growing popularity of networking, many manufacturers provide network kits, which package in one box all the essentials for setting up a small network. Ethernet kits, for example, usually include two NICs, a hub, and a couple of network cables.

The kits are a good value because they often cost less than the components purchased separately. For $50 to $100, you can buy a complete Ethernet kit that gives you everything you need to connect two computers. If you need to add computers, you can purchase additional cards and cables separately. Also, you can be relatively certain that all the parts have been designed to work together. Many network kits even come with a program that sets up Windows for networking, so you don't have to do any software configuration.

In addition, most of these kits include software that lets you share one Internet connection among all the people on the network. This feature means that everyone on the network can browse the Internet at the same time, using one phone line and one Internet account.

See Also

You'll learn how to share Internet accounts in Chapter 11, "Going Online Through the Network."

Kits do have some disadvantages, however. Although you might be able to find a kit that includes one internal NIC for a desktop computer and one PC Card for a laptop, almost all the kits offer two cards of the same type. That's fine if that's what you need, but otherwise, you might have to purchase a card of a different type separately. The other disadvantage is that if one of the cards is defective, you might have to return the entire kit, which means you'll have to remove both cards and the hub, even if only one component is malfunctioning.

As an alternative to a kit, you can purchase each component separately. You can then buy different cards for different machines and return individual pieces if necessary. Because all Ethernet cards work together, you can even purchase NICs and hubs from different manufacturers. Most 802.11b wireless cards are also compatible with each other.

Where to Shop?

Now that you've made some basic decisions about the type of components to buy, you're ready to get out your credit card and go shopping. But where?

You'll find the best prices at computer superstores—those large stores that carry only computer hardware and software—and through mail order. Superstores have a good selection of kits and individual components, you can purchase the kit and take it home the same day, and you'll have a local place to go if you must return anything. If you can't find items locally, you should opt for buying them through mail order.

Mail order companies and online retailers such as PC Connection, CDW, Insight, Outpost.com, and Buy.com also offer great prices and often a better selection than local stores. Although you do have to pay for shipping, most mail order and Internet companies don't charge sales tax. They offer the same return policy as local stores and often provide overnight or two-day shipping. You'll have to install the hardware yourself, however, and it'll take longer if you have to return or exchange something.

Note

If you decide to purchase hardware online or through a catalog, do some comparative online shopping first. Make certain that the product you plan to purchase is the most current version by checking the manufacturer's Web site. Current products will be supported with drivers for all versions of Windows, including Windows 2000 and Windows XP.

As an alternative, you can purchase hardware at large chain appliance stores, electronic boutiques in malls, and independent computer stores. However, although the prices at appliance stores might be good, you'll rarely get the sales help you need. Expect to pay slightly higher prices at electronic boutiques in malls that carry computer games, magazines, and some hardware. Again, the salespeople usually aren't computer experts, although they'll know a lot about the most awesome computer games.

Also expect to pay slightly higher prices at local independent computer stores. However, at your local computer store, you'll probably find the most knowledgeable salespeople and the most helpful technical support. Try to pick a shop that's been around for a while. Plenty of little computer stores pop up, only to go out of business by the time the stoplight on the corner changes. There's nothing wrong with these places, but it's nice to have a place to go if something goes wrong down the road.

You should consider one other place as a source for computer hardware: computer shows. If you live near a metropolitan area, look for computer shows periodically at convention centers, schools and colleges, or other meeting grounds. You might have to pay a small entrance fee, but you'll have access to a wide selection of vendors and products. Some vendors simply travel from show to show, but local computer stores often send their own representatives. If you need support, you might have difficulty tracking down a traveling vendor, or one from out of town.

My recommendation? Purchase a kit from a computer superstore in your area. Check the return policy, and install and test the hardware before the return period ends. If you don't want to install the hardware yourself, have the techies at the superstore do it for you.

If there's no superstore in your area, find a local computer shop that's been around for some time. Tell them what you want and that you want to spend as little money as possible.

Playing the Card Game

If you've chosen to install the network cards yourself, a little preparation will expedite the job. If you're installing an ISA network card, refer to the section "Installing ISA Cards," later in this chapter, before attempting the installation.

Make sure you have a Phillips screwdriver; a small one will usually do. Don't use a magnetic screwdriver because the magnetism in the screwdriver might scramble information stored in computer chips.

Find a small container, such as a paper cup. You'll be removing small screws and you'll want a place to put them so they don't get lost.

Although it may not be necessary, you might find it handy to have needle-nose pliers available in case you drop a screw and need to fish it out of the computer. You might also need a flat-bladed screwdriver to pry off a cover plate. And you'll need a scalpel and forceps (only kidding, of course).

Next, remove rings, necklaces, and any other metal jewelry that might hang down or make contact with the inner workings of the computer. Metal is a conductor of static electricity, and necklaces can get caught inside the computer.

Now find a place to work. Make sure the work area is as free from static electricity as possible. Rub your hands on your clothing and touch something metal. Did you get a shock? If so, static electricity is present, and it's a danger to the components in any computer. Work in a room without a carpet, if possible, and discharge any static electricity by touching the computer case before working inside. You can also purchase an antistatic band from a computer store or online that wraps around your wrist and connects to the computer case. Any static that is present flows through the band to the case rather than through the delicate electronic equipment inside the case.

You can work on a table or on the floor—whatever you do, don't try squeezing in beside the desk or balancing the computer on your lap. Make sure you use a bright lamp to illuminate the interior of the computer. In addition, it's best to find a spot near a phone because many manufacturers supply a telephone number that you can call for support. With the phone close to your workspace, you can describe to the support technician what you see and what you're doing.

If you work on a table, use a tablecloth or towel to protect its surface. Clear the table of other objects so they don't get in the way or get pushed off as you move the computer around.

You should have plenty of room on all sides of the computer, so if you decide to work on the floor, pick the center of a room or a hallway where you won't be disturbed by foot traffic. If you must work in a carpeted room, make sure the rug doesn't have a deep pile that will attract static electricity and make screws that fall on it difficult to find. Work on a towel or other piece of fabric to protect the floor (you'll be amazed how much dirt can accumulate inside a computer case).

Caution

To protect the NIC from static electricity, leave it in its antistatic packet until you're ready to insert it. Never touch the surface of the card or the metal connectors on the bottom, and handle the card only by its edges.

Installing the Card

When you're ready to start, work on just one computer at a time; don't take two or more computers apart at the same time because you might mix up their parts.

Follow these steps:

1. Unplug the computer.

Caution

Don't just turn off the computer or turn off the power strip it is attached to. The computer must be unplugged.

2. Unplug the wires from the keyboard, mouse, printer, scanner, and any other device. Think of this as a good opportunity to dust behind the computer and straighten out all the cables.

3. Move the computer case to the work area.

4. Remove the computer's cover and put any screws that you remove into the paper cup.
   If you have a desktop computer, you might need to remove only the top panel. Some cases have tabs on the back that you press to release and lift off the cover. In other cases (pardon the pun), you must remove several screws at the back of the

computer and slide the case forward to remove it. If you have a tower computer that sits on the floor, you can often remove one or both side panels. Look carefully at the case to determine whether the two side panels appear to be separate from the rest of the case. If they are, you need to remove the screws only on one side and slide the panel away. Which side? Sometimes you just can't tell. If you take off one side and you don't see the row of cards and slots, replace the panel and remove the other side.

The screws you need to remove are probably near the edge of the case. Don't remove any screws from the middle, especially ones near the power supply, where you plug in the power cord, because they might hold the power supply in place. The power supply is bulky and can damage the computer if it falls on a circuit board. With all of the wires attached to a power supply, it can also be difficult to reattach.

5. Remove the metal slot cover behind the empty slot in which you plan to place the NIC, as shown in Figure 5-1.

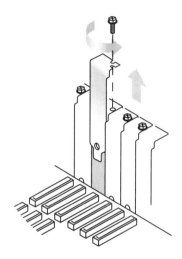

Figure 5-1.
Remove the cover plate for the slot.

You might need to either remove the screw that holds the cover in place or break off the small tab that holds the cover. Use a flat screwdriver to gently pry the cover away and then work the plate back and forth until it comes out.

6. Position the card so the connectors are toward the back of the computer. The metal back of the card will replace the blank slot cover that you've removed.

Note

If you're building a wireless network, the card might have a protrusion at the back that serves as the antenna. You might have to angle the card slightly to get the protrusion through the back of the computer before you straighten out the card so that it fits in the socket.

7. Line up the bottom edge of the card with the slot and confirm that they match. (Some ISA cards won't fill the entire ISA slot, just the front section.)

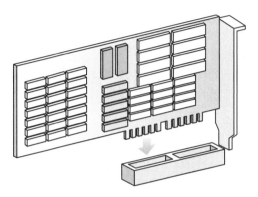

    If any wires or cables are in the way, gently move them aside without disconnecting them. Although most cables inside the computer are connected snugly, some are not, so make sure you don't dislodge the smaller and more delicate cables, such as those that connect a CD drive to the sound card, while moving them aside to access the slot.

8. Push the card down into the slot, exerting steady, firm pressure. As the card goes into the slot, the metal back should slide down and fit where the plate cover was. The top of the back should rest on the screw hole. If it doesn't, the card isn't down all the way.

    Try not to bend the card to either side, rock it back and forth, or touch its surface. Just hold the card by its edges and apply firm, downward pressure.

9. Being careful not to drop the screw into the computer, screw the metal back of the card into the frame of the computer. This screw is important because it keeps the card firmly seated in the slot.

10. Replace the computer cover and be careful not to trap any wires.

11. Before putting the computer case back in its place, clean around the area, straighten out the cables, and make sure you have no leftover screws in the paper cup.

12. Plug everything back in. Plug in the power cord last.

Installing ISA Cards

Using ISA cards often requires that you change special settings on the card, such as its IRQ and I/O address. IRQ stands for *interrupt request.* Imagine the IRQ as a telephone number. Each device in your computer has a different IRQ number that it uses to communicate with the computer. Your computer scans each IRQ line to see which device is requesting service—that is, to send or receive information through the computer bus. Only one device is allowed on an IRQ line at one time. If more than one ISA device uses the same IRQ, their signals might conflict.

> **Note**
>
> Some devices, such as PCI cards, can usually share an IRQ. If your network adapter doesn't work, however, check for an IRQ conflict. You'll learn more about this topic in the section "Troubleshooting Hardware Conflicts," in Chapter 7, "Installing the Software," on page 207.

The *I/O address* is the location in your computer's memory where the signals from the device are stored. No two devices can have the same I/O address or their signals will conflict.

The IRQ and the I/O address of an ISA device are changed either by hardware or software. If the card's documentation tells you that the IRQ and I/O address are set up through software, you can skip this section for now.

On some older cards, you make these settings by changing a small switch or moving a *jumper*, which is a small device with metal prongs, as shown in Figure 5-2. Notice the plastic cap that fits over two of the prongs. The pair of prongs that the cap is on determines the IRQ that is assigned to the device. The card's documentation will show you which switch or jumper to change.

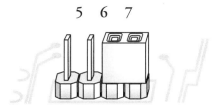

Figure 5-2.
Positioning a jumper to set the IRQ to 7.

Note

PCI plug-and-play cards share IRQs automatically, so no special setup is required.

Before you can pick an IRQ setting for the card, you must check to see what's available on your system to avoid a conflict. To check which IRQs are already being used, follow these steps:

1. Look at the documentation on the card for possible IRQ and I/O settings.

2. In Windows 95, Windows 98, Windows Me, and Windows 2000, right-click My Computer on the Windows desktop. In Windows XP, click Start on the desktop and right-click My Computer on the Start menu.

3. Click Properties on the shortcut menu to open the System Properties dialog box.

If you're using Windows 95, Windows 98, or Windows Me, continue with these next steps to see which IRQ and I/O settings are available:

1. Click the Device Manager tab in the System Properties dialog box.

2. Double-click Computer at the top of the list.

3. Click the Interrupt Request (IRQ) radio button. The IRQs, usually numbered from 0 to 15, are listed.

4. Look for an unused IRQ or one that is assigned to a device you don't plan to use, such as an unused COM port. Don't worry if some IRQs are used by more than one device in the list. Some devices can share IRQs.

Note

A PCI NIC can share an IRQ with an item called *PCI IRQ Steering* without a conflict.

5. Click the Input/Output (I/O) radio button.

6. Check to see which of the addresses are free for your card to use.

7. Click Cancel to return to the Device Manager tab.

8. Click Cancel again to close the System Properties dialog box.

If you're using Windows 2000 or Windows XP, follow these steps to check for available IRQ and I/O settings:

1. Click the Hardware tab in the System Properties dialog box, and then click the Device Manager button to open the Device Manager window.

2. Choose Resources By Type from the View menu.

3. Click the plus sign next to the Interrupt Request (IRQ) option. The IRQs, usually numbered from 0 to 15, are listed.

4. Look for an unused IRQ or one that is assigned to a device you don't plan to use, such as an unused COM port. Don't worry if some IRQs are used by more than one device in the list. Some devices can share IRQs.

5. Click the plus sign next to the Input/Output (I/O) option.

6. Check to see which of the addresses are free for your card to use.

7. Close the Device Manager window and then close the System Properties box.

8. Set the switches or jumpers on the card to settings that won't conflict.

9. Install the card and restart your system.

The Bottom Line

Your NIC is now installed. If you installed the NIC yourself, you must still install the NIC drivers and configure Windows, and that's the subject of Chapter 7, "Installing the Software." If someone else installed it, your network drivers and Windows software should also be set up and ready to go.

The next chapter covers how to run cable for your Ethernet network and how to connect phone-line and wireless networks.

Chapter 6

Connecting Your Network

Now that you have network interface cards (NICs) or external adapters installed in your computers, you're ready to connect them. Because a chain is only as strong as its weakest link, though, your network is only as reliable as the connections between computers, so you'll want to follow the suggestions in this chapter carefully to connect your network effectively.

Connecting an Ethernet Network

Because it requires cables and hubs, an Ethernet network is the most complicated network to set up. If you can run cables throughout the house, however, the speed and dependability of Ethernet might be well worth the trouble.

Running the Cable

You can often run cable between devices in the same room along the baseboard molding. In some rooms, you might be able to hide the cable by pushing it between the carpet and the bottom of the molding. If not, run the cable on top of the baseboard molding. Of course, it looks best if the cable is the same color as the molding. When you get to a corner, don't bend the cable sharply, even if it has to protrude slightly from the corner—sharp bends can damage the wires inside the cable so your computers can't communicate. *To learn more about selecting and purchasing network cable, see the section "Making the Grade," later in this chapter.*

Running Cable Between Rooms

Cabling together two or more computers in the same room is relatively easy, but when the computers are in different parts of the house, connecting them can be more of a challenge.

Running Cable Between Adjacent Rooms   If you need to connect two computers in adjacent rooms, you can drill a hole in the wall between the rooms and feed the cable through. Of course, if the computers are on opposite sides of the same wall, you won't have to run the cable along a baseboard. Alternatively, you can run the cable through the ceiling, between the ceiling joists. You'll then have to make two holes: one where the wire enters the ceiling in one room, and another where the wire exits the ceiling in the other room.

If a heating duct or a return runs between rooms, you can also run the cable through it, but if you make holes in the metal to get the wire into the duct, stuff some insulation around the wire to prevent air loss around the holes and to protect the cable from the sharp metal edges. You might find some space next to pipes or other wires that you can use for your network cable. If the space you must go through is insulated, be sure to replace any insulation that you remove. In some localities, the fire code requires that all spaces between floors be insulated as a fire-prevention measure.

When drilling holes through walls, be careful not to drill through pipes and electrical wires. Consider purchasing a device from your local home center or hardware store that you can use to detect wood studs, metal pipes, or electrical cable behind the surface of the wall. Drill holes only where the device indicates that no hidden items are present. If you are drilling through wallboard, you can make a preliminary hole with a small punch to determine whether any obstacle lies below the surface.

If you want to connect a computer that's directly upstairs, look for a closet. You might be able to drill a hole in the closet ceiling and run the cable through it. Because floors can be 8 inches (20 centimeters) thick or more, you might have to use a coat hanger to fish the cable through. After the cable reaches the other floor, you can run it along the baseboard.

Running Cable Between Nonadjacent Rooms   If the computers you want to connect aren't in adjacent rooms, you might need to run cable through an attic or basement. If you have a basement or crawl space, for example, you can run cable between the first-floor rooms by drilling through the floors in both rooms. You can then run the cable down one hole, across the basement ceiling, and up the other hole. Use an attic the same way. Drill through the ceiling in both rooms. Run the cable up one hole, across the attic, and down the other hole. *If you need custom cable lengths, see the section "Making Your Own Network Cables," later in this chapter.*

If you have more than two floors in your house, running wires between nonadjacent floors can be a real challenge because you don't want unsightly wires running up the wall. You can try routing cables through the walls using a coil of wire called a *fish*, which you can purchase at most hardware stores. The fish is more rigid than network cable and easier to feed through spaces. Once the fish is through, tie an end of the cable to it and pull it back through. However, you might have to make some holes in the walls to run the cable through, and then patch the holes when you're done. If you don't want to fish cables through walls, try to run the cables through closets from floor to floor.

Caution

Never run network cable along the exterior of your house. If the cable is hit by lightning, all the computers on your network can be damaged.

Using Twisted-Pair Cable

When you're using twisted-pair cable for the network, you must run a cable from the NIC at each computer to the hub. If you purchased an Ethernet kit, you probably have a hub and two lengths of cable. Simply plug in the cable just as you would a telephone cable.

Note

Lengths of twisted-pair cable with connectors at both ends are called *patch cables*.

If you have cable that is too short, you can join two lengths of cable end to end with a coupler, as shown below, which has two female RJ-45 jacks. Couplers for network cable resemble couplers for telephone cable, only bigger.

Making the Grade

You can purchase several categories, or *grades,* of twisted-pair cable. The higher the category, the better the cable and the more stable the connection. The standard grade for home networks is *Category 5*, or Cat 5. Fast Ethernet, which runs at 100 Mbps, requires Cat 5 cable, but for 10BaseT, which runs at only 10 Mbps, you might be able to get away with Cat 3 or Cat 4. Most stores sell only Cat 5 cable because the price difference between categories is negligible for short patch cables. Another category of cable, called enhanced Category 5 (or Cat 5e), falls between Cat 5 and Cat 6 in price and quality. You won't need to use Cat 6 or Cat 7 cable in your home because they're designed for high-speed networks that must span long distances.

Note

Cat 2 cable is used to wire alarm systems and telephone lines. Although you can use Cat 3 and Cat 4 cable for 10-Mbps networks, to achieve the best performance, you should use Cat 5 or Cat 5e whenever possible.

You can purchase twisted-pair cable in various lengths and colors. Most stores stock only one or two colors, but additional colors are available through mail order, from companies such as Data Comm Warehouse *(http://www.warehouse.com/datacomm),* Cables to Go *(http://www.cablestogo.com)* and Network Warehouse (*http://www.superwarehouse.com/networks*). You can also buy cable that has molded or booted ends: plastic or rubberized material covers the connection between the wire and the plug. This reinforcement strengthens the connections and makes the cable more suitable for installations that require you to frequently remove and reinsert cable.

Note

You can purchase inexpensive Cat 5 cable that has only four of the eight wires connected, but it runs only at 10BaseT speeds, not at 100BaseT.

Hubless Networking

If you want to network only two computers, you can avoid using a hub by connecting their NICs with special cable called *crossover* or *cross-pinned* cable. You plug one end of the crossover cable into the NIC of one computer and plug the other end into the NIC of the other computer. No other hardware is required, and the cable can be up to 328 feet (100 meters) long. Crossover cable is inexpensive: a 10-foot (3-meter) cable costs $20 or less.

Note

Two computers running Microsoft Windows XP that have FireWire adapters installed can network directly through the FireWire adapters. Windows XP automatically configures the network for the FireWire adapter, and the network runs as if two Ethernet network cards were installed and connected.

If you go to a computer store to purchase a crossover cable, make sure you don't get a regular patch cable, the standard cable for networking. A crossover cable has two of its wires switched, so it's different from a regular network cable.

If you can't find crossover cable at the local computer superstore, try ordering it from a mail order company, such as Data Comm Warehouse *(http://www.warehouse.com/datacomm).* You can also go to a small, local computer store where they might make one for you.

Tip

Because crossover and regular patch cables look the same, you might want to wrap a small piece of duct tape or adhesive tape on one end of the crossover cable and write *crossover* on it. This label will help you distinguish the crossover cable from your regular patch cable.

Placing the Hub

When you want to connect three or more computers or connect a printer directly to the network, you'll need a hub. Consider a hub even when you need to connect only two computers. Hubs are so inexpensive that buying one might cost less than having crossover cable custom made. Before connecting the hub to the network, however, consider its placement.

Note

You'll need a hub for any Ethernet network of three or more computers that uses twisted-pair cable, even networks with computers using external universal serial bus (USB) Ethernet adapters.

The hub must be plugged into an electrical source for power, so make sure the hub is near an outlet. Consider connecting the hub to an outlet that isn't controlled by a wall switch, because you'll probably want to leave the hub turned on at all times. The hub needs some air circulating around it, so don't put it an enclosed space, and be sure to keep it away from direct sunlight, heat, radios, fluorescent lights, or transmitters of any kind that can cause interference.

The main trick in placing a hub is to make it convenient to all your computers so that you can easily connect cables from the computers to the hub, passing through the fewest number of walls, floors, and rooms. If you're connecting two computers that are in the same room, place the hub near an electrical outlet and run the cables from each computer to the hub. If you're connecting computers in adjacent rooms, locate the hub near the hole you've made between the rooms.

If you live in a one story house with a basement, consider placing the hub in the basement. You can drill through the floor in each room that has a computer and run cables down to the hub in the basement, as shown below.

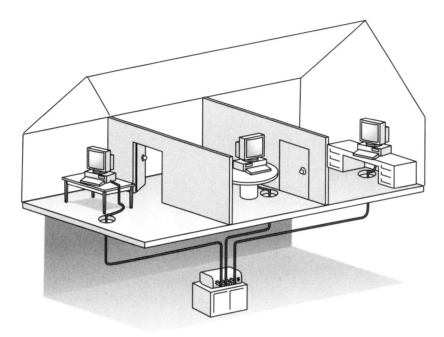

Because you have to run separate wires from every computer to the hub, sometimes the central location where you'd like to place the hub isn't ideal, especially when you have to run the cable through walls and along baseboards. Select a location that requires the least amount of cable and the least amount of fishing through walls, floors, and ceilings.

Making Your Own Network Cable

If you have a lot of wiring to do, you might want to consider making your own patch cable. That way, you can get cables that are just the right length and you can save some money, too. Rather than purchase patch cable that already has connectors on both ends, you can purchase *bulk cable*—long lengths of twisted-pair wire without any connectors. Although you must usually buy lengths of 250 feet (75 meters) or more to get bulk cable, cable at that length is relatively inexpensive. A 250-foot (75-meter) roll of bulk cable can cost about the same as two 50-foot (15-meter) patch cords. Buying bulk cable in longer lengths, 500 to 1000 feet (150 to 305 meters), is an even better bargain.

Note

You can also purchase patch cable, cut one end off to make it the proper length, and install a connector on the end yourself.

In addition to bulk cable, you'll need a supply of connectors and two special tools—a *stripper* and a *crimper*. The stripper cuts away the outer jacket around the cable so that you can place the wires inside the connector in a specific order. You'll have to remove about 0.5 inch (1.3 centimeters) of the outer cover but none of the insulation around the smaller wires within the cable.

The crimper secures the connector onto the wires in two locations, as shown below. Near the front of the connector, the crimper pushes the metal contacts through the wires so the wires make contact with the metal conductor inside each connector. Near the end of the connector, the crimper pushes a plastic wedge against the outer cover of the cable to lock it into place.

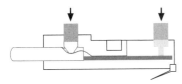

Complete kits of connectors and tools aren't expensive, but you need some dexterity to strip and crimp the cable. You must insert the wires into the connector so they stay in the proper order, so they fit all the way into the connector and the metal contacts touch the metal conductors, and so the wedge locks against the outer cover. It is easy for the wires to move as you insert them, changing their positions within the connector and either breaking the connections or making incorrect connections.

You can purchase more expensive two-piece connectors to simplify this job. With two-piece connectors, you can hold the wires in position when you insert the top piece and crimp them together. You then trim off any wire extending beyond the connector.

When you're running cable through walls, another option is to install *Ethernet jacks*. These are like phone jacks, but they're designed for network cables instead. They help to create a more attractive look and avoid clutter; if you plan to sell your home in the future, these features may prove especially beneficial. If you install network jacks, you can even purchase models that don't require a crimping tool. To install them, you'll need only a stripper to expose the wires in the cable and a faceplate to hold the jack on the wall, as shown in Figure 6-1. Some faceplates can hold two, four, or even more plugs. You'll need one of these faceplates for the location in which all the cables connect to the hub.

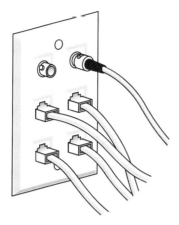

Figure 6-1.

Connecting cables to a faceplate.

The best jacks to purchase for the home are those that need no special tools. Simply place the wires on top of metal contacts and use a small screwdriver to push each wire down so the contacts penetrate the insulation. Some jacks have two pieces, so pressing the parts together creates the contact with the wires. However, some other jacks require special tools, called *punchdown tools*, that press the wires into place.

Note

If you're running cable along baseboards, you can purchase surface-mounted jacks that attach directly to the baseboard. You then plug the patch cable into the jack. Because the cable and jacks connect on the surface, you don't need to make holes in your walls, and it's easier to rewire than cables and jacks installed in the wall.

Ethernet Color Codes

When you make your own cables, you have to make sure that the wires are connected in the proper order. Two standards exist for arranging the order of cables, 568A and 568B, as shown in Figure 6-2. You can use either standard, and you can mix them in the same network, but not in the same cable. This restriction means that the wires must be in the same order at each end of the cable, looking at the connectors from the same side. So if you place the white/green wire on the first pin on one end of the cable, the white/green wire must be on the first pin on the other end of the cable, and so on.

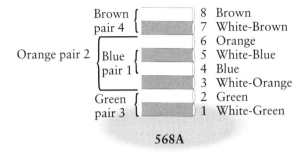

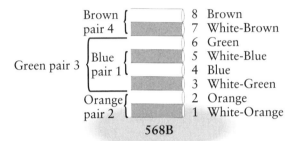

Figure 6-2.

Color codes for unshielded twisted-pair (UTP) connections.

A crossover cable is the only type of cable that has a different arrangement on each end. The colors do not match up on all of the pins on each side. As shown in the following illustration of a crossover cable, for example, the white/green wire is connected to the first pin on one end of the cable, but to the third pin on the other end.

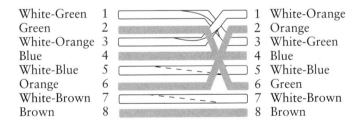

Testing Your Installation

You should test all cables that you make yourself before putting away your crimper and other tools. If you're running wires before completing the walls in a house you're building or remodeling, you should test the cables at least twice, whether or not you made the cables yourself:

- After you install the cables but before you put up the wall

- Immediately after putting up the wall and moldings, but before painting or wallpapering

    Cables can be damaged if you bend them sharply around studs or as you're nailing up the drywall or molding. Don't wait until you complete your remodeling before finding out that a network cable won't work.

    The best way to test cables is by using a two-piece cable tester. Cable testers start at about $100, but having one is a worthwhile investment, considering the cost of tearing down and refinishing walls.

    As shown in Figure 6-3, the cable tester includes two parts: a remote and a main unit. To test a patch cable, plug one end into the remote and the other end into the main unit. Then, depending on the tester, turn it on and watch as a series of lights indicate whether the cable works. Most testers identify which of the four pairs of wires work and whether the wires are in the proper order.

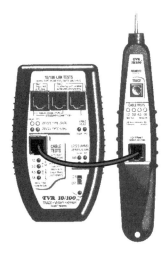

Figure 6-3.
Testing a cable.

You can also use the tester to check cables after they've been installed. Plug the remote into the jack in one room, and plug the main unit into the jack in the other room. You can then check the lights on either unit to determine a cable's status.

What if a cable turns out to be defective? The problem can originate in one of two places: at one of the ends, or somewhere along the cable itself.

First, check the tester lights to see which pair of wires is defective. Then inspect each end of the cable to look for a problem, such as a different color order on each end or a wire not making contact. If you aren't sure, remove the cable from the jacks or cut off the connector, and try again.

If you're sure the problem isn't at either end, the difficulty might be somewhere along the cable. When a cable is being installed in a wall, it might have been pinched by a bend that's too sharp or have been hit by a nail. If you find a defective cable after putting up the walls, you might be able to salvage your work. Cables for 10BaseT networks really need only two sets of wires, not all four. Only pins 1, 2, 3, and 6 of each end need to be connected. So long as at least two sets of wires are working, you can rewire the sockets or connectors. Just use whichever two sets are working to connect those four pins. You won't be able to run at the higher 100BaseT speed, but at least your network will be running.

For example, suppose you wired all eight pins of a cable, as shown at the top of Figure 6-4. After testing the cable, you find that something is wrong with the orange pair of wires connected to pins 3 and 6. Because the other pairs are working, you can rewire *both* ends of the cable, as shown at the bottom of Figure 6-4, by using the blue pair on pins 3 and 6. The cable will now work properly for your network running at 10BaseT speeds.

Numerous cable testers are available that range in price and in the number of features they offer. For example, the Ideal LinkMaster is easy to use, and it costs about $90. Although status lights are available only on the main unit, this product tests both unshielded twisted pair (UTP) and shielded twisted pair (STP) cables, and it reports shorts, miswires, reversed wires, and split pairs. Just plug each end of your cable into one of the units, press the Test button, and watch the indicator lights on the main unit. After 20 seconds of nonuse, the LinkMaster turns itself off to conserve battery life—another handy feature.

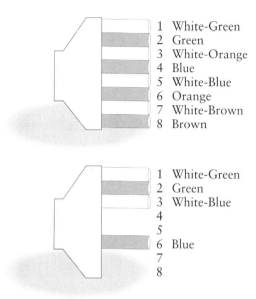

1 White-Green
2 Green
3 White-Orange
4 Blue
5 White-Blue
6 Orange
7 White-Brown
8 Brown

1 White-Green
2 Green
3 White-Blue
4
5
6 Blue
7
8

Figure 6-4.

Salvaging a defective cable by using only two pairs of wires.

The Paladin Tools LAN ProNavigator, available for about $100, tests UTP and STP cables as well as coaxial cable. It has status lights on both the remote unit and the main unit so you can check a cable's status from either end. In addition to reporting the status of each wire pair, shorts, bad wiring, reversals, and split pairs, this device includes a Pass/ Fail display for a quick indication.

The ByteBrothers TVR 10/100 costs a little over $200, but it provides an exceptional range of features for troubleshooting network problems. This device contains status lights on both the main unit and the remote unit, and the main unit has several connections for testing a cable by itself. So if the remote is in another room for testing a cable run through walls, you can still use the main unit to test an individual patch cable or to perform other tests.

For example, you can plug the main unit directly into the cable from a computer to verify that the network card is working. You can also place the main unit between a computer and another device, such as hub, to monitor the speed of network traffic and to determine whether a straight cable or a crossover cable is needed.

In addition, the TVR 10/100 remote unit contains a *tone probe*. When you plug a cable into the main unit, the unit transmits a tone that's carried along the cable. You can then use the probe to trace the cable anywhere along its length—just place the probe along a wire and press the remote's Trace button to listen for the tone.

For example, suppose you have several cables running together within a wall and need to determine which one is connected to a particular computer elsewhere in the house. Plug the main unit into the cable connected to the computer and run the remote probe along both cables. You'll hear the tone when you move the probe along the correct cable. You can also use the probe to quickly identify a cable at a hub without having to unplug each cable and insert it into the remote.

Using Thin Ethernet Coaxial Cable

When you use coaxial cable, you don't need to connect the network cables at a hub. Instead, simply connect cables from one NIC to another to form a continuous chain.

At the end of each length of coaxial cable is a male BNC connector (short for several different terms, including barrel node connector, British Naval Connector, and bayonet Neill-Concelman). The connector has a pin in the center and an outer ring that rotates. If you look into the end of the connector, you'll see that this ring has two grooves, as shown below.

The BNC male connector attaches to a BNC female connector, which has two small stubs and no outer ring, as illustrated below.

You join the male and female connectors by inserting the male connector into the female connector so the stubs fit into the grooves, and then rotating the ring on the male connector clockwise to lock the connectors together.

To connect a cable to a NIC, attach it to a T-connector and then attach the T-connector to the NIC. The T-connector has a BNC male connector at the base and a female connector at the end of each arm, as shown below.

Slide the male BNC connector of the cable onto one arm of the T and then rotate the connector clockwise so that it locks into place.

If you're connecting only two computers, connect the other end of the cable to the T-connector attached to the second machine. If the machines are in adjacent rooms, attach one end of the cable to the computer in one room, bring the cable through the wall, and connect it to the T-connector on the other computer. So for two computers, you'll need two T-connectors, one length of cable, and two terminators.

As you'll see in the following diagram, one arm of the T on each computer won't be connected to a cable, but you can't leave it empty because that would cause the electronic signals to be lost. So you must attach a terminator to each unused arm of the T.

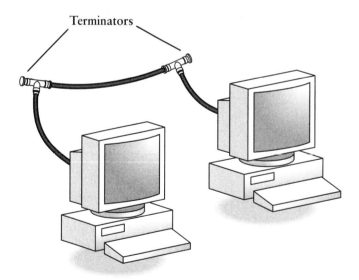

Terminators

After you've connected the cable to the T-connector, slide the T-connector onto the connector on the NIC and rotate it clockwise until it locks into place.

Just picture the network as a chain of computers with a coaxial cable running from the computer at the start of the chain to the computer at the end of the chain. Adding more computers to the chain is easy. You can add them to the unused connections at the ends of the chain or insert them in the middle of the chain. To insert a computer in the middle of the chain, just follow these steps:

1. Disconnect a cable going into one end of a T-connector of one of the computers.

2. Plug that end into the T-connector going to the computer you want to insert.

3. Connect the free end of the new computer's T-connector to the end you removed in the first step.

If possible, use continuous lengths of cable from one computer to the next. Connections are the most likely place for problems to occur, so eliminate as many as possible to make sure your network runs well. If you don't have a length of coaxial cable long enough, you can join cables end to end, the same way you'd use an extension cord. To join them together, you can use the two arms of a T-connector without attaching the connector at its base to anything. You can also use a *barrel connector*, which is the top part of a T-connector that has the two BNC female connectors.

Making Your Own Coaxial Cable

You can create your own custom lengths of coaxial cable by using bulk cable and connectors. There are even "twist-on" connectors that you can attach to the end of bulk coaxial cable without having to do any crimping. These connectors work like the twist-on connectors you can use on cable TV wire. Bulk thin Ethernet coaxial cable is about $80 for 500 feet (150 meters), and twist-on connectors are only about $2 each. If you want to run coaxial cable through walls, you can also purchase male connectors, sockets, and faceplates, which resemble cable TV outlets.

Good Cabling Equals Good Networking

Now that you're familiar with the basics of cabling your network, you should consider the overall rules outlined in the following sections.

Use Continuous Lengths

Whenever possible, use continuous lengths when you run twisted-pair cables from computers to the hub or when you run coaxial cables from computer to computer. Although you can join two cables end to end with a coupler, the connections at the coupler can come loose, and moisture or dust can disturb the contacts. Therefore, the coupler is the first place to look if something goes wrong with the network and the problem seems to be in the cable. If you do decide to use a coupler, don't place it in a wall, in case you need to reach or replace it.

Prevent Bends at Sharp Angles

As you run the cable, don't bend it at sharp angles. If you have to go around a corner, for example, don't bend the cable so that it folds or creases, and don't pull the cable tight. The wires inside cables are strong and flexible, but bending a cable back and forth during installation or sharply folding it in the corner of a room can break one of them. Although these wires might not break immediately, they can deteriorate over time.

Keep a Tidy Appearance

To preserve the appearance of your rooms, try to run cable in a wall or above the ceiling whenever possible. Try to avoid running it on the outside of a wall, along the baseboard. Many businesses have dropped ceilings just so network and other cables can be easily run from room to room, but you don't usually have that luxury in a home. If you must run cable along a baseboard or up a wall, secure it to the surface. Rather than nail or staple directly into the cable, use U-shaped standoffs that you can purchase at a hardware store or home center.

Never put a cable where it can be tripped over or kicked, and never put it under the carpet where people can step on it. Although you might be tempted to run the cable under an area rug rather than around the perimeter of a room, continuously walking on a cable, rolling over it with a chair, or vacuuming over it can wear it down and eventually ruin it. And no matter how thick your carpet is, you'll soon see the telltale sign of a cable bulging through.

Don't Force Cables

If you have to drill a hole in a wall to run the cable, make the hole larger than the connector at the end of the cable. Never force a cable through a smaller hole because you could damage the connector on the end. In fact, always be particularly careful with connectors at the ends of the cable. The plug at the end of a twisted-pair cable has small metal contacts and a plastic tab that helps hold the plug in place. Don't step on the end or break off that tab. Also, take care to avoid cutting or bending the small wire at the end of a coaxial cable.

Use a Fish or a Coat Hanger

The worst part of running cable is fishing it through walls: getting it to go from one location to another when you can't see where it's going. Sometimes fishing cable is easy, such as when you have to run it between two adjacent rooms, but sometimes fishing is so frustrating that you'll want to give up and send mail by carrier pigeon.

If you have trouble feeding the cable through a wall, you can open a metal coat hanger and push one end through. Otherwise, you can use a fish, as discussed earlier. Once you get the coat hanger or fish through the wall, tie the end of the cable to the end of the hanger or fish, and then pull the cable through the other end.

Accessorizing Your Installation

No matter which type of cable you use, you can purchase all sorts of accessories to help hide it throughout the house. Raceways and floor cable covers are the most common types of these accessories. *Raceways*, shown in the following diagram, are usually made of a nonconductive material such as vinyl, and they attach to walls, ceilings, or floors to hide cable and keep it safe. Most raceways have curves for the corners of rooms to keep the cable from bending too sharply, as shown below, and they are ideal for use with surface-mounted jacks.

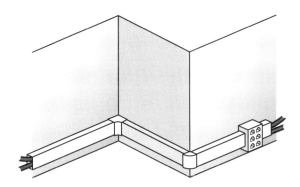

Floor cable covers, shown on page 136, are plastic or rubber, and they cover a cable that might otherwise be stepped on. Depending on their design, run the cable through them or under them.

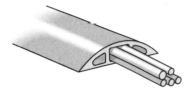

Many companies sell bulk cable, connectors, and the other accessories you'll need for a professional cabling job in your home. Unfortunately, most computer stores, even superstores, carry only a small selection of cabling supplies. An alternate source for the parts you'll need is a mail order catalog such as Data Comm Warehouse.

Because you must order the materials and wait for them to arrive, it pays to plan your detailed cable layout in advance. You can run lengths of string where you plan to run the cable to get measurements. You can also make the holes in advance and use the string later to fish the cable through the walls.

Expanding Your Ethernet Network

As your needs and your family grow, you might want to add more computers to the network. As you've seen, adding computers to a network that uses thin Ethernet coaxial cable is easy; just remove the terminator at one end of the chain and connect the cable from the additional computer. But networks connected by twisted-pair cable must have enough ports on the hub to accommodate all the computers that you want to connect. If you have a five-port hub, for example, you can connect only five computers. When your twisted-pair cable network exceeds the hub's capacity, you have two choices: you can purchase a hub that handles more computers, or you can link two or more hubs, as shown below.

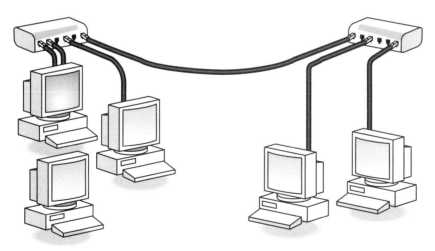

The two hubs you connect don't need to be in the same room of your house, so you can also consider using two hubs to connect different branches of your network where it's difficult to run cables or where you want to avoid running multiple cables along the same path. In Figure 6-5, two hubs are used to simplify a household network. With two hubs in different areas of the house, you need to fish only one cable between the areas.

Most of the ports on the hub are designed to be connected to a NIC using a standard twisted-pair cable. You can't use a regular cable to connect regular ports of two hubs. As a solution, many hubs have an extra connector called an *uplink port* that lets you connect hubs and link them in a chain. This port is designed so that you can connect it to a regular port of another hub to connect them together. In some cases, a switch on the hub changes a port from regular to uplink. Here are four ways to connect two hubs.

If both hubs have an uplink port, you have two choices:

- Use a regular twisted-pair cable to connect the uplink port of one hub to any regular port on the second hub. This system allows up to nine computers to be on the network if you have two five-port hubs with separate uplink ports.

- Use crossover cable to connect the uplink ports of both hubs. With this configuration, you can have 10 computers networked with a pair of five-port hubs with separate uplink ports.

If only one hub has an uplink port, do the following:

- Again, use a regular twisted-pair cable to connect the uplink port of one hub to any regular port on the second hub. This system allows as many as nine computers to be on a network of two five-port hubs, one of which has a separate uplink port.

If neither hub has an uplink port, you must use this method:

- Use a crossover cable to connect any port on one hub to any port on the other hub. This technique allows as many as eight computers to be networked with two five-port hubs.

Note

If your hub has an uplink port, check the hub's documentation. In some hubs, the uplink port shares the same resources as a regular port—usually the one next to it. This means that if you plug a cable into the uplink port to connect the hub, you can't use the shared port for a workstation. So if you have a five-port hub with an uplink port that shares resources, using the uplink port means that only four computers can be connected to the hub.

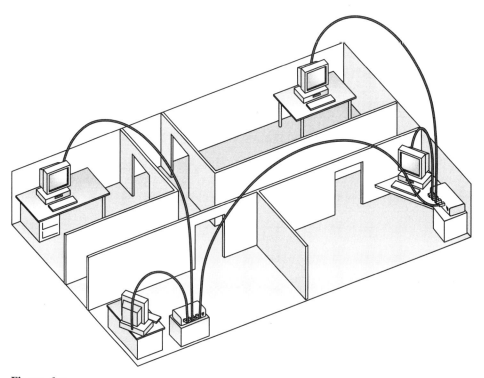

Figure 6-5.

Connecting hubs in different parts of the house.

You can even connect some hubs on twisted-pair networks with thin Ethernet coaxial cable. The documentation for your hub can tell you which type of cable and which ports to use.

If you have a hub that contains one or more coaxial connections, by the way, you can use it to combine twisted-pair and thin Ethernet cable in one network. As shown in Figure 6-6, connect the free end of the coaxial cable to the coaxial port of the hub.

Alternatives to Hubs

Most of the inexpensive hubs on the market are called *passive hubs.* They simply provide a means of linking all the computers through twisted-pair cable.

No matter how many passive hubs you have linked, all the computers and hubs are seen as one network, and all the computers are competing for the same space on the network cable, called the *bandwidth.* This situation is like driving along a narrow, one-lane highway with a high speed limit. No matter how fast you allow cars to travel, the road can handle just so much traffic before a traffic jam occurs.

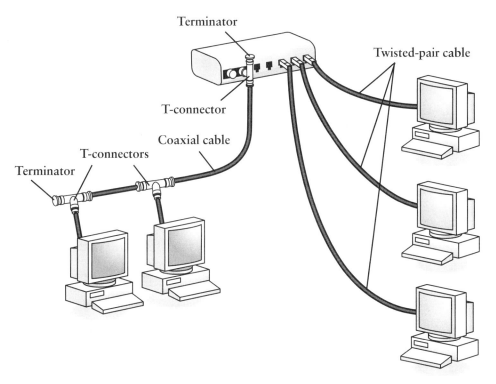

Terminator

Twisted-pair cable

T-connector

Coaxial cable

T-connectors

Terminator

Figure 6-6.

Combining twisted-pair and coaxial networks.

If several computers try to access the network simultaneously, a collision can occur between the information traveling through the cable. Such a collision slows the entire network and might result in some lost data.

One of the first options you should consider for increasing the performance of a small network is to replace the hub with a *switch* or *switching hub*. Switches work by transmitting information only to the computer it's being sent to. With a switch, the network appears to have a separate connection to each of the computers, so you get the full performance and speed from each device. Think of a switch as a mechanism that opens the traffic to multiple high-speed lanes, with each lane going to a separate destination—one specific computer. Simply remove the hub from your network and replace it with a switch; no additional setup or configuration is required.

You can consider other types of hubs and devices as well, but many are rather costly for a home network. A device called an *active hub* can amplify the signal to allow greater distances, and an *intelligent hub* can manage the network transmissions to increase performance. A *stackable hub* uses a special high-speed bus to carry network signals from one hub to another. A *repeater* allows the distance between devices to be extended by amplifying the network signal, and a *bridge* connects two sections of a network so that each appears as its own network without competing for the same space on the cable.

Boost Performance with Switches

Switches cost much more than a hub. They start at about $100 but are well worth the investment if you have a busy home network.

As an example, my network consisted of a five-port hub and an eight-port hub linked together in one location and an additional five-port hub in another location. When all my computers were running and the family was busy sharing files, printers, and modems, performance speed dropped noticeably. Accessing a resource on the network would sometimes take an unusually long time, and someone would occasionally get an error message that the network or a specific resource wasn't available.

I replaced the two linked hubs with one 16-port switch—a model AT-FS716E from Allied Telesyn. Not only did the error messages vanish, but the performance speed of the network also increased dramatically.

Switches are available with from five to 24 ports, and you can link as many multiple switches as you can hubs. You can get five-port switches that cost less than $70 from such companies as Allied Telesyn, D-Link, Linksys, and SMC.

Creating a Wireless Network

Physically connecting a wireless network is easy because you need to insert only the wireless network cards or USB devices. With the Wi-Fi 802.11b standard, you can mix devices from several manufacturers, taking advantage of sales and special offers to hold down the cost of your network.

Although you don't have to worry about running cables around the house, you do need to be concerned about the network's range. For example, two computers might not appear to be networked because they are too far apart or there are too many walls or other obstacles between them.

If two computers can't make contact, try moving them closer, or just move one computer to another location within the same room, such as on top of the desk or to one side of it. You might also place the computers next to their wireless devices to have a clear path to the doors of rooms, removing one or more walls as obstacles. Some wireless devices, but not all, also let you connect an optional external antenna. Connected to the device by a cable, the antenna can be moved around the room or even outside of it, to extend the network's reach.

Extending Wireless Networks

If you have a large house or one with several floors, however, you might not be able to get two wireless devices to communicate. In those cases, you might need an access point to extend the network's range.

As shown in Figure 6-7, you can create a wireless network in two general ways: peer-to-peer (also called ad hoc) and infrastructure. In a *peer-to-peer* wireless network, all computers communicate directly with each other so they must be within range. In an *infrastructure* arrangement, all data travels through a central location, which can be an access point or a residential gateway.

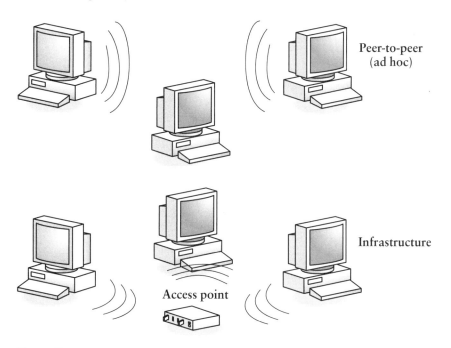

Figure 6-7.
Two ways to create a wireless network.

Access Points

An *access point* lets you link wireless computers with a wired Ethernet network. A *residential gateway* (described further in the next section) is designed primarily to let the entire network share a single Internet account, but it can also perform as an access point if it has a built-in hub or switch.

By strategically placing an access point, you can link computers that might otherwise be out of range. For example, suppose you have a three-story house with computers on the first and third floors that can't communicate. The solution might be to place an access point on the second floor, as shown in Figure 6-8. The access point is within the range of each computer, serving as a hub to carry the signals between them.

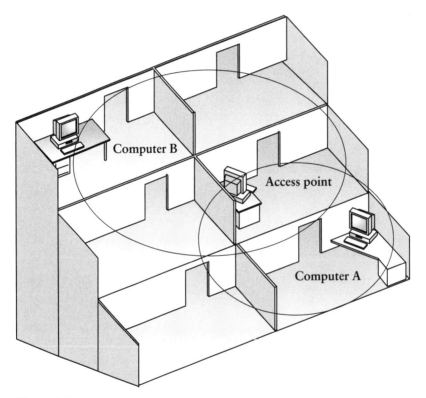

Figure 6-8.
Using an access point when wireless connections aren't possible.

If the computers still can't communicate, you might need to run a limited amount of Ethernet wire. Using the illustration on the left of Figure 6-9 as an example, suppose the wireless access point alone is not able to network the computers on the first and third floors. You might have to install an Ethernet device in one of the computers and run a cable between it and the access point, as shown on the right side of the figure. In this case, using an Ethernet cable between the access point and the computer on the first floor would allow the two computers to be networked. The data travels wirelessly between one computer and the access point, and then over Ethernet wire to the other computer.

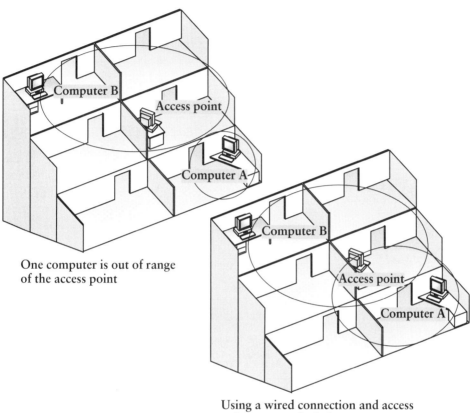

One computer is out of range of the access point

Using a wired connection and access point to extend wireless range

Figure 6-9.

Combining wired and wireless networking.

Figure 6-9 shows which computer is out of range of the access point, but how would you tell in your installation? Most access points have built-in Web pages that you can use for configuration. You either run a program provided with the access point, or use your Web browser to connect to the access point to change settings. When you set up the access point, try connecting to it with each computer. Move the access point and computers around until both computers connect to the access point and to each other. If you can get only one computer connected to the access point, the other is still out of range. You might need a second access point or an Ethernet cable to complete the network.

Residential Gateways

Access points let you connect your wireless computers to a wired network. Wireless residential gateways perform routing functions, letting everyone share an Internet connection.

You can use residential gateways that have only one Ethernet port as either an access point or as a router, but not both at the same time. The single Ethernet port can be connected to either a broadband modem or to an Ethernet hub or switch. If you connect it to a hub to connect to a wired local area network (LAN), it can't be connected to a broadband modem for shared Internet use. Using such a gateway to also share the Internet with a wired network requires a separate access point that links the wired LAN to the wireless gateway, as shown in Figure 6-10.

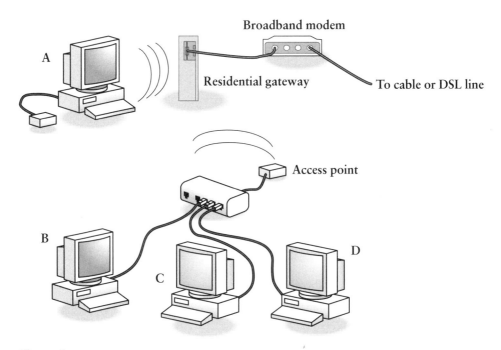

Figure 6-10.
Combining an access point and residential gateway.

You can use gateways that have a built-in hub or switch as both a router and as an access point, as shown in Figure 6-11. Some gateways include a print server for sharing your printer with everyone on the network, and some offer built-in dial-up modems for sharing a dial-up Internet account. Others have a serial port that you can connect to an external dial-up modem. You can then use the modem to share a dial-up account if you don't have broadband Internet, or as a backup if your broadband service fails.

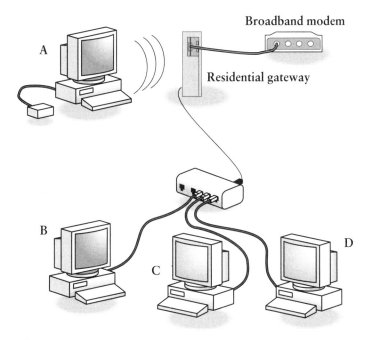

Figure 6-11.
Using a residential gateway with at least two Ethernet ports.

See Also

We'll look at sharing an Internet account with a wireless network in Chapter 11, "Going Online Through the Network."

Many access points and residential gateways exist on the market, including the products described in the following sections.

Note

The Ethernet port that is used to connect to the digital subscriber line (DSL) or cable modem might be labeled WAN (wide area network).

SMC Networks (*http://www.smc.com*)   This company offers both a stand-alone wireless access point with only one Ethernet connection as well as an access point/gateway combination called the Wireless Barricade. SMC Networks also sells a nonwireless Barricade model that serves as an Ethernet switch and broadband router but without the wireless capabilities.

The Wireless Barricade includes a Wi-Fi 11-Mbps wireless access point, a three-port 10/100-Mbps Ethernet switch, a separate Ethernet port with firewall security for sharing a broadband modem, and a serial communications port for connecting to an optional dial-up model for backup if your broadband service goes down. In addition, the Barricade includes a parallel printer port that lets you share a printer with all network users—both wired and wireless.

Buffalo Technology (*http://www.buffalotech.com*)   This company offers a variety of models in its AirStation line. The WLAR-L11-L (called the local router model) includes a Wi-Fi wireless port, a four-port Ethernet switch, and a separate Ethernet connection for a DLS/cable modem. Other models include the Standard, which functions like an access point to a wired network, the Cable/DSL, which offers only one Ethernet port for use as either a broadband router or an access point, and the Pro, which is designed for a large office environment.

Buffalo Technology also markets the AirStation Wireless Print Server. It includes a built-in Wi-Fi connection and a parallel printer port for direct connection to a printer, which any wireless computer on the network can use.

2Wire (*http://www.2wire.com*)   This company offers the HomePortal 100W, which has the widest array of connection options available today. In addition to the built-in wireless 802.11b port, the device includes the following: an Ethernet port for connection to a computer or Ethernet hub; an Ethernet port for sharing a broadband modem; a USB connection to the network through a computer's USB port; and a HomePNA 2 phone-line network port to communicate with computers by using a home phone-line network. One particularly useful feature of HomePortal is a configuration guide that provides step-by-step instructions for configuring other manufacturers' wireless Ethernet cards to work with it.

Agere Systems (*http://www.orinocowireless.com*)   This company offers the ORiNOCO product line, featuring the Residential Gateway, a product with a wireless port but only one Ethernet port for use as either an access point or with a DSL/Cable router. The unit also has a built-in 56K dial-up modem for those who don't have broadband Internet but still want to share an Internet connection across the wireless network.

Asanté Technologies (*http://www.asante.com*)   This company offers a full range of wired and wireless devices, including the FriendlyNet FR3002AL. This device includes an Ethernet connection for your broadband modem, an Ethernet connection to your wired LAN, and a parallel port that offers a built-in print server.

U.S. Robotics (*http://www.usr.com/*)   This company offers a wired router (USR 8000) as well as a stand-alone wireless access point (USR 2450). The router includes an Ethernet port for a broadband modem, a four-port Ethernet switch, a print server, and a serial port. Plug the wireless access point into the router's Ethernet port to link your wired and wireless networks and share broadband Internet.

D-Link Systems (*http://www.dlink.com*)   This company offers a wireless access point with a single Ethernet port (DWL 1000AP) as well as several wireless routers. The DI-714 router has a four-port switch, the DI-713P has a three-port switch and print server, and the DI-711 has only one port. D-Link also sells a wireless print sever with three parallel ports (DI-313).

ZyXEL Communications (*http://www.zyxel.com*)   This company offers the Prestige 316 Broadband Sharing Gateway with Wireless LAN. In addition to its wireless capabilities, the device has one 10/100 Mbps Ethernet port to connect to a computer and one WAN port for a broadband modem.

Linksys Group (*http://www.linksys.com*)   This company offers the one-port EtherFast BEFW11P1 Wireless AP + Cable/DSL Router with PrintServer, the four-port EtherFast BEFW11S4 Wireless AP + Cable/DSL Router Combination, and the Instant Wireless Network Access Point WAP11.

Connecting Other Network Types

Phone-line, power-line, and USB networks are easy to set up and connect, although your choices of manufacturers are limited. Although Ethernet and wireless are by far the most popular types of networks, these alternatives have their advantages.

Phone-Line Networks

Most homes have phone jacks in the places where you'll want to put a computer. All you have to do to create your network is to plug the computer's phone-line interface device into a phone jack and run the software supplied with your hardware.

A phone jack can then serve a dual purpose by also letting you connect computers on a network. If you need another phone jack, the phone company can install it for you—for a charge, of course. You can also purchase adapters, such as the one shown on page 148, to connect both a phone and a telephone NIC to the jack at the same time.

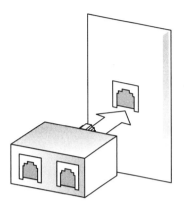

If you have more than one computer in the same room, you can usually connect their NICs with phone cables directly, as shown in Figure 6-12.

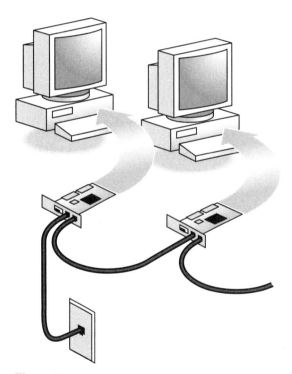

Figure 6-12.
You can link computers directly with HomePNA cards and regular telephone wire.

To connect a computer in a room that has no phone jack, use a regular telephone extension wire to connect the computer to a networked machine in another room. Telephone wire is much easier to hide along baseboards than twisted-pair or coaxial cable.

Some access points and residential gateways for phone-line networks let you communicate with wired Ethernet computers and share a single Internet account. The 2Wire HomePortal 100W, for example, lets you combine a phone line, Ethernet, and a wireless network. You can plug its phone jack into a phone outlet to use it as an access point to an Ethernet or wired network and to share a single broadband Internet account. Other phone-line access points include the Netgear Ethernet to Phoneline Bridge and the Linksys HomeLink Phoneline Ethernet Bridge. Both devices operate at 10 Mbps.

Power-Line Networks

Power-line network hardware connects your computer to a standard wall power outlet. Depending on the hardware, connect one end of the interface device to your computer through the USB, printer, or Ethernet port, and connect the other end into the power outlet.

To help avoid power-line interference, however, you should plug your computer, monitor, and other peripherals into a power strip or other device that also filters out any interference from the computer and monitor. Then plug that device into the wall. Until power-line networks begin to emerge, there is not much more to know about their use.

USB Networks

Networks that connect through their USB ports are perhaps the easiest to set up. Because of the limitations on the distance between computers and the number of computers that can be connected, however, USB networks have limited expandability. Consider a USB network only if you have two computers in the same room, or perhaps on opposite sides of a wall in adjacent rooms.

If you choose to create a USB network, the cable you need will be included with the network software, such as PCSync, LapLink, USB Direct Connect, and EZLink. You can also purchase extra USB network cables from LapLink and other companies for about $30.

See Also

All these programs were discussed in Chapter 4, "Types of Networks."

Getting Wired for the Future

If you're looking forward to the time when you can create a completely networked home, you'll have to plan to install a *structured wiring system* within your house. In a structured wiring system, all your network cables originate in a central location called the *distribution center, wiring closet,* or *hub.* The wires are then connected to wall outlets in the rooms of your house.

The central location can be any standard closet that provides enough room for you to maneuver and manipulate the wiring. As long as we're looking at the future, however, you might want to use a small room, about the size of a small bathroom, that has heating and cooling vents and enough space for you to access all four sides of a central wiring cabinet. Make sure the wiring closet has enough electrical outlets and that all electrical outlets, telephone lines, and video cables are protected against surges.

In this wiring cabinet, you could have the following:

- An Ethernet hub

- A video distribution panel for a home entertainment system

- A telephone system

- A security panel

- Central home automation controllers

- A controller for multiple-zoned heating and air conditioning

- A broadband router or LAN modem for sharing an Internet account

When you plan the electrical system for your home, make sure you include plenty of wall outlets. Carefully mark which outlets are connected to wall switches because you don't want to plug certain pieces of equipment into switched outlets. If you did, flipping the switch to turn off a light might also accidentally turn off a computer or hub.

Now run the following wires from the central location to each room of the house:

- Two coaxial video cables using a high-grade RG-6 quad-shielded coaxial cable. The RG-6 cable is more expensive than the standard coaxial cable used for televisions and cable transmissions, but it can handle more signals with higher quality. One of the cables is for downstream transmission from cable television, video cameras, VCRs, or DVD players to the rooms in the house. The other cable is for upstream transmission to feed signals from a room to the central hub or to other locations. You can then watch a video or DVD playing from any other room in the house, or you can set up your own closed-circuit video system.

- Three Cat 5e or Category 6 UTP cables. You can use one cable for your basic home network and reserve the others for maximum expandability so you can add networked printers, modems, and other equipment, as well as an intercom.

- Telephone cable for your telephone system, sufficient for four lines.

- Speaker wire that is 16-gauge for "surround sound" throughout the home.

- Thermostat cable for use with a multiple-zoned heating and cooling system.

- Fiberoptic cable for future expansion. If you don't want to run fiberoptic cable right now, consider running an empty conduit to each room. Then, you can run any type of cable through the conduit in the future.

Terminate all the cables into wall jacks, and label each jack to identify its use. Plan the arrangement beforehand for each room, based on where you intend to place computer desks, entertainment units, and other furniture. You might decide, for example, to have speakers built into the walls or ceilings. You'll need to plan their location so the speaker wire can be run properly. Thermostats are usually located away from windows and other sources of drafts. Plan their location carefully with a heating contractor.

Home entertainment networks provide a centralized source for video and audio. For example, you might plan for a thin, wall-mounted TV display and hidden speakers in every room. Using a universal, handheld remote control, you'll be able to tune into your favorite music or TV show or watch a video or DVD. A video distribution panel serves as a switchboard for video signals from your cable provider and also from your in-house video cameras and players. Much of this technology is available today. Some devices, for example, let you broadcast cable TV signals or display video from a VCR or DVD player—even a device in your computer—to any television in the house.

If an electrician is wiring your home, make sure that he or she uses the proper types of cable. Insist on Cat 5e, or, better yet, twisted-pair and RG-6 quad-shielded coaxial cable. Don't allow the electrician to talk you into using a lesser grade. Make sure you have enough separate electrical circuits to handle a high load, especially in the wiring closet and the kitchen.

If you plan to set up home automation, be sure the electrician runs a neutral wire to all wall-switch boxes because some home remote control devices need it. Also make sure that the boxes themselves are extra deep to accommodate remote control switches, which are usually bulkier than standard switches.

The X10 Files

There are a number of technologies for controlling your home, including CEBus and LonWorks, but much of today's home automation is performed through a power-line technology called X10. The communication between automated devices is carried through your existing home wiring, much like the power-line network. Simply plug the X10 devices into wall outlets and control the system from a control station or computer interface.

An X10 controller—either a wall-mounted device or a program that runs on your computer—can individually direct the operation of up to 256 devices. In addition, the technology is standardized, so you can control devices from various manufacturers through the same wiring and with the same controllers.

In an X10 system, you can use three types of units:

- A *transmitter* sends signals from a controller to another X10 device. An X10 switch, for example, sends a signal to an X10 device that turns on a light.

- A *receiver*, such as a device that turns on a light or television, accepts signals from X10 controllers.

- A *transceiver*, also called a two-way transmitter and receiver, can both send and receive signals. These devices are usually controllers that can send signals to units and simultaneously receive status information from other units.

X10 receivers can be given one of up to 256 codes. The controller uses the code to send a signal to the receiver telling it to switch on or off. You can have up to 256 devices, each controlled separately. You can also set several devices to have the same code so you can control them as a group with one signal from the controller.

You can control almost any electrical device with an X10 system. For example, X10 can underpin a security system that monitors access to your home and detects unauthorized entry. X10 security devices can include underground driveway sensors that alert you when a car enters the driveway, remote-controlled doors and gates, and video surveillance and alarm systems.

The system is ideal for controlling internal and external lights and appliances such as coffee makers, microwaves, ovens, and refrigerators. X10 can also automate television and stereo home entertainment systems and communications devices such as telephones and intercoms.

To get started with an X10 system, you can purchase X10 starter kits that control a few lights from a small panel for about $30. You can then add individual devices to build a complete home automation system. The most common and inexpensive of these (about $6) are switches, dimmers, and lamp modules that allow you to turn lights and small appliances on or off. Heavy-duty modules for 220-volt appliances such as air conditioners, dryers, water heaters, and pool pumps cost about $15.

Controllable thermostats are more expensive, costing up to $200. Among the available models is a telephone-controlled thermostat that you can remotely control from any phone. And multiple switch boxes exist for controlling speakers, sprinkler systems, and window treatments. For drapes and blinds, you'll need a motorized control that opens or closes the drapes or blinds when the X10 signal is detected.

An X10 system can be self-contained; wall-mounted or tabletop panels can control the devices on the system. But for the ultimate in control, you can control the entire system from your computer network. In fact, when you use a computer to automate your home, you can turn on the coffeepot so that the coffee is ready when you wake up, turn lights on and off according to a predetermined schedule, control a DVD player from any computer in the house, or check for mail.

The Bottom Line

Connecting your computers can be easy, but their location can sometimes pose challenges. In most cases, you can find ways to run cable that avoid making too many holes in the walls and running cable where it is unsightly.

In this chapter, you learned how to connect computers. In the next chapter, you'll learn how to install the software that gets your network up and running.

Part 3

Setting Up the Software

Chapter 7

Installing the Software

Now that you've installed the network hardware, you're ready to deal with the software. Your network interface card (NIC) won't do you any good unless you configure Microsoft Windows to use it and to communicate with other computers on the network.

Note

This chapter refers to network interface cards and external adapters collectively as NICs. When you see the term *NIC*, remember that it can refer to an internal card, a PC Card for a notebook, a universal serial bus (USB) network adapter, or any other device used to connect your computer to the network.

In this chapter, you'll learn how to install the software that controls your NIC and that allows your computer to communicate with the rest of the network. Before you do anything else, however, check the manual that came with your hardware. Some types of network hardware require several steps to set them up. Others come with a completely automatic setup program. Once you've run the setup program, you're ready to connect to your network without any further configuration.

Although not every networking system is automatic, many have their own special way of installing drivers and configuring Windows. It pays to look at the hardware manual first and run any installation program the manufacturer provides.

You'll also learn how to troubleshoot common network problems, including software issues and conflicts among hardware devices.

Installing Network Drivers

The first software you have to install is *network drivers*: the files that Windows needs to communicate with your NIC. If a disk or CD came with your hardware, it probably contains the network drivers.

Drivers are installed in one of three basic ways, depending on the type of hardware:

- **The Good:** Automatically, with plug-and-play devices that Windows recognizes and that provide the easiest installation

- **The Bad:** Manually, with Windows or special software that comes with the hardware

- **The Ugly:** Manually, with non–plug-and-play network cards that require special configuration to avoid hardware conflicts

Loading Drivers Automatically

In most cases, you can install the card or plug in the external network device, and Windows automatically senses that the adapter is installed and loads the software for it. For some network devices, the drivers are already on your hard disk; for others, you need to copy them from the Windows CD. (Have the CD handy, just in case.)

Note

Although Peripheral Component Interconnect (PCI) plug-and-play cards can usually share interrupt requests (IRQs) automatically, sometimes conflicts do occur. If you have problems with your network card, refer to the section "Troubleshooting Hardware Conflicts," later in this chapter.

In other cases, you'll get a CD with your NIC. Then, all you need to do to install the driver is to insert the CD into your computer and follow the instructions that appear on the screen.

Note

Depending on the version of Windows your machine is running, different wizard pages than the ones described next might appear, but the general process is the same regardless of the Windows version.

To install the drivers for your NIC on a Windows system, follow these steps:

1. Turn on your computer and watch the screen.

    Windows, sensing that a new card has been installed, briefly displays the New Hardware Found message on the screen and then starts the Add New Hardware Wizard. A *wizard* is a series of dialog boxes from which you select options. This wizard takes you step by step through the process of installing the drivers. The first page of the Add New Hardware Wizard identifies the new hardware that has been detected.

Note

If Windows doesn't detect your card, go to Control Panel. In Microsoft Windows 95, Windows 98, and Millennium Edition (Me), double-click Add New Hardware. In Windows 2000, double-click Add/Remove Hardware; and in Windows XP, double-click Add Hardware, or, if it is not visible, select Printers and Other Hardware, then select Add Hardware. Keep clicking Next and following the directions that appear until the wizard finds the card in your system.

2. Click Next.

3. The next wizard page asks whether you want Windows to search for new drivers or whether you want to select the driver from a list. Choose to search for new drivers, and then click Next.

4. Select the check boxes next to one or more of these locations to look for the drivers: Floppy Drive, CD-ROM, Microsoft Windows Update, and Specific Location.

5. If your NIC came with a floppy disk, select Floppy Disk and insert the disk in the floppy disk drive. If the NIC came with a CD, select CD-ROM and insert the CD in your CD-ROM drive.

    • If you select Microsoft Windows Update, you'll need to have an active Internet connection because this option will open the Windows Update Web site.

    • If you select Specific Location, you'll need to type the path of the drivers, such as D:\Win98.

6. Click Next, and the wizard will look for the appropriate drivers. Once the drivers are found, the next wizard page shows the folder where the drivers are located.

7. Click Next, and then click Finish.

    After the drivers are installed, you'll be asked whether you want to restart your computer. The drivers won't be recognized properly until you restart, so click Yes.

Installing Drivers Manually

If the Add New Hardware Wizard doesn't detect your NIC, you can load the drivers manually. You can also consider purchasing a new NIC that is advertised as plug and play. Internal network cards are not expensive, and getting a new one might save you a lot of time trying to configure an out-of-date card. If you need to install your drivers manually, however, follow these instructions.

Installing Drivers Manually in Windows 95, Windows 98, or Windows Me

To install NIC drivers manually in Windows 95, Windows 98, or Windows Me, follow these steps:

1. Double-click My Computer on the Windows desktop.

2. In the My Computer window, double-click Control Panel.

3. In Control Panel, double-click the Network icon.

4. Click Add to see the Select Network Component Type dialog box shown below.

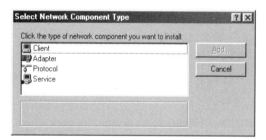

5. Click Adapter in the list, and then click Add to open the Select Network Adapters dialog box shown in Figure 7-1. On the left side of the dialog box is a list of manufacturers whose drivers are provided with Windows.

6. From the list of manufacturers, select the manufacturer of your NIC. On the right side of the dialog box, you see a list of network adapters made by that manufacturer.

7. From the Network Adapters list, select your card model.

8. Click OK.

9. Click Yes when Windows prompts you to restart your computer.

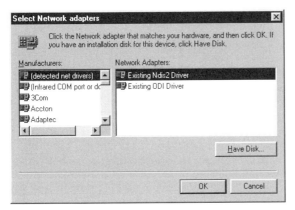

Figure 7-1.
The Select Network Adapters dialog box allows you to select the make and model of your NIC.

Installing Drivers Manually in Windows 2000

If you're using Windows 2000, follow these steps to install NIC drivers manually:

1. In Control Panel, double-click Add/Remove Hardware.

2. Click Next twice. Windows displays a list of devices.

3. Click Add A New Device and then click Next.

4. Select No, I Want To Select The Hardware From The List, and then click Next to display the Hardware Type list, as shown in Figure 7-2.

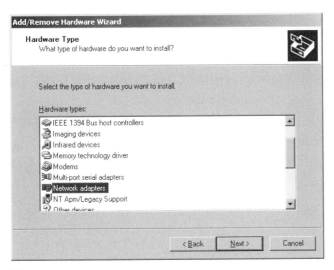

Figure 7-2.
Choose the type of hardware you want to install by using the Add Hardware Wizard.

5. Choose Network Adapters and then click Next. On the left side of the dialog box is a list of manufacturers whose drivers are provided with Windows.

6. From the list of manufacturers, select the manufacturer of your card. On the right side of the dialog box is a list of network adapters made by that manufacturer.

Note

If your manufacturer or card isn't listed, but the card came with a disk or CD that contains the drivers, click Have Disk in the Select Network Adapters dialog box and navigate to the disk or CD.

7. In the Network Adapters list, select your card model.

8. Click OK.

9. Click Yes when Windows prompts you to restart your computer.

Installing Drivers Manually in Windows XP

If you're using Windows XP, follow these steps to install NIC drivers manually when Windows XP does not automatically recognize the NIC:

1. In Control Panel, double-click Add Hardware. If the Add Hardware icon is not visible, select Printers And Other Hardware, then select Add Hardware.

2. Click Next, and then select Yes, I Have Already Connected The Hardware, and then click Next.

3. In the dialog box that appears, scroll to the end of the Installed Hardware list and choose Add A New Hardware Device.

4. Click Next.

5. Select Install The Hardware That I Manually Select From A List, and then click Next to display the Common Hardware Types list.

6. Choose Network Adapters and then click Next. On the left side of the dialog box is a list of manufacturers whose drivers are provided with Windows.

7. In the list of manufacturers, select the manufacturer of your card. On the right side of the dialog box is a list of network adapters made by the manufacturer.

Note

If your manufacturer or card isn't listed, but the card came with a disk or CD that contains the drivers, click Have Disk in the Select Network Adapters dialog box and navigate to the disk or CD, and then continue with Step 8.

8. In the Network Adapters list, select your card model.

9. Click OK.

10. Click Yes if Windows prompts you to restart your computer.

Installing Drivers for Non–Plug-and-Play NICs

In Chapter 5, "Installing Network Cards and Adapters," you learned how to install an Industry Standard Architecture (ISA) card and how to set switches and jumpers if the IRQ and input/output (I/O) addresses need to be set on the card itself. Some ISA cards, however, let you change these settings by using software. Such cards come with a setup or installation program on disk that either makes the settings for you or guides you through the process.

Tip

If other devices are already using all your IRQ addresses, you might encounter difficulties when setting up an ISA card. Exchanging the card for another ISA NIC might not solve the problem; you might need a PCI card or an external network device that connects to your USB or printer port.

Run the installation program that came with the software. The program might automatically check out your system and assign the best settings to the card. If the program asks you to select the settings, however, cancel the program so that you can check out which IRQs and I/O addresses are free. The NIC manual should include a list of the possible addresses to which you can set your card. Here's a quick reminder about how to find out which of these are actually available.

Checking the IRQ and I/O Addresses in Windows 95, Windows 98, or Windows Me

If you're using Windows 95, Windows 98, or Windows Me, check the IRQ and I/O addresses by following these steps:

1. Right-click My Computer on the Windows desktop, and choose Properties from the shortcut menu.

2. Click the Device Manager tab in the System Properties dialog box.

3. Double-click Computer at the top of the list of devices.

4. In the Computer Properties dialog box, make sure the Interrupt Request (IRQ) option is selected on the View Resources tab.

5. Write down the numbers of the unused IRQs. You might also be able to use the IRQ assigned to an unused serial port.

6. Select the Input/Output (I/O) option.

7. Write down the addresses that are not already in use.

8. Click Cancel twice to return to the desktop.

9. Run the installation program that came with the card, and select an IRQ that is not currently being used and an I/O address not in use by another device.

Checking the IRQ and I/O Addresses in Windows 2000 or Windows XP

If you're using Windows 2000 or Windows XP, check the IRQ and I/O addresses by following these steps:

1. In Windows 2000, right-click My Computer on the desktop and choose Properties. In Windows XP, click Start, right-click My Computer, and choose Properties.

2. On the Hardware tab, click Device Manager.

3. Select Resources By Type from the View menu.

4. Click the plus sign next to Interrupt Request (IRQ).

5. Write down the numbers of unused IRQs. You might also be able to use the IRQ assigned to an unused serial port.

6. Click the plus sign next to Input/Output (I/O).

7. Write down the addresses that are not already in use.

8. Close the window.

9. Run the installation program that came with the card, and select an IRQ and I/O address not in use by another device.

If you have problems with your network card, refer to the section "Troubleshooting Hardware Conflicts," later in this chapter.

Configuring Windows for Networking

The next step in creating your network is to configure Windows for networking. This process involves four steps:

1. Adding the network client

2. Installing the network protocol

3. Selecting network services

4. Identifying your computer on the network workgroup

Choosing a *network client* determines how users gain access to the network. In Windows 95, Windows 98, Windows Me, and Windows 2000, you can choose whether everyone who uses a networked computer must log on by entering a user name or by selecting the name from a list. In either case, users must enter a password for access to the network.

Installing a network protocol allows networked computers to send information back and forth and understand what other computers are saying. A *network protocol* is a sort of language, with its own vocabulary and rules of grammar, that all networked computers must "speak" to understand each other. If two computers are using different protocols, they can't communicate.

Selecting *network services* entails choosing the resources you want to share. For example, you can choose to share your files and to let other network users access your printer.

Then you must identify your computer on a *workgroup*: a collection of computers that can interact and communicate with each other on a network. Everyone on the network who wants to share resources with others in a particular workgroup must belong to that group and must be identified by a computer name. You must enter the workgroup name for each computer when you set up networking.

Using the Home Networking Wizard

Windows Me and Windows XP can take you through all the steps to create a network by running a wizard that determines how your computer connects to the Internet and to other computers on your network. *In all other versions of Windows, you must set up the network manually, as described in the section "Configuring Windows Networks," later in this chapter.*

The Windows Me Home Networking Wizard

If you have Windows Me, you can choose to set up and configure home networking and Internet Connection Sharing (ICS) by using the Home Networking Wizard. I recommend, however, that you set up your network without using the wizard and instead use the techniques that you'll learn in this chapter. Learning how to use the Network icon in Control Panel—along with learning other Windows features—gives you the tools to fine-tune and troubleshoot your network beyond the basic steps the wizard provides.

However, if you decide to run the wizard, perform the following steps:

1. Double-click My Network Places on the Windows desktop.

2. Double-click the Home Networking Wizard icon.

3. Follow the directions on the screen.

The wizard will ask whether you want to set up ICS to share your modem and Internet account with others on the network, enter your computer name and workgroup, specify the files and printers you want to share, and create a home networking setup disk to use with other Windows Me computers so that they're compatible with yours.

The Windows XP Network Setup Wizard

The Windows XP Network Setup Wizard offers many options that are unique to Windows XP, so I recommend using this wizard to get your network running if you're using Windows XP. You can step through the wizard to set up your network initially, and then you can fine-tune the settings as needed by following the steps in the next section, "Configuring Windows Networks."

To set up the network for the first time, follow these steps:

1. Click Start and then click My Network Places.

2. Click Set Up A Home Or Small Office Network to start the Network Setup Wizard.

Note

If you install a new network adapter, Windows XP automatically prompts you to begin the Network Setup Wizard.

3. Click Next twice. You see options that determine how your computer shares an Internet connection.

See Also

These options will be discussed in Chapter 11, "Going Online Through the Network."

4. Select Other and click Next. The option you select now depends on the type of Internet connection you have.

5. Select an option from the list and click Next. Use the wizard's Help feature if you need more information about the options that appear.

Note

At a certain point, if you have more than one network device connected to your computer, you can choose to bridge them. Among other functions, a *bridge* links computers networked over wired Ethernet with those using wireless devices. You'll learn more about bridging in the section "Windows XP Bridges," later in this chapter.

6. If you have more than one network device connected to your computer, select Determine The Appropriate Connections For Me, and click Next.

7. Enter the name for the computer, and click Next.

8. Enter the workgroup name. Windows XP uses the default name *MSHOME*. Other versions of Windows use the name *Workgroup*. If you're connecting to a network of other Windows versions, enter *Workgroup* (or the name of the workgroup, if is different), and click Next. You'll see a summary of the settings.

9. Click Next. Windows now takes a few moments to set up networking on your computer. You're then given options for creating a setup disk for other systems on the network, as shown in Figure 7-3. You can use the setup disk to configure the other computers.

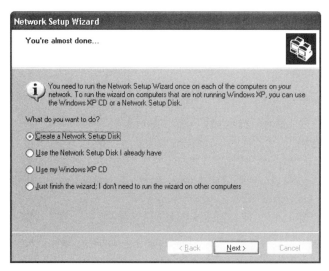

Figure 7-3.
Choose a setup disk option.

10. If you want the wizard to set up other computers for your network automatically, select Create A Network Setup Disk. Otherwise, select Just Finish The Wizard; I Don't Need To Run The Wizard On Other Computers.

11. Click Next and then click Finish.

Note

Windows XP automatically configures network settings for installed FireWire adapters.

Configuring Windows Networks

If you're using versions of Windows without a wizard—namely, Windows 95, Windows 98, and Windows 2000—you have to set up the network yourself. You might also want to make changes to a network created with a wizard in Windows Me and Windows XP.

Adding the Network Client

The first step in configuring Windows for networking is to determine how members of your family log on to the network when they start the computer or restart Windows. You do this by installing one of two network clients:

- **Client For Microsoft Windows** lets you start your computer and log on to the network by entering your name and password in a dialog box when Windows starts.

- **Microsoft Family Logon** lets you start your computer and log on to a network by selecting your user name from a list. You can use this option if more than one person uses a single computer. This option isn't available in either Windows 2000 or Windows XP.

Adding a Network Client in Windows 95, Windows 98, or Windows Me

Follow these steps to select your network client if you're using Windows 95, Windows 98, or Windows Me:

Note

You might need to insert your Windows CD later in the process, so have the CD handy.

1. On the Start menu, point to Settings, and then click Control Panel.
2. Double-click the Network icon to open the Network dialog box.
3. Look for either Client For Microsoft Networks or Microsoft Family Logon.
   If one of these clients is already installed and you don't want to change to the other, you can skip the rest of this procedure. If neither is installed or if you want to select the other client, continue with the next steps.
4. Click Add.
5. In the Select Network Component Type dialog box, click Client.
6. Click Add.
7. In the Select Network Client dialog box, click Microsoft in the Manufacturers list.
8. From the list of network clients in the Select Network Client dialog box, select Client For Microsoft Networks or Microsoft Family Logon.

9. Click OK to close the Select Network Client dialog box.

10. Click OK to close the Network dialog box. You might be asked to insert your Windows CD at this point.

11. Click Yes when you're asked whether you want to restart the computer.

You can have both Client For Microsoft Networks and Microsoft Family Logon installed at the same time. After adding one client, repeat the previous steps but choose the other client. To choose which client to use as the default, follow these steps:

1. On the Start menu, point to Settings, and then click Control Panel.

2. Double-click the Network icon to display the Network dialog box.

3. From the Primary Network Logon drop-down list, choose either Client For Microsoft Networks or Microsoft Family Logon.

4. Click OK.

Configuring a Network Client in Windows 2000 or Windows XP

If you have Windows 2000 or Windows XP, follow these steps to configure the network client:

1. Start by opening the Local Area Connection Properties dialog box in one of the following ways:

    - In Windows 2000, on the Start menu, point to Settings, and then click Network And Dial-Up Connections. In the window that appears, right-click the icon for your network adapter (labeled Local Area Connection) and choose Properties from the shortcut menu.

    - In Windows XP, click Start and then click My Network Places. Click View Network Connections. Right-click Local Area Connection and choose Properties from the shortcut menu.

    If Client For Microsoft Networks is listed, you can skip the rest of this procedure. If it isn't installed, continue as follows:

2. Click Install to open the Select Network Component Type dialog box.

3. Select Client, and then click Add to display the Select Network Client dialog box.

4. Select Client For Microsoft Networks and click OK.

5. Click Close to close the Local Area Connection Properties dialog box.

Installing Protocols

Your next step is to install one or more protocols that will allow your computer to communicate with other computers. Three basic protocols are used in home networks:

- **Transmission Control Protocol/Internet Protocol** (TCP/IP) is used to dial in to an Internet service, so odds are you already have it installed. However, it's not often used in smaller home networks because it requires a few more steps to set up than the other protocols do.

- **Internet Packet Exchange/Sequenced Packet Exchange** (IPX/SPX) was originally developed for an office networking system called Novell NetWare, although it can be used for any type of network.

- **NetBIOS Extended User Interface** (NetBEUI) is a network protocol for smaller networks that's easy to set up. This protocol isn't supported in Windows XP.

Note

If you plan to extend your network to shared modems and network printers, consider using TCP/IP because it's often required for connecting devices directly to the network. See the section "Configuring TCP/IP," later in this chapter, for more information.

You can actually have all three protocols installed at the same time, which would provide compatibility with any type of network that you connect to. In fact, the manufacturer might already have installed them in Windows. Some NIC installation programs set up and configure all three protocols when they install the network drivers.

With all three protocols installed, your home network will probably work perfectly well, choosing the best protocol when the computers begin communicating. The IPX/SPX and NetBEUI protocols require virtually no special configuration. However, TCP/IP is the protocol of choice for most networks, especially because Windows XP doesn't even support NetBEUI.

Installing Protocols in Windows 95, Windows 98, or Windows Me

To see which protocols are already installed and to add new ones, follow these steps for Windows 95, Windows 98, or Windows Me:

1. On the Start menu, point to Settings, and then click Control Panel.

2. In Control Panel, double-click the Network icon to display the Network dialog box shown in Figure 7-4. Any network protocols and services already installed are listed.

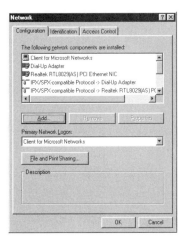

Figure 7-4.
The Network dialog box lists the protocols installed in your system.

3. Click Add.

4. In the Select Network Component Type dialog box, select Protocol and click Add to open the Select Network Protocol dialog box.

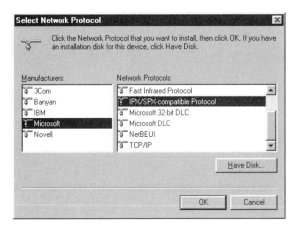

5. Choose Microsoft from the list of manufacturers.

6. Click a protocol in the Network Protocols list—IPX/SPX, NetBEUI, or TCP/IP.

7. Click OK to close the Select Network Protocol dialog box. Now repeat steps 3 through 7 for any other protocols you want to add.

8. Click OK to close the Network dialog box. You might be asked to insert your Windows CD at this point.

9. Click Yes when you're asked whether you want to restart your computer.

10. Open the Network dialog box again. You should see a listing for each of the protocols followed by the name of your network card in this form: TCP/IP→NETGEAR PCI Fast Ethernet, for example.

Installing Protocols in Windows 2000 or Windows XP

To see which protocols are already installed and to add new ones if you're using Windows 2000 or Windows XP, follow these steps:

1. Open the Local Area Connection Properties dialog box in one of the following ways:

    • In Windows 2000, on the Start menu, point to Settings, and then click Network And Dial-Up Connections. In the window that appears, right-click the icon for your network adapter and choose Properties from the shortcut menu.

    • In Windows XP, click Start and then click My Network Places. Click View Network Connections. Right-click Local Area Connection and choose Properties from the shortcut menu.
    Any network protocols and services already installed are listed.

2. Click Install.

3. In the Select Network Component Type dialog box, select Protocol and click Add to open the Select Network Protocol dialog box.

4. Click a protocol in the Network Protocols list—IPX/SPX, NetBEUI, or TCP/IP.

5. Click OK to close the Select Network Protocol dialog box.

6. Click Close to exit from the Local Area Connection Properties dialog box.

7. Click Yes if you're asked to restart your computer.

8. Open the Network dialog box again. The check mark next to the protocol indicates that the protocol is associated (bound) with your NIC.

Selecting Network Services

Network services allow you to share the resources on your network—primarily files and printers—among all the computers. File sharing lets other network users access your files. If you don't allow file sharing, other users can tell that you're on the network, but they won't be able to use any of your folders or files. Because sharing files is one of the main reasons to set up a network, it makes sense to activate this feature. You always have the option to specify which folders can be shared and how the files in these folders can be accessed.

Because sharing a printer is another big advantage of networking, you'll want to activate printer sharing as well. Before you can activate file sharing and printer sharing, however, you have to install the Windows service that allows sharing in the first place.

Selecting Network Services in Windows 95, Windows 98, or Windows Me

Here's how to add network services in Windows 95, Windows 98, or Windows Me:

1. On the Start menu, point to Settings, and then click Control Panel.

2. In Control Panel, double-click the Network icon to open the Network dialog box.

3. In the list of network components that are installed, look for File And Printer Sharing For Microsoft Networks.

    If File And Printer Sharing For Microsoft Networks is installed, you can skip the rest of these steps. If not, continue.

4. Click Add.

5. In the Select Network Component Type dialog box, click Service.

6. Click Add.

7. In the Select Network Service dialog box, click File And Printer Sharing For Microsoft Networks.

8. Click OK.

9. Click OK to close the Network dialog box. You might be asked to insert your Windows CD at this point.

10. Click Yes when you're asked whether you want to restart your computer.

After your computer restarts, you're ready to activate file and printer sharing.

1. On the Start menu, point to Settings, and then click Control Panel.

2. In Control Panel, double-click the Network icon to display the Network dialog box.

3. In the Network dialog box, click the File And Print Sharing button.

4. Select both check boxes in the File And Print Sharing dialog box.

5. Click OK.

6. Click OK to close the Network dialog box.

Completing this procedure doesn't mean that your files and printer are already shared. It means only that the service that allows sharing is now activated.

Selecting Network Services in Windows 2000 or Windows XP

Follow these steps to select services in Windows 2000 or Windows XP:

1. Open the Local Area Connection Properties dialog box in one of the following ways:

   - In Windows 2000, on the Start menu, point to Settings, and then click Network And Dial-Up Connections. In the window that appears, right-click the icon for your network adapter and choose Properties from the shortcut menu.

   - In Windows XP, click Start and then click My Network Places. Click View Network Connections. Right-click Local Area Connection and choose Properties from the shortcut menu.

2. In the list of network components that are installed, look for File And Printer Sharing For Microsoft Networks. If it's already installed, make sure File And Printer Sharing For Microsoft Networks has a check mark in the box to its left, and then skip the rest of these steps. Otherwise, continue.

3. Click Install to open the Select Network Component Type dialog box.

4. Select Service and then click Add to open the Select Network Service dialog box.

5. Select File And Printer Sharing For Microsoft Networks and then click OK.

6. Click OK to close the Select Network Component Type dialog box.

7. Click Yes if you're asked whether you want to restart your computer.

Identifying Your Computer on the Network

The final step in configuring Windows for networking is to make sure that your computer has a name and that you're a member of the same workgroup as the other computers on the network.

Identifying Your Computer in Windows 95, Windows 98, or Windows Me

If you're using Windows 95, Windows 98, or Windows Me, identify your workstation by following these steps:

1. On the Start menu, point to Settings, and then click Control Panel.

2. In Control Panel, double-click the Network icon to open the Network dialog box.

3. In the Network dialog box, click the Identification tab. You'll see the options shown in Figure 7-5.

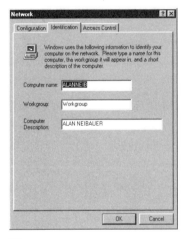

Figure 7-5.

Identify yourself and your workgroup on the Identification tab of the Network dialog box.

4. If you want, change your computer's name.

5. Make sure the workgroup name is the same one you use for other computers on your network. Windows suggests the name *Workgroup* by default.

6. Enter an optional description that others who browse the network can see.

7. Click OK to close the Network dialog box.

8. Click Yes when you're asked whether you want to restart the computer.

Identifying Your Computer in Windows 2000

If you're using Windows 2000, identify your workstation by following these steps:

1. Right-click My Computer and choose Properties from the shortcut menu to open the System Properties dialog box.

2. Click the Network Identification tab.

3. Click the Properties button on the Network Identification tab to open the Identification Changes dialog box.

4. If you want, change the name of your computer.

5. Make sure the workgroup name is the same one you use for other computers on your network. Windows suggests the name *Workgroup* by default.

6. Click OK to close the Identification Changes dialog box, and then click OK to close the System Properties dialog box.

7. Click Yes if you're asked whether you want to restart the computer.

Identifying Your Computer in Windows XP

If you're using Windows XP, identify your workstation by following these steps:

1. Right-click My Computer on the Start menu and choose Properties from the short-cut menu to open the System Properties dialog box.

2. Click the Computer Name tab to see your computer's name and workgroup.

3. Click the Change button to open the Computer Name Change dialog box.

4. If you want, change your computer's name.

5. Make sure the workgroup name is the same one you use for other computers on your network. Windows suggests the name *MSHOME* by default.

6. Click OK to close the Identification Changes dialog box, and then click OK to close the System Properties dialog box.

7. Click Yes if you're asked whether you want to restart the computer.

Configuring TCP/IP

Once installed, the NetBEUI network protocol usually doesn't require any further configuration to get it working. With TCP/IP, however, you must check some settings to make sure that the computers on the network can communicate.

If you have a dial-up Internet account, your computer is probably already using TCP/IP to connect to the Internet. In the Network dialog box, you'll see a listing for TCP/IP→Dial-up Adapter showing that the protocol is installed.

Note

If you get a message stating that file sharing is turned on when you first connect to the Internet, turn it off and restart your computer. This precaution will protect your files from unauthorized use—or even sabotage—by Internet hackers.

TCP/IP requires that each computer on the network have its own *IP address*—a string of numbers that identifies every computer linked to the Internet and every computer linked to a home TCP/IP network. No two computers on the Internet or two computers on your home network can have the same IP address. If you have a dial-up Internet account, most Internet service providers (ISPs) assign an IP address to your system each time you connect.

For a home network using TCP/IP, you can have Windows automatically assign an IP address to your computer every time your computer is started, or you can assign an IP address to it that will be unique on the network. Letting Windows assign the IP address is called *dynamic addressing* because the address assigned to your computer might change each time you connect to the network depending on which other computers have connected before you. Some Internet sharing software, which you'll learn about in Chapter 11, "Going Online Through the Network," requires that Windows assign the IP addresses.

Note

Network servers and some other hardware, such as Internet sharing routers and wireless gateways, can act like a Dynamic Host Configuration Protocol (DHCP) server that assigns IP addresses to computers.

You'll need to assign a specific IP address, however, if you plan to use your computer with peripherals, such as a network modem or a print server that requires a specific address. This address is called a *static address* because it will be the same each time you start your computer.

Note

You should learn both methods of assigning IP addresses. For a home network, I recommend assigning your own addresses, but be prepared to switch to dynamic addressing if the need arises.

An IP address is composed of four sets of numbers, each between 0 and 255, and each set of numbers is separated by a period. When you type an IP address, you must type all four sets of numbers, even if the number is 0, as in **192.168.0.25**. Because no two computers on the Internet are allowed to have the same IP address, your ISP will assign you an IP address when you connect. (After you log off, the IP address you just used becomes available for the ISP to assign to another user.)

If you have a digital subscriber line (DSL) or cable modem, your ISP has already assigned you an IP address for connecting to the Internet. You have to select a network IP address that's guaranteed not to conflict with your Internet IP address. To simplify this task, the Internet Engineering Task Force (IETF), the organization that determines Internet standards, set aside three ranges of numbers that can't be used as Internet addresses, and you can safely choose any IP address for your network in these ranges:

- 10.0.0.0–10.255.255.255

- 172.16.0.0–172.31.255.255

- 192.168.0.0–192.168.255.255

For your home network, you can use IP addresses starting with 192.168.0.1 and just add 1 to the last number for each computer. (To set up the second computer in your network, for example, enter **192.168.0.2** as the IP address.) Type a period between each number to separate the numbers into the four sections.

Note

When setting up Internet Connection Sharing (ICS), Windows assigns the address 192.168.0.1 to the computer that is sharing its connection. If you plan to use ICS, don't assign that IP address to a computer on your network.

You also have to designate a subnet address. To add further flexibility, another set of numbers, called the *subnet mask*, is used to modify how each address is interpreted. The subnet mask determines which portion of the entire IP address is used to specify the network and subnet numbers and which portion specifies an individual computer on the subnet. Because all your computers will be in the same subnet, they must all have the same numbers in the Subnet Mask field.

Setting IP Addresses in Windows 95, Windows 98, or Windows Me

To set the IP address of a Windows 95, Windows 98, or Windows Me computer on the network, follow these steps:

1. On the Start menu, point to Settings, and then click Control Panel.

2. In Control Panel, double-click the Network icon to open the Network dialog box.

3. In the list of network components, click the TCP/IP setting for your NIC, and click Properties to see the options in Figure 7-6.

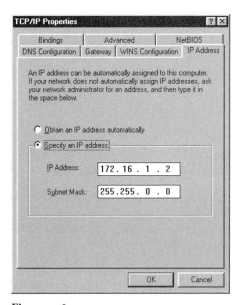

Figure 7-6.
The TCP/IP Properties dialog box displays two TCP/IP settings: IP Address and Subnet Mask.

Caution

If you're connected to the Internet through a DSL or cable modem, you might have two TCP/IP settings for Ethernet devices shown in the Network dialog box. One is for your Ethernet connection to the Internet; the other is for your Ethernet connection to the network. In setting up your network, be sure to select the TCP/IP setting for the NIC connected to the network. When you click Properties, if a specific IP address is already shown in the dialog box that appears, you've probably selected the Internet TCP/IP setting. Click Cancel and choose the other TCP/IP setting in the Network dialog box. Check with your ISP if you have any questions.

4. Make sure Obtain An IP Address Automatically is selected if you want Windows to assign an IP address to your computer whenever it's started, and then click OK.

   If you want to assign your own IP address, continue with the following steps:

5. Click Specify An IP Address in the TCP/IP Properties dialog box.

6. Enter an IP address in the text box.

Tip

When you enter an IP address or subnet mask, Windows will move from one set of numbers to the next when you enter the third digit. If you want to put only one or two digits in a set, either type a period to move to the next set, or click in the spot where the next set of numbers is located.

7. Enter **255.255.255.0** as the subnet mask for this and every other computer on the network.

8. Click OK to close the Network dialog box.

9. Click Yes when you're asked whether you want to restart your computer.

Configuring TCP/IP in Windows 2000

To configure TCP/IP on a Windows 2000 workstation, follow these steps:

1. On the Start menu, point to Settings, and then click Network And Dial-Up Connections.

2. Right-click Local Area Connection and choose Properties from the shortcut menu to display the Local Area Connection Properties dialog box.

3. In the list of network components, click Internet Protocol (TCP/IP) and click Properties.

4. Make sure Obtain An IP Address Automatically is selected if you want Windows to assign an IP address to your computer whenever it's started, and then click OK.

   If you want to assign your own IP address, continue with the following steps:

5. Click Use The Following IP Address.

6. Enter an IP address in the text box.

7. Enter **255.255.255.0** as the subnet mask in this and every other computer on the network.

8. Click OK to close the TCP/IP Properties dialog box.

9. Click OK to close the Local Area Connection Properties dialog box.

10. Click Yes when you're asked whether you want to restart your computer.

Configuring TCP/IP in Windows XP

To configure TCP/IP in Windows XP, follow these steps:

1. Click Start and then click My Network Places.

2. Click View Network Connections.

3. In the window that appears, right-click the icon for your network adapter and choose Properties from the shortcut menu to display the Local Area Connection Properties dialog box.

4. In the list of network components, click Internet Protocol (TCP/IP) and click Properties to see the options in Figure 7-7.

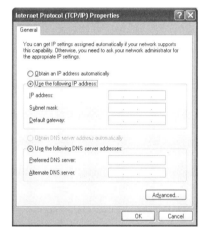

Figure 7-7.

The Internet Protocol (TCP/IP) Properties dialog box displays two TCP/IP settings: IP Address and Subnet Mask.

5. Make sure Obtain An IP Address Automatically is selected if you want Windows to assign an IP address to your computer whenever it's started, and then click OK.
    If you want to assign your own IP address, continue with the following steps:

6. Click the Use The Following IP Address option.

7. Enter an IP address in the text box.

8. Enter **255.255.255.0** as the subnet mask in this and every other computer on the network.

9. Click OK to close the TCP/IP Properties dialog box.

10. Click OK to close the Local Area Connection Properties dialog box.

11. Click Yes if you're asked whether you want to restart your computer.

Alternate IP Addresses   Windows XP offers a unique feature to assign multiple IP addresses to the same computer. If a network connection can't be established using one of the addresses, Windows automatically tries one of the other ones that you designated.

Two choices exist for multiple IP addresses:

- Obtain a dynamic address and assign one alternate static IP. If the computer can't obtain its IP address dynamically, it'll use the static IP.

- Assign multiple static IP addresses, without obtaining a dynamic address.

To use a dynamic address with a static IP for a backup, follow these steps:

1. Open the Local Area Connection Properties dialog box.

2. In the list of network components, select Internet Protocol (TCP/IP) and click Properties.

3. Click Obtain An IP Address Automatically. A new tab—Alternate Configuration— appears in the dialog box.

4. Click the Alternate Configuration tab to see two options: Automatic Private IP Address and User Configured.

   These are two different ways to assign the static backup address. Using the Automatic Private IP Address option, Windows XP selects the static address for you when a dynamic address isn't found. The static address will be in the range 169.254.0.1–169.254.255.254 and the subnet mask will be 255.255.0.0. To select this option, just click on it and click OK.

   That range may not fit in with your network, however, so the User Configured option lets you specify the static address yourself. If you want to select the User Configured option, continue with these steps.

5. Click User Configured.

6. Enter an appropriate IP address and subnet mask for your network.

7. Click OK.

To assign multiple static IP addresses, follow these steps:

1. Open the Local Area Connection Properties dialog box.

2. In the list of network components, click Internet Protocol (TCP/IP) and click Properties.

3. Click Use The Following IP Address.

4. Enter the first static IP address you want to assign the computer.

5. Enter the subnet mask for that address.

6. Click the Advanced button to open the Advanced TCP/IP Settings dialog box, shown in Figure 7-8.

Figure 7-8.
Assigning multiple IP addresses.

7. Click Add.

8. Enter another IP address and subnet mask, and click Add.

9. Repeat the steps for each additional IP address that you want to assign the computer.

Windows XP Bridges

Some computers have more than one type of NIC installed. It is not uncommon, for example, for a laptop computer to have a built-in Ethernet port in addition to a wireless PC Card.

You can easily network two laptops without using wires if they both have wireless PC Cards, but you might also want to connect one of the computers to another network through its Ethernet port. You might also have a desktop computer connected to an Ethernet network but want to install a wireless NIC or USB adapter to communicate with other systems wirelessly.

When a computer is connected to two different networks in that way, as shown in Figure 4-12 in Chapter 4, the two networks are not actually connected. To link the two networks, you need a hardware device or software program called a bridge. A *bridge* connects two or more networks of any type and combination—wired, wireless, phone-line, or FireWire. You can view the bridge whenever you want, and you can remove, create, or modify a bridge if you later add or remove a network adapter.

Creating a Bridge Using the Wizard

If you have more than one network device on your computer, the Windows XP Network Setup Wizard offers you two options to create a bridge, as shown below.

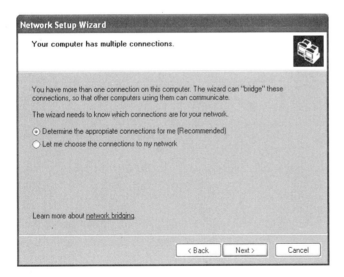

If you select the first option, Windows XP automatically creates a bridge between your active adapters. When you have more than two NICs, however, you might want to choose which should be bridged. To choose the adapters, select the second option to display a list of adapters as shown below.

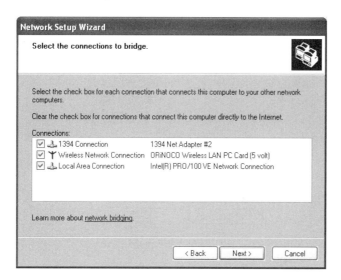

Remove the checkmarks next to the adapters you don't want bridged, and then click Next to continue the Network Setup Wizard

To see the installed network adapters and bridge, such as those shown in the following illustration, click Start and then click My Network Places. Then click View Network Connections.

Creating A Bridge Manually

If you didn't create the bridge using the wizard, or if you just recently added another network adapter, you can create the bridge manually. To create a new bridge, when viewing the network connections, select the first adapter you want to add to the bridge, and then hold down the Ctrl key and select the other adapters. Then select Bridge Connections from the Advanced menu.

To quickly add an adapter to an existing bridge, right-click it and select Add To Bridge from the shortcut menu.

When an adapter is bridged, you might not be able to make any changes to its settings, such as changing its IP address or adding a protocol. You have to first remove the adapter from the bridge, make the changes, and then add it back to the bridge. To remove an adapter from the bridge, right-click its icon and choose Remove From Bridge from the shortcut menu.

You can also adjust some properties of the bridge itself, adding and removing adapters from it. Right-click the icon for the bridge and choose Properties to see the available options.

Setting Up Wireless Networks

Wireless network adapters need the same general setup as Ethernet adapters. But in addition to setting up protocols and network clients, wireless adapters and access points have their own unique settings. With wireless adapters, you need to specify the type of network connection, the name of the network it's connecting to, and the encryption level and Wired Equivalent Privacy (WEP) code, as explained in the following list:

- The network type determines whether the adapter is communicating directly with other wireless adapters (called *peer-to-peer* or *ad hoc*) or through an access point (called *infrastructure*).

- The network is called the *Service Set Identifier (SSID)*. The SSID is included with all transmissions to designate which network accepts the data. Most adapters let you specify the network name as ANY so the card will connect to any 802.11b network that it finds within its range.

- The WEP level and encryption key code help secure a network by allowing only wireless adapters that know the key to communicate with the network. *(WEP is discussed in more detail in the section "Setting Up Wireless Networks," earlier in this chapter.)*

Note

Wireless adapters have other settings, too, but they're usually best left at the default values.

In this section, we'll look at how to set up five different types of wireless adapters: four laptop PC Cards and a USB device. All the adapters are Wi-Fi 802.11b–compliant, and they can all work together on the same network. We'll first look at some general setup options, and then compare the way the adapters are set for WEP security.

All the companies that manufacture a wireless PC Card, by the way, also market a PCI adapter. The adapter is an Internet PCI card that fits inside your computer, to which you plug in the wireless PC Card. The combination gives your desktop computer wireless networking capabilities.

The SMC EZ Connect and U.S. Robotics wireless PC Cards use similar setup routines, including the Configuration Utility shown in Figure 7-9. On the Configuration tab, you can select between infrastructure and peer-to-peer modes, set the network ID, and set other options as well.

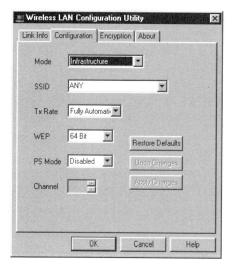

Figure 7-9.
Setting up the SMC PC Cards.

The Configuration tab of the SMC utility also lets you choose the encryption level; that option is available on the Encryption tab of the U.S. Robotics dialog box. Use the Restore Defaults button to quickly return to the default settings provided by the software, or use the Undo Changes button to cancel any changes you made.

The Link Info tab reports the status and strength of the signal and the speed at which data is transmitted and received. And the Rescan button forces the adapter to look for other wireless devices in its range.

The ORiNOCO PC Card's Client Manager program lets you create up to 99 profiles, so you can switch between networks as you roam. Each profile can be set up for an access point, residential gateway, or peer-to-peer group. For example, suppose you connect to a wireless access point at work, but you have a peer-to-peer wireless network at home. You would create a profile for each, so when you move from home to work, you need only select the profile needed to connect to the network without making any other changes to the configuration. The Client Manager then reports the status of the connection and lets you quickly change the profile when you move into another network, as shown in Figure 7-10.

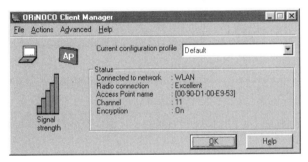

Figure 7-10.
Selecting profiles with the Orinoco Client Manager.

Once the Buffalo Technology AirStation PC Card is installed, set it up by using the Windows Control Panel. Open the Network icon in Control Panel, select the Melco Adapter listing, and click Properties to set its options. Enter the network ID and select the Infrastructure check box if you're connecting to an access point using infrastructure mode. (Clear the Infrastructure check box if you're connecting peer-to-peer.)

Connection to the network is automatic, but a separate Client Manager program is provided that lets you manually connect to a network, changing settings as needed, as shown in Figure 7-11. You can use the Client Manager to create a list of frequently used network IDs, so you can quickly switch among them as you change locations.

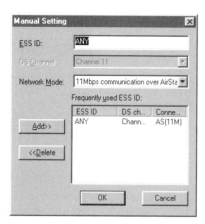

Figure 7-11.

Connecting with the Buffalo Technology card.

Setting up the D-Link USB wireless adapter is similar to how you set up the PC Cards just described. A configuration utility allows you to set the SSID, choose between infrastructure and peer-to-peer networking, and other options. The program's Status tab, shown in Figure 7-12, reports the signal strength, the number of packets that have been transmitted and received, and other details about the connection.

Figure 7-12.

Checking status of the D-Link USB wireless adapter.

Setting Up Wireless Encryption

To create a secure wireless network, you should enable WEP encryption.

Note

Much controversy exists over how much security WEP encryption provides. Many experts think it's much easier to detect a network's WEP code than previously believed. WEP encryption does offer some level of security against casual interlopers, but it should be combined with the use of passwords for file access and firewall software. We'll look at firewall protection in Chapter 11, "Going Online Through the Network."

Using WEP makes your wireless network a little more difficult to manage, but it's well worth the increase in security. Just because a wireless network is limited in range doesn't mean it's protected against interlopers. In fact, hackers are taking some imaginative steps to break into wireless networks, including wireless sniffers and war driving.

Wireless sniffers are devices that intercept and analyze the data packets that are transmitted within a wireless network. They can determine and copy the SSID and WEP key to allow a hacker access to your network. *War driving* is the technique of "driving around the streets" with a wireless computer to detect wireless networks. A war driver who detects a network that isn't protected with a WEP key can then access the network without authorization.

Note

War driving derives its name from the term *war dialing,* inspired by the Matthew Broderick film *WarGames.* War dialing is the technique of using a computer program to randomly dial hundreds or thousands of phone numbers looking for an unprotected computer dial-up network.

To increase your network's security, always enable WEP. You might also want to change your WEP keys periodically for an extra measure of safety.

When all your wireless hardware is from the same manufacturer, you can enter the WEP key by using whichever techniques the hardware allows: either as a series of alphanumeric characters (called a *passphrase*) or in hexadecimal values. If you enter a passphrase, the configuration program automatically converts it into an equivalent hexadecimal value, as explained in the sidebar "The Hexadecimal System" on page 192. The length of the key is determined by the WEP level:

- **64-bit WEP** allows 5 alphanumeric characters or 10 hexadecimal values.

- **128-bit WEP** allows 10 alphanumeric characters or 20 hexadecimal values.

The Hexadecimal System

Hexadecimal numbering is a base-16 system. It consists of the numbers 0–9 and the letters A–F. Counting from 0 to 15 in hexadecimal is 0 1 2 3 4 5 6 7 8 9 A B C D E F.

So the decimal number 10 is A in hexadecimal, the number 11 is B, and so on. To avoid confusion, hexadecimal numbers are usually preceded by either 0x or followed by the letter h, as in 0xA or Bh. The number 16 is represented by the digits 0x10; the number 17 is 0x11.

If this concept is confusing, think about the base-10 decimal number system that includes the digits 0 through 9. Two digits, 1 and 0, represent the value after 9. In this case, the 1 means the number of 10s and the 0 means the number of 1s. So the decimal value 25 means two 10s and five 1s.

The same process is used for hexadecimal numbers, except using base 16. In the hex value 0x10, the 1 means the number of 16s and the 0 means the number of 1s. One 16 (1 x 16) and no 1s (0 x 1) is 16. Likewise, the hex number 0xA5 is equal to the decimal number 165—that is, ten 16s (remember, 0xA is decimal 10) and five 1s—160 plus 5.

The technique that programs use to convert alphanumeric keys to hexadecimal is not always the same. For example, the same passphrase could be converted to different hexadecimal values by different programs. When you're using hardware from a mix of manufacturers, always enter the key in hexadecimal for all devices to insure that the same key is being used.

Now let's take a look at how to set WEP keys in our sample wireless adapters.

Setting WEP Keys in Wireless Adapters

The Encryption tab of the SMC Configuration Utility, shown in Figure 7-13, lets you enter the WEP code as either a passphrase or hexadecimal values. If you enter a passphrase, click the Generate button to convert it into hexadecimal; otherwise, enter actual hex values in the Key boxes. When you click Write, the key is saved so the adapter can use it.

Note

Before you click Write, by the way, you'll see the actual hexadecimal values rather than a series of asterisks as you usually see when you enter a password, so you can copy the values for use with other systems.

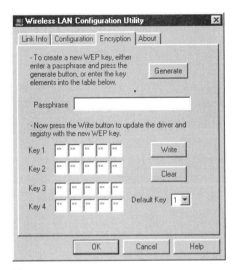

Figure 7-13.

Setting WEP code with SMC wireless adapters.

The Encryption tab of the U.S. Robotics Configuration Utility is similar to the SMC program, except it lets you select the encryption level as well. Rather than have Generate and Write buttons, however, you enter a passphrase or hex code and then click the Apply button.

The ORiNOCO configuration program lets you enter up to four keys that you can use for the profiles, as shown below. You can choose to enter the keys as either alphanumeric characters or hexadecimal values. There are two ORiNOCO cards: the Silver uses 64-bit encryption, and the Gold uses 128-bit encryption.

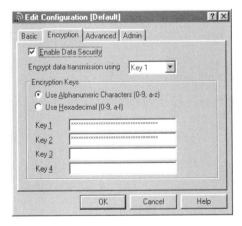

The Buffalo Technology AirStation configuration program also lets you enter up to four keys. No option exists that would let you select either alphanumeric or hexadecimal entry. Rather, to enter a passphrase, just type the characters; to enter hexadecimal values, type **ox** before the key, as in **ox34f3f6ae45**.

The D-Link configuration program allows you to enter only hexadecimal values as the WEP key. This "restriction" isn't a drawback, however. If you're using a mix of hardware, you should use hex values anyway. The D-Link configuration program does include two advanced options not found on many adapters—you can choose whether WEP encryption is mandatory or optional, and you can set the authentication type. Although you should generally use the default settings, these two security options are becoming available on many wireless systems, so it pays to understand them.

When WEP is set to Optional, the D-Link adapter can communicate with other computers that don't have WEP enabled. When set to Mandatory, matching WEP keys are required. Setting the card to Optional allows easier movement between networks.

The authentication type options are Shared Key and the default, Open System. When set to Open System, any computer is allowed to join the network, although the WEP settings must match to share data. When set to Shared Key, a wireless client computer must request authentication to access the network. When the network receives that request, it sends a random number to the client that it has encoded with the shared key. The client must decode the number using its copy of the shared key and transmit the result back to the network. When the number received by the network matches the random number it generated, the client is authenticated and allowed to join the network.

Windows XP Wireless

Windows XP has built-in support for wireless networks. In many cases, wireless NICs will automatically be recognized and the built-in drivers used, so you do not need to install drivers supplied by the NIC's manufacturer.

You configure the wireless NIC from the Network Connections window by performing the following steps:

1. Right-click the listing for the NIC and select Properties to open the Wireless Network Connection Properties box.

2. Click the Wireless Networks tab to see the options in Figure 7-14.

3. To set the type of network, click the Advanced button to see these options:

    - Any available network (access point preferred)

    - Access point (infrastructure) networks only.

    - Computer-to-computer (ad hoc) networks only.

4. Make your selection and then click Close.

Figure 7-14.
Setting wireless network properties in Windows XP.

To set the encryption level, click Properties to see the options shown in Figure 7-15 and then follow these steps:

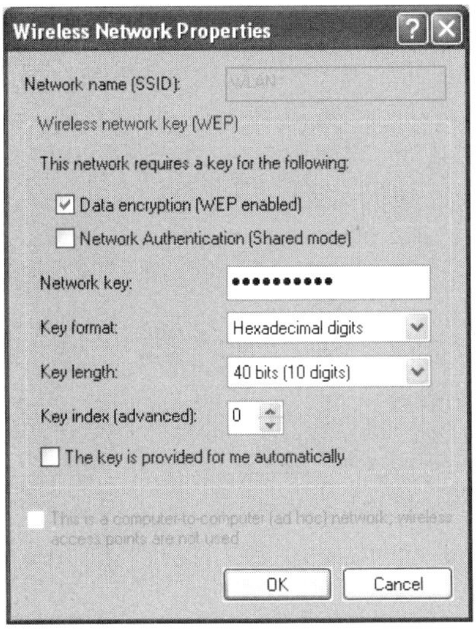

Figure 7-15.
Setting WEP code with Windows XP.

1. Select Data encryption (WEP enabled).

2. Select either Hexadecimal digits or ASCII characters from the Key Format list.

3. Select either 40 bits or 104 bits from the Key Length list.

4. Enter the key in the Network key box.

5. Click OK.

Access Points

If your wireless network is using an access point, it too must be configured. Usually, you have to first assign to the access point an IP address that fits into your network.

Three basic scenarios exist:

*   The access point has no preassigned IP address.

*   The manufacturer has assigned an initial IP to the access point.

*   The access point has been set up to provide dynamic IP addresses.

When the access point hasn't yet been assigned an IP address, you have to run a setup program provided with the access point to set its IP so the IP is compatible with your network. The program scans your network looking for the hardware, and then it lets you enter an IP address and subnet mask. The program then records the IP address and subnet mask into the access point's memory so the access point can be part of your network.

If the manufacturer has already assigned an address to the access point, you have three options:

*   In some cases, a configuration program will allow you to connect to the access point even if the IP isn't compatible with your current network settings. You can then use the configuration program to change the IP address and subnet mask.

*   You have to change the network settings of the computers on the network to be compatible with that of the access point.

*   You have to change the network settings of one computer temporarily so you can use it to communicate with the access point's built-in Web page to change its settings. You then reset the computer's settings so the computer can connect to the rest of the network again.

Some access points are preset as a *DHCP server*, which assigns the IP addresses to computers that have been set up for dynamic addressing. If you want to use static IP addresses on the network, you must change one computer to dynamic addressing temporarily so it can communicate with the access point. You can then use the access point's built-in Web page to turn off its DHCP function and assign it a compatible static IP address and subnet mask. You then have to reset the computer you used to its original static IP.

The SMC and U.S. Robotics access points are examples of devices that have both a configuration program and a built-in Web page. You can assign the access point a static IP address or have it act as a DHCP server to your network. The access points are Wi-Fi compatible so they can be used with any Wi-Fi adapter, and they have one Ethernet port for connecting to an Ethernet hub or a switch for connecting to a wired Ethernet network.

Except for the title bar, the configuration program used by both types of access points is identical. (See Figure 7-16.) The program searches your network for an access point and displays its current configuration information. You then select the Set IP option on the AP menu to give the access point a temporary IP address that fits into your network.

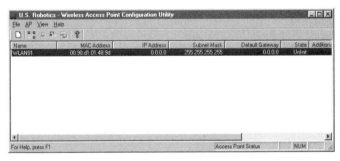

Figure 7-16.
Setting up the U.S. Robotics access point.

Once the temporary IP is set, you configure the access point by using its built-in Web pages. To display the built-in Web page shown in Figure 7-17, either double-click the listing for the device in the Configuration Utility, or use your Web browser to go to the IP address assigned to the device.

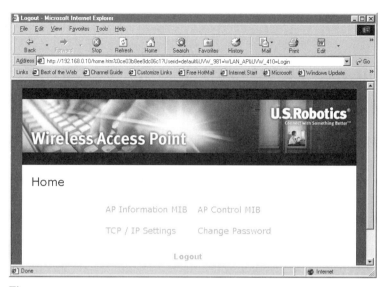

Figure 7-17.

Built-in configuration Web page.

To use your browser, enter *http://* in the address or location text box, followed by the IP address of the access point. (You might need to turn off the Automatic Connect feature of your browser to prevent it from trying to go online.) The Web page appears once you enter a user name and password. Default values are given in the manual, but you can change them for security purposes. Using these options, you can display or change the access point's TCP/IP settings, configuration settings, and password.

The encryption options for the access points are shown in Figure 7-18. The WEP level and key must match the settings of the wireless adapters. Notice that the access point gives you the option of entering the key as a passphrase or by manually entering the hexadecimal values. You can enter either a 64-bit or 128-bit key to be compatible with the wireless adapters.

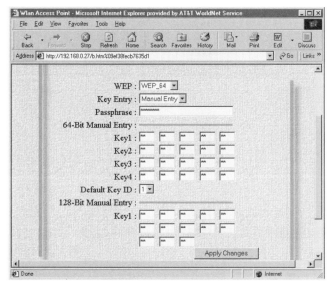

Figure 7-18.

Setting the access point WEP level and key.

See Also

In Chapter 11, "Going Online Through the Network," we'll look at a number of devices that combine wireless access points and Internet sharing routers.

MAC Address Filtering

In addition to WEP security, some access points allow Media Access Control (MAC) address filtering. The *MAC address* is a unique number assigned by the manufacturer to every Ethernet adapter, so it's sometimes called the *Ethernet address* or the *adapter address*. Your computer keeps track of all MAC addresses and the corresponding IP address of every device connected to it.

MAC addresses are written as a series of six hexadecimal values, such as 00 e0 39 9a 3a 3b. You can usually find your adapter's MAC address on a label somewhere on the adapter, or you can use these steps:

1. Click Start and then click Run.

2. Type **winipcfg** and press Enter to open the IP Configuration dialog box.

3. Click the drop-down list at the top of the dialog box and select your network adapter. The MAC address appears in the box labeled Adapter Address.

MAC address filtering lets you specify the MAC addresses of adapters that might connect to the access point. Adapters with MAC addresses that you don't specify won't be able to communicate with the access point and access the network. You'll see a specific example of MAC address filtering in Chapter 11, "Going Online Through the Network."

Welcome to the Neighborhood!

With all your hardware and software properly installed, your network is now complete. All the computers on the network are ready to communicate, and they should be able to "see" each other.

Accessing the Network in Windows 95 or Windows 98

If you're using Windows 95 or Windows 98, double-click the Network Neighborhood icon on your Windows desktop to find other computers on the network. You should see icons for each of the computers on the network, as well as one labeled Entire Network, as shown in Figure 7-19.

Figure 7-19.

Network Neighborhood displays an icon for each computer on the network.

Note

Your computer might take a few minutes to "see" the other computers on the network. If no other computers appear in Network Neighborhood, close the Network Neighborhood window and try again in a few minutes.

To access one of the computers on the network, double-click its icon in Network Neighborhood. You should see all the resources listed on that computer that can be shared. Don't worry if nothing appears when you try this now—you'll learn how to share resources in Chapter 10, "Printing Across the Network."

If you double-click the Entire Network icon in Network Neighborhood, you'll see an icon representing the workgroup. Double-click that icon to display the computers in your workgroup.

Network Neighborhood will appear in Windows Explorer and in the File Open dialog box and the File Save As dialog box of Windows applications. If you're using Microsoft Word, for example, you can open or save a file on a connected computer by choosing Network Neighborhood in the Look In list that appears in the Open or Save dialog box, as shown below.

Another way to access a computer on the network in Windows 95 or Windows 98 is by using the Find command. Here's how:

1. On the Start menu, point to Find, and then click Computer.

2. Enter the name of the computer in the Find: Computer dialog box, and click Find Now.

Accessing the Network in Windows Me

If you're using Windows Me, you access the network by using My Network Places on the Windows desktop. Here's how:

1. Double-click My Network Places on the Windows desktop.

2. Double-click Entire Network to see an icon for the workgroup.

3. Double-click the Workgroup icon to see a list of computers in the workgroup.

4. Double-click a computer to see its shared resources, such as disk drive and shared folders. (Once you perform these steps, by the way, the network resources that you accessed will automatically appear in My Network Places.)

See Also

In Chapter 10, "Printing Across the Network," you'll learn how to add shortcuts to specific shared drives and how to add folders to the My Network Places window.

Accessing the Network in Windows 2000

To find other computers in Windows 2000, follow these steps:

1. Double-click the My Network Places icon on your Windows desktop to reveal these two options:

    -   **Entire Network** includes your workgroup and a server domain.

    -   **Computers Near Me** includes computers in your workgroup.

2. Double-click Computers Near Me to see icons for each of the computers in your workgroup. If you double-click Entire Network and click the text to view the entire contents of the network, you can then double-click Microsoft Windows Network to see an icon labeled with your workgroup name. Double-click the icon for the computer you want to locate.

3. To access one of the computers on the network, double-click its icon. You should see all the resources listed on that computer that can be shared.

    My Network Places will appear in Windows Explorer and in the File Open and File Save As dialog boxes of Windows applications.

Accessing the Network in Windows XP

To find other computers in Windows XP, follow these steps:

1. Click Start and then click My Network Places.

2. If the other computers on the network aren't shown, click View Workgroup Computers in the Network Tasks section.

3. Double-click the icon for the computer to which you want to connect. You should see all the resources listed on that computer that can be shared.

My Network Places will appear in Windows Explorer and in the File Open and File Save As dialog boxes of Windows applications.

Troubleshooting

Theoretically, every part of your network should be humming along now. But sometimes, even with the best planning, problems can occur. If you can't access the other computers on your network, you'll have to take some time and check out each aspect of the installation.

Browsing the Network

First, give your computers a few minutes to recognize each other before opening Network Neighborhood (or My Network Places). It often takes a minute or so for the networking software to find the other computers. If no computers appear, or if you get an error message saying that the network can't be browsed, wait a few minutes and try again.

If you know the name of another computer, try locating it using Find: Computer (or Search in Windows Me, Windows 2000, and Windows XP) on the Start menu. You can often access a computer this way before it shows up in Network Neighborhood (or My Network Places).

You can also try restarting your computer and making sure that you log on when asked for your network password before the Windows desktop appears. If you click the Cancel button in the Enter Network Password dialog box when starting Windows, you won't be able to access the network.

If that fails, check all the cable connections at the computers and at the hub. Make sure the hub is plugged in and turned on and that all the cables are securely connected.

If you have a wireless network, try moving the computers closer to each other or closer to the access point. If the network works when the machines are closer, you might need to adjust the position of the access point, or see whether the manufacturer of your adapters sells an antenna or other range-extending device.

If you still can't access the network, the problem might be the configuration of the NICs.

Checking Network Settings

The next place to troubleshoot the network is in the Network dialog box. Make sure that you're using the same workgroup name for each computer, with the same spelling and the same combination of uppercase and lowercase characters. If any computer is using a different workgroup name, change it to match the others, restart the computer, and try Network Neighborhood (or My Network Places) again.

Next, make sure that you have all three protocols installed and that you have the same protocols on every computer on the network.

If you're using TCP/IP, make sure that either you're assigning IP addresses automatically or that each machine has a different address. Check that the subnet mask is the same for every machine.

If you have a wireless network, make sure that all of the adapters and the access point (if any) are set properly, as follows:

- Peer-to-peer (ad hoc) or infrastructure mode

- WEP enabled or disabled

- The same WEP hex code set for every device.

Note

The problem might be related to one or more of the different protocols you're using. If all else fails, remove all the protocols except NetBEUI from all the computers and try again. NetBEUI is the easiest protocol to get started with because it requires no special configuration.

Checking the Master Browser

If you still can't browse the network, the trouble might lie in the Master Browser setting. Even though all computers are equal in a peer-to-peer network, one computer is a little more important than the others.

Windows automatically assigns one computer on the network the role of browse master. The *browse master* keeps track of every shared resource on the network. When you use Network Neighborhood or My Network Places to look for network computers, Windows checks with the browse master for the list. If the computer assigned as browse master is turned off, it takes Windows some time (as long as 15 or 20 minutes) to assign a new browse master and update the list of network computers and shared resources. Only systems that are logged on to the network and that are sharing some resource (such as a drive or folder) can act as the browse master.

Windows 2000 computers have browse master priority. If you turn on a Windows 2000 computer on an existing Windows 95, Windows 98, or Windows Me network, the browse master will be reassigned and your network resources might seem unavailable during that process.

When you first start your computer and try to connect to another computer, you might get an error message reporting that you can't browse the network. This error usually occurs because Windows is still assigning a computer to be the browse master, or the browse master is still building a database of network resources.

Although the browse master is automatically assigned, you can override the setting in versions of Windows other than Windows 2000 and Windows XP by designating a specific computer as the browse master. When you do this, however, you must set all the other computers so they don't try to assign an automatic browse master.

Note

Modifying the browse master settings in Windows 2000 and Windows XP requires a change to the Windows registry, which is beyond the scope of this book.

To check or set the browse master in Windows 95, Windows 98, or Windows Me, follow these steps:

1. On the Start menu, point to Settings, and then click Control Panel.

2. In Control Panel, double-click the Network icon to open the Network dialog box.

3. In the list of network components that are installed, select File And Printer Sharing For Microsoft Networks.

4. Click the Properties button.

5. In the Properties dialog box that appears, shown in Figure 7-20, click Browse Master in the Property list.

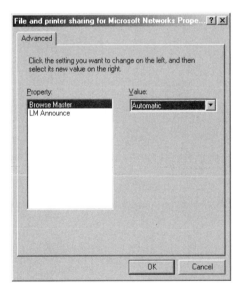

Figure 7-20.
Setting the browse master.

To have Windows assign the browse master for you, make sure the Automatic option appears in the Value drop-down list. If Automatic isn't displayed and you want Windows to assign the browse master, click on the Value drop-down list and select Automatic. You'll need to do this for every computer in the network.

If you want to assign one computer to be the browse master manually, click on the Value drop-down list on that computer and select Enabled. Then on every other computer on the network, select Disabled. The machine that you designated as the browse master must be running before any other computer can access the network.

Troubleshooting Hardware Conflicts

Finally, if your network still doesn't work, check for conflicts between the NIC and other hardware on your computers. After you install the drivers, your NIC should operate properly. If you're unable to get your network going, however, a conflict might exist between the NIC and other hardware. To determine whether a hardware conflict exists, follow these steps:

1. In all versions of Windows except for Windows XP, right-click My Computer on the Windows desktop, and choose Properties from the shortcut menu. In Windows XP, click Start, right-click My Computer, and choose Properties.

2. In Windows 95, Windows 98, or Windows Me, click the Device Manager tab in the System Properties dialog box. In Windows 2000 or Windows XP, click the Device Manager button on the Hardware tab.

In all versions of Windows, if your network device isn't working properly, you'll see an exclamation point or X next to its name. Follow these steps to troubleshoot the problem:

1. In the list of devices on the Device Manager tab, click the name of your NIC under Network Adapters. In Windows 95, Windows 98, or Windows Me, click Properties. In Windows 2000 or Windows XP, click the Properties button on the toolbar.

2. In the Properties dialog box for your network device, look in the Device Status section of the General tab. If you see a message that says This Device Is Either Not Present, Not Working Properly, Or Does Not Have All The Divers Installed, you have either a bad card or a conflict.

3. Click the Resources tab of the Properties dialog box. The Conflicting Device List section shows where the conflict is occurring.

Another way to check for conflicts in Windows 98, Windows Me, Windows 2000, or Windows XP is with the System Information program. To do this, follow these steps:

1. On the Start menu, point to Programs (All Programs in Windows XP), point to Accessories, point to System Tools, and then click System Information.

2. In the Microsoft System Information window, click the plus sign next to Hardware Resources.

3. Under Hardware Resources, click Conflicts/Sharing and see whether any conflicts are listed in the right pane of the window or whether your network card is using the same IRQ as another device. Note that PCI-bus network cards can share an IRQ with other devices without causing a problem, but ISA cards can't.

4. Click Forced Hardware. This folder will show devices that you set up manually using settings other than those chosen by a plug and play device.

5. Click I/O and look for addresses that are shared by two devices.

6. Click IRQs and scan the list for any possible conflicts involving ISA devices.

7. Click the plus sign next to Components.

8. Under Components, click Network.

9. Scroll through the list on the right to confirm that your network card, TCP/IP, and network clients are all listed. If any of them isn't listed, go back and reinstall the missing elements as described in the beginning of this chapter.

   With PCI cards, you might be able to correct a hardware conflict by moving the card to another empty PCI slot in your computer. If you then restart Windows, the card will be assigned a different IRQ number that might not conflict with other hardware.

Note

A PCI network card can share an IRQ with an item called *PCI IRQ Steering* without conflict.

If moving the card doesn't correct the problem or you're using an ISA network card, try rerunning the card's installation program and selecting other settings. If that doesn't work, change the settings manually in the device's Properties dialog box.

Caution

Changing the settings yourself is a last-ditch option. There's no guarantee that you'll get the NIC to work, and you could create a new conflict with another device, such as a modem or printer, causing that device to fail as well.

If you do want to try changing the settings manually, follow these steps:

1. Select Control Panel and point to System.

2. Click the Device Manager tab and select the hardware you want to change.

3. Click Properties, and then select the Resources tab.

4. On the Resources tab of the Properties dialog box, make a note of which settings are being used.

    This information will allow you to restore the original settings, if necessary. Restoring the original settings won't do anything for the NIC, but it might restore some other device that you disabled by changing settings manually.

5. Click the Use Automatic Settings check box to clear it.

6. In the Resource Type list, click the setting you want to change.

7. Click Change Settings.

8. In the Edit Resource dialog box that opens, change the setting, and then click OK.

9. Restart your computer and test all your devices.

If the new configuration doesn't work, repeat the process but restore the original settings. Perhaps it's time to take your computer to a shop for the installation or remove the card and exchange it for a plug-and-play PC model.

The Bottom Line

Depending on your NIC, setting up your hardware can be either a breeze or a windstorm. Fortunately, almost all NICs available these days are either plug and play or include software that guides you through the process.

In the next chapter, you'll learn how to create profiles to personalize your computer if you share it with other members of your household.

Chapter 8

Creating User Profiles

Even if you have more than one computer in the house, more than one person probably uses each computer. With Microsoft Windows, individual users can have their own settings that go into effect whenever they log on to the network. Such settings specify screen displays, such as screen savers and desktop themes, and they also maintain other preferences, such as which folders and files to share with other users.

These personal settings are stored in a feature called a *profile*. Each user creates a profile, which is associated with a user name. When each person enters or selects a user name upon starting Windows, the correct profile is used automatically. One set of default settings is reserved for users who don't have their own profiles.

To use profiles, you must create a user name for each person using your computer.

What's in a Profile?

In addition to the user name and password, a personal profile might include the following items:

- Display settings such as the screen saver, Windows desktop theme, and the Windows color scheme

- Icons and other items on the Windows desktop

- Internet cookies and downloaded files

- The files contained in the My Documents folder

- Recently used files on the Documents menu

- Programs on the Start menu

- Favorites in the Favorites folder (if Microsoft Internet Explorer is your Web browser)

- E-mail shown in certain e-mail programs, such as Microsoft Outlook Express

You can probably see, just from this list, how useful the profiles feature can be. For example, when you have your own user profile, your Web browser saves all your Internet cookies in a file reserved just for you. A *cookie* is a small file that a site on the Internet saves on your hard disk. When you later revisit that site, your browser reads the information in the cookie file to identify you and any settings or options that you selected on your last visit.

Your own settings will show up when you return to many Web sites because your browser retrieves your cookies rather than the cookies stored for other users. Sites that sell books, such as Amazon.com, save your book-buying preferences in a cookie. When you log on to the site, you might see a list of books that matches your interests. If other users of your computer also used your profile, you'd see books of interest to them, as well—but the books would all be listed under your name.

The My Documents folder in all versions of Windows, and the Documents list on the Start menu in Microsoft Windows 95, Windows 98, Windows Millennium Edition (Me), and Windows 2000, show only your files, so you can quickly open files that you've worked on instead of having to see a multitude of files from other users.

If you share your computer with another avid game player, your profile lets you avoid seeing a long list of somebody else's games on the Start menu. Those games appear only when the other player logs on with a different user name and password.

Having a personal Favorites list means that only the Web sites you want to visit are listed on the Favorites menu—both on the Start menu and in Internet Explorer. You won't need to scroll through a long list of favorites chosen by other users.

The same notion applies to e-mail messages in programs such as Outlook Express. Each user sees only his or her messages in the Inbox and Sent Items folders; every other user's mail is kept private.

Using Profiles in Windows 95, Windows 98, or Windows Me

To use the profile feature in Windows 95, Windows 98, or Windows Me, you have to first specify that you want other users to have their own settings. Otherwise, Windows displays the same desktop and uses the same settings for everyone who uses your computer. You then create a separate profile for each user of the computer.

Note

This section discusses profiles in Windows 95, Windows 98, and Windows Me only. For creating and using profiles with the most recent versions of Windows, see the sections "Using Profiles in Windows 2000" and "Using Profiles in Windows XP," later in this chapter.

Turning On Profiles

To activate the profiles feature in Windows 95, Windows 98, or Windows Me:

1. On the Start menu, point to Settings, and then click Control Panel.

2. In Control Panel, double-click the Passwords icon to open the Passwords Properties dialog box, shown in Figure 8-1.

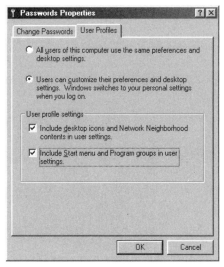

Figure 8-1.

The Passwords Properties dialog box lets you change your Windows password and set up user profiles.

3. Click the User Profiles tab.

4. Click Users Can Customize Their Preferences And Desktop Settings.

5. Select the two check boxes in the User Profile Settings section on the User Profiles tab. These settings allow individual users to add icons to the desktop and add programs to the Start menu that appear only when they select their profile.

6. Click OK to close the Passwords Properties dialog box.

7. Click Yes when you're asked whether you want to restart your computer.

8. After Windows restarts, enter your user name and password, and then click OK.

9. Click Yes when you're asked whether you want to retain the individual settings in your profile.

You now have your own profile, containing all the settings you created when you were the computer's only user.

Adding Users

The next step is to specify who the users of your computer will be so that each one can have a personal profile. You can add as many users as you like, whenever you like, or users can create their own profiles, which allows them to keep their passwords confidential.

You can add a new user in two ways: Simply enter a new name and password when you start Windows, or go to Control Panel and double-click Users.

Note

You can add a new user through Control Panel only if you have Internet Explorer version 4 or later on your computer.

Adding Users When You Log On

It's easy to add a new user when you start Windows, but then you'll have to go to Control Panel to select options. Here's how to do it:

1. When you start Windows or use the Log Off option on the Start menu to log on as another user, enter a new name and type a new password in the Enter Network Password dialog box, and then click OK. (With some versions of Windows 95, Log Off is an option in the Shut Down dialog box rather than on the Start menu.) Because you've entered a new user name, the Set Windows Password dialog box appears, asking you to retype your password to confirm it.

Note

A password is optional. If you don't want to use one, just leave the Password text box blank. Using a password, however, provides some security by controlling users' access to the network.

2. Enter a password, and then click OK.

3. When a message appears asking whether you want to save your desktop settings, click Yes.

Adding Users Through Control Panel

If you have Internet Explorer version 4 or later, you can add users and select certain profile settings through Control Panel. The first time you add a user this way, Windows runs the Add User Wizard, which takes you through the process step by step.

1. On the Start menu, point to Settings, and then click Control Panel.

2. In Control Panel, double-click the Users icon to open the User Settings dialog box, shown in Figure 8-2.

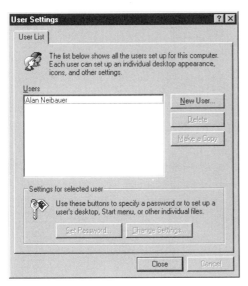

Figure 8-2.
Start the Add User Wizard in the User Settings dialog box.

3. Click New User to start the Add User Wizard.

4. Read the explanation shown on the first page, and then click Next.

5. On the Add User page, enter a new user name, and then click Next.

6. On the Enter New Password page, enter the password in both the Password and Confirm Password text boxes, and then click Next.

7. On the Personalized Items Settings page, shown in Figure 8-3, select each of the check boxes for the items that you want in your personal profile. If you leave a check box cleared, you won't have a custom copy of that item.

Figure 8-3.
The Personalized Items Settings page allows you to choose the contents of your profile.

8. Select one of the two option buttons near the bottom of the page to determine how you want your personal profile set up.

   If you select the first option button, Windows will make a copy of all the items in the profile currently being used as the basis for your personal profile. If you select the second option button, you'll have to create all of the items yourself from scratch.

9. Click Next, and then click Finish. Windows creates your personal desktop and displays the User Settings dialog box.

10. Click Close in the User Settings dialog box.

If you prefer to use the desktop settings of another user, it's possible to copy those settings to a new personal profile that you can use. Follow these steps to start a new profile using someone else's settings:

1. Double-click the Users icon in Control Panel.

2. Click the user's name whose settings you want to copy.

3. Click Make A Copy to start the Add User Wizard.

4. Follow the steps of the wizard, selecting only the items you want to copy on the wizard's Personalized Items Settings page. For example, you can clear the My Documents Folder check box if you don't want to see the other user's documents displayed in your My Documents folder.

5. Click Finish on the last page of the wizard.

Changing User Settings

Changing your password and profile settings is as easy as adding a new user.

1. Double-click the Users icon in Control Panel.

2. In the User Settings dialog box, click your user name.

3. Click Set Password to change your password. You'll have to enter your current password, and then enter and confirm the new one.

4. Click Change Settings to open the Personalized Items Settings dialog box, and then change your settings.

If you're not using Internet Explorer version 4 or later, see the section "Changing Passwords," later in this chapter, to learn how to change your password.

You can also delete a user profile, eliminating not only the user name and password, but also all the folders associated with the user name, such as the My Documents and Favorites folders. If you don't want to delete the contents of these folders, copy the files or favorites you want to save to another location before deleting the user. Then click the user name in the User Settings dialog box and click Delete.

Note

You can't delete a user who is currently logged on.

Logging On as a Different User

You can start Windows on any computer by logging on with your user name. If you forget your password, you can bypass the logon process and use the default desktop—the desktop that existed when the profile feature was originally enabled.

To log on to any computer, start the computer and enter your user name and password in the Enter Network Password dialog box. Leave the Password text box blank if you didn't enter a password when you created your profile.

If you want to log on using the default desktop, click Cancel in the Enter Network Password dialog box or press the Esc key. Windows will start using the settings of the default profile. Any files that were in the My Documents and Favorites folders of your personal profile won't be available on the default desktop.

If your computer is already started and you want to switch to another user profile, you must log off and then log on again using the other profile. You might want to do this if you bypassed the logon when you first started and you now want to access your personal profile files. To switch profiles in some versions of Windows 95, and in Windows 98 and Windows Me, follow these steps:

1. On the Start menu, click Log Off.

2. Click Yes when asked whether you're sure you want to log off. The Enter Network Password dialog box appears.

3. Enter the user name and password you want to log on with, and then click OK. You can also click Cancel or press Esc to log on using the default profile.

If you're using Windows 95 and Log Off is not an option on the Start menu, follow this procedure to switch profiles:

1. On the Start menu, select Shut Down.

2. In the Shut Down dialog box, click Close All Programs And Log On As A Different User. Windows will restart so that you can enter another user name and password.

If a number of family members are using your computer, you can save them—and yourself—the trouble of typing in user names by choosing the Microsoft Family Logon feature. In Chapter 7, "Installing the Software," you learned how to install Microsoft Family Logon as a network client when setting up Windows for your network.

When a family member starts a computer on the network, a dialog box lists the profile names of all users. The family member can choose a user name from the list, enter a password, and then click OK to log on using the correct profile.

If you installed Microsoft Family Logon and want to use it, follow these steps to select it as the default logon option:

1. On the Start menu, point to Settings, and then click Control Panel.

2. In Control Panel, double-click the Network icon to open the Network dialog box.

3. In the Primary Network Logon drop-down list, select Microsoft Family Logon, and then click OK.

Note

If you no longer want to use the Microsoft Family Logon feature, select Client For Microsoft Networks instead.

Locating Your Folders

The profiles that are set up on a computer are stored in folders in the Profiles folder, which is in the Windows folder. To locate a profile folder, use either My Computer or Windows Explorer to navigate to the Profiles folder. In the Profiles folder, you'll see folders with profile names, as shown below.

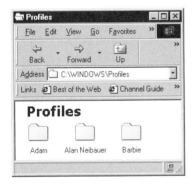

Double-click the profile name you're looking for to display all the folders in that user's profile, as shown below.

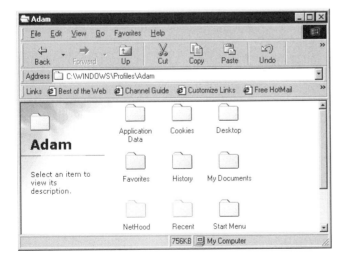

Changing Passwords

If you're using Internet Explorer version 4 or later, you can set and change your password in the Users dialog box. But no matter which version of Internet Explorer you're using, you can always change passwords with the Password icon in Control Panel. Here's how:

1. In Control Panel, double-click the Passwords icon to display the Password Properties dialog box.

2. Click the Change Passwords tab.

3. Click Change Windows Password.

4. In the text boxes, enter your current password, then type and confirm your new password.

Note

The Change Other Passwords option, which is not available on all systems, lets you change the passwords you use to log on to a network server. On a family network, you probably won't be using a network server, so you can forget about this option.

See Also

You'll learn how to password-protect individual folders and files in Chapter 9, "Learning to Share."

Surviving Password Forgetfulness

What happens if you forget your password? What you *don't* want to do is log on as a different user and delete your entire profile. This action will delete settings and files that you probably want to retain.

After the initial panic wears off, you can easily delete your old password and start over. Passwords are stored in files with a .pwl extension. To locate your password file, follow these steps:

1. On the Start menu, point to Find, and then click Files Or Folders. In Windows Me, point to Search and click For Files Or Folders.

2. Make sure the Look In box is set at C: so you'll search your entire hard disk.

3. Type *.pwl* in the Named text box and click Find Now. (Click Search Now in Windows Me.) You'll see a list of files with the .pwl extension.

4. Click the file that has your user name, press Delete, and click Yes to confirm the deletion.

Note

After you delete your password file, you'll have to reenter the password for your Internet service provider (ISP) when you next log on to the Internet or check your e-mail.

You can now log on using your own user name and no password. You can also create a new password—one that you might not forget so easily. Either enter a new password in the Enter Network Password dialog box or create the new password in the Users or Passwords dialog box from Control Panel. *If you don't want to worry about remembering passwords, see the sidebar "Avoiding Password Forgetfulness," later in this chapter.*

Deleting All Profiles

If you ever decide that you no longer want to share your computer, you can delete all user profiles from Windows. To do so, however, you need to use the Windows Registry Editor, and this can be tricky. Because the registry is where Windows stores all its settings, you must be extremely careful not to change a setting you don't want to change.

Warning

Read these steps closely and be sure you are performing each one correctly before going to the next. Making the wrong changes to the registry could cause your computer to stop working and might require you to reinstall Windows.

If you decide to delete all your profiles, follow these steps carefully:

1. Restart your computer and click Cancel when the Enter Network Password or Microsoft Family Logon dialog box appears.

2. Double-click the Password icon in Control Panel.

3. On the User Profiles tab, click All Users Of This PC Use The Same Preferences And Desktop Settings.

4. Click OK and restart your computer.

   When the computer restarts, follow these steps:

1. On the Start menu, click Run.

2. In the Run dialog box, type **regedit**, and then click OK. The Registry Editor starts, as shown in Figure 8-4.

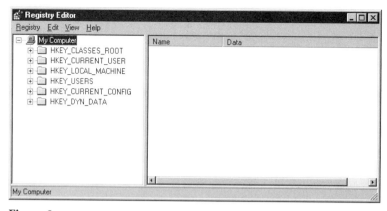

Figure 8-4.

The Registry Editor lets you change settings in the registry.

3. Click the plus sign in front of HKEY_LOCAL_MACHINE to expand this section, as shown below.

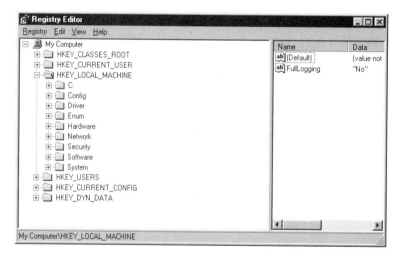

4. Click the plus sign in front of Software.

5. Click the plus sign in front of Microsoft.

6. Click the plus sign in front of Windows.

7. Click the plus sign in front of Current Version.

8. Click ProfileList. The status bar at the bottom of the Registry Editor should look like this:

My Computer\HKEY_LOCAL_MACHINE\Software\Microsoft\Windows\CurrentVersion\ProfileList

222

9. Press Delete, and then press Enter if you're asked to confirm the deletion.

10. From the Registry menu, choose Exit.

   Now that you've edited the registry, follow these steps:

1. Double-click My Computer on the desktop.

2. Double-click the icon for your hard disk.

3. Open the Windows folder. In Windows 95, the contents of the folder are displayed automatically. In Windows 98, click Show Files to display the contents of the folder. In Windows Me, click View The Entire Contents Of This Folder.

4. Click the Profiles folder.

5. Press Delete to delete the folder.

6. Click Yes to confirm that you want to move the folder to the Recycle Bin.

Avoiding Password Forgetfulness

If you share your computer with others in the house but don't want to deal with profiles and passwords, then go biometric! You can use some neat little gadgets to allow access to your computer and its folders and files, by using your fingerprints.

The U.are.U Fingerprint Recognition System *(http://www.digitalpersona.com)*, for example, is a small device that plugs into your computer's universal serial bus (USB) port and that contains a small scanner the size of your fingertip. You configure the device to recognize one or more of your fingerprints and then scan your fingertip whenever a password is required.

When you try to log on to the Internet, for example, a message appears telling you to put your finger on the U.are.U sensor. The sensor scans your fingerprint and inserts your ISP password only if the scanned print matches the one that you programmed into it. Some models of U.are.U also include a feature called Private Space—an encrypted folder on your hard disk, network server, floppy drive, or removable drive. The file can be decrypted only by your fingerprint authorization.

If you use a laptop computer and you don't want to worry about an external USB device, you can use the Ethenticator MS3000 from Ethentica *(http://www.ethentica.com)*. Ethenticator fits all the way into your notebook's card slot, with a small fingerprint sensor that snaps out when you need it. You "enroll" your fingers in the program, and then you use your fingerprints to start Windows, access password-protected shares, and browse the Internet.

Using Profiles in Windows 2000

If you're using Microsoft Windows 2000, profiles work about the same way as in previous versions of Windows. The main difference is that Windows 2000 lets you assign users to groups. A *group* defines the rights of users who have been assigned to the group, saving you the trouble of specifying permissions for each user individually.

Windows creates the following default groups:

- **Administrators** have full access to the computer or network domain.

- **Guests** and **Users** can use the computer and save their documents, but they can't install programs or change system files and settings. The groups are similar, except that Guests can't shut down the system or undock a laptop from a docking station.

- **Backup Operators** can back up files and folders only onto the computer.

- **Power Users** can install programs and change computer settings, but they can't read other users' files.

- **Replicators** can support file replication.

To add a new user, you have to be logged on as the Administrator. When you first set up Windows 2000 and log on, you will automatically be made the Administrator. Once you've logged on to Windows 2000 in this way, follow these steps to add a new user:

1. Open Users And Passwords in Control Panel to see a list of currently defined users, as shown in Figure 8-5. Windows automatically creates a user called Administrator and an account called Guest for others with whom you want to share the computer. If you set up your computer by entering your own name as the user rather than the default name of Administrator, you'll also see your own user account name.

Figure 8-5.

Windows 2000 users and groups.

Note

Depending on the features of Windows 2000 that you installed, you might also see other accounts in the Users and Passwords dialog box that are used for a corporate Web server.

2. To require that users sign on with their name and password, select the check box labeled Users Must Enter A User Name And Password To Use This Computer.

3. Click Add to see this dialog box.

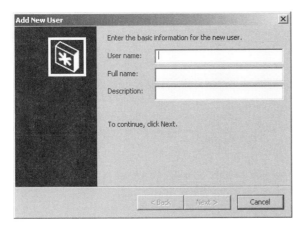

4. Enter the information requested and then click Next.

5. In the dialog box that appears, enter and confirm the password, and then click Next to see the dialog box in Figure 8-6.

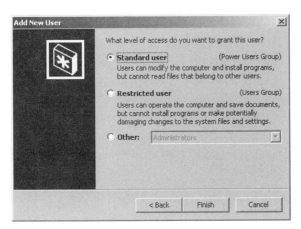

Figure 8-6.

Assigning a user to a group.

6. Select the group to which you want to assign the users; the options are Standard User, Restricted User, and Other. Choose Standard User to add the person to the Power Users Group, or select Restricted User to add the person to the Users Group. Otherwise, click Other and select the group from the list.

7. Click Finish.

The new user will be listed in the Users And Password dialog box and can now log on to the system. If you need to change the user's name or group assignment, select the user's name and then click Properties.

You can create new groups and make other changes to the user's profiles in the Computer Management dialog box shown in Figure 8-7.

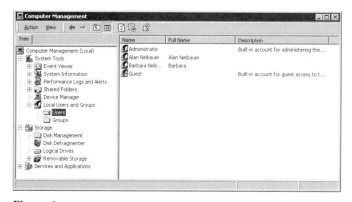

Figure 8-7.
The Computer Management dialog box.

To display this dialog box, open Administrative Tools in Control Panel, and then open Computer Management. To change a profile, click the plus sign next to Local Users And Groups and then click Users to list the users on the right of the window. Select the user whose profile you want to change, and then from the Action menu, select Properties. The user's Properties dialog box appears, as in Figure 8-8.

On the General tab of the dialog box, you can designate whether each user has to change his or her password the first time he or she logs on to the computer, whether the password ever expires, or whether the account is disabled. Use the Member Of tab to change the groups to which the user belongs.

Figure 8-8.
The Properties dialog box for a user's profile.

The Profile tab lets you create a roaming or mandatory profile location. A *roaming profile* allows a user to log on to the computer remotely and download the profile information from the server to the remote computer. A *mandatory profile* is one that the administrator creates and that the user can't change.

To create a new group in the Computer Management dialog box, click Groups in the Local Users And Groups section, and then choose New Group from the Action menu. In the box that appears, enter the group name and then click Create.

Note

Setting the permissions assigned to a group is more complicated than setting an individual user's permission and is beyond the scope of this book.

Using Profiles in Windows XP

User profiles in Windows XP are called *user accounts*. Although they work about the same way as in previous versions of Windows, they provide a more graphic way to change accounts and see a user's individual files.

Adding a User

To add a new user in Windows XP, you must be logged on as a Computer Administrator. When you first set up Windows XP and log on, you'll automatically be made a Computer Administrator. Once you've logged on to Windows XP in this way, follow these steps to add a new user:

1. Open User Accounts in Control Panel to see a list of currently defined users, as shown in Figure 8-9. Windows automatically creates a user called Computer Administrator under the name you used to set up Windows. It also creates an account called Guest for others with whom you want to share the computer. Windows chooses the pictures shown next to each account, but you can select other pictures to replace them at any time.

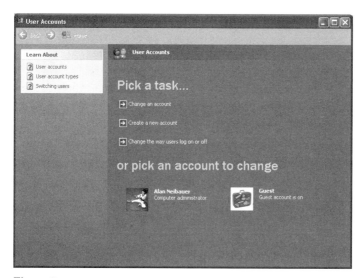

Figure 8-9.
User accounts in Windows XP.

2. Click Create A New Account.

3. Enter the user name and click Next.

4. Select the account type. The options are Computer Administrator and Limited. A Computer Administrator user can manage user profiles and make any other changes to the computer. A Limited user can change only her own files and programs.

5. Click Create Account. The account will now be shown in the User Accounts window, as seen on page 229.

Modifying a User Account

Once the account is created, you can make changes to the default settings that Windows provides for it. To change an account, use either of these techniques in the User Accounts window:

- Click the account name that you want to change.

- Click Change An Account, and then click the account you want to change.

  You can then select from these options:

- Change The Name

- Create A Password

- Change The Picture

- Change The Account Type

- Delete The Account

Logging On a Different User

Now that you've created a new user, when you start Windows XP, you'll see the Welcome screen with icons for all the users and the Guest account. Each icon, by the way, will show the number of unread messages, if any, in the user's inbox. Just click the user that you want to sign on as. If you set up a user password, you'll be prompted for it before Windows begins.

Note

Anyone who has not been assigned a user account can use the Guest account.

You can quickly switch users at any time without restarting your computer.

1. On the Start menu, click Log Off.

2. Click Log Off when asked whether you're sure you want to log off. Windows saves the settings for the current user account and displays the list of users.

3. Click the user you want to sign on as.

The name of the current user appears on the top of the Start menu, as shown below.

By default, when Windows XP starts, icons for each user appear on the Welcome screen. To use the classic logon prompt used by previous versions of Windows, in which users must type their user name and password, follow these steps:

1. Open User Accounts in Control Panel.

2. Click Change The Way Users Log On Or Off.

3. In the window that appears, clear the check mark from the Use The Welcome Screen option.

4. Click Apply Options.

The logon options also include a check box labeled Use Fast User Switching. When you select this option and then choose Log Off from the Start menu, you'll see the Switch User option, in addition to the Log Off option. The Switch User option lets you select another user account without logging off the current user profile and closing any of your open programs. This is a much faster way to change users. Windows saves the status of all open program windows before letting you choose another user profile. When you return to a previous user, program windows appear just as you left them, so you don't need to reopen files. In essence, you can have multiple users logged on to one computer at the same time and quickly switch between them. When you switch back to the original profile, the open windows appear just as you left them. To actually log off a user account, select Log Off from the Start menu and choose Log Off rather than Switch User.

Shared and Private Folders

If you are logged on as a Computer Administrator, when you open My Computer from the Windows XP Start menu, you'll see icons such as the ones shown below in the Files Stored On This Computer section.

Each user has a separate folder, and each user can access a folder called Shared Documents.

To prevent other users from gaining access to your files, you need to use the *NT file system (NTFS)*. This file system is an organization of files originally used in the Microsoft Windows NT operating system that's also available for Windows 2000 and Windows XP. NTFS provides greater file security than the FAT or FAT32 file systems used for previous versions of Windows. When you install Windows XP on your computer, you'll have the opportunity to convert the drive on which it's installed to NTFS.

Note

You can also convert the drive containing Windows XP to NTFS later by using the command Convert X: /FS:NTSF, where X: is the drive containing the Windows XP system.

If you're not using NTFS, any user can access your user files. If you are using NTFS, someone logged on as a user with limited access can access only Shared Documents and their own document folders. The icon for Computer Administrator folders won't even appear in the Files Stored On This Computer section. However, every Computer Administrator can access your documents.

To prevent other Computer Administrators from gaining access to your files when using NTFS, you can declare your profile folders to be private by following these steps:

1. Log on using your name, with a Computer Administrator account.

2. Click Start and then My Computer.

3. Right-click your document folder in the Files Stored On This Computer section, and choose Sharing And Security.

4. On the Sharing tab of the My Documents Properties dialog box that appears (as shown below), select the Make This Folder Private option, and then click OK.

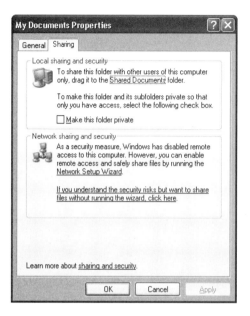

5. If you don't have a logon password, you'll be reminded that anyone can log on using your name and access your files. Click Yes to create a password at that time, or click No to skip creating a password.

When another user tries to access your files, they will get an error message such as this one.

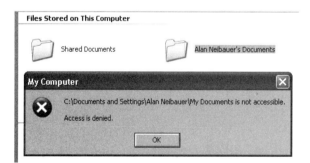

If you have files that you want to share with every user, store them in the Shared Documents folder.

The Bottom Line

User profiles are important when you share a computer with others. Profiles allow individual users to personalize their desktops and have a sense of ownership without changing other users' settings. In the next chapter, you'll learn how to share files and folders across the network.

Chapter 9

Learning to Share

One of the main advantages of setting up a home network is that it gives you the ability to share files. In all versions of Microsoft Windows except Windows XP, however, sharing doesn't come automatically. (Windows XP turns on sharing when you run the Network Setup Wizard.) You not only have to turn on the file-sharing service when you configure your network; you must also specify which resources you want to share with other users. In this chapter, you'll learn how to share disks, folders, and files.

Turning On File Sharing

Before you can activate file sharing, you must install the Windows service that allows sharing. You probably already installed this service along with your network drivers and software, as described in Chapter 8, "Creating User Profiles," but just in case you didn't, here's how to do it.

In Microsoft Windows 95, Windows 98, and Windows Millennium Edition (Me), follow these steps. (*To share resources with other versions of Windows, see the sections "Sharing in Windows 2000" and "Sharing in Windows XP," later in this chapter.*)

1. On the Start menu, point to Settings, and click Control Panel.

2. Double-click the Network icon to open the Network dialog box.

   In the list of network components that are installed, look for File And Printer Sharing For Microsoft Networks. If it's listed, you can skip the rest of these steps. If the service isn't installed, continue with these steps.

3. In the Network dialog box, click Add.

4. In the Select Network Component Type dialog box, click Service.

5. Click Add.

6. In the Select Network Service dialog box, click File And Printer Sharing For Microsoft Networks.

7. Click OK.

8. Click OK again to close the Network dialog box. You might be asked to insert your Windows CD.

9. When you're asked whether you want to restart your computer, click Yes.

Now that the service is installed, you're ready to turn on file and printer sharing by following these steps. (In Windows Me, the Home Networking Wizard performs this task for you, but you'll need to follow these steps if you created your Windows Me network manually.)

1. On the Start menu, point to Settings, and click Control Panel.

2. Double-click the Network icon to open the Network dialog box.

3. Click the File And Print Sharing button to open the File And Print Sharing dialog box, shown below.

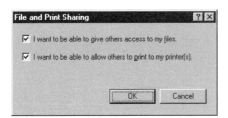

4. Select both check boxes to allow access to your files and your printers.

5. Click OK.

6. Click OK again to close the Network dialog box.

Caution

By default, the Transmission Control Protocol/Internet Protocol (TCP/IP) is configured to allow file and printer sharing across the network. However, you don't want to share files over your connection to the Internet using TCP/IP, either through a dial-up connection or a network adapter for a digital subscriber line (DSL) or cable modem. Enabling file and printer sharing over the Internet will make your computer and its contents vulnerable to Internet hackers. See the section "Turning Off Internet File Sharing," in Chapter 11, "Going Online through the Network," on page 364, to learn how to disable file and printer sharing over the Internet.

Sharing and Accessing Network Resources

Installing the hardware and configuring Windows for sharing doesn't make the information on your computer instantly available to everyone. Before someone else can access a folder on your hard disk, you must first specify that the folder is shared. (Windows XP automatically creates a shared document folder.)

Note

Shared resources, also known as *shares*, include disk drives, folders, and printers.

Windows organizes disks, folders, and files hierarchically as follows:

- Disks contain folders.
- Folders contain subfolders and files.
- Subfolders contain files.

When you share a disk or a folder on a network, the contents within it are also shared. For example, if you allow a disk to be shared, all folders and files on that disk are shared as well. If you allow only a folder to be shared rather than the whole disk, all subfolders and files within that folder can be shared but not other folders on that disk. So if you want everything on your hard disk to be available on the network, turn on sharing for your hard disk.

Once you share the disk, you don't have to turn on sharing for any of the individual folders within that disk—they're automatically shared across the network. You can also share a floppy disk, a CD-ROM, or a Zip disk. When you share a disk, all users on the network will have access to it through an icon that appears in either Network Neighborhood or My Network Places.

Note

Throughout this chapter, you'll see references to Network Neighborhood and My Network Places. Windows 95 and Windows 98 users should use Network Neighborhood; Windows Me, Windows 2000, and Windows XP users should use My Network Places.

Even though a folder on a shared disk is automatically available to network users, it won't appear as a separate icon in Network Neighborhood or My Network Places in Windows 95, Windows 98, Windows 2000, or Windows Me unless you specifically share that particular folder, and not just the disk on which the folder resides. If you want the folder to be seen in Network Neighborhood or My Network Places so that network users can easily access it, turn on sharing for the folder even if you've already turned on sharing for the disk.

In addition to turning on sharing, you can also specify how you want the disk or folder to be shared. There are three levels of sharing:

- **Read-Only** sharing means that users can open files in the shared folders and copy them to their own computers, but they can't change, delete, or add files on the shared disk or folder.

- **Full** sharing means that other users can do anything to shared disks or folders that you can do.

- **Depends On Password** sharing means that the password a user enters determines the level of sharing—Full or Read-Only—granted to the user. (Passwords for file sharing aren't available in Windows XP Home Edition.)

If you select the Read-Only or Full access options to a disk or folder, a password is optional. You can do without one and allow all members of your family to access a resource on your computer at whatever level of sharing you've specified for that resource. Or you can create a password and limit access—again, at the level of sharing you've specified—to whom you've given the password.

If you select the Depends On Password sharing option, you can selectively grant Read-Only or Full access to members of your family. You create two passwords: a read-only password and a full password. Users to whom you give the read-only password can read and copy your files, but they can't change or delete them or add new ones. Users with the full password can do anything they want to your files.

Sharing a Hard Disk

To turn on sharing for an entire hard disk and give only certain people access to it, follow these steps:

1. Double-click My Computer on the desktop.

2. Right-click the disk that you want to share.

3. Select Sharing from the shortcut menu to open the Properties dialog box shown in Figure 9-1.

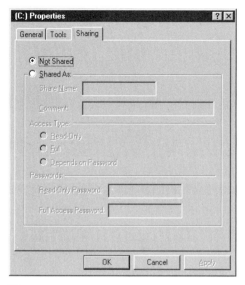

Figure 9-1.

The Properties dialog box allows you to turn on sharing for a resource and limit access to it by password.

4. Click Shared As.

   Windows places a default name in the Share Name text box, usually the same letter as the disk. (The *share name* is what appears when network users access your computer.)

5. Leave the share name as it is or change it to better identify the disk, as in *Alan's Zip disk*.

6. In the Comment text box, you can enter an optional description.

7. Click one of the three access types—Read-Only, Full, or Depends On Password.

8. Enter an optional password in the Read-Only Password text box, in the Full Access text box, or in both text boxes if you want the level of access to be determined by the password that the person enters.

9. Click OK.

10. If you specified one or two passwords, reenter each in the Confirm Passwords dialog box, and then click OK.

Now the icon for the disk will show, with a cradling hand, that the disk is shared, as shown below.

(C:)

When another member of your family is connected to your computer and opens either Network Neighborhood or My Network Places, an icon for your disk appears. If you've granted Full access without a password, that family member can access your disk just as if it were a local hard disk on his or her computer rather than a disk in your computer.

If you turn on sharing for a floppy disk or a removable disk, such as a Zip disk, the drive itself is actually shared rather than a particular disk. Turning on sharing for a floppy disk, for example, means that any floppy in the drive is shared. You might want to think twice about sharing removable drives if they contain sensitive information.

If you want to make a shared drive or folder available to everyone on a network, you can leave the password for the resource blank. If you do enter a password, however, make sure you remember it. Let's say you're at a computer other than your own, and you want to access your own files across the network. Your system won't know that it's you at the computer and will require the same password it does from the computer's primary user.

Note

Windows XP Professional Edition provides greater security than other versions of Windows. A person holding an Administrator account can control access to files, folders, and other shared resources.

If you forget the password that you've assigned to a shared resource, you can easily change it so long as you log on to your own computer. Unlike some passwords, you can change a sharing password without knowing the current one. To change a password, right-click the shared disk or folder, and choose Properties from the shortcut menu. Type the new password in place of the old one and click OK. You'll have to reenter the password to confirm it.

Note

To erase a password so that a shared disk or folder is no longer password-protected, just delete the asterisks in the password text boxes. You'll have to click OK without typing anything in the Confirm box that appears.

Sharing Folders

If you don't want to allow complete access to your disk, you can turn on sharing for only certain folders and not for the entire disk.

To turn on sharing for a folder, follow these steps:

1. Double-click My Computer.

2. Double-click the disk containing the folder you want to share.

3. Right-click the folder you want to share. You might have to navigate through folders to display the subfolder you want to share.

4. Select Sharing from the shortcut menu to open the Properties dialog box.

5. Click Shared As.

6. Accept the default share name or enter a new one.

7. Enter an optional comment.

8. Choose an access type.

9. Enter an optional password in the Read-Only Password text box, the Full Access Password text box, or both.

10. Click OK.

11. If you specified one or two passwords, reenter each in the Confirm Passwords dialog box, and then click OK.

You can also turn on sharing from any window that displays the folder, such as Windows Explorer, the Find or the Search dialog box, or the Save As or the File Open dialog box in an application such as Microsoft Word. To turn on sharing, right-click the folder icon, select Sharing from the shortcut menu, and follow the rest of the steps in the previous procedure.

Note

You can't turn on sharing for the My Documents folder from the Windows desktop. If you want to set sharing for that folder, in My Computer, double-click the disk on which you've installed Windows, right-click the My Documents folder, and choose Sharing from the shortcut menu.

Accessing Shared Disks and Folders

Once disks and folders are shared, network users can access them in much the same way as they would access disks and folders on their own computers. The trick is for them to locate the disk or folder on the remote computer.

Note

A *remote computer* is a computer on the network other than the one you're using.

Once you access a shared folder on a remote computer, you can use the files in that folder just as if you were on that computer, but only at the level of sharing you've been granted. If you have Read-Only access, you'll be able to open or copy files only from the shared folder. You won't be able to change or delete files or add new files to the folder. If you attempt to do so, you'll see the following dialog box:

Windows 95 and Windows 98

In Windows 95 and Windows 98, you can always access remote computers using Network Neighborhood, so let's start from there:

1. Double-click Network Neighborhood on your desktop.

    Remember, your computer might take a few minutes after you turn it on to recognize the remote computers on the network. You'll see icons representing all the computers on your network, as well as an icon for the Entire Network, as shown in Figure 9-2.

Figure 9-2.

Network Neighborhood displays icons for each computer connected to the network and an icon for the Entire Network.

Note

Double-clicking the Entire Network icon lets you access other workgroups that are connected to your network.

2. Double-click the icon for the computer you want to access. You'll see icons representing shared drives and printers as well as folders that you've shared.

3. Double-click the disk or folder you want to access. If you see no individual folders at this point, the entire drive is shared.

Windows Me

Windows Me uses My Network Places rather than Network Neighborhood to access shared drives and folders:

1. Double-click My Network Places on the desktop.

2. Double-click Entire Network to see an icon for the workgroup.

3. Double-click the Workgroup icon to see a list of computers in the workgroup.

4. Double-click a computer to see its shared resources.

Once you access a shared drive on another computer from My Network Places, Windows Me will insert a shortcut to that resource in the My Network Places window, like this:

You can just double-click the shortcut to access the drive. You can also add a short-cut to a specific folder for quick access to its files. Follow these steps to add a shortcut to a folder in My Network Places:

1. In My Network Places, double-click Add Network Place to open the Add Network Place Wizard.

2. Click Browse to see the contents of My Network Places, as shown here.

3. If you see a listing for the disk that contains the folder you want to insert as a short-cut, as in *c on Piii* in the previous illustration, click the plus sign to display the folders contained on the disk. Otherwise, click the plus sign next to Workgroup to see a list of networked computers, and then click the plus sign next to the computer to access its resources. Navigate through the directory tree until you see the icon for the folder you want to add to My Network Places, such as the following:

4. Click the folder you want to add, and then click OK to return to the Add Network Place Wizard.

5. Click Next.

6. Enter the name for the resource as you want it to appear in My Network Places.

7. Click Finish to open a window with the contents of the folder.

8. Close the window. You'll now see an icon for the folder in My Network Places, as shown here.

Home Networki...   Entire Network   My Documents on Piii

Accessing Resources from Windows Explorer

Another way to access shared disks is from Windows Explorer or any Windows file management dialog box, such as the File Open dialog box in Word. Let's look at Windows Explorer:

1. In Windows 95 or Windows 98, on the Start menu, point to Programs, and click Windows Explorer. In Windows Me, point to Programs, point to Accessories, and then click Windows Explorer.

2. In the list of remote computers, click the plus sign next to Network Neighborhood or My Network Places.

3. Click the plus sign next to the remote computer you want to access.

4. If the disk in the computer is shared, click the plus sign next to the disk to display its contents. You can then access any of the files as if they were on your computer.

Note

The Network Neighborhood icon or My Network Places icon appears in the Open and Save dialog boxes of most Windows applications that let you access disks and folders. You can always use the icon to access remote computers.

Accessing Resources by Using the Run and Find Commands

Although using Network Neighborhood, My Network Places, and Windows Explorer are the most common ways to access a remote computer, Windows offers two other options: the Run command and the Find or Search command on the Start menu.

If you know the name of the remote computer, you can use the Run command by following these steps:

1. Select the Run command from the Start menu. The Run dialog box opens, as shown below.

2. Enter the path to the resource by typing the Universal Naming Convention (UNC) in the Run dialog box. You start the UNC with two backslashes (\\) followed by the name of the computer, as in \\Joe.

3. Press Enter or click OK to open a window showing the shared resources on that computer. If you know the name of the specific disk and folder you're looking for on the remote computer, you can open it directly by adding its resource name to the UNC, as in \\Joe\C:\Budget.

You can also search for a computer on the network. In Windows 95 and Windows 98, use the Find command on the Start menu. Just follow these steps:

1. On the Start menu, point to Find, and click Computer.

2. In the Find: Computer dialog box, enter the remote computer's name, and press Enter or click Find Now.

3. When the computer is located and listed in the Find dialog box, double-click its icon to access its shared resources.

In Windows Me, use the Search command on the Start menu by following these steps:

1. On the Start menu, point to Search, and click For Files And Folders.

2. In the Search For Other Items section of the Search Results window, click Computers.

3. In the Computer Name text box that appears, enter the remote computer's name, and press Enter or click Search Now.

4. When the computer is located and listed in the Search Results window, double-click its icon to access its shared resources.

Accessing Resources with Passwords

When a resource requires a password in order to be shared, you must enter the password before you can open the disk or folder—or at least you must enter it the first time you try to access the resource. As you'll see, there's a way to save the password so that you don't have to enter it each time you open a password-protected disk or folder.

When you first try to access a resource, you'll see the Enter Network Password dialog box, shown below.

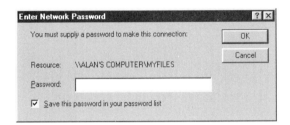

Before you enter the password and click OK, you can select the check box labeled Save This Password In Your Password List. Windows maintains this password list in a file whose name is your user name plus the extension .pwl, as in *alan.pwl*. If you select this check box, the name of the shared resource and the password will be saved in your .pwl file. The next time you access the same disk or folder, Windows automatically locates the password so that you don't have to enter it again.

Caution

Don't select the Save This Password In Your Password List check box if you want to prevent other network users from accessing shared resources with your password.

When the Enter Network Password dialog box opens, type in your password, and then click OK. If the password you've typed is incorrect, a message appears telling you so. Click OK to clear the message, and then reenter the correct password.

Making Sharing Easier

Navigating through Network Neighborhood or My Network Places to locate a folder or file can be time-consuming. Fortunately, Windows offers a number of ways to simplify network life.

Creating a Desktop Shortcut

The easiest way to access a remote disk, folder, or file is to add an icon for it to your desktop. To do this, follow these steps:

1. Use Network Neighborhood or My Network Places to locate the disk, folder, or file on the remote computer.

2. Right-click the disk, folder, or file, and then hold down the right mouse button while you drag the icon to your desktop.

Note

To create a shortcut to the remote computer itself, click the remote computer icon and hold down the right mouse button as you drag it to your desktop.

3. Release the mouse button and select Create Shortcut(s) Here from the shortcut menu.

Windows 98 and Windows Me also allow you to drag the shortcut icon you placed on your desktop to your Quick Launch toolbar so that you can access it with a single click. The Quick Launch toolbar is located next to the Start button on the Windows taskbar.

Adding Shared Resources to Favorites

If you're using Windows 98 or Windows Me (or Windows 95 with Microsoft Internet Explorer version 4 or later), you can store frequently used folders and files in a Favorites folder, which is quickly accessible from the Start menu.

You'll also find a Favorites menu item in Windows Explorer, My Computer, Network Neighborhood, My Network Places, and dialog boxes in Windows that let you manage files. After you've added a folder or file shortcut to your Favorites list, you can open Favorites and double-click the shortcut to open the folder or file.

To add a resource to the Favorites list, follow these steps:

1. Use Network Neighborhood or My Network Places to locate the folder or file.

2. Double-click the folder or file so that its path appears in the Address field on the Address toolbar.

3. From the Favorites menu, choose Add To Favorites to open the Add Favorite dialog box, shown on page 249.

4. Click OK. You can also click the Create In button if you want to add the item to a folder within Favorites or to create a new subfolder of Favorites.

Mapping Network Disks and Folders

Another way to gain easy access to a disk on a remote computer is to assign it a drive letter on your own machine. This technique is called *mapping* the disk. For example, suppose you have the following disks in your computer:

- A floppy disk drive, designated as A:
- The hard disk, designated as C:
- A CD-ROM or DVD disk drive, designated as D:

If you frequently access a hard disk, CD-ROM, or other drive on a remote computer, you can map it so that it appears as E: or F: on your computer. Even better, you can map to a specific folder on a remote computer, giving it a drive letter, so long as the folder has been enabled for sharing. Let's say you often access a folder named Budget on a remote computer. You can map to the folder so that it shows up on your computer as F: in My Computer, as seen below.

Myfiles on
'Alan's
computer' [F]

To map a shared disk or folder in Windows 95 or Windows 98, follow these steps:

1. Use Network Neighborhood to display the icons for each of the disks and folders on the remote computer that have been shared.

2. Right-click the icon for the resource you want to map to, and then choose Map Network Drive from the shortcut menu to see the Map Network Drive dialog box shown on page 250.

3. In the Map Network Drive dialog box, select the Reconnect At Logon check box if you want Windows to map to this resource every time you start your computer.

4. Click OK. A window opens showing the contents of the drive or folder; the address box on the Address toolbar shows that the resource is now mapped to a drive on your computer.

To map a shared drive or folder in Windows Me or Windows 2000, follow these steps:

1. Double-click My Network Places.

2. In Windows Me, double-click Entire Network and then the icon for your workgroup. In Windows 2000, double-click Computers Near Me. You'll see icons for each of the computers on the network.

3. Double-click the icon for the computer that has the resource you want to map.

4. Right-click the icon of the resource you want to map to, and then choose Map Network Drive from the shortcut menu to open the Map Network Drive dialog box. If Map Network Drive isn't on the shortcut menu, you can select it from the Tools menu.

5. In the Map Network Drive dialog box, select the Reconnect At Logon check box if you want Windows to map to this resource every time you start your computer.

6. Click OK in Windows Me; click Finish in Windows 2000.

If you close the window and open My Computer, you'll see the shared resource listed as a drive. Just double-click the icon as you would any actual disk to access its contents on the remote computer.

When you select Reconnect At Logon, Windows browses the network looking for the mapped disk or folder each time you start your computer. If the remote computer isn't turned on, Windows starts normally but doesn't map to the shared resource. You'll have to remap to it after the remote computer joins the network.

If you don't select Reconnect At Logon, the drive you mapped to is disconnected when you turn off your computer or restart Windows. You'll have to repeat the previous procedure to map to the drive again.

Browsing for mapped resources takes some time, and it will slow down the logon process, so if you don't need to map to the resource every time you use your computer, don't select the Reconnect At Logon check box.

To accelerate the process of mapping resources, an alternative is to tell Windows not to browse the network automatically when your computer starts. With the Quick Logon feature, Windows displays the icons for mapped resources in Network Neighborhood or My Network Places, My Computer, and Windows Explorer without checking to see whether the resource is really available. Windows waits until you first try to use the resource before actually connecting to it. To turn on the Quick Logon feature, follow these steps:

1. On the Start menu, point to Settings, and click Control Panel.

2. In Control Panel, double-click the Network icon to open the Network dialog box.

3. In the list of installed network components, select Client For Microsoft Networks.

4. Click Properties to open the Client For Microsoft Networks Properties dialog box shown in Figure 9-3.

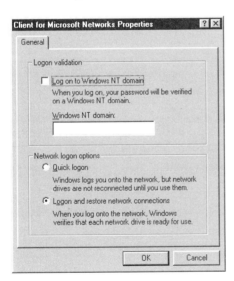

Figure 9-3.
You can change logon options in the Client For Microsoft Networks Properties dialog box.

5. Click Quick Logon.

If you were to select the other option, Logon And Restore Network Connections, every time you started Windows, it would map and connect to shared resources you've mapped.

6. Click OK to close the Client For Microsoft Networks Properties dialog box.

7. Click OK to close the Network dialog box. You might be asked to insert your Windows CD at this point.

8. Click OK if you're asked whether you want to restart your computer.

Working with Remote Files

Once you've accessed a drive or folder on a remote computer, you can start working with its files in Network Neighborhood, My Network Places, My Computer, or Windows Explorer. Here's how to access a file with Network Neighborhood, My Network Places, or My Computer:

1. Open Network Neighborhood or My Network Places, or double-click My Computer if the disk on the remote computer has been mapped.

2. Double-click the icon for the computer you want to access.

3. Double-click the disk or folder you want to open.

4. Select the file you want to work with.

To access the file with Windows Explorer, follow these steps:

1. On the Start menu, point to Programs, and click Windows Explorer. In Windows Me, point to Programs, point to Accessories, and then click Windows Explorer.

2. Click the plus sign next to Network Neighborhood or My Network Places in the Folders list on the left.

3. Click the plus sign next to the remote computer you want to access.

4. Click the plus sign next to the disk you want to open on the remote computer.

5. Click the folder containing the file you're looking for. If the folder contains subfolders, click the plus sign next to the folder to display its contents, and then select the subfolder containing the file.

After you've accessed a file, you can do anything with it that your level of sharing allows. If you have Read-Only access to the folder, you can open the file or copy it to another location. You can make changes to the file, but you can't replace the original; you must save the changed file in another folder where you have Full access. If you have Full access, you can change, delete, or move the file.

Let's take a closer look at how to work with files on remote computers.

Opening Remote Files from Within Applications

On the network, you can open a file on a remote computer just as you'd open it on your own computer. In Windows 95, Windows 98, and Windows Me, you can locate the file in My Computer, Network Neighborhood, My Network Places, or Windows Explorer, and open it by double-clicking its icon.

You can also open files from within Windows applications, such as the programs in Microsoft Office. Because Network Neighborhood and My Network Places are integrated parts of the Windows file system, one or the other (depending on your version of Windows) appears in all the lists you see whenever you try to access files. Consequently, you can treat a remote computer as you would any drive: Locate it in the application's Open dialog box, choose the drive, choose the folder, and then choose the document you want to access.

For example, suppose you're working in Word and need to open a file in the My Documents folder of a remote computer. Here's how to do it:

1. From the File menu, choose Open to display the Open dialog box.

2. In the Look In drop-down list, select Network Neighborhood or My Network Places. A list of computers on the network appears in the Open dialog box, as shown below.

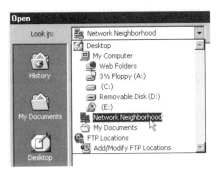

3. Double-click the icon for the computer whose drive contains the file you want. A list of shared resources on the remote computer appears in the Open dialog box.

4. Double-click the hard drive that contains Windows on the remote computer. It's usually designated as C:.

5. Double-click My Documents or the folder in which the file is saved.

6. Double-click the file you want to open.

Saving Remote Files from Within Applications

Saving a remote file from within a Windows application is even easier than opening it, so long as you have Full access privileges. If you've made changes to an existing remote file, save it just as you would any other document by clicking the Save button on the application's Standard toolbar or by choosing Save from the application's File menu.

You can also use the Save As command on the application's File menu to save the document to another location or with a new filename. When the Save As dialog box opens, it shows the folder from which you opened the document. Choose another location from the Save In list in the Save As dialog box, a folder either on your own computer or on any other computer on the network.

If you're working on a new document and want to save it on a remote computer, use the Save In list in the Save As dialog box to select Network Neighborhood or My Network Places, choose the remote computer, and then select the destination folder.

Saving a Read-Only File

If you've made changes to a file that you opened from a read-only folder, you can't save it to the same location. If you try to do so, you'll see a warning message such as the one below.

However, you can still make changes to the file; you just can't replace the existing version in the shared folder with your edited version. (Remember that when a folder has been designated as read-only, you can't change its contents.) To save your changes, you must use the Save As command and save the file as a new document in a folder to which you have Full access. The folder can be on your own hard disk or on a disk in a remote computer.

To save a file to a remote computer, follow these steps:

1. From the application's File menu, choose Save As to display the Save As dialog box.

Note

In some Windows programs, clicking Save when a file is read-only automatically opens the Save As dialog box.

2. In the Save In drop-down list, choose Network Neighborhood or My Network Places. A list of computers on the network appears in the Save As dialog box.

3. Double-click the icon for the remote computer to which you want to save the file to see a list of its shared resources.

4. Double-click the disk drive.

5. Double-click the folder in which you want to save the file.

6. Click Save.

Avoiding Double Trouble

It doesn't make sense for two people to work on the same file at the same time. The result can be lost work and confusion.

Suppose, for example, that you and your spouse want to work on the family budget using two different computers. Here's what might happen:

1. You and your spouse both open the document and see that Entertainment is set at $100 per month.

2. You change Entertainment to $200.

3. Your spouse changes it to $50.

4. You save the document. The $200 amount you designated for Entertainment is recorded on the disk.

5. Your spouse saves the document after you do. The $50 figure is recorded on the disk, and your changes to the budget are lost! If your spouse had saved the document before you did, your $200 choice would have prevailed.

To avoid such situations, only one person at a time should work on a document in a folder to which Full access has been granted. What happens, however, when one person opens a document that's already being used by another person depends on the version of Windows and the application you're both using.

For example, you might receive a message that the document you're trying to open is already in use and you might get the option to open it in read-only mode. Although this option will allow you to make changes to the document, you won't be able to save it back to the same location, using the same name.

Note

There are exceptions to the one-person-at-a-time rule. With a program such as Microsoft NetMeeting, or Remote Assistance in Windows XP, two people can collaborate on a document at the same time and see each other's changes as they're made. You'll learn more about this type of simultaneous file sharing in Chapter 14, "Networking for Road Warriors."

Some applications provide safeguards against opening a document in use. Microsoft Word 2000, for example, displays this message if you try to open a file that's being used.

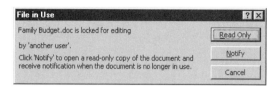

In the File In Use message box, click Read Only to open the document in read-only mode. Clicking Notify opens the document in read-only mode too, but you'll also see a message such as this when the other user closes the file.

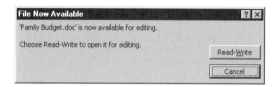

Click Read-Write to reopen the latest version of the document with the other user's changes. If you made any changes to the document, you'll see a message that tells you so, like this one.

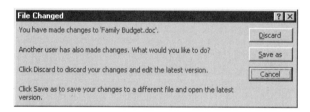

- Click Discard to ignore your changes and to reopen the latest version of the document.

- Click Save As to save your document using a new name and to open the latest version of the original file.

Copying and Moving Remote Files

You move or copy a file between computers on a network the same way you move or copy a file between folders on your own hard disk.

When you copy a file, you leave the original in its location and place a duplicate on another computer. Copying a file is smart when you want to make changes to a document without deleting the original version. Just remember that if someone changes one of the copies, two different versions of the same file will exist on the network.

When you move a file, you delete the original from its location and place it on another computer. If you move a file that someone else might want to work with, let the other user know where you're putting it. You can't move a file from a read-only folder because moving it would be the same as deleting it from that folder, and Read-Only access doesn't permit deletion of files. If you try to move such a file, you'll get an error message.

You can move and copy files between a remote computer and your own using Windows Explorer, Network Neighborhood, or My Network Places.

Copying Files Between Computers

Whether you're copying a file between the folders on your own hard disk or between computers on the network, you can use three basic methods. You can drag the file from one location to another, you can use the copy-and-paste method, or you can copy a file using the Send To feature.

Dragging Files   To copy a file by dragging it, you need to have open both the folder that contains the file and the folder to which you want to copy it. This process is easiest with Windows Explorer, so let's start there.

Let's assume that you want to copy a file from a remote computer to your own computer.

1. On the Start menu, point to Programs, and click Windows Explorer. In Windows Me, point to Programs, point to Accessories, and then click Windows Explorer.

2. In the Folders list on the left, locate the folder in which you want to place the file.
   For example, if you want to place the file in the My Documents folder, make sure you see the folder in the list. If necessary, click the plus sign next to the C: drive.

3. To locate the file you want to copy, click the plus sign next to Network Neighborhood or My Network Places in the list on the left.

4. Click the plus sign next to the remote computer you want to access.

5. Click the plus sign next to the disk on the remote computer that contains the file.

6. Click the folder containing the file you're looking for.
   If the folder contains subfolders, click the plus sign next to the folder to display its contents, and then select the subfolder containing the file. You should see the file you want to copy in the list on the right.

7. Now scroll through the list on the left until you see the folder to which you want to copy the file, *but do not click it.*

     Being able to see the icon for the folder is enough for now. You should still see the file you want to copy on the right.

8. Drag the icon of the file you want to copy from the list at the right to the destination folder in the Folders list on the left. As you drag, a small plus sign appears next to the mouse pointer indicating that you are copying, rather than moving, the file.

In Figure 9-4, the file named Budget in the Excel Book folder on a remote computer is being copied to the My Files folder on the local computer.

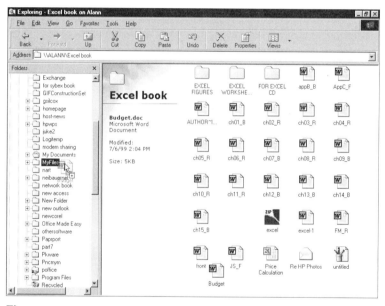

Figure 9-4.

To copy a remote file, drag it from its current location to the proper folder in the Folders list.

Note

You can also drag a file by holding down the right mouse button as you drag. Using the right mouse button causes a shortcut menu to appear, from which you can choose Copy Here when you release the mouse button.

In addition, you can copy a file using a combination of My Computer and Network Neighborhood or My Network Places. With this approach, you drag the file to be copied between two windows on your screen: one that shows the file's original location, and another that shows its destination. This time, you'll copy a file from your computer to a remote one following these steps:

1. Double-click My Computer on the desktop and double-click the drive containing the file.

2. Double-click the folder containing the file.

3. If the folder window fills the screen, click the Restore button to make the window smaller.

4. Drag the window to the left side of the screen.

5. Double-click Network Neighborhood on the Windows desktop or open My Network Places.

    Network Neighborhood or My Network Places appears in a new window. If the two windows overlap, drag the Network Neighborhood window to the right.

6. In the Network Neighborhood or My Network Places window, double-click the icon for the computer you want to access.

7. In the Network Neighborhood or My Network Places window, double-click the disk, and then double-click the folder in which you want to place the file. The Network Neighborhood screen should resemble the one shown in Figure 9-5.

Figure 9-5.

Copy a file by dragging it between the My Computer and Network Neighborhood windows.

8. Drag the file from the Network Neighborhood or My Network Places window on the left to the My Computer window on the right.

Copying and Pasting   If copying a file by dragging seems too time-consuming, you can always do it the old-fashioned Windows way, by using the Copy and Paste commands. You'll still need to open both a window showing the file in its original location and a window showing the new location, but you don't need to have both open at the same time.

You can copy and paste using Windows Explorer, Network Neighborhood, My Network Places, or My Computer. Here's how:

1. Open the folder containing the file you want to copy and select the file.

2. Right-click the file and choose Copy from the shortcut menu. You can also click Copy on the Windows Explorer toolbar, choose Copy from the Edit menu, or press Ctrl+C.

3. Open the folder to which you want to copy the file.

4. Right-click and choose Paste from the shortcut menu. You can also choose Paste from the Edit menu or from the toolbar.

Note

If you periodically access a file on a remote computer, you can create a shortcut to it on your machine by dragging it to your desktop while holding down the right mouse button and choosing Create Shortcut(s) Here from the shortcut menu that appears.

Copying Files to Remote Disks Using the Send To List   One handy Windows feature is the Send To list. If you need to save a file on a floppy disk, for example, you can right-click its icon on the desktop or in any folder, and then point to Send To to see a list of possible destinations, as shown below. Click 3½ Floppy (A) at the top of the list to copy the file to the floppy disk, for example.

You can add your own destinations to the Send To list so that you can copy files quickly to a remote computer of your choice.

To do so with Windows 95, Windows 98, or Windows Me, you must first create a desktop shortcut to the disk or shared folder on the remote computer that you want to add to the Send To list. *(For more information, see "Creating a Desktop Shortcut," earlier in this chapter.)* Next, right-click the shortcut you've created to the remote computer and choose Rename from the shortcut menu. Type a name that you'd want to see in the Send To list and press Enter. Finally, drag the icon to the C:\Windows\SendTo folder.

Using Windows 2000 or Windows XP, add a SendTo destination by performing the following steps:

1. In My Computer or Windows Explorer, double-click the drive where Windows is installed.

2. Double-click the Documents and Settings folder.

3. Double-click your user name.

4. Select Folder Options from the Tools menu, and click the Folder Options tab.

5. Select the option Show Hidden Files and Folders.

6. Click OK.

7. Double-click the SendTo folder.

8. Select New from the File menu, and click Shortcut.

9. Follow the instructions on your screen.

Now, whenever you want to copy a file to the remote location, right-click the file, point to Send To, and click the listing for the remote location.

Moving Remote Files

You move a file between computers almost exactly the same way you copy a file. To move a file by dragging, follow the steps for copying, but hold down the Shift key when you release the left mouse button. While you hold down the Shift key, the small plus sign next to the pointer disappears, indicating that you're moving, rather than copying, the file. You don't have to hold down the Shift key while you're dragging the mouse, only when you release it.

If you prefer not to move a file by dragging it, you can move the file by using the cut-and-paste method, rather than the copy-and-paste method. Right-click the file and choose Cut from the shortcut menu instead of Copy. Open the folder to which you want to move the file, right-click again, and choose Paste from the shortcut menu. When you paste the file into its new location, it's removed from its original folder.

Note

As with copying, it's also possible to drag the file by holding down the right mouse button instead of the left. In this case, choose Move Here from the shortcut menu that appears when you release the mouse.

Deleting Remote Files

When you have Full access to a remote folder, you can delete it or delete the files within it. But before you delete anything, you should be aware that the Recycle Bin doesn't work across the network.

The Recycle Bin, on the Windows desktop, is a holding tank for files or folders that you delete from your hard disk. If you change your mind about deleting an item, you can open the Recycle Bin, select the deleted file or folder in the Recycle Bin window, and choose Restore from the File menu.

When you delete a file that's on another computer on the network, however, it's immediately deleted from the disk without making a protective stop at the Recycle Bin of either computer. Even dragging the file to the Recycle Bin of your computer erases it automatically.

Note

The Recycle Bin also doesn't work for files and folders deleted from floppy disks or removable disks, such as Zip disks.

With these caveats in mind, if you're sure you want to delete a remote file, just locate it by using Network Neighborhood, My Network Places, Windows Explorer, or any other method. Select the file and press the Delete key, or right-click the file and choose Delete from the shortcut menu. When you're asked whether you really want to delete the file, click Yes if you do or click No if you've changed your mind.

Note

You can delete an entire folder from a remote computer by using this procedure.

Sharing in Windows 2000

The general concept of file sharing and accessing shared files is the same in Windows 2000 as it is in Windows 95, Windows 98, and Windows Me. However, Windows 2000 has inherited the file-sharing capabilities of Windows NT. With Windows 2000, you can set permissions for specific users and encrypt folders and files for added security.

In Windows 98, for example, you can limit access to a folder by assigning it a password. Anyone who has the password can then access the folder. If an unauthorized user learns the password, he or she can access the folder from any computer on the network.

Windows 2000 doesn't use passwords because it offers user-level access, which means you can assign specific permissions to each user individually or in groups. To assign permission to an individual, you use the Users And Passwords icon in Control Panel to create a user account for the individual and then set his or her permissions. The user must log on to the network with his or her name and password to access the folders you've allowed.

The level of security that you choose depends on your network and office requirements.

Turning On File Sharing

If you need to install the file-sharing service in Windows 2000, follow these steps:

1. On the Start menu, point to Settings, and then click the Network And Dial-Up Connections icon.

2. Right-click Local Area Connection and choose Properties from the shortcut menu.

3. In the list of network components that are installed, look for File And Printer Sharing For Microsoft Networks. If it's installed, you can skip the rest of these steps.

4. Click Install to open the Select Network Component Type dialog box.

5. Select Service and then click Add to open the Select Network Service dialog box.

6. Select File And Printer Sharing For Microsoft Networks and then click OK.

7. Click OK to close the Select Network Component Type dialog box.

8. Click Yes when you're asked whether to restart your computer.

Sharing Drives

To turn on sharing for an entire drive and give only certain people access to it, follow these steps:

1. Double-click My Computer on the Windows desktop.

2. Right-click the drive that you want to share and select Sharing from the shortcut menu to see the dialog box shown in Figure 9-6.

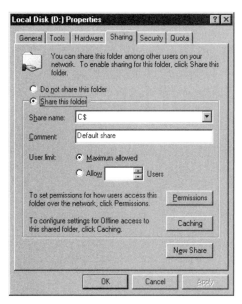

Figure 9-6.

The Properties dialog box allows you to activate sharing for a resource.

The Share This Folder option might already be enabled and an entry with a dollar ($) sign, such as C$, might appear in the Share Name box. The dollar sign indicates a special shared resource that Windows needs for administrative purposes. You can't remove this type of sharing, but network users won't be able to see it when they browse the network to access your computer.

3. If the disk is assigned for sharing, click New Share, type the share name, and click OK. If no default name exists for the drive, click Share This Folder. Windows places a default name in the Share Name text box, usually the same letter as the drive.

4. In the User Limit section, select either Maximum Allowed, or Allow, and enter the number of users allowed to access the drive at one time. The maximum is 10.

5. Click Permissions to see the dialog box shown in Figure 9-7.

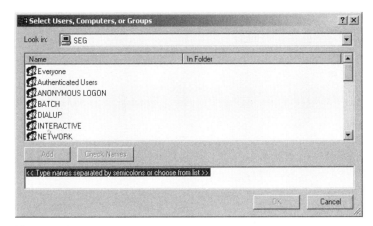

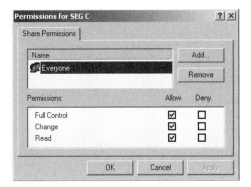

Figure 9-7.
The Permissions dialog box.

6. The default is set to Everyone, meaning that permissions are granted to every network user accessing your computer. In the Permissions section, select Allow or Deny for the specific permissions you want to allow to everyone: Full Control, Change, and Read.

If you want to limit access to certain groups or users, you can remove Everyone (the default) from the access list and add specific users or groups. Create a user account for network users you want to access the system. Click Add to open the dialog box shown in Figure 9-8. Double-click the user or group, and click OK. Then set the permissions for the individual or group.

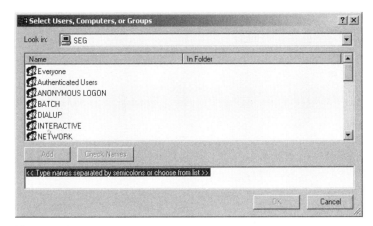

Figure 9-8.
Setting permissions for sharing.

For even more control over permissions, click the Security tab on the Local Disk Properties dialog box to set permission options.

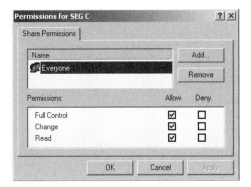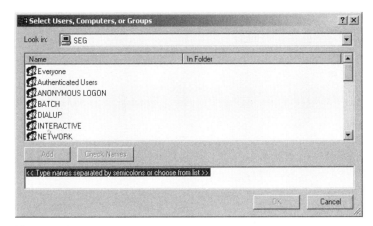

Note

If you want to change permissions, display the Share Name list by clicking the down arrow to the right of the selected name, and choose the new share you created. You can't set or change permissions for shares whose names include the dollar sign.

Sharing Folders

If you don't want to allow complete access to your disk, you can designate sharing privileges only for certain folders and not for the entire disk.

In fact, each user of the computer has a folder assigned with his or her name in the Documents And Settings folder of the hard disk. Granting access to the disk doesn't automatically grant access to these personal folders. If you want to grant access to a personal folder, you must activate sharing for it specifically.

To designate sharing for a folder, follow these steps:

1. Double-click My Computer on the Windows desktop.

2. Double-click the disk containing the folder you want to share.

3. Right-click the folder you want to share. You might have to navigate through folders to display the subfolder you want to share.

4. Select Sharing from the shortcut menu to open the Properties dialog box.

5. Click Share This Folder.

6. Click Permissions if you want to specify the rights and users, as you learned to do for disks.

Sharing in Windows XP

Although Windows XP inherits its file-sharing capabilities from Windows NT and Windows 2000, the methods used to share files are slightly different.

Windows XP Home Edition supports a feature called Simple File Sharing that has two options:

- Share This Folder On The Network

- Allow Network Users To Change My Files

The first option turns on sharing but provides just Read-Only access to files. Selecting the second option as well provides Full access, so other network users can also modify or delete your shared files.

Windows XP Professional offers the Simple File Sharing feature as well as Advanced File Sharing. Using Advanced File Sharing, you can determine the number of users and set individual permissions as you can in Windows 2000.

Turning On File Sharing

The Windows XP Network Setup Wizard activates file sharing for you automatically. However, if you didn't use the wizard to create your network, you must install the Windows service that allows sharing. Here's how to do it:

1. Click Start and then click My Network Places. Click View Network Connections. (If you don't see the View Network Connections options, run the Networking Setup Wizard to initially setup your network.)

2. Right-click Local Area Connection and choose Properties from the shortcut menu.
   In the list of network components that are installed, look for File And Printer Sharing For Microsoft Networks. If File And Printer Sharing For Microsoft Networks is installed, make sure that the check box next to it is selected, and you can skip the rest of these steps.

3. Click Install to open the Select Network Component Type dialog box.

4. Select Service and then click Add to open the Select Network Service dialog box.

5. Select File And Printer Sharing For Microsoft Networks and then click OK.

6. Click OK to close the Select Network Component Type dialog box.

7. Click Yes if you're asked whether you want to restart your computer.

Sharing Drives

To turn on sharing for an entire drive, follow these steps:

1. Click Start and then click My Computer.

2. Right-click the drive that you want to share and select Sharing And Security from the shortcut menu. You can also select Properties from the shortcut menu and click the Sharing tab.

3. Click the message If You Understand The Risk But Still Want To Share The Root Of The Drive, Click Here. You'll see the options shown in Figure 9-9.

Figure 9-9.
Setting permissions for shared folders in Windows XP.

4. Select Share This Folder On The Network.

5. In the Share Name text box, enter a name that will identify the drive on the network.

6. If you want users to be able to change the contents of the files on the drive, select Allow Network Users To Change My Files.

7. Click OK.

Advanced File Sharing

Windows XP Home Edition allows you to select only Simple File Sharing. In Windows XP Professional, however, you can select Advanced File Sharing to use options similar to those in Windows 2000, shown in Figure 9-6 and Figure 9-7.

To select Advanced File Sharing in Windows XP Professional, follow these steps:

1. On the Start menu, point to Settings, and click Control Panel.

2. Double-click the Appearance and Themes, then click Folder Options icon to open the Folder Options dialog box.

3. Click the View tab.

4. Scroll the Advanced Settings list and when you find the Use Simple File Sharing (Recommended) option, clear the check box.

5. Click OK.

For detailed information about how to use the Advanced File Sharing option in Windows XP Professional, refer to the section "Sharing in Windows XP," earlier in this chapter.

Sharing Folders

The procedure for sharing only a folder within a disk is about the same as for sharing the entire disk. Rather than right-clicking the disk icon, however, navigate to the disk containing the folder and right-click the folder's icon.

Select the Share This Folder On The Network check box, enter a share name, and select the Allow Network Users To Change My Files check box if you want.

Note

Running the Network Setup Wizard automatically creates a Shared Documents folder that can be shared among all network users.

Windows XP Home Edition doesn't offer options to set individual user permissions for file access. All network users are granted Guest access, and you can't create an individual account for network users or create groups. Windows XP Professional also forces all users to have Guest status, but it has some options similar to those in Windows 2000 that let you create groups of users for more control over network access.

Monitoring Network Connections

One way to protect your data is to monitor your network connections periodically. In Windows, you can see who is connected to your computer and which resources they are accessing. You can then continue to allow their connection, or choose to close the connection or just the file that they're using.

Monitoring Your Network in Windows 95, Windows 98, or Windows Me

To monitor your network connections in Windows 95, Windows 98, or Windows Me, perform the following steps:

1. Click Start, point to Accessories and then System Tools, and click Net Watcher. The Net Watcher window will appear, showing which users are connected, which shares they are accessing, and any files they have open. Figure 9-10 displays the By Connection view.

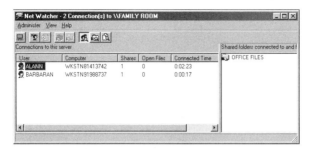

Figure 9-10.
Monitoring the network with Net Watcher.

Note

If Net Watcher isn't an option, you can install it from the Windows Setup tab of the Add/Remove Programs icon in Control Panel. It's listed under System Tools.

2. You can change the way the list is organized by using the View menu. To organize the list by folders, select By Shared Folders; to organize the list by open files, select By Open Files. Select By Connections to return to the organization shown in Figure 9-10.

3. From here, you have several options:

   • In the By Connections view, you can select Disconnect User from the Administer menu to close the user's connection so he or she no longer has access to your files.

   • In the By Open Files view, you can select Close File from the Administer menu to close the file. The user will lose any changes he or she has made.

   • In the By Shared Folders view, the Administer menu gives you these options: Add Shared Folder, Stop Sharing Folder, and Shared Folder Properties.

Monitoring Your Network in Windows 2000 or Windows XP

You can also monitor connections in Windows 2000 or Windows XP. Here's how:

1. Open Administrative Tools in Control Panel and double-click Computer Management. In Windows XP, open Administrative Tools from the Performance and Maintenance option in the Control Panel.

2. Click the plus sign next to Shared Folders.

3. Click Sessions to see which users are connected, along with the number of open files and connection times for each person, as shown in Figure 9-11. Click Open Files to see the list of open files, find out who has each file open, and find out the mode (Read-Only or Write And Read).

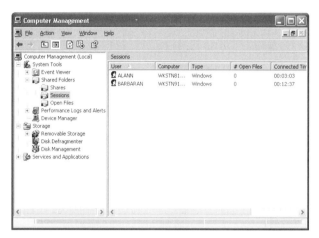

Figure 9-11.
Monitoring connections in Windows XP.

4. Use the Action menu to close connections or files. To close a specific user's connection, select By Sessions from the View menu, click the user in the right side of the window, and choose Close Session from the Action menu. To close all open sessions, click Sessions on the left side of the window, and select Close All Sessions from the Action menu. Use the same method to close a specific open file or all open files.

Sharing CDs Virtually

Ever want to listen to a music CD but it's in some other area of the house? Need to get a file from a CD, or install a program from a CD-ROM that someone else is using?

Sharing a music or computer CD across a network is as easy as sharing any disk or folder. The user who has the CD must turn on sharing for his or her CD-ROM drive. Then any other network users can access the files on the CD from their computers.

But sharing a CD has some serious limitations:

- The CD must remain in the CD drive so other users can access it. This restriction means that the drive can't be used for another CD while it's being made available to the network.

• Some programs that are supplied on a CD can be run only from a CD drive; they can't be run remotely across the network. In other words, the entire CD must be made available to the computer locally, in its own drive.

You can overcome both of these limitations by using a technique called *virtual CD emulation*. When you create a virtual CD on your computer, the computer treats the information as though an actual CD is inserted into a CD-ROM drive. In reality, the information from the CD—the music tracks or programs—are actually stored on your hard disk, or on some hard disk elsewhere on the network.

Here's how it works:

1. Install a program (such as those described in the following sections) that creates one or more virtual CD drives on your computer. The CD drive will appear in My Computer just like any other drive, as shown below.

(H:)

2. Use the program to create an image file of a CD. The image file contains all the information on the CD, but in one large file on your hard disk or on some other hard disk on the network.

3. Tell the emulator program to "insert" the image file into a virtual CD drive.

As far as your computer is concerned, an actual CD is now inserted into an actual CD drive. You can run the CD to play music, open the CD to list and access files, and eject the CD. Of course, with a virtual CD, ejecting merely disassociates the image file from the CD so it no longer appears to be inserted.

You can store the image file anywhere on the network. So you can create an image file of a music CD on one computer, and then insert it into the virtual CD drive of another computer to play. While you play the virtual CD, someone else can listen to the actual CD. If you have a network version of the virtual CD emulator program, more than one person can use the image file at the same time, so multiple family members can listen to the same CD or run the same program.

Several popular virtual CD emulator programs are available. As examples, the following sections will look at Paragon CD Emulator and Virtual CD 3.

Paragon CD Emulator

Paragon CD Emulator from Paragon Software (*http://paragon.ru*) comes in a personal version and a network version. The only differences between them are that the network version allows simultaneous access to a CD image file, and a network administrator can create permissions to control access to the image file. If you need only one person to access a virtual CD at a time across the network, you can save money and purchase the less-expensive personal version.

Figure 9-12 shows the Paragon program window. The pane on the left shows that the computer has one virtual drive, H:, and two actual drives, E: and G:. The image files that have been loaded into the computer are shown on the right. Both of these files, however, were created using Paragon on another computer and are being stored on that computer.

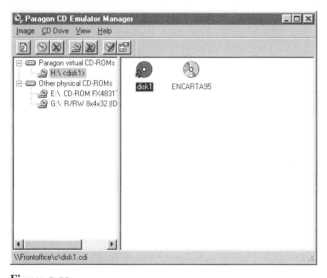

Figure 9-12.
Virtual CD drives in Paragon CD Emulator.

To use the program, you first create an image file, insert the image file into the Paragon program, and then load the file to a virtual CD drive.

To create the image file, follow these steps:

1. Insert the CD that you want to load into a virtual drive into a computer on which Paragon is installed.

2. Start Paragon and click the Create New CD Image button.

3. In the dialog box that appears, designate the drive containing the CD and click OK. Paragon copies the contents of the CD into an image file.

After the image file is stored on a computer, add it to the Paragon program on the computer on which you want to use the image file as a virtual CD, by performing the following steps:

1. Click Add A CD Image File on the Program toolbar.

2. Navigate to the location where the image file is stored. If it's on another computer on the network, you can use the Network Neighborhood or My Network Places option in the Open box's Look In list to browse the network, locating the computer and folder on which the image file is stored.

3. Select the image file and click Open.

The image file now appears in the Paragon window, regardless of its actual physical location. To "insert" the image file into the virtual CD, just drag it from the right side of the Paragon window to the virtual drive on the left.

In My Computer, you'll see the CD listed with its virtual drive letter. You can now play or open the CD just as if it were in an actual CD drive.

Eject the virtual CD from within the Paragon program or from My Computer. Right-click the virtual drive icon and select Eject from the shortcut menu as if it were an actual CD.

Virtual CD 3

Virtual CD 3 (*http://virtualcd-online.com*) also comes in two versions: personal and network. In this case, however, you must buy the network version to access CD image files across a network.

With this program, you create an image using the Image Wizard. The wizard takes you step by step through the process of converting a CD into an image file, including changing the format of audio tracks.

You work with images and virtual CDs in the program window shown in Figure 9-13. Use the toolbar to create new image files, add image files to the program window, and insert image files into the virtual drives. The Editor feature lets you customize the contents of the image file, which is particularly useful for creating custom audio or picture virtual CDs.

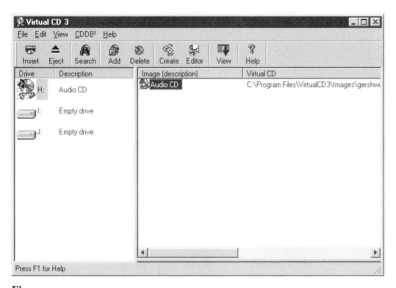

Figure 9-13.
Creating virtual drives with Virtual CD 3.

After you've created image files, however, you can quickly insert files into the virtual drives using the Virtual CD 3 menu in the system tray on the right of the taskbar, as shown below. Open the menu, point to Insert, point to the drive, and then click the image file you want to insert into the drive.

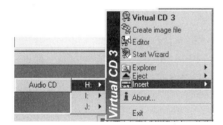

The first time you create an audio image file, by the way, you can register for a free account with CDDB, a company that maintains an Internet database of audio CDs. After you register with CDDB, Virtual CD 3 will retrieve detailed information about your audio CD and its individual tracks for your reference.

Sharing Programs

So far, we've looked rather generically at sharing files, primarily documents, graphics, sounds, and other files that aren't programs. Sharing a program on a network is a slightly different matter.

What Can Be Shared?

Sharing programs on a network might have legal ramifications:

- It's not always legal to purchase one copy of a program and install it on each computer on your network.

- It's not always legal to purchase one copy of a program, install it on one computer, and then let more than one person on the network run the program at the same time.

Remember that software is usually licensed, and many software companies prohibit program sharing as part of their licensing agreement. This limitation means that all you're really purchasing is a license to use the software and, according to the rules, you don't own the software. By opening and using a piece of software, you're agreeing to abide by the terms of your software license agreement.

Many licensing agreements require you to purchase a separate copy or license for every computer on which you want to run the software, even if you're using the software on just one computer at a time.

Some programs can't be shared. Many older versions of programs, particularly those that run on MS-DOS rather than Windows, can be run only on the computer on which they're installed. These programs are designed to access additional files within the same computer. When you try to run such programs remotely, they can't find the files they need and either display an error message or don't work at all.

Running a Program Remotely

Running a program on a remote computer is essentially the same as opening it on your own computer. You locate the program file and then open it by double-clicking it. When you run a program that's on a remote computer, the program runs on your computer, but its files remain on the remote computer.

See Also

In Chapter 12, "Playing Games," you'll learn how to share and play games across a network.

Because some programs frequently draw information from the disk as they run, you might find that running a remote program uses up quite a bit of your network resources. You might also encounter problems with programs that won't run properly across a network. If you get error messages when you start the program or while you're using it, you won't be able to run it remotely. You'll either have to install the program on your computer (if the licensing agreement allows), or go to the computer on which it's installed and run it from there.

Sharing a Data File

Sometimes you must share access to certain files, such as calendars and databases, on other computers. The shared data file might be a calendar, for example, that each member of the family accesses to check for appointments and special events. You want only one copy of this calendar on the network so that everyone sees the same information and so that changes made to it are available to everyone.

You can open a data file by simply navigating to it and opening it, as you've learned in this chapter, or you can set up your program to access the file on a remote computer automatically.

If you want to share a document or data file with other network users, think about the best location in which to keep the file. For example, storing it on the computer that's turned on most often increases the odds that the file will be available when someone needs to access it.

Security is another issue to consider. If you want to use a password to limit access to a file, you'll need to store the file in a folder that is password-protected, which might limit your placement options. The computer in your child's room might be on almost all the time, for example, for game-playing, doing homework, and chatting online, but you wouldn't want to store a personal or parents-only file there. The tradeoff for security might be to store the file on a computer that's used less frequently, but mainly by adults.

Another factor to consider when sharing files on different computers is that many programs expect to see files in specific places. They're set up to look in a default folder for the files they need to open. When you need to use this type of program, you have two choices: place the files where the program expects to see them, or tell the program where you've chosen to keep the files.

Microsoft Money, for example, which lets you keep track of your bank accounts and even transfer funds and pay bills online, uses a data file named Mymoney.mny. The program stores this file in a reserved folder on the hard disk.

To change where Money should look for Mymoney.mny, just copy the file to wherever you want to store it, and then double-click Mymoney.mny to start the program.

Because Money always uses the last data file you opened, the new data file in its new location becomes the default.

You can share a Money file between computers on the network so that anyone who runs the program can have access to the most current bank account data. Just copy the Mymoney.mny file to the computer where you want the shared file to be located, and then have all network users start their copy of Money by navigating to the remote computer and opening the Mymoney.mny file.

Other applications let you set the default location for documents in a dialog box, such as Word's Options dialog box, shown in Figure 9-14.

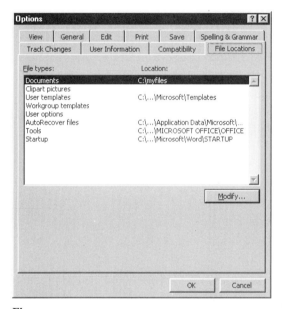

Figure 9-14.

In Word, the default location for documents is set in the Options dialog box.

If you want Word to automatically look for new documents on a remote computer or to save new documents to a remote computer, enter the UNC path as the document's location. Here's how to do it:

1. Start Word, and from the Tools menu, choose Options.

2. In the Options dialog box, click the File Locations tab.

3. Click Documents in the File types list, and then click Modify.

4. In the Modify Location dialog box, type the full path for the folder on the remote computer, such as \\Barbara\C:\Myfiles. You can also browse for the location by choosing Network Neighborhood or My Network Places in the dialog box's Look In list.

5. Click OK to close the Modify Location dialog box.

6. Click OK to close the Options dialog box.

Backing Up Important Files

When it comes to backing up, the best rule of thumb is to back up what you don't want to lose. Unfortunately, backing up is one of those tasks we all know we should do but too often don't.

Backing up means making a copy of important files in some location other than your hard disk. That way, if your hard disk decides it's had enough of your interference and departs to never-never land, your important files are safe somewhere else. Sounds logical, only many of us forget to back up important files or we just get too lazy to do it.

When you're sharing files on a network, backing up is even more important for two reasons:

- The more people who access your disk, the greater the chance an important file will be deleted or corrupted. This possibility is especially true if you allow Full access to your network's resources.

- More people depend on being able to use a given file and will be affected by its loss. It's not just you anymore.

All network users should take some precautions to safeguard important files that would be difficult or impossible to recreate. Backing up programs isn't as critical because you can always reinstall them from their original disks. But your documents, database files, spreadsheets, banking files, and other data files might be unique and difficult to replace.

Some programs, such as MECA's Managing Your Money and Microsoft Money, automatically create a backup file each time you exit them. Although the setup procedure varies, in most cases, the backup option is available as a menu choice or in a dialog box that opens when you choose to exit the program. You can usually specify the backup location, including a disk on a remote computer.

Using Removable Disks

The best choice for quick and easy backup of files and folders is a Zip, Jaz, or other type of removable disk anywhere on your network. Removable disks hold at least 100 megabytes (MB) of information, the equivalent of about 70 floppy disks. That's not as much storage as you have on a hard disk or tape drive, but it can certainly accommodate a lot of files. Because the disk is removable, you can use multiple disks to store as much information as you like.

If the disk is attached to your computer, it will appear as a disk icon in My Computer. Just drag the files or folders you want to back up to this icon. If your computer has a built-in removable disk or tape drive, it might appear automatically in your Send To list. If it doesn't, create a shortcut to the disk on the desktop and add it to the SendTo folder yourself. *(For more information, see the section "Sending Files to Remote Drives," earlier in this chapter.)*

When the disk is attached to a remote computer, consider mapping to the disk so that you can access it from My Computer, or else creating a shortcut to it in the SendTo folder.

Storing Files Remotely

Another option worth considering is backing up your files to the hard disk of a remote computer. One of the computers on the network might be newer and have a much larger hard disk than the disk in your own computer. Or it might not be used quite as much as other computers in the house, so it has extra hard disk space that can be shared among the family.

Create a folder on that computer with your name so that you can easily identify it. Create a shortcut to the folder on your desktop, and then add the shortcut to the SendTo folder. You'll now be able to back up folders and files to that remote disk quickly and easily.

Using Microsoft Backup

As an alternative to backing up individual files and folders, you can automate the backup process with Microsoft Backup. The program comes with Windows, so you can't beat the price, and it works with floppy disks, tape backup drives, and most removable disks. It's great for a network because you can use it to back up files from your own or any other computer on the network and store the backup on a remote computer.

Note

Backup is supplied with Windows 95 and Windows 98, but it isn't included with Windows Me.

Using Backup in Windows 95 or Windows 98

Backup isn't usually installed in Windows 95 and Windows 98, so you'll have to do it yourself. But don't worry, it's easy. Just follow these steps:

1. Insert your Windows CD into the CD-ROM drive.

2. On the Start menu, point to Settings, and click Control Panel.

3. In Control Panel, double-click Add/Remove Programs.

4. In the Add/Remove Programs Properties dialog box, click the Windows Setup tab. After a moment or two, you'll see a list of Windows components.

5. Scroll through the list and click System Tools. Make sure you don't remove the check mark from the check box to the left.

6. Click Details to see a list of items in the System Tools category.

7. In the System Tools dialog box, select the Backup check box to enable it.

8. Click OK to close the System Tools dialog box.

9. Click OK again to close the Add/Remove Programs Properties dialog box.

10. Click Yes when you're asked whether you want to restart your computer.

After your computer restarts, you're ready to configure and run Backup. The process varies slightly, depending on the type of drive you're using for backup—tape, removable disk, or floppy disk.

Using Backup in Windows 2000 or Windows XP

The Backup program included with Windows 2000 and Windows XP Professional is similar to the version for Windows 95 and Windows 98 discussed here, but it has a different look. (Windows XP Home Edition doesn't come with the Backup program.) To start the program, click Start, point to Programs (All Programs in Windows XP), point to Accessories, point to System Tools, and then click Backup.

In Windows 2000, the Welcome page appears with three choices, as shown here.

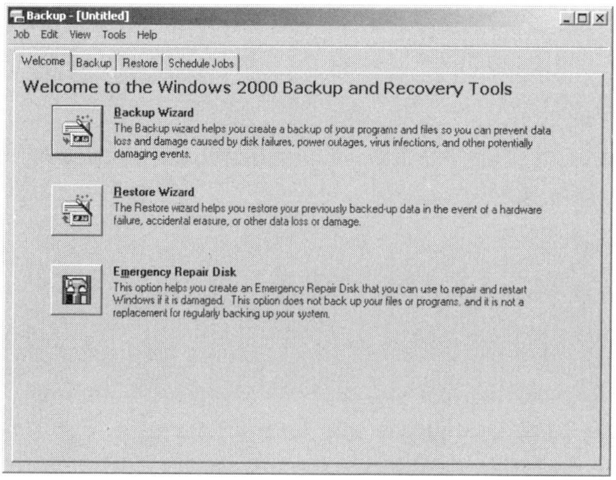

You can use the Backup Wizard to automate your backup, or click the Backup tab to specify the files you want to back up and their destination. Use the Restore Wizard or the Restore tab to restore files. The Emergency Repair Disk option creates a floppy disk that you can use to start your computer if Windows is damaged on your hard disk. The Schedule Jobs tab lets you schedule backup operations for specific dates and times.

In Windows XP Professional, the Backup Or Restore Wizard begins. Click Next to see these options:

- Back Up Files And Settings
- Restore Files And Settings

Select the option for the task you want to perform and then follow the instructions in the remainder of the Backup Or Restore Wizard.

Note

If you don't have a tape backup drive or another device that Backup automatically recognizes as a backup device, the first time you run the program, you might be asked whether you want it to search for a backup device. Click No.

Creating Backup Jobs

Microsoft Backup lets you create a *backup job* that defines which files you want to back up and where you want them stored. You can have any number of backup jobs defined, and you can easily repeat a backup to save updated files.

To start the program in all versions of Windows, follow these steps:

1. On the Start menu, point to Programs, point to Accessories, point to System Tools, and then click Backup. The Microsoft Backup dialog box appears, as shown in Figure 9-15.

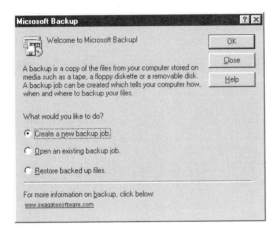

Figure 9-15.
The Microsoft Backup dialog box prompts you to create a new backup job, which starts the Backup Wizard.

2. Select Create A New Backup Job to define a backup job, and then click OK to start the Backup Wizard.

The wizard takes you step by step through the process of defining a backup job and performing the backup itself. You can choose options such as these:

*   The name of the backup job

*   Whether to back up your entire computer or only selected files

*   The storage location for backup files

*   Whether backups and originals are compared to verify their accuracy

*   Whether backup files are compressed to save space

Using the Backup Wizard isn't the only way to define a backup job. You can also use the main Backup window, shown in Figure 9-16. This window allows you to specify what to back up, where to store it, and how to save it. Then you just click the Start button. To back up important files from a remote computer, for example, scroll through the What To Back Up list and click the plus sign next to Networks to access remote computers.

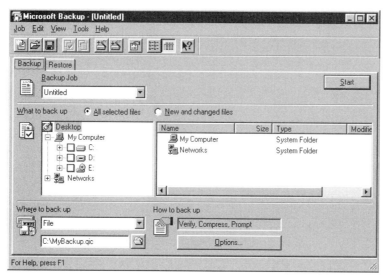

Figure 9-16.

Using the controls in the Microsoft Backup window is an alternative to using the Backup Wizard.

Microsoft Backup doesn't store files individually. Instead, it combines them in one large file or a series of large files spread over several disks. Therefore, you can't use standard Windows or MS-DOS techniques to access individual files in a backup. If you want to retrieve files from the backup, you have to perform a *restore* operation.

To restore files, choose the Restore Backed Up Files option when you start Backup. The Restore Wizard opens. You can also click Close in the Microsoft Backup dialog box after you start Backup and use the controls on the Restore tab to specify restore options. If you choose to restore selected files, you'll see a list of the individual files in the backup from which to choose.

Using Tape Backup

Tape backup devices, although they're slower than external hard disks, are usually less expensive and provide more storage.

When tape backup devices first appeared on the market, they were strictly sequential: to add something to the tape, the device first had to run through the tape to find the end of the recorded data, and you couldn't delete a specific file in the middle of the tape without rewriting the entire tape. A disk, on the other hand, provided random access, so you could add and delete files anywhere.

Tape backup has come a long way from those early days, now offering many of the same advantages as disks. External tape backup devices are even more useful because, although they are slower than internal models, you can easily move the devices from one computer to another to back up and restore files as needed.

The Echo OnStream USB tape drive is one example. With a capacity of up to 30 gigabytes (GB), the device plugs into your computer's USB port and works as both a backup/restore program, such as Backup, and as a disk drive. After installing the software, for example, you'll see two new "drives" in My Computer. As the illustration shows, drive V: is the Echo Catalog and drive T: is the removable disk.

The Echo Catalog on drive V: is a copy of all your tape's directories stored on your hard disk. You can access the directories even if a tape cartridge isn't loaded into the tape drive, so you can always see which files are backed up. When you access a file in the catalog, the catalog tells you which tape to insert into the drive and locates the files on the tape.

Drive T: in My Computer represents the current tape inserted into the external drive. You can open drive T: just as you would any hard disk or floppy drive. You can then drag files onto the drive for storage, open files, or copy files from the tape to your hard disk. It works the same way as any hard disk except that the file might not actually be written to the tape until you either eject the tape or shut down your computer.

In addition to accessing the tape as you would a disk drive, Echo includes a complete backup and restore program, as shown in Figure 9-17.

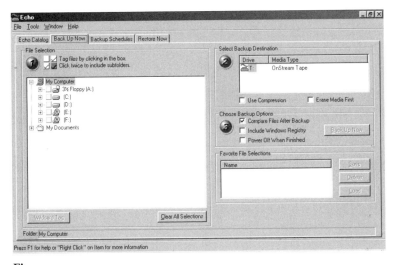

Figure 9-17.
Echo OnStream backup.

Echo also includes a quick-access Echo Express program designed for making backups, shown here.

All the software options are available on a menu on the Windows taskbar, as illustrated below.

Network Attached Storage

Sharing a file that's stored on a computer has one major drawback: that computer must be turned on to access the file. If that computer is off, it won't appear in Network Neighborhood (or in My Network Places), and its files won't be accessible to anyone on the network. If you mapped the drive to appear automatically when you start Windows, you'll get an error message that the drive can't be located.

A solution to this problem is network attached storage (NAS). NAS is a hard disk that's connected directly to the network hub, rather than to any specific computer on the network, as shown in Figure 9-18. The device is fundamentally a hard disk with a network interface card (NIC), and it has built-in software, so it looks like a computer to other systems on the network. However, it has no keyboard, monitor, or mouse.

You plug the NAS into your network hub or switch and then configure the device to be seen by your network. You must run a special setup program or access a Web page built into the device, to configure its TCP/IP address to fall within the range of your network.

At one time, network attached storage devices were quite expensive—beyond the budget range of most home networks. With the drop in hard disk and other hardware prices, however, adding NAS to a home network is realistic, particularly if you depend on shared files.

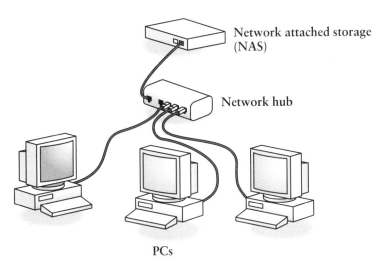

Figure 9-18.

Network attached storage (NAS).

The NETGEAR (*http://www.netgear.com*) network disk drive is a good example of a NAS device. The 8-GB model (ND508) costs less than $200. The drive uses TCP/IP and is initially configured to get its IP address automatically. If you use dynamic IP addressing, simply plug the device into the hub and access it without any additional setup.

If you use static IP addresses on your network, you assign the network drive its own IP address using the TCP/IP Configuration Utility supplied by NETGEAR, shown in Figure 9-19. Enter the media access control (MAC) address of the drive in the MAC Address text box, specify the IP address and subnet mask, and then click Next twice. Notice that you can also use the drive as a DHCP server to assign IP addresses to your network.

To access the drive, open Network Neighborhood. You can also map the drive so it appears as a local hard disk in My Computer. In fact, a program called FirstGear for Network Drives is provided with the drive, which automatically assigns the drive your computer's next available drive letter.

Using a Web page built into the drive, which you access with your Web browser, you can create any number of public or private folders. A *public folder* is accessible to everyone on the network; a *private folder* is protected with a password to control access.

In addition to the 8-GB model, Netgear offers the 20-GB ND520 for about $400. Other NAS devices include SNAP servers, which start at $500 for a 20-GB model, and the Maxtor MaxAttach, which starts at about $1,000 for an 80-GB model.

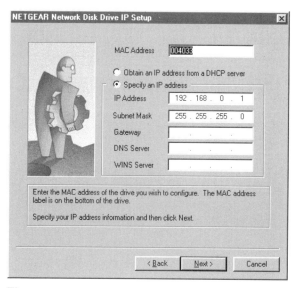

Figure 9-19.
Assigning an IP address to the NetGear network drive.

Sending and Receiving Pop-Up Messages

The easiest and least formal way to communicate over the network is to send and receive pop-up messages. You can send a message to a specific family member or "broadcast" it to everyone on the network.

See Also

Windows XP lets you send and receive messages over the Internet with Windows Messenger, which you'll learn about in Chapter 14, "Networking for Road Warriors."

With a program named WinPopup, which comes with Windows 95, Windows 98, and Windows Me, you can announce that dinner is ready, tell your daughter that the phone call is for her, or send out a reminder or words of wisdom to your loved ones. Your message simply pops up in a window on the recipient's screen. Keep in mind that WinPopup doesn't save your messages after you close it or after you shut down your computer.

Note

Although WinPopup isn't included with Windows 2000 or Windows XP, you can down-load programs over the Internet that let these versions of Windows send and receive pop-up messages. These programs include Net Hail at *http://www.nethail.com*, Realpopup at *http://www.realpopup.it*, and e/pop at *http://www.wiredred.com*.

Starting WinPopup

WinPopup is usually installed when you set up Windows, but it's not listed with other programs on the Start menu. If you plan to use WinPopup regularly, you can add it to the Start menu, to your desktop, or to your Windows taskbar.

To locate WinPopup and add it as a shortcut on your Windows desktop, follow these steps:

1. On the Start menu, point to Find, and click Files Or Folders. In Windows Me, point to Search on the Start menu and click For Files Or Folders.

2. Make sure the Look In box is set at C: (or Local Hard Drives in Windows Me) so your entire drive is searched.

3. In the Named text box (or the Search For Files Or Folders Named text box in Windows Me), type *winpopup*. In the Look In drop-down list, choose the drive on which Windows is installed (usually the C: drive) and then click Find Now (Search Now in Windows Me).

    Windows then searches your disk and locates the WinPopup program, as illlustrated below. *If Windows doesn't locate the program, see the next section, "Installing WinPopup."*

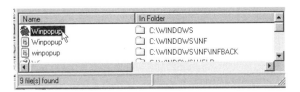

4. In the list of files, right-click WinPopup and choose Create Shortcut from the shortcut menu.

5. Click Yes when a message appears reporting that you can't add the shortcut to the current location and asking whether you want to add the shortcut to your desktop.

6. Close the Find window (the Search Results window in Windows Me). You now have on your desktop a shortcut to the program, as shown below.

Shortcut to
Winpopup

If you're using Windows 95, Windows 98, or Windows Me and you have Internet Explorer 4 or later installed, you can add the shortcut to your Quick Launch toolbar on the taskbar so that you can access it from within any application. To perform this task, drag the shortcut icon to the Quick Launch toolbar, which is just to the right of the Start button. Now you can delete the shortcut from the desktop if you want by right-clicking it and choosing Delete from the shortcut menu.

Note

If the Quick Launch toolbar is now too narrow to fit all the icons it needs to display, you can bring them all back into view by dragging farther to the right the vertical line beside the last icon.

Because WinPopup must be running for someone to send or receive messages, you should have everyone on the network copy the WinPopup shortcut to the Startup folder, usually located in C:\Windows\Start Menu\Programs\StartUp. When the shortcut is in that folder, it automatically starts whenever Windows is started.

Installing WinPopup

If the WinPopup program isn't already installed on your computer, you'll have to install it yourself. Insert the Windows CD into your CD-ROM drive just in case you need it, and then follow these steps:

1. On the Start menu, point to Settings, and click Control Panel.

2. In Control Panel, double-click Add/Remove Programs.

3. In the Add/Remove Programs Properties dialog box, click the Windows Setup tab.

4. In the list of components, click System Tools (in Windows 95, click Accessories), but be careful not to remove the check mark in the check box to its left.

5. Click Details.

6. In the System Tools dialog box (the Accessories dialog box in Windows 95), scroll through the components list and select the check box next to WinPopup, as illustrated below.

7. Click OK to close the System Tools dialog box or the Accessories dialog box.

8. Click OK again to close the Add/Remove Programs Properties dialog box.

Note

If you don't have a Windows CD, the installation program might already be on your hard disk.

Using WinPopup

WinPopup must be running for you to send or receive a message. If the WinPopup short-cut isn't in the Startup folder on your machine, which starts WinPopup automatically when you start Windows, you must run WinPopup by double-clicking the icon you placed on the desktop or on your Quick Launch toolbar.

When WinPopup starts, you see the window shown in Figure 9-20. If you're not ready to send a message, minimize the window so that WinPopup appears on the taskbar.

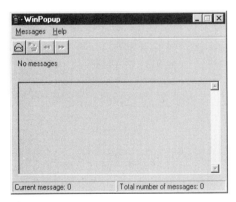

Figure 9-20.
The WinPopup window allows you to send or receive messages on the network.

Here's how to send a message:

1. Click the WinPopup button on the taskbar to open the WinPopup window.

2. Click the Send button on the toolbar, which shows a picture of an envelope, or choose Send from the Messages menu to open the Send Message dialog box shown below.

3. To send a message to everyone on the network, click Workgroup. To send a message to a specific person on the network, click User Or Computer.

4. If you want to send a message to everyone and the workgroup name doesn't appear automatically, enter the name of the workgroup in the text box in the To area of the Send Message dialog box. If you want to send a message to one person, enter that person's user name or computer name.

5. In the Message box, type the message (which can be up to 127 characters if you're sending the message to a workgroup, or 500 characters if you're sending the message to an individual). Then click OK. A complete message might look like this.

Note

To paste text into the message from the clipboard, right-click the Message text box and choose Paste from the shortcut menu.

A message box reports that the message was sent successfully.

6. Click OK.

When you receive a message from another computer on the network, you'll hear a beep. If the WinPopup window is open, the message appears in the window, as shown in Figure 9-21.

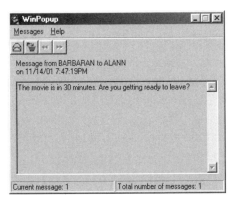

Figure 9-21.

A received message appears in the WinPopup window.

If the window is minimized, click its button on the taskbar to display the message. The WinPopup icon on the taskbar indicates whether you have pop-up messages to read. When you have no messages, the icon looks like this.

As you receive messages, the icon indicates how many you have. Here's how the icon looks when you've received a message.

If you want the WinPopup window to open automatically when a message arrives, select Options from the Messages menu and select the Pop Up Dialog On Message Receipt check box. Other options allow you to turn off the beep that sounds when a message arrives and to keep the WinPopup window in the foreground in front of other program windows.

When you have more than one message, click the Previous button or the Next button on the WinPopup toolbar to switch from one message to the next. Click the Delete button on the toolbar to delete a displayed message.

When you close the WinPopup window, a message reminds you that you can't send or receive any more messages unless the window is open. If you still have undeleted messages, the message box also reminds you that all messages will be discarded when you close WinPopup because the program doesn't save messages from session to session. If you decide you still want to exit the program, click OK to close the WinPopup window.

The Bottom Line

In this chapter, you learned to share disks, folders, files, and programs among computers on the network so that everyone can use them. You also learned how to back up important files to a different computer, and how tape drives and network attached storage devices can be used. This chapter also discussed using virtual CD drives to get the most use out of programs on CDs, and how to share messages using WinPopup with Windows 95, Windows 98, and Windows Me. In the next chapter, you'll learn how to share another important resource on a network: the printers connected to the computers.

Part 4

Running the Network

Chapter 10

Printing Across the Network

Sharing files and folders is one great advantage of connecting computers on a network; sharing printers is another. When you share printers, everyone on the network can access them. You might need to walk to the printer in another room to retrieve your printed copies, but the pages will be there, ready and waiting for you.

Here are a couple of scenarios in which sharing printers can be a great benefit:

- You don't have a printer for each computer.

- You want to use a feature of a printer that's connected to a remote computer.

Let's say you purchased printers for some but not all the computers in your home. If your computers aren't connected to a network, you'll need to perform one of two actions to get a printout from a computer that doesn't have a printer:

- Save your documents on a disk and take the disk to a computer that's connected to a printer (and install the necessary software on that computer, if it isn't already loaded).

- Disconnect the printer from one computer and hook it up to the computer from which you want to print (and load the appropriate printer driver on that computer, if necessary).

If you've set up a home network, it doesn't matter whether all your computers are linked to printers. You can send a document to printers connected to other computers on the network.

Even if you do have a printer for each computer, the printers might not all be of the same type. For example, you might have a laser printer connected to your computer for printing business documents, whereas your children have a color printer for school reports and kids' stuff. If your computers are connected on a network, you can get to your kids' color printer whenever you want, and the kids will be able to print with your laser printer.

See Also

Chapter 2, "Getting Connected Without a Network," covered ways to share printers without a network.

You can link a printer to a network in two basic ways. The cheaper and easier method is simply to connect the printer to the parallel or universal serial bus (USB) port of one of the computers on the network. The other way is to connect the printer directly to the network. Although this second option is more expensive, connecting a printer directly has many advantages. *You'll learn about these advantages in the section "Connecting Printers Directly to the Network," later in this chapter.*

Sharing Printers

When you print to a printer connected to a remote computer, your print job travels over the network, through the remote computer, and then to the printer attached to it. The remote computer, rather than your computer, produces the print job.

Let the Printer Beware!

Sharing printers attached to computers connected on a network is a great time-saver, but there's one big gotcha: both the printer and the computer it's attached to must be turned on, and the printer must be online, stocked with paper, and ready to go. Otherwise, it's no go!

So before you print to a printer on the network, you have to ensure the printer is ready. If no one is using the computer that's attached to the printer, you might have to go to the computer, turn on both the computer and the printer, and set up the printer for printing.

Even if the computer and printer are turned on and ready, they might be busy with someone else's print job. When the printer completes the job, it'll start printing your document and others that are waiting on a first in, first out (FIFO) basis, which means the first job in line is printed first. Another problem can occur if the person using the computer attached to the printer shuts down the computer before the printer starts printing your work. A little coordination among the family is clearly needed here.

You might suggest to everyone on the network that anyone who wants to print to someone else's shared printer should first send a short message to make sure the printer is on and ready. You could also try yelling from room to room, but that's not always the best approach.

Setting Up Printer Sharing

Before you can share your computer's printer on the network, you must have installed the File And Printer Sharing For Microsoft Networks service. Chances are, you already installed the service when you set up file sharing. But you should make sure that you've enabled the printer sharing part of the service. If you use the Home Network Wizard in Microsoft Windows Millennium Edition (Me) or the Network Setup Wizard in Microsoft Windows XP, print sharing will already be set up for you.

See Also

For more information about installing the File And Printer Sharing For Microsoft Networks service on your system, see the section "Turning on File Sharing," in Chapter 9, "Learning to Share," on page 235.

If you're using Microsoft Windows 95, Windows 98, or Windows Me, follow these steps to enable printer sharing:

1. On the Start menu, point to Settings, and then click Control Panel.

2. In Control Panel, double-click the Network icon to open the Network dialog box.

3. Click the File And Print Sharing button to open the File And Print Sharing dialog box.

4. Make sure the I Want To Be Able To Allow Others To Print To My Printer(s) check box is selected.

5. Click OK to close the File And Print Sharing dialog box.

6. Click OK to close the Network dialog box. Depending on how Windows is set up on your computer, you might be asked to insert your Windows CD so the files necessary for sharing are installed.

If you're using Windows 2000, follow these steps to enable printer sharing:

1. On the Start menu, point to Settings, and then click Network And Dial-Up Connections.

2. In the Network And Dial-Up Connections dialog box, right-click a connection and choose Properties from the context menu to open the Properties dialog box for the connection.

3. On the General tab, in Components Checked Are Used By This Connection, select File And Printer Sharing For Microsoft Networks.

4. Click OK, and close the Network And Dial-Up Connections dialog box.

If you're using Windows XP and you didn't use the Network Setup Wizard to create your network, follow these steps to enable printer sharing:

1. Click Start and then click My Network Places. (If My Network Places doesn't appear on the Start menu, select My Computer, and then click My Network Places.) Click View Network Connections.

2. Right-click Local Area Connection and choose Properties from the shortcut menu.

3. In the list of network components that are installed, make sure File And Printer Sharing For Microsoft Networks is selected.

4. Close the Properties dialog box.

Installing a Printer

The next step in setting up a printer is to check that it's actually installed on your computer and working properly. If you can't use the printer that's directly attached to your computer, no one else will be able to use it over the network.

To make sure that your printer is installed in Windows 95, Windows 98, Windows Me, or Windows 2000, point to Settings on the Start menu, and then click Printers. In Windows XP, open Control Panel and double-click Printers and Other Hardware. Then click Printers And Faxes. If you see a listing for your printer, it's already installed and you can close the Printers window. If your printer isn't listed in the Printers window, you'll have to add the printer now.

If your printer came with a floppy disk or CD, it might have its own special printer drivers and installation program. Take a quick look at the documentation that came with the printer. If the printer came with a CD, look at the CD too—sometimes instructions are printed right on the CD.

Depending on the type of printer, running its special installation program can be as simple as inserting the CD into the computer and waiting for the installation program to start by itself. If nothing happens when you insert the CD, go to My Computer and double-click the icon for the CD. If that doesn't start the installation program, you might have to run the Setup or Install program on the CD. When the installation program starts, just follow the instructions that appear on the screen.

Note

In Windows XP, inserting a plug-and-play USB printer into the USB port will automatically begin the installation process.

In many cases, however, setting up your printer doesn't require running a special installation program. Instead, you can set up the printer using the Add Printer Wizard in Windows. Here's how:

1. Insert your Windows CD into the CD-ROM drive. (Depending on how your computer was set up, this step might not be necessary, but it can't hurt.)

2. In Windows 95, Windows 98, Windows Me, or Windows 2000, on the Start menu, point to Settings, and then click Printers. In Windows XP, open Control Panel and double-click Printers and Other Hardware. Then click Printers And Faxes.

3. To start the Add Printer Wizard, double-click the Add Printer icon in Windows 95, Windows 98, Windows, Me, or Windows 2000. In Windows XP, under Printer Tasks, click Add Printer.

4. Click Next. The Add Printer Wizard will take you through the steps of installing the printer.

Using the Add Printer Wizard in Windows 95, Windows 98, or Windows Me

If you're using Windows 95, Windows 98, or Windows Me, follow these steps to complete the installation with the Add Printer Wizard:

1. When the wizard asks whether you want to install a local printer or a network printer, select Local Printer, and then click Next.

    You'll now see a dialog box similar to the one shown in Figure 10-1, which contains lists of printer manufacturers and printer models. *If your printer model isn't listed, see the next section, "Handling Problem Printers."*

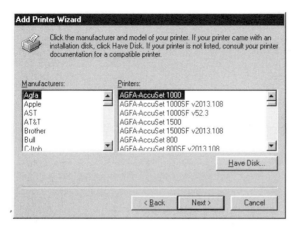

Figure 10-1.

Select your printer's make and model in the Add Printer Wizard.

2. Click the manufacturer of the printer on the left, click the model of the printer on the right, and click Next.

3. If your computer already has a driver for your printer, Windows will ask you whether it should keep the existing driver or replace it. (You should keep the existing driver unless you've experienced problems with your printer.) Click Next.

4. You'll now be asked to select the port to which the printer is attached. In most cases, your printer is attached to the LPT1 port, the standard parallel printing port on most PCs. If your computer has more than one printer port, the ports will be labeled LPT1, LPT2, and so on. If you have a USB or serial printer, it might be connected to the USB or a serial (COM) port instead. Click the port that your printer is attached to, and click Next.

5. Type in a new name for the printer if you want, such as *Dad's laser printer*, or leave the default name.

6. If you're installing the first printer on your computer, that printer will automatically be the default. If other printers are installed on the computer, Windows asks whether you want the new printer to be the default. Click Yes if you want the printer to be the default printer in all Windows programs. Click No if you want to leave another printer as the default. If you click No, you can still select the printer when you're ready to print. *See the section "Selecting a Different Printer on the Network," later in this chapter, for more information.* Click Next.

7. The wizard now asks whether you want to print a test page. Make sure your printer is turned on and loaded with paper, and then click Yes to print a test page. Printing a test page isn't really necessary, but it's a good idea to confirm that everything is working properly rather than waiting until you have an important document to print.

8. Click Finish.

    Windows loads the appropriate printer drivers and prints the test page. A dialog box opens to ask whether the page printed correctly.

9. Click Yes if the page printed without a problem. If the page didn't print correctly, click No to start the Print Troubleshooter. Follow the dialog boxes that appear, selecting the answers that best explain the problem you're having.

Using the Add Printer Wizard in Windows 2000 or Windows XP

If you're using Windows 2000 or Windows XP, follow these steps to complete the installation with the Add Printer Wizard:

1. The wizard asks whether you want to install a local printer or a network printer.

    *   In Windows 2000, select Local Printer. If your printer is plug-and-play compatible, also select Automatically Detect and Install My Plug and Play Printers, then click Next.

    *   In Windows XP, select Local Printer Attached To This Computer. If your printer is plug-and-play compatible, also select Automatically Detect and Install My Plug and Play Printers. Click Next.

2. Windows 2000 and Windows XP now ask you to select the port to which your printer is attached.

3. Select the port, and click Next.

    You'll now see a dialog box similar to the one shown on page 304, which contains lists of printer manufacturers and printer models. *If your printer model isn't listed, see the next section, "Handling Problem Printers."*

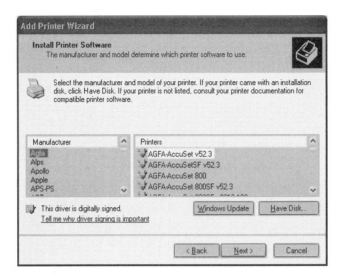

4. Click the manufacturer of the printer on the left, click the model of the printer on the right, and click Next.

5. If your computer already has a driver for your printer, Windows will ask you whether it should keep the existing driver or replace it. (You should keep the existing driver unless you've experienced problems with your printer, or if you know your current driver is not suitable for use with Windows XP.) Click Next.

6. Type in a new name for the printer if you want, such as *Dad's laser printer*, or leave the default name.

7. If you're installing the first printer on your computer, that printer will automatically be the default. If other printers are installed on the computer, Windows asks whether you want the new printer to be the default. Click Yes if you want the printer to be the default printer in all Windows programs. Click No if you want to leave another printer as the default. If you click No, you can still select the printer when you're ready to print. *See the section "Selecting a Different Printer on the Network," later in this chapter, for more information.* Click Next.

8. The wizard now asks whether you want to share the printer on the network. Select Share As, type in a name for the shared printer, and click Next. You can now type in a location and a comment for the printer. This information can help other users determine the printer location and its capabilities.

   The wizard now asks whether you want to print a test page. Make sure your printer is turned on and loaded with paper, and then click Yes to print a test page. Printing a test page isn't really necessary, but it's a good idea to confirm that everything is working properly rather than waiting until you have an important document to print.

9. Click Next and then click Finish.

    Windows loads the appropriate printer drivers and prints the test page. A dialog box asks whether the page printed correctly.

10. Click Yes if the page printed without a problem. If the page didn't print correctly, click No to start the Print Troubleshooter. Follow the dialog boxes that appear, selecting the answers that best explain the problem you're having.

Handling Problem Printers

If you run the Add Printer Wizard and your printer's model doesn't appear on the list, don't give up hope. Many new printer models and many old ones might not be listed.

If your printer is new, insert its accompanying floppy disk or CD into the appropriate drive before you start the Add Printer Wizard. When you see the dialog box in the Add Printer Wizard that prompts you to select the printer's manufacturer and model, click the Have Disk button. In the dialog box that appears next, specify the location of the disk and then continue following the prompts. You might have to specify a subfolder on the disk that contains the proper drivers for your printer or browse the disk to locate the drivers.

If your printer is older, it might not be listed in the Add Printer Wizard, and you might not have its installation disk. Even if you have the installation disk, the printer drivers might not be compatible with newer versions of Windows, such as Windows XP.

If your printer model is not listed, try selecting the same manufacturer as your printer's and choosing one of the older models listed for that manufacturer. If that doesn't work, look for information in the printer's manual about other printers that yours can emulate. Many laser printers, for example, use the same drivers as some Hewlett-Packard (HP) printers. If you have an older laser printer with no documentation or software, try selecting the LaserJet Plus, LaserJet II, or LaserJet III models from the HP list.

If you still can't get the printer to work, try searching the Internet. You might be able to download from a Web site the drivers you need to install the printer. On the Web, look for the printer manufacturer's home page, and look for drivers that are compatible with your version of Windows. If specific drivers are not listed for Windows XP, try using Windows 2000 drivers instead. If the manufacturer is out of business, search the Microsoft Web site, *http://www.microsoft.com/downloads/search.asp*, for driver information. (Select Keyword Search and enter *printer driver* as keywords.) You can also perform general Web searches using your printer's make and model as keywords.

Sharing a Printer

Sharing a printer is similar to activating sharing for a disk drive or folder.

Sharing Printers in Windows 95, Windows 98, or Windows Me

Follow these steps to activate printer sharing in Windows 95, Windows 98, or Windows Me:

1. On the Start menu, point to Settings, and then click Printers.

2. In the Printers window, right-click the printer you want to share.

3. Choose Sharing from the shortcut menu.

4. On the Sharing tab of the Properties dialog box, click Shared As, as shown below.

5. In the Share Name text box, enter a name for the printer that will identify it to other network users.

    You also have the option of entering an identifying description of the printer in the Comment text box. To make it easier for other users to select the printer, include its type, such as Canon Color InkJet or HP LaserJet Printer, in the description.

6. If you want to allow sharing only for users with a password, enter a password.

7. Click OK.

8. If you entered a password, type it again to confirm it, and then click OK.

    The printer's icon now shows, with a cradling hand, that it's a shared resource, as shown on page 307.

HP DeskJet
895C Seri...

The check mark next to a printer icon in the Printers window indicates that the printer is the default in all Windows applications. To make a different printer the default, right-click its icon and choose Set As Default from the shortcut menu.

Separating Print Jobs   Once other people start using your printer, don't be surprised if it starts churning out pages that you're not expecting. Windows will print documents in the order in which they're received, so if another network user starts a job before you do, you'll have to wait for your document to print.

If you're not careful, you might wind up with several documents in the printer's output tray at one time. And you certainly wouldn't want to grab your quarterly report and your kid's homework and distribute both to the board members later in the morning. You also wouldn't want your document to disappear with someone else's job.

To avoid this problem, you can have Windows automatically print a separator page between documents. The page prints at the start of each job and shows the name of the person who printed it, making it easier for you to find your document in the printer's output tray.

Here's how to turn on the Separator Page feature:

1. On the computer to which the printer is attached, click Start, point to Settings, and then click Printers.

2. Right-click the printer that's being shared, and choose Properties from the shortcut menu. The General tab of the printer's Properties dialog box appears, as shown in Figure 10-2.

3. Choose either Full or Simple from the Separator Page drop-down list. Both options print the user's name, document name, and current date and time. The Full option just prints it larger.

Note

Choose None from the Separator Page list if you no longer want to print separator pages.

4. Click OK.

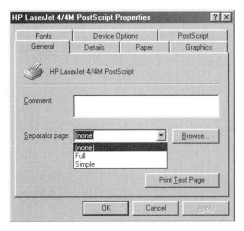

Figure 10-2.

You can turn on separator pages on the General tab of the printer's Properties dialog box.

Sharing Printers in Windows 2000 or Windows XP

The concepts you learned for sharing printers in previous versions of Windows also apply to Windows 2000 and Windows XP, although the dialog boxes to allow sharing are somewhat different.

The Sharing tab in Windows 2000, for example, is shown in Figure 10-3. The options are similar in Windows XP. If Windows 2000 or Windows XP is sharing your printer with computers that run another version of Windows, click Additional Drivers to select and install the drivers for their systems.

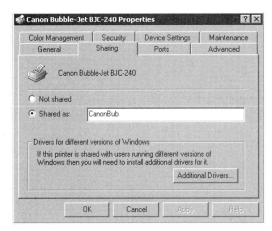

Figure 10-3.

Sharing printers in Windows 2000.

In Windows 2000, after enabling sharing you must set the permissions. (InWindows XP, access is controlled by user profiles, as explained in Chapter 8, "Creating User Profiles.") Click the Security tab to display the options shown in Figure 10-4.

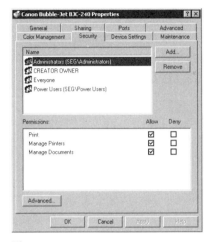

Figure 10-4.
Setting permissions for printer sharing.

As with sharing files, you can choose the users or groups to which you want to assign permissions. Three levels of permissions are possible:

- **Print** allows users to print documents.

- **Manage Printers** allows users to change printer properties.

- **Manage Documents** lets users delete print jobs and manage the printer queue.

Accessing a Shared Printer

The printer you've set up for sharing is now available to all the computers on the network. But before the other computers can access it, you must first install the printer on the other computers as a remote network printer rather than as a directly connected local printer. The procedure for installing a network printer is similar to that for a local printer, but with a few twists along the way. And you must be sure that everyone who wants to add the network printer to a computer has access to the printer drivers.

To install a network printer on a computer, follow these steps:

1. Insert the Windows CD into the CD-ROM drive. (This step might not be necessary because the drivers might already be on the computer's hard disk, but it can't hurt.)

2. In Windows 95 and Windows 98, double-click Network Neighborhood and then double-click the computer connected to the shared printer. In Windows Me and Windows 2000, use My Network Places to access the network computer. In Windows XP, click Start and then click My Network Places; click View Workgroup Computers, and double-click the computer connected to the shared printer.

3. In Windows 95 and Windows 98, right-click the icon for the shared printer and choose Install from the shortcut menu, shown below, to start the Add Printer Wizard. In Windows Me, Windows 2000, and Windows XP, choose Connect from the shortcut menu. (Windows 2000 and Windows XP are smart about adding network printers; they'll probably install the correct drivers for the printer without any further intervention on your part.)

     If your computer is running Windows 95, Windows 98, or Windows Me, you now must specify whether you want MS-DOS programs, such as an older version of WordPerfect or dBASE, to be able to print to the network printer. Normally, MS-DOS programs can't print to printers across the network; they can print only to local printers. But when you tell Windows to provide network printing capability to MS-DOS programs, Windows captures the information the MS-DOS program is trying to print and then channels it to the network printer.

4. If you want to print from MS-DOS programs to network printers, click Yes. If you don't use MS-DOS programs or you want to print with them only to a local printer, click No.

5. Click Next.

6. If you chose to capture MS-DOS printing, you'll be asked to select a port. Click the Capture Printer Port button, select LPT1, click OK, and then click Next.

7. If your computer is running Windows 95, click the manufacturer of the printer on the left, click the model of the printer on the right, and then click Next.

8. Enter a name for the printer if you want, such as *Mom's color printer*, or leave the default name, which is usually the printer's model name.

9. If you're installing the first printer on your computer, that printer is automatically the default. If other printers are installed on the computer, Windows asks whether you want the new printer to be the default. In all versions of Windows, click Yes if you want the printer to be the default printer. Click No if you want another printer as the default. You can still select the printer when you're ready to print. *See the next section, "Selecting a Different Printer on the Network."*

10. Click Next.

11. When you're asked whether you want to print a test page, make sure the printer is turned on and loaded with paper, and then click Finish in Windows 95, Windows 98, and Windows Me. (Click Yes in Windows 2000 and Windows XP.)

12. Click Finish. A dialog box then asks whether the page printed correctly.

13. Click Yes if the page printed without a problem. If the page didn't print correctly, click No to start the Print Troubleshooter. Follow the dialog boxes that appear, selecting the answers that best describe the problem you're having.

Selecting a Different Printer on the Network

Whenever you set a printer as the default—either your local printer or one of the printers on the network—all your documents are directed to that printer unless you choose a different printer. To change which printer is the Windows default, click Start, point to Settings, and then click Printers to open the Printers window, right-click the printer you want as the default, and then choose Set As Default from the shortcut menu.

You can also choose to print a particular document at a printer other than the default printer. How you perform this task depends on the application you're using. In many programs, such as Microsoft Word, clicking the Print button on the toolbar automatically prints the document to the default printer. If you want to choose a different printer, you must select the printer in the Print dialog box.

For example, suppose your own laser printer is the current default, but you want to print a document in color. Your kids have a color printer that's been set up as a network printer. Here's how you'd print a document on your kids' printer:

1. Choose Print from your application's File menu.

2. Click the drop-down arrow next to the Name box, which shows the default printer, and choose the printer in your kids' room from the drop-down list.

3. Click OK.

4. Go and get your document before the kids turn it in as homework!

Using Printer Shortcuts

Normally, you start an application and then print a document. But with all versions of Windows, you can use several shortcuts for printing documents.

In My Computer or Windows Explorer, you can right-click a document's icon and choose Print from the shortcut menu. Windows opens the application that was used to create the document, sends the document to the printer, and then closes the application.

You can also drag a document onto a printer icon that you've placed on the Windows desktop. To place a printer icon on the desktop, follow these steps:

1. In Windows 95, Windows 98, Windows Me, or Windows 2000, on the Start menu, point to Settings, and then click Printers. In Windows XP, open Control Panel and double-click Printers And Other Hardware, then click Printers And Faxes.

2. Right-click a printer and choose Create Shortcut from the shortcut menu.

3. When a message tells you that you can't place a shortcut in the Printers folder and asks whether you want to place the shortcut on the desktop instead, click Yes.

Connecting Printers Directly to the Network

Because a printer that's connected to a computer on the network works only when the computer to which it's connected is on, you might want to use an alternative: connecting the printer directly to the network. Connecting a printer directly to the network also frees a computer's printer port so that you can hook up an external Zip drive, scanner, or other parallel device without a conflict.

In a twisted-pair network, you use twisted-pair cable to connect a printer to the hub. In a thin Ethernet network, you use coaxial cable to connect the printer to the network interface card (NIC) of the nearest networked device. Because the printer isn't connected to the printer port of a computer, anyone on the network can access it directly so long as the printer is turned on.

The disadvantage of connecting printers directly to the network is expense. Most printers are designed only for standard parallel connections. To connect them directly to the network, you'll need to purchase either a network-ready printer or a *print server*, a device that makes your printer network-ready.

Network-ready printers, which feature a built-in NIC, cost more than standard printers and can be a little harder to find. The print server is equipped with an Ethernet connection on one side and a parallel, or possibly serial, connection on the other.

The least expensive print servers are called *pocket servers*. About the size of a pack of cigarettes, a pocket server plugs directly into a printer's parallel port. The twisted-pair cable from the network hub or the coaxial cable from another networked device plugs into the other end of the server.

Another type of print server connects to a printer with a cable. These external servers are usually more expensive than pocket servers, but they might include additional features. Some models, for example, have more than one parallel port, allowing them to connect several printers to the network at the same time.

Note

For some HP LaserJet printers, you can purchase an internal print server that fits inside the printer, much the way some NICs fit inside a computer.

When selecting a print server, make sure it matches your cable type—either twisted pair or coaxial. Some print servers, but not all, can accommodate both types.

The print server must also support the protocol you're using on your network. Some print servers support only IPX/SPX; others require either Transmission Control Protocol/Internet Protocol (TCP/IP) or NetBEUI.

Finally, although most printers have a standard-sized parallel port, called a *Centronics* port, some models, such as the LaserJet 1100, have a smaller mini-Centronics port. The standard-sized connection on a pocket print server won't fit a mini-Centronics port. If you're using such a printer, you'll need an adapter for the print server.

Note

To install an external print server, just connect the cable that came with the printer to the server's parallel connection. Connect the network cable to the server's network connection.

Setting Up a Print Server

Many different models of print servers exist. Although they all operate in about the same way, their setup procedures vary. Most servers are sold with software that helps them connect to the network, but the process really depends on the type of protocol the server supports.

The easiest type of printer server to set up uses the NetBEUI protocol. In fact, sometimes, you don't even have to load any special software because the network computers automatically recognize the server as another networked device.

See Also

If you're using Windows XP, which doesn't support the NetBEUI protocol, see the section "Using a TCP/IP Print Server," later in this chapter.

The MiLAN print servers *(http://www.milan.com)*, for example, can use either the TCP/IP, NetBEUI, or IPX/SPX protocols. By using NetBEUI or IPX/SPX, however, you don't need to install or configure any special software or be troubled with setting IP addresses; therefore, they're among the easiest print servers to install. After you connect the server to your network hub, an icon for it will appear in Network Neighborhood or My Network Places, like this:

Fp04a3d2

Double-click the item to see the port that Windows will use for the printer, as shown below.

parallel1

Right-click the icon and choose Install or Connect, depending on your version of Windows, to start the Add Printer Wizard.

Note

The MiLAN print servers also include all the software and instructions you need to install when you're using TCP/IP as your protocol.

MiLAN manufacturers a number of print servers, including the two pocket servers, MIL-3410X, and MIL-P3720. The 3410X model is a 10-megabit-per-second (Mbps) server with one parallel port to connect to the printer, and one Ethernet port. The P3720 model is a dual-speed 10-Mbps and 100-Mbps server that also contains a serial port for connecting to a printer that uses a serial connection rather than a parallel connection. The company also manufactures a number of desktop units including those with one to four parallel ports.

If you want an easy-to-install desktop server, consider PowerPrint for Networks from Strydent Software *(http://www.strydent.com)*. When you run the server's setup software, you'll be asked whether you want to install the NetBEUI or TCP/IP drivers. Select NetBEUI and follow the instructions on the screen to install the driver. You'll need to run the setup program on each computer that you want to connect to the printer. Once the software is installed, you'll see an icon for the server in Network Neighborhood or My

Network Places. Double-click the icon to display four possible ports, as shown below, and then right-click the port you want to use and select Install or Connect to add the printer.

d1prn   d2prn   d3prn   d4prn

See Also

PowerPrint for Networks also lets you share your PC printer with Macintosh computers. You'll learn more about that in Chapter 13, "Networking PCs and Macs."

Using a TCP/IP Print Server

Using TCP/IP on a print server requires more setup than NetBEUI does. If you have a Windows peer-to-peer network, you'll probably need to assign the server and each of your computers a static IP address, or use the print server's built-in DHCP server, if it has one. Check the literature that came with your server for step-by-step directions. Some TCP/IP print servers are quite complicated to configure.

Most manufacturers provide programs to help you through the process. The Microplex Ethernet Pocket Print Server, for example, offers two programs for configuring the print server: IPAssign and Waldo. The IPAssign program, whose main dialog box is shown in Figure 10-5, accesses the print server through the Ethernet address and assigns it an IP address of your choice.

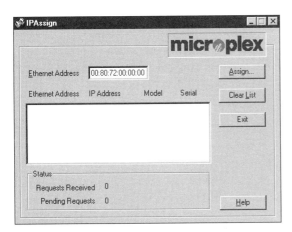

Figure 10-5.

The IPAssign program for a Microplex print server assigns an IP address to the server.

The Waldo program is Java-based, so you must have the Java run-time files installed on your computer. When you run Waldo, it searches for a Microplex print server on the network and displays its Ethernet address, as shown below.

You can then click the Assign button in the Waldo window to associate an IP address and subnet mask to the Ethernet address, as shown below.

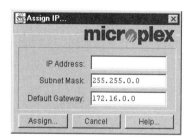

Once you assign an IP address to your server, you then configure Windows to communicate with the printer. You first have to associate the server with a printer port. The default port most printers use is called *LPT1*, the parallel connector that the printer cable plugs into. When you configured your printer, as you learned earlier in the section "Installing a Printer," you associated the printer with the port so Windows knows where to send the information to be printed—to the LPT1 port and then out to the printer.

When you connect a print server to the network, you must create a port with which the IP address is linked. When you associate a printer to that port, Windows sends the information to be printed through the network and the Ethernet address of the print server.

How you associate a printer port to the print server depends on the print server itself. With Microplex servers, for example, the server appears as a device in Network Neighborhood or My Network Places and has four ports associated with it. When you configure the printer, you browse to the port you want to use in the same way you would browse to a workstation, as explained earlier in the section "Accessing a Shared Printer."

Other manufacturers handle port assignments differently. The pocket print servers from Axis Communications, for instance, don't appear in Network Neighborhood or My Network Places. Instead, you use the NetPilot program to associate the server with a port, and then you use a program called Axis Print System to add the printer to Windows.

Microplex and Axis certainly aren't the only makers of print servers. Table 10-1, on page 319, lists other print server makes and models.

Hewlett-Packard's JetDirect print servers, for example, work with virtually any printer equipped with a parallel port—not just HP's brand. The line includes two models that have three parallel connections and a one-printer model, the 170X, that's more suitable for home networks. The servers use either the TCP/IP or the IPX/SPX protocols.

Setting up an HP print server is easy. After you connect the server both to the printer and to your network hub, you press a small button on the back of the server to print out a page of configuration information, including the electronic hardware address built into the device.

You then install the JetAdmin program supplied with the server and use the HP JetDirect Printer Wizard to configure the device. Figure 10-6 shows the wizard page in which you select a protocol and enter the unit's hardware address.

Assigning a Printer to the Server Port

If you have a printer that requires its own CD and installation routine, you might not be able to install the driver directly when setting up the print server.

You can still easily use the printer with a print server by following these steps:

1. Use the printer's CD to install the printer to the standard parallel printer port.

2. Use the print server's installation routine to install any printer that's listed by the Add Printer Wizard.

3. Open Control Panel and double-click Printers (Printers And Faxes in Windows XP).

4. Right-click the printer that you installed in step 2 and choose Properties.

5. Click the Details tab and make a note of the printer port shown. This port is the one your print server is installed in Windows.

6. Close the Properties dialog box.

7. Right-click the printer that you installed in step 1, and choose Properties.

8. Click the Details tab and select the port that you noted in step 5.

9. Make your actual printer the default, and delete the printer that you installed in step 1.

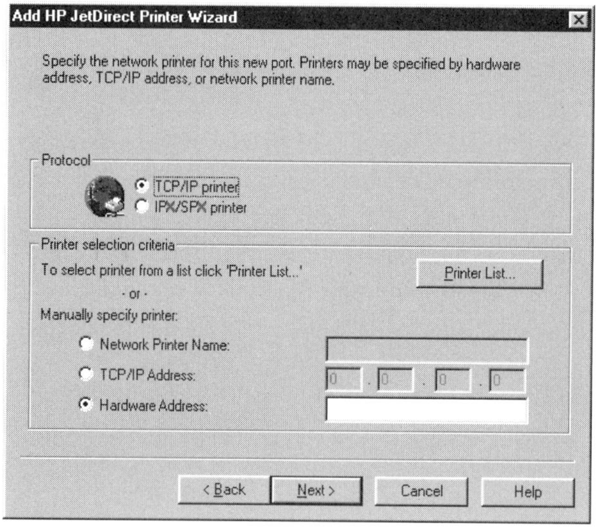

Figure 10-6.
The HP JetDirect Printer Wizard prompts you to select a protocol and enter the server's hardware address.

Using the address, JetAdmin locates the printer and displays a dialog box in which you can specify an IP address if you're using the TCP/IP protocol. After a few additional steps, JetAdmin starts the Add Printer Wizard in Windows, which opens a dialog box that prompts you to assign an IP address, as shown below.

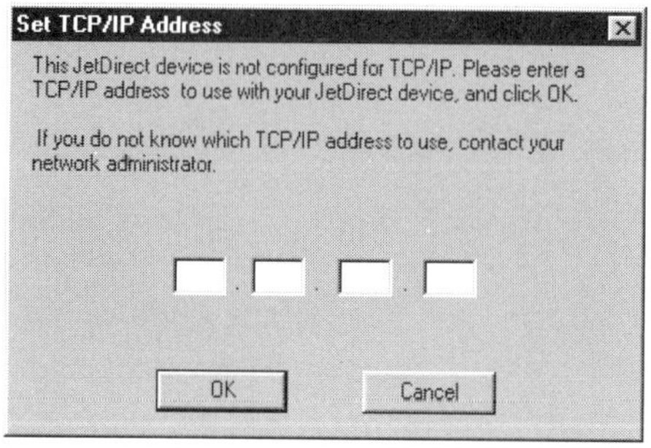

After the JetAdmin setup, you can send documents to the printer from your computer, and other network users can select the printer as their network printer and print documents even when your computer isn't on.

Many manufacturers of print servers exist, so you have plenty of choices. Table 10-1 lists print server models and each manufacturer's Web address.

Table 10-1. **Print Server Manufacturers and Models**

Manufacturer	Models	Web site
Axis Communications	Pocket, one-port, and two-port models, some with both parallel and serial ports	*http://www.axis.com*
Emulex	Pocket, two-port, and three-port models	*http://www.emulex.com*
Hewlett-Packard JetDirect	One-port and three-port models, external and internal, and one model for sharing over home telephone lines	*http://www.hp.com*
Intel NetPort Express	One-port and three-port models	*http://www.intel.com*
Lantronix	Pocket and external print servers, up to six-port models (four parallel and two serial)	*http://www.lantronix.com*
Linksys EtherFast	One-port and three-port models	*http://www.linksys.com*
MicroPlex	Pocket, and a four-port model (two parallel and two serial)	*http://www.microplex.com*
MiLAN	Two pocket models, and multiple-port desktop models	*http://www.milan.com*
NETGEAR	One- and two-port models, some with built-in four-port hub	*http://www.netgear.com*

Gateway Print Servers

Adding a print server to the network is so useful that many wired and wireless residential gateways have print servers built in. The gateway then serves as a router to share an Internet account, a network hub or switch, and a print server in one unit. Wireless print servers can even be used with Wi-Fi wireless networks.

The Asanté FriendlyNET cable/digital subscriber line (DSL) router (FR3004LC), the U.S. Robotics Broadband Router, and the SMC Barricade Wireless Broadband Router are examples that use the same basic setup. These devices let you share a broadband Internet account across a wired network because they have built-in Ethernet switches. The Barricade also acts like an access point for Wi-Fi wireless computers as well.

See Also

You'll learn more about the Asanté, U.S. Robotics, Barricade, and other Internet sharing devices in Chapter 11, "Going Online Through the Network."

Setting up the printer port in these devices is easy:

1. Plug in the router and connect Ethernet cables to your computers or to another hub. Plug in your printer's cable to the parallel port on the router.

2. On each computer, run the setup program provided on the CD that came with the device.

3. Right-click the icon for your printer in the Printers window, and select Properties.

4. On the Details tab, from the Port list, select PRT: (FriendlyNET Print Server) for the Asanté router, USRPRTSHR for the U.S. Robotics router, or PRTmate: (All-In-1) for the Barricade router.

5. Click Port Settings and enter the IP assigned to the router; the default issued by each of the devices is 192.168.123.254. You'll learn how to install a router and configure its IP address if you don't want to use the default setting in Chapter 11, "Going Online Through the Network."

6. Click OK.

The AirStation Print Server from Buffalo Technology (*http://www.buffalotech.com*) offers another unique alternative. This Wi-Fi–compatible device connects to a printer by a standard cable but communicates wirelessly with Wi-Fi–enabled computers. A switch on the server lets you select either peer-to-peer or infrastructure mode.

If you have all wireless computers, the print server operates in peer-to-peer mode, communicating directly with each wireless computer, as shown in Figure 10-7.

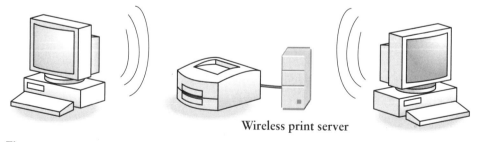

Wireless print server

Figure 10-7.

Using a wireless print server in peer-to-peer mode.

If you have a wireless access point or wireless broadband router, however, you can use the print server with your wired Ethernet computers as well, as shown in Figure 10-8. The print server is set up to communicate through the access point, so it can print documents from wired as well as wireless computers.

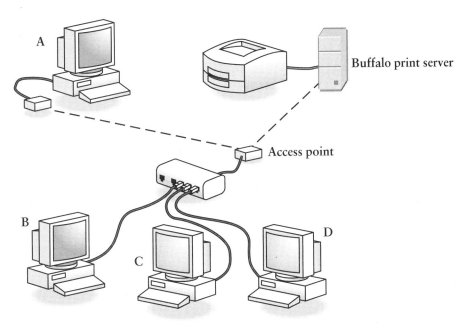

Figure 10-8.
Using a wireless print server in infrastructure mode.

Setting up the AirStation Print Server for infrastructure mode takes a few steps. You must configure one wireless computer with the IPX/SPX protocol for peer-to-peer communications using no WEP code. You can then connect to the print server to set it for infrastructure mode and enter the WEP code used by the wireless network. Finally, reset the computer to infrastructure mode and restore the WEP code.

If you want to use the NetBEUI protocol for printing, that's all the setup required. An icon for the printer appears in Network Neighborhood, and you can assign it to a printer the same way you would for other NetBEUI print servers.

If you want to use the TCP/IP protocol for printing, you have to use the software provided with the server to set its IP address and subnet mask. You then use the software to add a new network client to the computer, TCP/IP Network Printing, which adds a printer port for the server's IP address. The port will then appear as an icon in Network Neighborhood that you can select as the port for your printer.

The Bottom Line

Sharing printers on a network can be a great time-saver and step-saver. You'll no longer need to carry a disk to another computer to print a document or carry a printer to another computer. With Windows, you don't have to purchase any additional software or hardware unless you want to connect your printer directly to the network.

Sharing files and printers isn't the only benefit of connecting computers on a network, however. You'll learn in the next chapter that you can use your network to share an Internet account and a single modem (DSL, cable, or dial-up) with every member of the family.

Chapter 11

Going Online Through the Network

One great advantage of connecting your home computers through a network is that it allows you to share one modem and one Internet account with everyone in the household. You can look up stock quotes, for example, while someone else is downloading software or surfing the Web for fun or profit.

If you're still using a dial-up modem, sharing means that you'll need only one phone line. No more waiting until someone else in the house goes offline before you can connect. If you have a broadband account, everyone in the house can take advantage of the high speed that cable and digital subscriber line (DSL) modems provide.

Note

With modem-sharing now so easy and popular, many Internet service providers (ISPs) have fine-tuned the small print in their customer agreements to discourage simultaneous sharing of an account. Many ISPs, however, will allow you to share an access line for an additional charge.

Sharing a phone line is especially useful when one computer on the network has a modem that's faster than the others, such as a 56-kilobit-per-second (Kbps) modem or an ultrafast DSL or cable modem. When you're connected on a network, you don't need a modem on more than one machine. All the computers on the network can share the high-speed modem that's connected to a single computer.

When a modem is shared on a network, only one user is logged on, and that user can be anyone on the network. Other users who want to access the Internet piggyback onto the existing connection through the network. As far as the ISP is concerned, only one person is logged on.

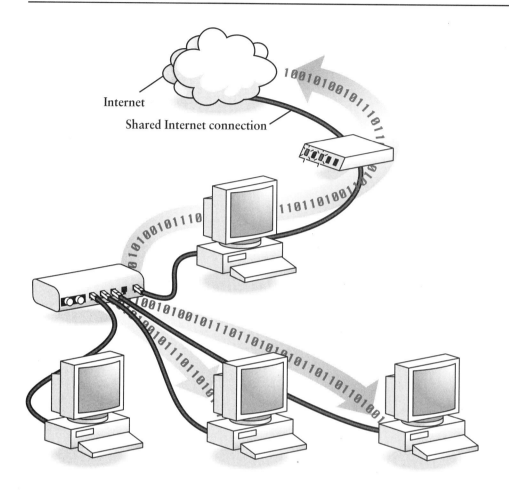

Internet Sharing Alternatives

You can share a modem and an Internet account in two basic ways—by using software or by using hardware.

When you use software to share a modem, you have to designate one computer on the network as the *host*. The other computers on the network, called the *clients*, will then share the host computer's modem. The Internet Connection Sharing feature of Windows and the modem-sharing programs described in this chapter reconfigure the network to accept Internet requests from the client computers and channel them to the shared modem on the host computer. The host computer's modem connects to the Internet; the client computers are reconfigured to connect to the ISP through the host rather than through their own dial-up connections and modems.

If the host computer is already online, a client computer can go online without dialing. If the host computer is turned on but isn't online, the client computer requests that the host computer make the connection so the client can access the Internet through the host's modem.

The shared modem can be any of the following types:

- A standard modem

- An Integrated Services Digital Network (ISDN) modem

- A DSL modem

- A cable modem

The main disadvantage of using software to share a modem is that the host computer must be turned on for its modem to be shared. If the computer is turned off, a client computer will get an error message when it tries to connect to the Internet through the host on the network.

You can work around this problem, however. The fastest solution is to go to the room with the shared modem and turn on the computer. An alternative to sharing a modem with software is to buy and install special hardware. You can purchase a local area network (LAN) modem that shares a 56-Kbps dial-up modem with everyone on the network, or a router that shares a dial-up, DSL, cable, or ISDN modem.

Both the LAN modem and router connect directly to the network in much the same way a printer can be connected to a network, as you learned in Chapter 10, "Printing Across the Network." So long as the modem or router and network hub are turned on, anyone on the network can access the Internet at any time.

The downside of LAN modems and routers is cost. Both are more expensive than standard modems, and they can be difficult to set up. In addition, if the router doesn't have built-in firewall protection, you'll need to install firewall software on every computer accessing the Internet so that your network is protected from unauthorized use by outsiders. A *firewall* prevents unauthorized outsiders from getting into your computer from the Internet.

Getting Ready to Share a Modem

If you're considering using software to share an Internet connection, make sure that the modem on the host computer works and that you can use the host computer to connect to the Internet. The network connections between computers must also be working properly. Each computer should be able to see the others in Network Neighborhood (or My Network Places) and communicate with them.

Making Sure TCP/IP Is Installed

Almost all Internet connection sharing requires that you have Transmission Control Protocol/Internet Protocol (TCP/IP) installed on each computer connected to the network. You'll need TCP/IP installed even if it's not the primary protocol you use for the network.

TCP/IP in Windows 95, Windows 98, or Windows Me

To determine whether TCP/IP drivers are installed on computers running Microsoft Windows 95, Windows 98, or Windows Millennium Edition (Me), follow these steps:

1. On the Start menu, point to Settings, and click Control Panel.

2. In Control Panel, double-click the Network icon.

3. On the Configuration tab of the Network dialog box, look for an entry in the installed network components list showing TCP/IP followed by your network card, as shown below.

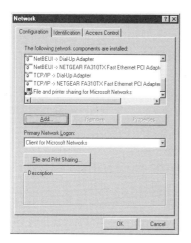

If the listing isn't present, you'll need to install TCP/IP.

See Also

Chapter 7, "Installing the Software," provides complete instructions for setting up a network protocol in the section "Installing Protocols," on page 171.

Here's a quick recap of the steps:

1. In the Network dialog box, click Add.

2. In the Select Network Component Type dialog box, click Protocol, then click Add.

3. In the Select Network Protocol dialog box, choose Microsoft from the list of manufacturers.

4. Select TCP/IP from the Network Protocols list.

5. Click OK to close the Select Network Protocol dialog box.

6. Click OK to close the Network dialog box. You might need to insert your Windows CD at this point so Windows can install the necessary files.

7. Click Yes when you're asked whether to restart your computer.

You'll have to configure TCP/IP, but how you do it depends on the particular software you're using for sharing an Internet connection, and it also depends on whether you're using TCP/IP as your network protocol.

See Also

For more information, consult the section "Configuring TCP/IP," in Chapter 7, "Installing the Software," on page 177.

TCP/IP in Microsoft Windows 2000 or Windows XP

If TCP/IP isn't installed in Windows 2000 or Windows XP, you'll have to install it.

See Also

You'll find complete instructions for setting up a network protocol in the section "Installing Protocols in Windows 2000 or Windows XP," in Chapter 7, "Installing the Software," on page 173.

Here's a brief recap of the steps to determine whether TCP/IP is installed and to install it if necessary:

1. Open the Local Area Connection Properties dialog box as follows:

   • In Windows 2000, on the Start menu, point to Settings, and then click Network And Dial-Up Connections. In the window that appears, right-click the icon for your network adapter, and choose Properties from the shortcut menu.

- In Windows XP, click Start and then My Network Places. Click View Network Connections. Right-click Local Area Connection and choose Properties from the shortcut menu.

    Any installed network protocols and services are listed. If TCP/IP is not installed, you must continue with these steps.

2. Click Install.

3. In the Select Network Component Type dialog box, select Protocol and click Add to open the Select Network Protocol dialog box.

4. Click the TCP/IP protocol in the Network Protocols list.

5. Click OK to close the Select Network Protocol dialog box.

6. Click Close to close the Local Area Connection Properties dialog box.

7. Click Yes if you're asked to restart your computer.

8. Open the Network dialog box again.

    The check mark next to the protocol indicates that the protocol is associated (bound) with your network interface card (NIC).

9. Close both dialog boxes. If you're asked to restart your computer, click Yes.

Using Modem-Sharing Software

Many programs let you share a modem and an Internet connection (subject to the terms of your ISP agreement) over a network. In fact, a modem-sharing feature is built into Windows 98 Second Edition, Windows Me, Windows 2000, and Windows XP. If you have any of these versions of Windows, you don't need to download or purchase additional modem-sharing software. (If you have Windows 95 or the first edition of Windows 98, you'll need to download or purchase a separate modem-sharing program.) You'll also find modem-sharing software in most network starter kits, although the programs vary in the way they are set up.

Some modem-sharing programs are also available as *shareware*, which means that you can download them from the Internet and try them out for free during a trial period. If you like the program, you can then register it for a fee. When you register, you'll get a password or serial number that enables the program to work beyond the trial period.

For information on modem-sharing programs for use with Windows 95 and other versions of Windows, refer to the section "Other Software Solutions for Internet Connection Sharing," later in this chapter.

Internet Sharing in Windows 98 or Windows Me

Internet Connection Sharing is a feature of Windows 98 Second Edition and Windows Me, but it isn't installed automatically when you install or upgrade to these Windows versions. You'll need to add it as an additional component to the Windows installation on the computer you plan to use as the host. Here's how to do it:

1. Make sure the Windows 98 Second Edition or Windows Me CD is in your CD-ROM drive.

2. On the Start menu, point to Settings, then click Control Panel.

3. In Control Panel, double-click the Add/Remove Programs icon.

4. In the list of components on the Windows Setup tab, click Internet Tools (or Communications in Windows Me) to select it, as shown below. Don't clear the check box to the left of Internet Tools or Communications.

5. Click the Details button to see a list of the items in the Internet Tools or Communications category, as shown in Figure 11-1.

Figure 11-1.

Select Internet Connection Sharing from the list of components in the Internet Tools dialog box in Windows 98 Second Edition.

6. In the list of components, select the Internet Connection Sharing check box.

7. Click OK to close the Internet Tools or Communications dialog box.

8. Click OK in the Add/Remove Programs Properties dialog box. Windows installs the Internet Connection Sharing feature and then starts a wizard that takes you through the rest of the process.

The wizard changes the IP address of the computer designated as the server to 192.168.0.1 and assumes that your client computers use *dynamic* IP addresses assigned by the Dynamic Host Configuration Protocol (DHCP) each time a computer accesses the Internet, rather than *static* IP addresses that you assign and always stay the same. If you set up your network so that computers obtain their TCP/IP addresses automatically, they'll all be able to communicate after you install Internet Connection Sharing.

If you're using static TCP/IP addresses that you entered, however, Internet Connection Sharing might no longer be able to communicate with the other computers on the network. When you configure the client computers, as explained in the section "Setting Up the Client Computers," later in this chapter, they'll be set to automatic IP addresses so your network will work again.

If you want to use static network addresses with Internet Connection Sharing using Windows 98 Second Edition or Windows Me, see the section "Static Network Addresses for Windows 98 or Windows Me," later in this chapter.

The Windows 98 Second Edition and Windows Me wizards are different, so we'll look at each one individually.

Windows 98 Second Edition

Installing Internet Connection Sharing in Windows 98 Second Edition displays the Internet Connection Sharing Wizard, which starts the process of setting up connection sharing.

1. Read the information on the opening page and then click Next.

2. Make sure the adapter you want to use for the connection is selected. Click Next on the next page. The wizard explains that it will create a floppy disk to set up the client computers for Internet sharing through the host computer.

3. Click Next.

4. Insert a formatted floppy disk that has at least 200 kilobytes (KB) of space into your floppy disk drive, and then click OK.

5. When the wizard tells you to do so, remove the disk, and then click OK.

6. Click Finish.

7. Click Yes when you're asked whether to restart the computer.

Windows Me

Installing Internet Connection Sharing in Windows Me starts the Home Networking Wizard, shown in Figure 11-2.

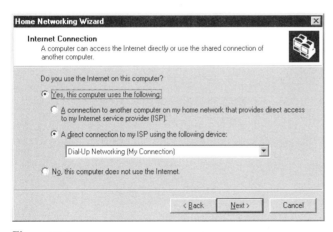

Figure 11-2.

Configuring your computer as the host.

1. Click Next on the first page of the wizard.

2. Because you'll be using this computer as the sharing host, select the option A Direct Connection To My ISP Using The Following Device.

3. Display the device list and select your Internet dial-up networking account.

4. Click Next.

5. You'll be asked whether you want other computers on the network to share this computer's Internet connection. Click Yes and then choose your network interface from the list box.

6. Click Next.

7. You'll be asked whether you want to create a home networking setup disk. You need to create this disk only if you want to share the connection with a computer running Windows 95 or Windows 98. If you want to share the connection, click Yes, click Next, and continue with the next steps. Otherwise, click No to complete the wizard.

8. Insert a formatted floppy disk into your floppy disk drive, and then click Next.

9. Click OK in the message box that appears.

    Windows now creates the setup disk for other computers on your network.

You'll learn how to use the disk in the section "Setting Up the Client Computers," later in this chapter.

Adjusting Internet Connection Sharing

After you install Internet Connection Sharing, you can make the following adjustments to its settings:

- Turn Internet Connection Sharing on or off.

- Place an icon for changing Internet Connection Sharing in the system tray.

- Select which connection the host will use to access the Internet if you have more than one Internet account.

- Choose which NIC to use for the network if you have more than one.

    To change any of these settings, follow these steps:

1. On the Start menu, point to Settings, and then click Control Panel.

2. In Control Panel, double-click the Internet Options icon.

3. In the Internet Properties dialog box, click the Connections tab.

4. Click Sharing in the Local Area Network (LAN) Settings section of the dialog box.

5. Change options in the Internet Connection Sharing dialog box, and then click OK. If you choose to show the icon on the taskbar, you can right-click the taskbar icon to see a shortcut menu, as shown below.

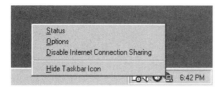

You can then choose Status to see which computers are sharing the Internet connection, or choose Options to change your connection and NIC. If you find that sharing your connection significantly slows Web surfing or program downloading, you might want to turn off Internet Connection Sharing. To do so, select the Disable Internet Connection Sharing option.

Setting Up the Client Computers

After you've installed Internet Connection Sharing on the host computer, the next step is to configure each client computer to access the Internet through the network rather than through its own dial-up connection and modem. But first, you need to set up each client computer so that its TCP/IP gets an IP address automatically. Here's how:

1. On the Start menu of each client computer, point to Settings, and then click Control Panel.

2. In Control Panel, double-click the Network icon.

3. On the Configuration tab of the Network dialog box, select the TCP/IP listing for your NIC.

4. Click Properties.

5. On the IP Address tab of the TCP/IP Properties dialog box, select Obtain An IP Address Automatically.

6. Click the WINS Configuration tab, shown in Figure 11-3.

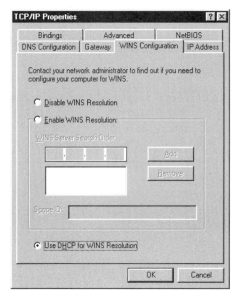

Figure 11-3.

The WINS Configuration tab of the TCP/IP Properties dialog box.

7. Make sure the Use DHCP For WINS Resolution option is selected. (The Disable WINS Resolution option must be selected before you can choose this option.)

8. Click the Gateway tab.

9. Make sure the Installed Gateways list is empty. If you see entries in the Installed Gateways list, select each entry and then click Remove.

10. Click the DNS Configuration tab.

11. Make sure the Disable DNS option is selected.

12. Click OK.

13. Click OK to close the Network dialog box.

14. Click Yes when you're asked whether to restart your computer.

Running the Internet Connection Setup Wizard

When you installed Internet Connection Sharing on the host computer, you created a floppy disk containing a program that configures client computers. You now need to use this disk to configure each of the client computers so that they access the Internet through the network.

Note

If the host and client computers are running Windows Me, you don't need to use the floppy disk. Start the Home Networking Wizard by double-clicking My Network Places on the Windows Me desktop and then double-clicking Home Networking Wizard. Choose the first option under Yes in the initial dialog box: A Connection To Another Computer On My Home Network That Provides Direct Access To My Internet Service Provider. Click Next and complete the wizard.

Configure the computers on your network by performing the following steps:

1. Start the host computer and use it to connect to the Internet.

2. Insert the disk into the floppy drive of a client computer.

3. On the Start menu, click Run.

4. In the Run dialog box, type **A:\Icsclset.exe** if you used Windows 98 Second Edition; type **A:\Setup.exe** if you used Windows Me. Click OK.

5. Click Next until the last wizard page appears, and then click Finish.

6. Repeat the process on each client computer.

Once you've configured the client computers, you'll be able to access the Internet from any of them through the host computer's modem. If, however, you try to connect to the Internet from a client computer and receive an error message, the host computer might be turned off. In this case, you can change the client computer's settings to connect through its modem rather than through the host's. How you perform this task depends on your browser. In Microsoft Internet Explorer, follow these steps:

1. Right-click the Internet Explorer icon on the client's desktop and choose Properties from the shortcut menu. If there's no icon, double-click the Internet Options icon in Control Panel.

2. Click the Connections tab.

3. In Internet Explorer 5, select Always Dial My Default Connection. You can also click Setup and use the Internet Connection Wizard to select your dial-up connection. In Internet Explorer 4, select Connect To The Internet Using A Modem on the Connections tab, or click Connect to start the wizard.

The Browser Connection Setup Wizard doesn't change the settings of other programs that access your ISP, including e-mail programs such as Outlook Express. If you want these programs to connect through the network as well, you have to change their setup. Most of these programs have a dialog box or menu option that allows you to specify a type of connection. As an example, let's run through the process for the Microsoft Outlook Express program.

Click the Outlook Express icon on the taskbar, or start the program as you would normally, and then follow these steps:

1. From the Tools menu, choose Accounts.

2. In the Internet Accounts dialog box, click your account, and then click Properties.

3. On the Connection tab of the Properties dialog box, click Always Connect To This Account Using.

4. Click the down arrow next to the drop-down list and choose Local Area Network.

5. Click OK.

6. Repeat the process for each account and then click Close to close the Internet Accounts dialog box.

Note

Versions of Outlook Express earlier than 5 have an option button on the Connection tab that you can click to connect through the network.

Static Network Addresses in Windows 98 and Windows Me

Internet Connection Sharing is set by default to use dynamic IP addresses. If you want to specify IP addresses on the client computers, you'll need to assign them addresses in the range 192.168.0.2 to 192.168.0.253 and with the subnet address of 255.255.255.0, as explained in the section "Configuring TCP/IP" in Chapter 7, "Installing the Software," on page 177.

First, however, you'll need to know the Domain Name System (DNS) server address that your ISP uses. If you don't know this number, follow these steps:

1. Connect to the Internet on the computer serving as the Internet Connection Sharing host.

2. Click Start and then click Run on the taskbar.

3. Type **winipcfg** and click OK to see the box shown on page 337.

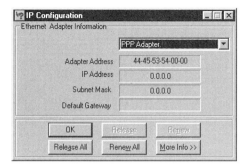

4. From the drop-down list at the top of the box, select ICShare Adapter.

5. Click More Info>> and write down the DNS server address that appears.

6. Click OK, and then disconnect from the Internet.

You can now configure the client computers to connect to the Internet through the Internet Connection Sharing host computer. On each client computer, follow these steps:

1. Open Control Panel and double-click Network.

2. Click the Identification tab.

3. Write the name in the Computer Name box. Names are case-sensitive, so copy the name exactly.

4. Click the Configuration tab.

5. Double-click the TCP/IP setting that's followed by the name of your NIC.

6. On the IP Address tab, select Specify An IP Address.

7. Enter an IP address in the range from 192.168.0.2 through 192.168.0.253—making sure that no other computer on the network is using the address you've chosen.

8. Enter the subnet mask **255.255.255.0**.

9. Click the DNS Configuration tab.

10. Click Enable DNS.

11. In the Host box, enter the name of the computer that you copied in step 3.

12. In the DNS Search Order box, type your ISP's DNS server address, and click Add.

13. Click the Gateway tab.

14. In the New Gateway box, enter **192.168.0.1** and click Add.

15. Click OK twice and then click Yes to restart your computer.

Disabling DHCP

If Internet Connection Sharing doesn't seem to work in Windows 98 Second Edition after you assign static addresses, you should disable the Dynamic Addressing feature. Follow these steps to perform this task in Windows 98 Second Edition:

1. Using the computer that will be the Internet Connection Sharing server, insert the Windows 98 Second Edition CD into the CD-ROM drive.

2. Double-click My Computer, right-click the Windows 98 CD, and choose Open from the shortcut menu.

3. Go to the Tools\Mtsutil\Ics folder.

4. Right-click the file Dhcp_off.inf and click Install on the shortcut menu.

5. Restart your computer.

Connecting to the Internet Through Internet Connection Sharing

When you're ready to connect to the Internet, start your browser as you normally would. If you're on a client computer, it'll connect through the network, dialing the modem on the host computer if the host isn't already connected.

Note

If you get an error saying that the site can't be found in your browser when it first connects through the server, enter the address of a site you want to access in the browser's address box and press Enter.

If you're on the host computer, don't disconnect from the Internet unless you're certain no one else is connected through the network.

To check whether anyone is online, use the Sharing option to place the icon in the system tray, the area of the taskbar adjacent to the clock. Then right-click the Internet Connection Sharing icon in the system tray, and choose Status. A box appears reporting the number of computers using the connection. The number includes your own computer even if you aren't connected, so don't disconnect if the number is greater than 1. If you do, you'll disconnect the other members of your family who are connected.

If no one else is connected to the Internet, you can disconnect. If you're used to seeing a message asking whether you want to disconnect when you close your browser, don't be surprised if it no longer appears. The message is turned off to avoid disconnecting when someone else is using the modem.

Internet Connection Sharing in Windows 2000

Internet Connection Sharing is installed automatically when you install Windows 2000 on your computer. You have to enable sharing, however, before other network users can access the modem and Internet account. To enable Internet Connection Sharing on your computer, you must be logged on as a member of the Administrators group.

To enable Internet Connection Sharing, follow these steps:

1. Open Control Panel and double-click Network And Dial-Up Connections.

2. Right-click your dial-up connection and choose Properties from the shortcut menu.

3. Click the Sharing tab and select the check box labeled Enable Internet Connection Sharing For This Connection, as shown in Figure 11-4.

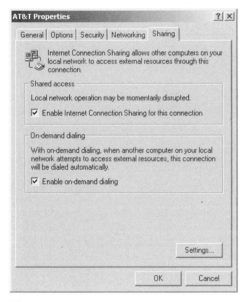

Figure 11-4.
Enabling Internet Connection Sharing in Windows 2000.

Note

If you have more than one network adapter in your computer, the Sharing tab contains a list box labeled For Local Network. In this list box, select the adapter connected to your LAN.

4. Select the check box labeled Enable On-Demand Dialing if you want network computers to use this connection for all their dial-up needs.

5. Click OK. A box appears warning you that the IP address of the computer will be changed to 192.168.0.1.

6. Click Yes.

   To use Internet Connection Sharing with the default settings, the other computers on the network can't use static IP addresses. Merely configure their TCP/IP settings to obtain an IP address automatically. *If you want to use a static address, see the section "Static Network Addresses in Windows 2000 or Windows XP," later in this chapter.*

Internet Connection Sharing in Windows XP

Internet Connection Sharing is installed automatically when you install Windows XP on your computer. You must enable sharing, however, before other network users can access the modem and Internet account.

You can set up to share the Internet by running the Network Setup Wizard or by changing Windows XP settings. Using the wizard is recommended for all but the most experienced Windows users.

See Also

For more details on using this wizard, see the section "The Windows XP Network Setup Wizard" in Chapter 7, "Installing the Software," on page 166.

To use the Network Setup Wizard in Windows XP, follow these steps:

1. Click Start and then click My Network Places. Click View Network Connections. (If My Network Places is not visible, select My Computer, then select My Network Places.)

2. Click Set Up A Home Network Or Small Office Network.

3. Click Next twice.

4. Select the option This Computer Connects Directly To The Internet. The Other Computers On My Network Connect To The Internet Through This Computer.

5. Click Next. You'll see a list of network connections.

6. Choose the dial-up account if you have an analog modem, or select the Ethernet connection for your broadband modem.

7. Click Next.

8. Enter the name for the computer, and click Next.

9. Enter the workgroup name.

   Windows XP uses the default name MSHOME. Other versions of Windows use the name Workgroup. If you're connecting to a network of other Windows versions, enter **Workgroup** (or the workgroup name, if it is different), and click Next. You'll see a summary of the settings.

10. Click Next.

    Windows now takes a few moments to set up networking on your computer. You're then given options for creating a setup disk for other systems on the network.

11. If you want the wizard to automatically set up other Windows 95, Windows 98, Windows Me, or Windows 2000 computers for your network, choose Create A Network Setup Disk. Otherwise, click Just Finish The Wizard; I Don't Need To Run The Wizard On Other Computers.

12. Click Next and then click Finish.

    The wizard sets the IP address of the computer to 192.168.0.1.

To set up Windows XP for sharing manually, follow these steps:

1. In Windows XP, click Start and then My Network Places. Click View Network Connections.

2. Right-click the icon for your Internet connection and select Properties from the shortcut menu.

3. Click the Advanced tab to see the options shown in Figure 11-5.

Figure 11-5.
Enabling Internet Connection Sharing in Windows XP.

4. Select all three check boxes in the Internet Connection Sharing section of the dialog box.

5. Select the check box in the Internet Connection Firewall section.

6. Click OK. A box appears warning you that the IP address of the computer will be changed to 192.168.0.1.

7. Click Yes.

Setting Up Client Computers for Windows 2000 or Windows XP Sharing

Now you're ready to set up the computers that will be sharing your Internet account. If you're using Windows 2000, set its TCP/IP protocol to get its IP address automatically, as you learned in the section "Configuring TCP/IP in Windows 2000" in Chapter 7, "Installing the Software," on page 181.

If you're using Windows XP, you can set up sharing by running the Network Setup Wizard. First, make sure that the computer set as the Internet Connection Sharing host is turned on. Then run the wizard, select the option This Computer Connects To The Internet Through Another Computer On My Network Or Through A Residential Gateway, and then complete the wizard as described previously. The client will be set up to get its IP address from the host computer and share its Internet account.

Static Network Addresses in Windows 2000 or Windows XP

Using the Windows XP Network Setup Wizard to set up Internet Connection Sharing sets the host computer's IP address as 192.168.0.1 and sets the client computers to obtain their IP addresses automatically. In Windows 2000, client computers are also usually set for automatic IP addressing. If you want to use static IP addressing in Windows 2000 or Windows XP, you have to make the following changes to the TCP/IP settings of the client computers.

First, open the TCP/IP Properties dialog box of the Internet sharing host computer and write down the host's IP address. In Windows 2000 and Windows XP, you can change the host IP address from the default 192.168.0.1 to another address that fits into the range that the network uses.

Next, open the TCP/IP Properties dialog box of each client computer and make the necessary changes. You do this by performing the following steps:

1. Open the Local Area Connection Properties dialog box by performing either of the following:

   • In Windows 2000, on the Start menu, point to Settings, and then click Network And Dial-Up Connections. In the window that appears, right-click the icon for your network adapter and choose Properties from the shortcut menu.

- In Windows XP, click Start and then My Network Places. Click View Network Connections. Right-click Local Area Connection and choose Properties from the shortcut menu.

2. Select Internet Protocol (TCP/IP) and click Properties. The TCP/IP Properties dialog box appears.

3. Select Use The Following IP Address.

4. Enter the IP address that you want to assign the client and a subnet mask of 255.255.255.0. If the host's IP address is 192.168.0.1, the client computers' IP addresses must be in the range 192.168.0.2 to 192.168.0.255.

5. In the Default Gateway section, enter the IP address of the host computer.

6. Select the option Use The Following DNS Server Addresses.

7. In the Preferred DNS Server section, enter the IP address of the host.

8. Click OK. A complete setting appears, as shown in Figure 11-6.

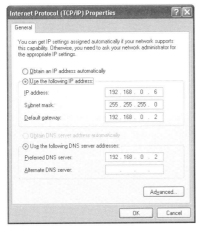

Figure 11-6.

Setting static addresses in Windows XP.

Disconnecting from the Internet

If you're sharing a dial-up Internet account, as compared to an "always on" broadband connection, you have to consider how to disconnect the line.

In Windows 95, Windows 98, Windows Me, or Windows 2000, you'll need to disconnect through the host computer. To accomplish this, you must go to the host computer and break the connection by right-clicking the icon in the system tray on the right of the Windows taskbar that represents the active connection and selecting Disconnect from the shortcut menu.

In Windows XP, however, you can disconnect from the client computer. Click Start and then My Network Places, and then click View Network Connections. You'll see an icon representing the shared Internet connection, shown below.

Right-click the icon and choose Disconnect from the shortcut menu. Just keep in mind that this action disconnects the line on the host, closing the connection for anyone else using the shared connection at that time.

Other Software Solutions for Internet Connection Sharing

Other software solutions for sharing an Internet connection are similar in concept to Internet Connection Sharing in Windows, but they're set up differently. Table 11-1 lists some of the Internet Connection Sharing programs you can download from the Internet.

Table 11-1. Other Internet Connection Sharing Software

Software	Internet Address
aVirt Soho Server	*http://www.avirt.com*
Internet Gate	*http://www.maccasoft.com*
MidPoint	*http://www.midcore.com*
PPPShar	*http://www.pppindia.com*
RideWay	*http://www.itserv.com*
SyGate	*http://www.sygate.com*

All these programs require that TCP/IP be installed on the computers on the network and that you install their Internet sharing software on the host computer. The main difference among the programs is how the client computers are configured to access the shared modem.

Using Internet Sharing Hardware

As an alternative to using software to share an Internet connection, you can purchase a *router*—hardware that provides a modem-sharing solution. Most routers are designed to share a broadband modem, but others also share an external 56 Kbps analog modem or even have an analog modem built in.

When you use a router, you set up your hardware so that the router is turned on whenever your network hub or switch is turned on. That way, the modem will be available to everyone on the network all the time regardless of which computers on the network are turned on.

In addition, many routers let you create a firewall between your network and the Internet. The router can prevent unauthorized access to your network by hackers, and it can control the type of access allowed to each family member. As you can with some of the Internet Connection Sharing software, you can limit a family member to only sending and receiving e-mail, for example, without allowing him or her to surf the Internet. Some router models also let you use Web content filtering to control the type of sites your family members can access. These models are ideal if you'd like to limit access to gaming, auction, and other sites that you feel aren't appropriate for younger members of the family.

Sharing a Dial-Up Modem

If you connect to the Internet over the telephone through a dial-up account, consider a *LAN modem*: a router with a 56-Kbps modem built into it.

The OfficeConnect LAN modem from 3Com *(http://www.3com.com)*, for example, also includes its own four-port hub, which allows it to serve as the network's modem and hub at the same time. After connecting the device, you can set it up just by starting your browser and connecting to a configuration Web page that's stored within the modem, as shown in Figure 11-7. Use the information on the Web page to set up the modem for your ISP.

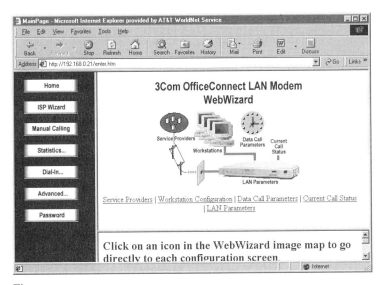

Figure 11-7.

Configuring the 3COM OfficeConnect LAN modem.

As an alternative, consider a broadband router that has the ability to share a dial-up line. If you don't yet have a broadband account, you can use the router to share a dial-up line. Once you get broadband, use the same router for your high-speed Internet, with the dial-up ability as a backup if your broadband service goes down.

Broadband routers that let you connect an external modem to the router's serial port are made by U.S. Robotics, SMC Networks, Asanté Technologies, and others. The ORiNOCO Residential Gateway, a wireless router, has a built-in 56-Kbps modem, so no external modem is required for dial-up Internet. *In the section "Sharing Broadband Internet," later in this chapter, we'll look at several routers that let you share a dial-up modem.*

If you already have an external modem, you can purchase a device called a *modem server* that, in effect, turns your external modem into a LAN modem. In that setup, the server connects to the network and your modem connects to the server. A modem server doesn't usually have its own modem built in, but some models provide that option. Companies such as Atronics, Lantronix, Netgear, and others make a variety of models. A modem server, however, is more expensive than a LAN modem, and you still need to connect it to an external modem.

Sharing Broadband Internet

Both DSL and cable modems offer speed that makes the Internet a great experience. You can download files in just minutes and watch videos online as if you were watching television. If you're networked, you can share the high-speed DSL or cable modem with everyone, and there are several ways to do it.

The easiest way to share a high-speed modem is to connect the modem to one computer and use Internet Connection Sharing software, as explained earlier in this chapter. The computer to which the modem is attached becomes the host; the other computers are the clients. The host computer must have two Ethernet connections: one for the network, and another for the modem. The disadvantage is that the computer to which the modem is attached must be running for anyone on the network to access the modem.

As an alternative, you can connect the modem directly to the network. How you connect it, however, depends on the number of IP accounts you purchase from your ISP.

DSL and cable modems communicate on the Internet through an IP address. When the ISP connects the modem to your computer, it assigns the computer a unique IP address that is either static or dynamic, and which identifies your computer on the Internet.

Most DSL and cable ISPs let you connect the modem directly to a network hub or switch, as shown in Figure 11-8. However, you'll need to pay a monthly fee for an IP address for each computer that you want to access the Internet.

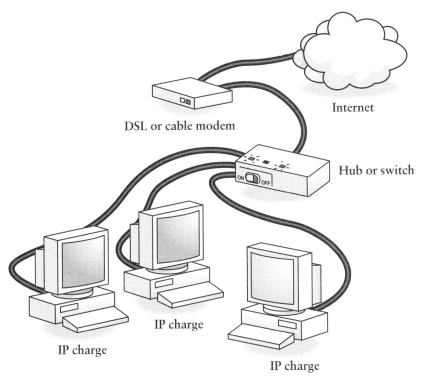

Figure 11-8.
Connecting a broadband modem to the hub requires multiple IP addresses.

If you want to connect your modem to the network but not pay for additional IP addresses, you'll need a *broadband router (residential gateway)*, a device that lets everyone on a network access the same DSL or cable modem. You connect the router to the network hub or switch, and then connect the modem to the router, as illustrated in Figure 11-9. You have to pay for only one IP address, as if the modem were connected directly to a computer.

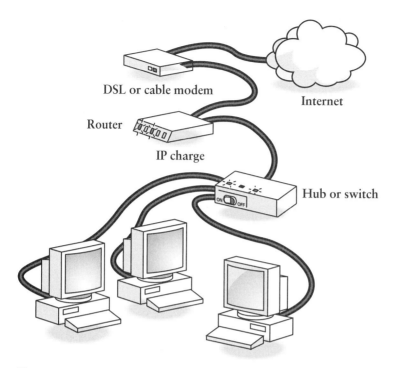

Figure 11-9.

Using a broadband router avoids extra IP charges.

Routers work using a system called *network address translation* (NAT). When a computer makes a request to display an Internet site, the router replaces the IP address of the network computer with the IP address assigned by the ISP and retrieves the site from the Internet. As far as the ISP is concerned, the IP address of the computer making the request is always the same regardless of which computer on the network is accessing it.

A number of companies manufacture routers, and the setup and configuration of the different routers vary. In general, you transfer the settings provided by your ISP from your computer to the router. You then set up the computer to access the Internet through the router. You typically perform this procedure in four steps:

1. Install the router on your hub or switch.

2. Connect the modem to the router.

3. If your ISP assigns you an IP address dynamically, you set the router for dynamic addressing. If the ISP assigns you a static IP address, you configure the router with the same address that your ISP assigned to your computer during installation.

4. You use the DHCP service provided with the router to assign IP addresses to all your computers on the network, or you manually assign IP addresses in the proper range to each of your computers.

We'll look at several broadband routers that work with both DSL and cable modems to illustrate their various features. After installing and configuring either router, everyone on your network can share the high-speed connection.

Broadband routers exist for both wired Ethernet and wireless networks.

- A wired router connects to the hub or switch, and it can be shared by all network computers. If you also have some wireless computers on your network, you'll need a separate access point to link the wireless computers with the network to share the wired router.

- A wireless router can be used by all wireless computers, and by wired computers if the router contains at least two Ethernet connections.

See Also

For more information about connecting access points and gateways, see Chapter 6, "Connecting Your Network."

Most routers let you use their built-in DHCP server or assign your computers static IP addresses. The first step is to get your computers to communicate with the router. You usually accomplish this task by setting one computer to automatic addressing to get its IP from the router's DHCP server, or by setting the computer's IP to one in the router's range. The instructions for the router tell you the default IP address. Once you're communicating with the router, you use its internal Web page, or a special setup program provided with the router, to change its network IP and set up its WAN port for your ISP.

If you continue to use the router's DHCP function, set every computer in the network to get its IP address automatically. If you turn off the router's DHCP server, you need to adjust the client computers. Using the appropriate directions given in either "Static Network Addresses in Windows 98 or Windows Me" or "Static Network Addresses in Windows 2000 or Windows XP," earlier in this chapter, set the gateway to the IP address of the router and set the DNS server to the DNS address assigned by your ISP.

Routers for Wired Networks

Let's first look at some routers designed for wired Ethernet networks. You can use these routers for wireless networks if you have a wireless access point.

The Asanté FriendlyNET Cable/DSL Router   The Asanté FriendlyNET router from Asanté Technologies (*http://www.asante.com*) comes in several varieties, with models having both a dial-up modem serial port and a built-in print server. All of these models have a four-port Ethernet switch and a separate WAN connection for your broadband modem.

Note

Asanté also sells a wireless router.

The Asanté is remarkably easy to install and set up. Just follow these steps:

1. Using the instructions in the Asanté manual, record your computer's TCP/IP settings that have already been set to use the broadband modem directly connected to that computer.

2. Set up one computer on the network to get its LAN IP address automatically.

3. Connect the router to a computer or to another hub or switch to which the computer is connected.

4. Connect the broadband modem to the WAN port of the router, then restart the computer. The router's DHCP server assigns the computer an IP address.

5. Use your Web browser to access the router's built-in Web page at its default IP, *http://192.168.123.254.*

6. After logging on (the default password is admin), click Setup to select the type of Internet account, as shown in Figure 11-10, and then click Save & Next.

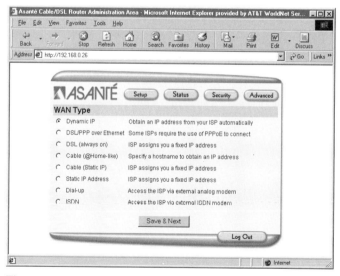

Figure 11-10.
Setting the ISP type with the Asanté FriendlyNET router.

Note

Select the Dial-Up option to use an external analog modem connected to the router's serial port.

7. Enter the information requested on the page that appears.

8. If you want to use static IP addressing for your computers, click the Advanced button on the Asanté Web page. On the page that appears, you can change the router's IP address and turn off its DHCP server.

The router is now ready to share your Internet account with client computers that are configured for it.

The U.S. Robotics Broadband Router   U.S. Robotics (*http://www.usr.com*), known for its modems, markets the Model 8000 broadband router for Internet sharing. The router includes a four-port Ethernet switch as well as a separate WAN connector for your broadband modem. It also includes an uplink port for connecting to another hub or switch, a serial port for an external dial-up modem, and a print server port.

The router is set up through its internal Web page at the default address of 192.168.123.254. To access the Web page and configure your computers, perform the following steps:

1. Set one computer to the router's default IP range (such as 192.168.123.253), and then use your Web browser to go to *http://192.168.123.254*.

2. Log on with the default password admin. The System Status page appears, as shown in Figure 11-11.

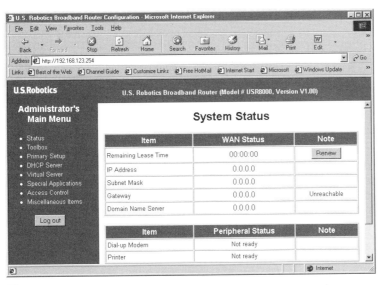

Figure 11-11.

Configuring the U.S. Robotics broadband router.

3. Click Primary Setup on the Administrator's Main Menu, shown below, to change the router's LAN IP address, to select the WAN type from the available options, and to configure the broadband connection.

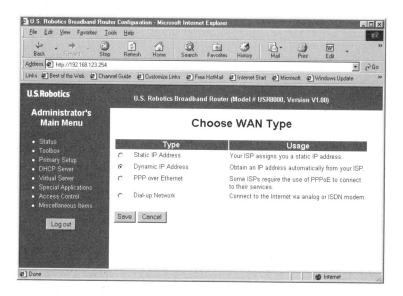

Note

Select Dial-Up Network to use an analog modem connected to the router's serial port.

4. Use the DHCP Server option on the Administrator's Main Menu to turn off the router's DHCP feature if you want to assign static IP addresses to your computers.

The ZyXEL Prestige 310 Router   The ZyXEL Prestige 310 router from ZyXEL Communications (*http://www.zyxel.com*) has two Ethernet ports. Connect one port of the router to your hub or switch; connect the other port to your cable or your DSL modem. The port for your modem is labeled WAN, for wide area network.

Note

Older versions of ZyXEL routers use a special program, called the Prestige Network Commander, for configuration.

The router is set by default at the IP address of 192.168.1.1 and a subnet of 255.255.255.0. Configure your computers as follows:

1. Temporarily set up one computer for dynamic addressing or assign it an IP in the range 192.168.1.2 to 192.168.1.255.

2. Start your Web browser and go to *http://192.168.1.1*.

3. Sign in using the default user name (admin) and password (1234) to access the router's built-in Web page. The page has three main menu options: Wizard Setup, Advanced, and Maintenance.

4. Use the Wizard Setup option to follow a series of windows to set up the router for your ISP.

As an alternative to using the Wizard to configure the router, you can use the Advanced option to set up the router manually in one of two ways:

- By choosing LAN from the Advanced page, you can change the router's local network settings, such as DHCP server status and IP address, as shown in Figure 11-12.

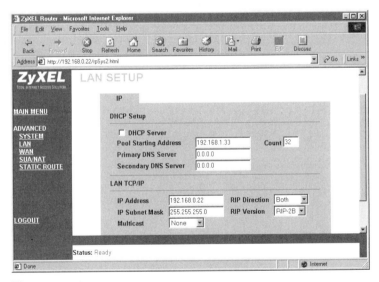

Figure 11-12.
Setting the network IP of the Prestige router.

- The WAN option on the Advanced page lets you set up the router for your ISP, as shown in Figure 11-13. Start by selecting the overall type of service from the Encapsulation list. The appropriate options will display for that type of service. Then use the ISP, IP, and MAC tabs to configure the router as necessary.

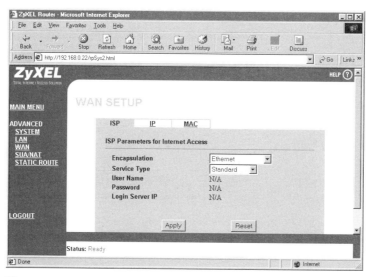

Figure 11-13.

Configuring the Prestige router for your ISP.

The Netopia 9100 Router   The Netopia 9100 router from Netopia (*http:// www.netopia.com*) includes its own eight-port Ethernet hub that lets you perform both the hub and routing functions. Plug the Ethernet cable from each computer into the router's ports, and plug your DSL or cable modem into the port provided for it on the router. If you already have a hub or switch that you want to continue using, connect it to the router's uplink port.

The router includes an installation and configuration program called SmartStart. The program guides you through the setup process using either a dynamic or fixed IP Internet address, and either a dynamic or fixed network address. When you start the program, for example, you'll be asked whether you want to perform the Easy installation using the default router address and settings, or the Advanced installation. If you select Advanced, you'll be able to enter the IP address you want to assign to the router on the network, as shown in Figure 11-14.

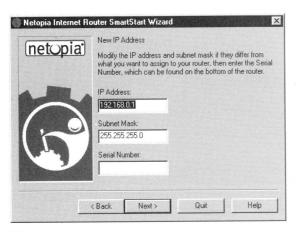

Figure 11-14.
Setting the IP of the Netopia router.

The WatchGuard SOHO Router   The WatchGuard SOHO router from WatchGuard Technologies (*http://www.watchguard.com*) includes its own four-port Ethernet hub, in addition to a WAN port for your DSL or cable modem. There's no uplink port to connect the router to another hub, but you can use a crossover cable between two regular ports, or a patch cable between the router and an uplink port on another hub. To set up the router, you connect it to your network and then connect to the WatchGuard installation site on the Internet (*http://www.watchguard.com/pubs/install*) and get complete instructions for configuring your network to share the Internet. Perform the configuration by doing the following steps:

1. Determine whether your ISP uses a static or dynamic address by using the Network icon in Control Panel to check the TCP/IP properties for the NIC to which the modem is attached to your computer. If the properties show a static IP address, make a note of the address and the subnet mask.

2. Configure your computer to communicate with the router. The router is set by default to obtain its Internet IP address dynamically from your ISP and to serve as a DHCP host to assign IP addresses to computers on the network. You use the Network icon in Control Panel to set your computers to obtain their IP addresses automatically.

3. If your ISP has assigned you a static IP address, set up the router for your ISP by starting your Web browser and entering the router's address, *http://192.168.111.1*, to open a form built into the router, as shown below.

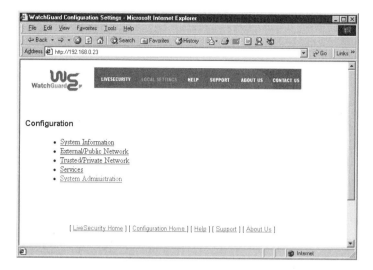

4. Complete the procedure using the following options:

- Use the Trusted/Private Network option to turn off the DHCP server and to change the router's local network address.

- Use the External/Public Network option to set up the router for your ISP by designating the IP address you are assigned.

The WatchGuard router includes a one-year subscription to an online service called LiveSecurity. Once you register your router, WatchGuard periodically provides you with security notices and warnings, software updates, and technical support. The notices include Threat Responses, which are alerts of threats that might require a software update or configuration change, and Virus Alerts, about potentially harmful viruses.

As an option, you can also purchase WebBlocker software, which prevents access to locations that you have placed in a database of questionable sites. The feature is password-controlled, so you can give the password to family members who should have full access to the Internet.

Wireless Routers

If you have wireless computers, or a combination wireless-and-wired network, consider a wireless router. Just keep these points in mind:

- A wireless router that has at least two Ethernet ports can be used as both an access point to link the wireless and wired computers, as well as a gateway for sharing a broadband modem.

- A wireless router with only one Ethernet port can be used only as an access point or as a gateway. This limitation is fine if your network is entirely wireless. If not, you'll need either a separate access point or a wired router, in addition to the wireless router.

The SMC Wireless Barricade   The SMC Wi-Fi 11-Mbps Wireless Barricade from SMC Networks (*http://www.smc.com*) includes a three-port 10/100-Mbps Ethernet switch, a separate Ethernet port for a broadband modem, and a serial port for connecting an external dial-up modem. In addition, the Barricade includes a parallel printer port that lets you share a printer with all network users, both wired and wireless.

To set up the Barricade, configure one computer for an automatic IP address, and then use your Web browser to access the router's built-in Web page, shown in Figure 11-15.

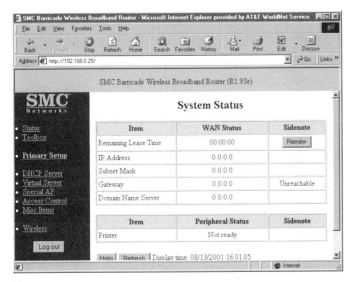

Figure 11-15.
Setting up the SMC Wireless Barricade.

Use the Primary Setup option to configure the router for your network and your ISP, and use the DHCP Server option to turn off the DHCP feature.

The Barricade also offers you the option of Media Access Control (MAC) access filtering. As explained in Chapter 7, "Installing the Software," MAC address filtering lets you specify the MAC addresses of adapters that can connect to the access point. As shown in Figure 11-16, you can enter the MAC address of each client computer and its corresponding IP address. You can also select the Connection Control setting to allow some unspecified MAC addresses to access the router from specific IP addresses.

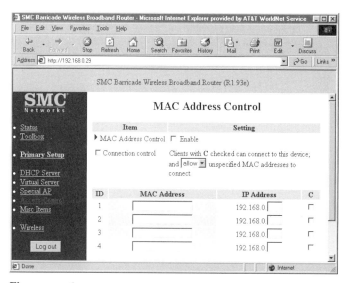

Figure 11-16.
Barricade MAC address filtering.

For example, suppose you have a laptop computer for which you have several wire-less PC Cards. You use only one card at a time, so each card has been set up with the same IP address. Because each card has a different MAC address, you'd want to allow access from any MAC address at that IP to access the router.

Because the Barricade is a wireless router, you'll also need to specify its Wired Equivalent Privacy (WEP) security and encryption code, using the Wireless option on the Web page.

The Buffalo AirStation Router   The Buffalo AirStation WLAR-L11-L from Buffalo Technologies (*http://www.buffalo-technology.com*) includes a Wi-Fi wireless port, a four-port Ethernet switch, and a separate Ethernet connection for a DSL/cable modem.

The router's built-in Web page, shown on page 359, offers two main options: Standard Setup and Custom Setup. The Standard Setup option lets you set a basic configura-tion, including the IP address for the WAN (ISP) and LAN.

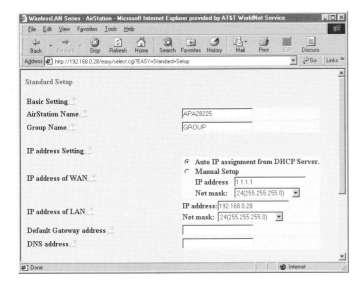

The Custom Setup option presents more advanced configuration choices, as shown in Figure 11-17.

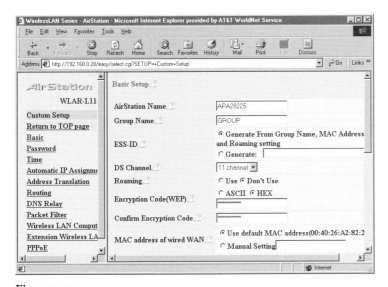

Figure 11-17.

Custom setup options for the Buffalo AirStation.

The wireless settings, for example, let you enter the WEP code as either a passphrase or hex, as shown below.

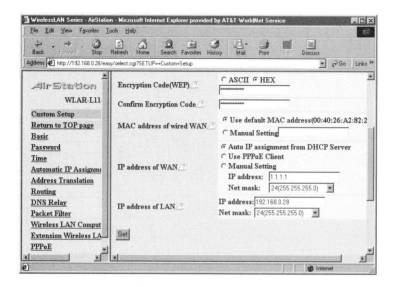

The 2Wire HomePortal Router   The 2Wire HomePortal 100W from 2Wire (*http:// www.2wire.com*) includes a wireless 802.11b port. The device includes an Ethernet port for connection to a computer or Ethernet hub, an Ethernet port for sharing a broadband modem, a universal serial bus (USB) connection to the network through a computer's USB port, and a HomePNA 2 phone network port to communicate with computers using a home phone-line network.

You configure the device by using the HomePortal Setup Wizard, which takes you step by step through the process of setting up the router. As part of the setup, you enter a key code that gives the router information about your ISP. When you order the Home-Portal, you'll be asked some information about your ISP that helps 2Wire create your key code. Otherwise, you can obtain the key code at *http://www.2wire.com/keycode*, as shown in Figure 11-18.

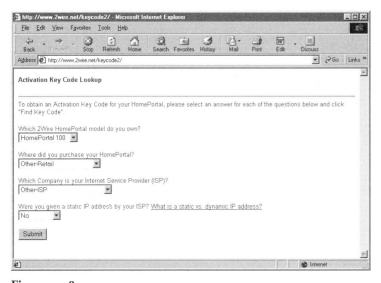

Figure 11-18.
Obtaining the 2Wire HomePortal key code online.

If you don't have access to the Internet when you're setting up the router, or you didn't give 2Wire any information when you ordered the router, use the generic key code on the CD box to set up the router initially, and then use the HomePortal Setup Wizard to complete the configuration.

The ORiNOCO Residential Gateway Router The ORiNOCO Residential Gateway router from Agere Systems (*http://www.wavelan.com*) includes a wireless port but only one Ethernet port for use as either an access point or with a DSL/cable router. To use the router for wired computers, you'll need a separate wireless access point. (The unit also has a built-in 56-KB dial-up modem for those who don't have broadband Internet but still want to share an Internet connection across the wireless network.)

You configure ORiNOCO Residential Gateway by using a setup utility program, shown in Figure 11-19.

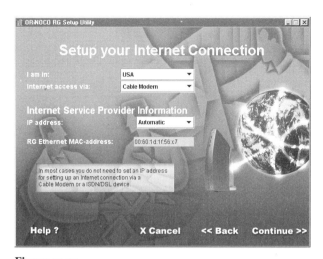

Figure 11-19.
The ORiNOCO Residential Gateway setup utility.

As part of the setup, you can adjust the router's local network and WAN settings, as shown here.

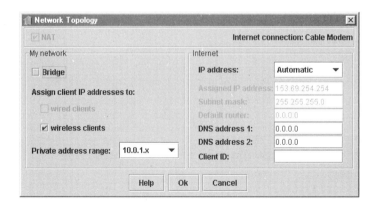

The My Network section, for example, lets you control the router's DHCP server individually for wired and wireless clients. The Internet section determines how your ISP is accessed.

Internet Security

Part of the reason you decided to create a home network is that you want to share your folders or disks with other family members. In Chapter 9, "Learning to Share," you learned how to turn on file sharing so family members could access your computer's resources.

When you connect to the Internet, however, sharing isn't always advisable. Whenever you go online, you open the door to hackers and viruses that have the potential to damage your computer. High-speed Internet is even more susceptible to problems because DSL and cable modems are always connected, and hackers have a better chance of learning your IP address.

When you're networked, the potential damage is even greater. A hacker can reach into not only your own computer, but also into other computers that are connected to your network.

The Windows XP Firewall

Windows XP has its own Internet firewall to protect your network. The firewall keeps track of all traffic from your computers to the Internet, such as requests to display Web pages. Only incoming traffic in response to such requests is allowed past the firewall and into your computers.

When you run the Network Setup Wizard, Windows XP automatically enables the firewall to protect your network. If you didn't use the wizard to set up your network and share the Internet, however, you can enable the firewall manually by following these steps on the computer that is sharing its Internet connection:

1. Click Start and then My Network Places. Click View Network Connections.

2. Right-click the icon for your Internet connection and select Properties from the shortcut menu.

3. Click the Advanced tab.

4. Select the option Protect My Computer And Network By Limiting Or Preventing Access To This Computer From The Internet.

   More advanced users can click the Settings button to control which services are allowed through the firewall.

Turning Off Internet File Sharing

Before using your computer to connect to the Internet, you should turn off file sharing through the TCP/IP protocol that you use for the Internet. In Windows 95, Windows 98, or Windows Me, follow these steps:

1. Open Network in Control Panel.

2. Click TCP/IP –> Dial-Up Adapter on the Configuration tab of the Network box.

3. Click Properties to open the TCP/IP Properties dialog box.

4. Click the Bindings tab.

5. Make sure the check box for the option File And Printer Sharing Using Microsoft Networks is not selected.

6. Click OK twice, and then click Yes if you're asked to restart your computer.

In Windows 2000 or Windows XP, follow these steps to turn off file sharing over the Internet:

1. Open the Local Area Connection Properties dialog box by performing one of the following:

   - In Windows 2000, on the Start menu, point to Settings, and then click Network And Dial-Up Connections. In the window that appears, right-click the icon for your network adapter and choose Properties from the shortcut menu.

   - In Windows XP, click Start and then My Network Places. Click View Network Connections. Right-click Local Area Connection and choose Properties from the shortcut menu.

2. Make sure the check box for the option File And Printer Sharing For Microsoft Networks is not selected.

3. Click OK, and then click Yes if you're asked to restart your computer.

Creating a Firewall

Before connecting to the Internet, especially if you have an "always on" broadband connection, you should have some sort of firewall protection. Internet Explorer has some protection features built in. To access the settings for these features, open the Internet Options icon in Control Panel and click the Security tab to see the options shown in Figure 11-20.

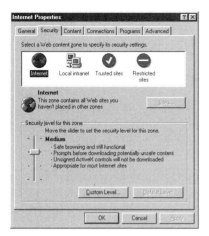

Figure 11-20.

Security settings in Internet Explorer.

At the top of the box are icons representing four zones:

- **Internet**   determines security settings for all sites not in another zone.

- **Local Intranet**   determines security settings for Web pages on your network.

- **Trusted Sites**   determines security settings for Web sites that you know are safe to access.

- **Restricted Sites**   determines security settings for Web sites that you don't trust.

I recommend that you leave the setting for the Internet zone at Medium, the Trusted Sites zone at Low, and the Restricted Sites zone at High. Select a zone and then drag the slider in the Security Level For This Zone section to the level of security that you want. Moving it to the top sets security at High. The High setting provides the maximum security Internet Explorer offers, but it might cause some elements of Web sites to appear incorrectly.

To add a potentially hazardous site to the Restricted Sites zone, follow these steps:

1. Click Restricted Sites.

2. Click the Sites button.

3. In the box that appears, type the address of the site and click Add.

If you know that a particular Web site is safe, you can add it to the Trusted Sites zone by following these steps:

1. Click Trusted Sites.

2. Click the Sites button.

3. In the box that appears, type the address of the trusted site and click Add.

Although these security features are helpful, they can't protect you from all the hazards on the Internet. Programs known as *Trojan horses*, for example, can infiltrate your computer and transmit information about you to the hacker's Web site when you're online. So for greater security, consider any of the many security programs that you can download or purchase, such as Norton Internet Security and ZoneAlarm.

ZoneAlarm, from *http://www.zonelabs.com*, is free for downloading and nonbusiness use. ZoneAlarm, whose opening screen is shown in Figure 11-21, prevents Trojan horses from sending information by prompting you to confirm whenever a program tries to access the Internet. It also prevents Web sites from obtaining information about you through requests to your system, and it can prevent access to the Internet after periods of inactivity.

Figure 11-21.
Using ZoneAlarm for Internet security.

Note

Some Internet security programs might interfere with normal network connections. If you have difficulty accessing a network computer after a security program has been installed on it, disable the program to confirm that it's the cause of the problem. If it is, check the documentation that came with the program for steps to solve the problem.

Router Internet Security

Routers that use Network Address Translation (NAT)—and most of them do—have built-in security because NAT blocks all traffic to your computer except traffic that's in direct response to information from within the network. The router hides the IP address of your computers, so a hacker doesn't know the IP address of the computer actually requesting information; only the router knows.

Most routers also let you fine-tune the firewall by configuring Internet Protocol ports. An *IP port* is an entrance point into your computer. The Internet uses certain ports for specific features. For example, port 80 is used to browse the Internet, 110 is used to receive e-mail, 25 is used to send e-mail, 119 is used to read Internet newsgroups, and 21 is used to transfer files using FTP.

By letting you deny access to these ports for specific IP addresses, you can control which services your computers can access. For example, if you want to allow a computer to browse the Internet but not send and receive e-mail, you would block ports 110 and 25 to that computer.

Routers such as Asanté and U.S. Robotics let you create four groups of users and block or allow specific ports to each group. Figure 11-22, for example, shows the Access Control options of the U.S. Robotics router.

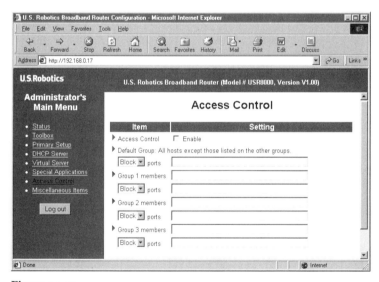

Figure 11-22.
Blocking and allowing ports for groups of users.

The last section of a computer's IP address determines membership in a group. So suppose you want to prevent two specific users from accessing Internet newsgroups and transferring files using the File Transfer Protocol (FTP). The IP addresses of this group are 192.168.0.25 and 192.168.0.26. The settings for this would appear like this.

Group 1 members   25-26

Block ▾ ports   21, 119

As another example, here's a group of 50 users (192.168.0.100 through 192.168.0.149) who can send e-mail (port 25), receive e-mail (port 110), and browse the Internet (port 80), but nothing else.

Group 1 members   100-149

Allow ▾ ports   25,80,110

Finally, use the Default group to assign permissions to every IP not included in another group. This Default group, for example, simply states that any other IP address is not allowed access to any port, so users in that group have no Internet rights.

Default Group: all hosts except those listed on the other groups.

Allow ▾ ports

The WatchGuard router controls ports using a different interface. You use the Services option on the WatchGuard SOHO router's Web page to access the Allowed Incoming Services and Blocked Outgoing Services pages. Using the Blocked Outgoing Services page, shown in Figure 11-23, you select which service you want the router to block from all users. You then use the Allowed Incoming Services page to authorize specific users, by their IP addresses, to access specific ports—opening a hole in your firewall for those users.

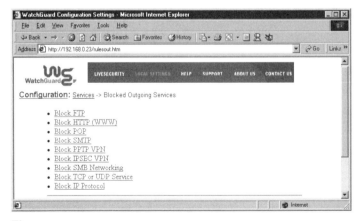

Figure 11-23.
Blocking services using WatchGuard SOHO.

Windows XP and NAT Traversal

NAT is a useful security feature, but it can create some problems. Many popular Internet applications need to access service ports to send and receive information. If you want to manually configure a router to allow controlled access to these ports by specific programs, the procedure can be complicated. In addition, if you incorrectly open a port, you might expose your computer to hackers.

Windows XP supports a feature called *NAT Traversal* that, when combined with compatible routers, automatically configures service ports. Using NAT Traversal, a network-aware application can discover that it's behind a NAT router and automatically configure port mappings so it can communicate with the Internet.

NAT Traversal, however, requires a router that conforms to the Universal Plug and Play Internet Gateway Device (IGD) specification. A number of manufacturers have announced such routers, and even more will be available in the future.

The Bottom Line

By sharing a modem and Internet connection, you can save a lot of money, even if you purchase a LAN modem rather than a purely software solution. You can also avoid having to wait for the telephone line in your home to be free. With the time you save waiting, you can play some of those cool computer games on the network with other members of your family, which is the subject of the next chapter.

Chapter 12

Playing Games

Playing games across a network encourages communication and competition and can be a great stress reliever—especially if you win! But even if you don't win, network game playing can be a great family experience. You can share a virtual world with your family, fighting a common foe or going head-to-head in the spirit of friendly competition.

Solo vs. Network Games

Solo games on a computer can be fun and exhilarating, but you're playing against the computer. The computer represents your foe—whether it's a galactic warrior, a World War II dogfighter, or a chess player at the other end of the board.

Although the computer can make all the right moves to keep a game interesting, it has no personality. When you're playing against a real person, you can try to anticipate your opponent's moves based on previous games or on what you know about his or her way of thinking. Human players provide more drama and a keener sense of competition. You can gently gloat over your win and someone else can gloat when you lose, making rematches all the more interesting.

Because many computer games allow more than two players, several members of the family can play. Usually, in fact, as many people can play as there are computers on your home network. Games that require more players than you have available can sometimes create computer-generated competitors, so you can still practice your skills when other members of the family are busy.

When you don't feel competitive, you can play games that simply allow you to share experiences with other family members. With Microsoft Midtown Madness 2, for example, you and another family member can race each other through detailed models of streets in San Francisco and London.

Preparing for Network Play

You can play hundreds of games over a network. Microsoft Windows 95, Windows 98, and Windows Millennium Edition (Me) even come with one, a game named Hearts. If you purchased a network kit, the accompanying CD might have network games on it, too. Check the documentation that came with the kit for a list of the games, or insert the CD into the drive and browse through its folders to learn which games are included.

Note

Windows 2000 doesn't include any network-enabled games, and Windows XP offers only Internet games, not multiplayer games for a network.

Selecting the proper games for you and your family and installing them on your network are the first steps toward network playing. But before you purchase or install any games, make sure your network is up and running.

To accommodate as many games as possible, you should make sure all three popular protocols are installed: TCP/IP, IPX/SPX, and NetBEUI. Check that all the computers on the network show up in Network Neighborhood (or My Network Places in Windows Me and Windows 2000) and that you can transfer information among them.

Selecting Games for Network Play

When choosing games, make sure that they fit your family's interests and standards and that they can be run on every computer on your network.

Many computer stores offer previews of popular games on special computers set up just for that purpose. You can play the game in the store before purchasing it to see whether it meets your standards. Bring your children with you and let them preview the game as well. You can also visit many sites online to read about games and download demonstration versions, such as *http://gamespot.com/gamespot*.

You also need to make sure that your computers and network are capable of running the game you want. The minimum and recommended hardware requirements are usually listed on the game's box. The minimum requirements are those that are absolutely necessary for the game to run, although its performance might be unsatisfactory. The recommended requirements are those that the game's manufacturer suggests for good game play. The box might also list optional hardware, such as advanced sound and display systems, that will provide higher quality video or audio.

Note

Network play normally requires greater resources than single-player action. For network play, your computers should meet the recommended speed and memory requirements rather than just the minimum requirements.

The following are some of the hardware requirements you'll need to consider:

- **Processor type and speed:** Most of the sophisticated action games require at least a Pentium or a Pentium-compatible processor, running at a certain speed or above. Older Pentiums running at 90 megahertz (MHz) are often too slow for the newest games. In fact, new games are designed for high-speed processors, so don't be surprised to see 300 MHz or more listed as the minimum or recommended processor speed.

- **Amount of RAM:** Some games, especially those with lots of graphics, require 32 megabytes (MB) or more of memory. Microsoft's Midtown Madness, for example, requires 64 MB.

- **Available disk space:** Programs that feature sound and video require a lot of storage space. A typical game might require 40 MB of disk storage or more, even when you run the program from the CD rather than installing it on your hard disk. Some graphics-intensive games require much more space; Midtown Madness, for example, needs at least 200 MB.

- **Sound card:** To hear the sound effects that help make many computer games so exciting, you'll need a sound card and speakers for your computer. Most newer computer systems come with sound cards. Older computers might not be able to generate a game's sounds unless you add a sound card and speakers.

- **Display requirements:** Look on the game's box for the minimum and recommended color and screen resolution settings. Many games require your system to be set at 256 colors or more, with a screen resolution of at least 800 by 600 pixels. In some cases, the game will start with lower settings, but the display won't be very clear. In other cases, you won't be able to start or play the game until the display is adjusted to the minimum settings. Although many games recommend advanced 3D or graphics accelerator cards, they're usually not part of the minimum requirements.

- **Joystick:** For flight simulators, combat games, and other action games, a joystick or yoke is highly recommended. You can still play the game using the keyboard or mouse to control movement, but you won't experience the same sense of control.

If some of your computers don't meet a game's minimum or recommended requirements, consider playing the game on only the computers that do meet them. Or you can use the most advanced computers in the house to play the game on the network, leaving less sophisticated computers for solo action.

Most network games require that a single computer serve as the host, starting and organizing the game, and running its CD while the game is played. (The other computers on the network don't have to run the game CD during play.) For maximum performance, choose as the host the computer with the greatest memory, speed, and storage space.

Installing Games for Network Play

In most cases, you don't have to do anything special to install a game for network play. The usual setup process installs both the single- and multiple-player versions of the game. If you're presented with options to install the single- or multiple-player version, choose the multiple-player version.

Install the game separately on each computer on the network. For games on CD or floppy disk, insert the CD or disk into each computer and run the installation program. If you downloaded the game from the Internet, copy the file to each computer in Network Neighborhood or My Network Places, and then run the installation program on each machine.

At installation, most games present a series of dialog boxes that prompt you to select hardware options. Make sure you choose options appropriate for the machine on which you're installing the game.

If you're not asked to select options during the installation process, you might have to do so when you first start the game. For example, you might have to select from a menu of input devices used to manipulate objects, such as a keyboard, mouse, or joystick. Be sure to start and set up the game on each computer before playing it on the network.

Playing Games on the Network

To play a network game that was supplied on a CD, you usually need to insert the CD into the host computer's drive. Once the host starts the game and sets its options, other computers on the network can join in.

The procedure for starting games varies. The installation process might place an icon on the desktop, add a listing to the Start menu, or both. To begin playing, double-click the icon or select the program from the Start menu.

With some older games, the Start menu listing accesses the CD directly and can be used only on the host. To start the game on the other computers, each player has to find the game program in its folder.

Once you start the game, you'll be asked to choose whether you want the computer you're playing on to be the host or whether you want to join a game that's already in progress. Again, the process varies widely. In the dialog box shown here, from the game HyperBlade, you can select the type of network you're using, choose to host a new game, or wait until a game in progress appears in the Open Games list and choose to join that game.

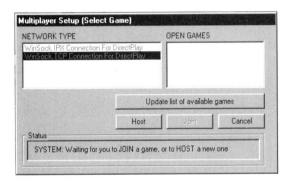

To introduce some of the possibilities for network game playing, we'll look at two examples of network games.

Hearts

Hearts is a fun four-player card game that comes with Windows 95, Windows 98, and Windows Me. To see whether Hearts and the other Windows games are installed on your computer, click Start, and then point to Programs, point to Accessories, and finally, point to Games.

Note

Windows XP includes a version of Hearts that can't be played across a network. It does, however, include Internet Hearts and other multiplayer games that can be played on the Internet.

If the Windows games aren't installed on your computer, follow these steps:

1. Insert the Windows CD into your CD-ROM drive.

2. On the Start menu, point to Settings, then click Control Panel.

3. In Control Panel, double-click the Add/Remove Programs icon.

4. In the Add/Remove Programs Properties dialog box, click the Windows Setup tab.

5. Click Accessories. (Don't select the check box to the left of Accessories or you'll clear the check mark.)

6. Click Details to see a list of the items in the Accessories category.

7. In the list of components, click the Games check box to enable it.

8. Click OK to close the Accessories dialog box.

9. Click OK to close the Add/Remove Programs Properties dialog box. Windows then installs the games.

To start Hearts, point to Programs on the Start menu, point to Accessories and then to Games, and then click Hearts. You'll see the following dialog box:

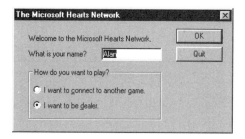

Enter your name, if it's not already shown in the What Is Your Name? text box, and choose whether you want to connect to a game in progress or be the dealer (the host) of a new game.

To start a new game, choose I Want To Be Dealer, and then click OK. The Microsoft Hearts Network window appears, as shown in Figure 12-1, with your name as the dealer at the bottom of the window. As other members join the game, their names are added to the window. If you want to play against three computer-generated opponents, you can press the F2 key.

To join a game that someone has already started, select I Want To Connect To Another Game, and then click OK to open the Locate Dealer dialog box. You must enter the name of the computer that the dealer is using and click OK to join the game. The Microsoft Hearts Network window appears and shows you as one of the players.

Figure 12-1.

The Microsoft Hearts Network window displays the name of the dealer when you start a new game.

When another member joins the game, the new player's name appears in the Hearts window of all the other players. After all the network players are signed in, the host presses the F2 key to start play. If there are fewer than four human players, the program adds its own players to bring the total to four, as shown in Figure 12-2. (If four people are already playing, you won't be able to join the game, and you'll see a message saying The Dealer Is Not Ready Or The Game Is Already In Progress.)

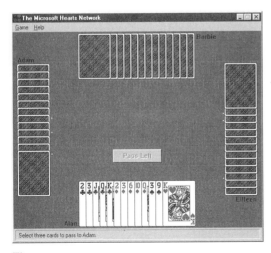

Figure 12-2.

Hearts can be played by a combination of human and computer-generated players.

To change the name of the computer-generated players for the next game, select Options from the Game menu to see the Hearts Options dialog box.

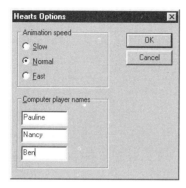

In the Hearts Options dialog box, you can also change the speed at which the animation runs in the game. Choose Sound from the Game menu to turn sound effects on or off, and choose Score to see the current score.

Midtown Madness 2

A number of popular games let you play against other members of the family across your network. Microsoft's Midtown Madness 2, for example, lets you race through the streets of San Francisco and London in your choice of 20 different vehicles—from the sleek Audi TT and Aston Martin DB7 to the fun-to-drive Mini Cooper. The landscape is rendered in detail, so you can see the sights of Fisherman's Wharf or drive past the Tower of London and Big Ben.

If you're on a network, you can also race against other members of the family, each player in his or her own car. You can do some sightseeing or try to outmaneuver each other through the streets and back alleys of town.

After you start Midtown Madness 2, click the Multiplayer button to see the Multiplayer Sessions options, shown in Figure 12-3.

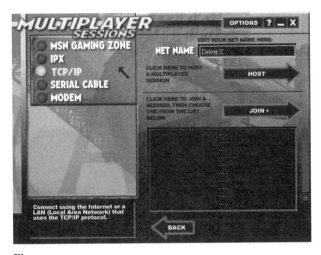

Figure 12-3.
Before starting a Midtown Madness 2 session, you need to choose your network protocol.

Enter the name you want to use to identify yourself, and then select the type of network connection you're using from the following choices:

- MSN Gaming Zone
- IPX
- TCP/IP
- Serial Cable
- Modem

On a home network, choose either IPX or TCP/IP, depending on your network protocol. Now choose whether you want to host a session, join one that's already started, or search the Internet for a session in progress.

If you want to join an ongoing game on your network, the IPX protocol will automatically search for current sessions. If you're using TCP/IP, you can enter the computer name or IP address of the computer hosting the session, or you can leave the address blank and have Midtown Madness 2 search the network for a hosted session. When a hosted session appears, click it to begin the game.

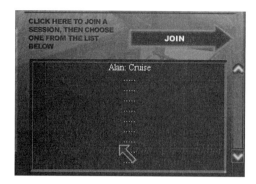

If you choose to host a new session, you can specify the maximum number of players that you'll allow, and then you'll see the Multiplayer Lobby screen shown in Figure 12-4, in which you can set session options such as these:

- Eject A Player Who Has Joined The Game.

- Select Another Vehicle.

- Change Host Settings. This option allows you to select the location, time of day, weather, and pedestrian density.

- Set Program Options. This option allows you to select the type of video display, controlling device, and sound settings.

Figure 12-4.

The Multiplayer Lobby screen allows you to set the session options.

The Multiplayer Lobby screen also includes a chat area in which you can send messages to and receive messages from other network players. Enter your message in the text box of the chat area, then press Enter to send the message.

As you play, you'll be able to see other players' vehicles on the city map, and you'll see their vehicles if they're in the same area.

Playing Internet Games

You can play lots of games with other people across the Internet. The Games menu of Windows Me and Windows XP includes the Internet games shown below.

- Internet Backgammon
- Internet Checkers
- Internet Hearts
- Internet Reversi
- Internet Spades

When you select one of these Internet games, you'll see the screen shown in Figure 12-5. Click Play to be connected to the Internet and paired with another player somewhere in the world.

Figure 12-5.

Starting an Internet game from Windows XP.

If you're sharing an Internet connection at home through a router or using a firewall for security, however, you might find that some games don't perform well or can't be played at all.

The Network Address Translation (NAT) feature of your router, for example, might interfere with your game. If so, consider paying your broadband ISP for separate IP addresses for your computers rather than having them all share one address. You can then eliminate the router and connect your broadband modem directly to your network hub or switch. Because NAT will no longer be used, however, you'll need to install and configure a firewall program on each computer.

Note

If you're using Windows XP, you can overcome the problems of NAT by using a Universal Plug and Play (UPP) gateway that takes advantage of NAT Traversal, as explained in Chapter 11, "Going Online Through the Network."

Another solution to these problems is to place your computer outside the router's firewall. Some routers let you designate the IP address of a computer that you don't want to be protected by its firewall, as in these options from the U.S. Robotics router.

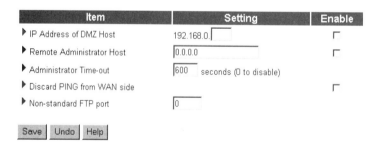

This solution should be a last-ditch effort, however, because it exposes that computer to hackers. The computer outside the firewall is said to be in the *perimeter network*—a neutral area between your firewall-protected network and the Internet, previously called the demilitarized zone (DMZ). Access is granted to the computer within the perimeter network but not to any other computers on the network.

Firewall software also often prevents you from playing Internet games. Many online games require access to your computer that is normally denied by firewall software. Rather than turning off your firewall, you might be able to adjust it to allow the game but still provide some security. Sometimes this process is as easy as changing a setting from high to medium, but it often requires fine-tuning the firewall to allow access to certain ports.

A Few Final Tips

Because network and Internet games are played in real time, family members might want to practice on their own before joining a multiple-player game. They should learn the rules and be able to control movement and play. It's no pleasure to win too easily or to wait while a novice player stops the action to learn the rules.

Game-playing requires a lot of system resources, so don't be surprised if the sound or video sometimes slows down during a game. The game might be accessing more information on the CD, or another player on the network or over the Internet might pause a game, which sometimes slows the action for other players. Still, playing games on the network or over the Internet can be fun and challenging, and it's a great way to compete within the family.

In the next chapter, you'll learn how to link PCs and Apple Macintosh computers on the same network to share files, printers, and even an Internet connection.

Chapter 13

Networking PCs and Macs

Many families these days have both Microsoft Windows and Apple Macintosh (Mac) computers in the home. Although the two types of computers are quite different, they can be connected on the same network. Windows and Mac users can share files, printers, and an Internet connection.

In this chapter, you'll learn how to add Mac computers to your Windows network, or vice versa. Any Mac with an Ethernet port can function on a Windows network because the port is totally compatible with Ethernet hubs and switches on that network. The popular Apple iMac computer and all new Macs come with a built-in Ethernet port, so you don't need to install an Ethernet card or worry about add-in adapters. Following the guidelines in this chapter, you can network a Mac with computers running any version of Windows.

Transferring Files by Disk

If you need to move only an occasional file between a Mac and Windows computer, you can transfer a file using a disk. Utilities such as TransMac from *http://www.asy.com* and MacDisk from *http://www.macdisk.com* allow a Windows computer to read a Mac floppy disk.

You can take advantage of the universal serial bus (USB) ports on your Mac and Windows computers to transfer files using a CompactFlash, SmartMedia, or MultiMedia card. These cards are the same ones used by many digital cameras, so you can use them not only to transfer files, but also to transfer digital photographs to either a Mac or Windows computer.

Devices such as the ZiO reader/writer (*http://www.microtech.com*), for example, include both Windows and Mac drivers that allow your computers to recognize the card reader as a disk drive. The USB bus powers the device, so it doesn't need batteries or power plugs. Once you install the drivers, plug the ZiO into one computer, insert the card that your ZiO accommodates, and copy files to it from your hard disk. Then plug in the ZiO to the other computer and transfer the files to the hard disk.

Planning for Networking

Two major steps are involved in networking a Mac with a Windows computer:

- Configure the protocols.
- Share and access resources.

Setting up and configuring a protocol enables the Mac to send and receive signals that are compatible with the other computers on the network using the same protocol. Mac computers use three main protocols: AppleTalk, Transmission Control Protocol/Internet Protocol (TCP/IP), and Internetwork Packet Exchange (IPX).

AppleTalk is the original protocol developed for Apple computers, and it's usually used for an all-Mac network. The protocol is easy to set up and can be used to network older Mac computers to the newer models.

TCP/IP is the protocol that the Internet and many Windows networks use. Macs include TCP/IP support through the Control Panels list on the Apple menu. Most Windows computers can run several instances of TCP/IP at the same time—one TCP/IP for connecting to the Internet, and another for the network, for example. Mac computers, on the other hand, use one instance of TCP/IP at a time. So if you use TCP/IP, you might not be able to connect to the Internet through your Mac's modem and share files over the network at the same time. You can circumvent this limitation, however, by letting your Mac connect to the Internet through a Windows computer set up as the Internet Connection Sharing host, as explained in the section "Sharing an Internet Connection," later in this chapter.

Finally, the IPX protocol on the Mac is used primarily to connect to Novell NetWare networks, but it might also be required on Mac networks to play multiple-player games.

MacIPX

The software that allows you to use IPX on a Mac, known as MacIPX, isn't included with the Mac operating system. If you want to use the IPX protocol, you must download it from the Internet. It's available at many locations, including *http://www.prosofteng.com/download.asp*.

Because the IPX protocol isn't included with the Mac, it's not covered in this chapter. However, if you're interested in learning more about MacIPX networking, perform a Web search for MacIPX, or visit this site on the Internet: *http://ftp.cioe.com/~galanti/mac.html*.

The Windows and Mac operating systems have totally different file structures. Therefore, just because the protocol is set up for a physical connection doesn't mean that either machine will be able to access the resources on the other. In fact, neither type of computer can recognize that the other one is on the network.

To communicate with each other and share resources, you'll need to use one of two techniques:

- Install software on one of the machines to make it compatible with the others.

- Share files using a Web browser by designating your Mac and Windows computers as Web servers.

The software solution takes one of two approaches: Either install a program on the Mac that enables it to be part of a Windows network using TCP/IP or NetBEUI, or install a program on the Windows computer that enables it to be part of a Mac network using AppleTalk. In both cases, all the computers on the network will then be able to share disks and files, communicate, and perhaps even share printers.

The software solution you choose depends on the number of Windows and Mac computers in your home. If you have only one Mac and one Windows machine, for example, either solution is just as effective. If you have several of one type of computer and just one of the other, however, choose the solution that requires you to install less software.

For example, if you have one Mac and several Windows computers, select the Mac-based software. This way, you need install the program only on the Mac. On the other hand, if you have one Windows computer and several Macs, choose the Windows-based software. This way, you have to install the program only on the Windows machine.

If you want to share files without purchasing additional software, consider the Web-server approach. In this solution, configure your Mac as a Web server and connect it to the network using TCP/IP. Any other computer on the network that also uses TCP/IP can then access the Mac using a Web browser. This solution is limited only to file sharing, however, and no other network services.

Because the setup and configuration of the protocol depends on the solution that you choose, we'll look at three kinds of Mac and Windows networking solutions: Mac-based networks, Windows-based networks, and Web-server networks.

Files That Can Be Shared

Although you can easily network a Mac and a Windows computer and make their files available to each other, not all types of files can be shared.

Program files designed for one type of computer can't be run on the other. If you download a program that runs under Windows, for example, you won't be able to run it on the Mac, and vice versa. Many programs, however, are available in both Windows and Mac versions. With some programs, both versions are on the same CD; but with others, you might have to purchase separate versions for each type of computer.

You can use most graphics files on both types of computers. If you have a JPEG or GIF graphic on one computer, for example, you'll be able to copy it and display it on the other. One popular Mac graphics format, PCT or PICT, isn't supported by most Windows programs, but you can download programs that will display these graphics formats on your Windows computer.

You can open plaintext files on either computer, as well as Web pages in the HTML format using a Web browser. Other types of files depend on the programs you've installed. Microsoft Office, for example, comes in both Windows and Mac versions. If you have Office installed on both computers, you can share Word documents, Excel worksheets, PowerPoint presentations, and Access databases.

DAVE 3.1: A Mac-Based Solution

If you have one Mac that you'd like to connect to a Windows network, consider the program DAVE 3.1, from Thursby Software Systems (*http://www.thursby.com*). The program is remarkably easy to set up and requires no special configuration or setup on the Windows computers on the network.

DAVE 3.1 configures your Mac so it appears on the network as another Windows computer. You'll be able to share files, access the Mac from the Windows computers, and place a shortcut to network resources on the Mac desktop. You'll also be able to share a PostScript printer that's connected to Windows computers. PostScript is a language used by some printers. *If you want to share a non-PostScript printer, see the section "Sharing a Printer," later in this chapter.*

To use DAVE, you must configure TCP/IP on your Mac, then install and configure the DAVE program.

Note

To connect to a Mac computer running the DAVE software, your Windows computers should be configured to use TCP/IP with static IP addresses. Refer to Chapter 7, "Installing the Software," for details on setting up TCP/IP.

Configuring TCP/IP on the Mac

You can set up TCP/IP as part of installing and configuring DAVE. In this chapter, however, you'll first learn how to configure TCP/IP on the Mac manually for a peer-to-peer home network. Complete the following steps.

Note

If you'd rather use the NetBEUI protocol for your Mac and PC network, consider the program MacSOHO, also from Thursby Software Systems, Inc. MacSOHO allows file sharing between Windows and Mac computers, but not printer sharing or instant messaging.

1. Open the Apple menu, point to Control Panels, and click TCP/IP to open the TCP/IP control panel, as shown in Figure 13-1.

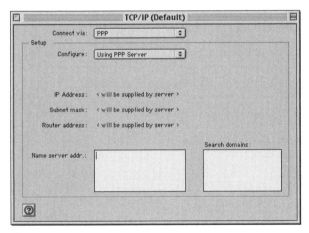

Figure 13-1.
The TCP/IP control panel.

Let's assume that you have your Mac set up for connecting to the Internet, so you'll see the TCP/IP settings for your Internet service provider (ISP). You must add and configure a new instance of TCP/IP to use for your network connection. If you're not using TCP/IP for the Internet, skip to step 7 to configure the existing default setting.

2. Choose Configurations from the File menu to open the Configurations window, shown in Figure 13-2.

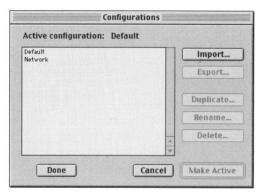

Figure 13-2.
Configuring TCP/IP for networking.

3. Select the default active configuration and then click the Duplicate button. A box appears in which you can change the name of the copy.

4. Type a name to identify the setting for your network, such as Network, then click OK.

5. Select the setting you just created and click Make Active.

   You now have to configure TCP/IP for your network by performing the following steps:

1. Pull down the Connect Via list and click Ethernet. (In some versions of the Apple operating system, this option is Ethernet Built-In.)

2. Pull down the Configure list and click Manually.

   The other options let you assign the IP address dynamically using a DHCP server, a BOOTP server, or a RARP server.

3. Enter a valid network IP address not already being used by another computer on the network.

4. Enter the subnet mask that your Windows network uses, such as 225.255.255.0.

5. Delete any addresses in the Router Address and Name Server Addr: boxes that might remain from the Internet configuration.

The completed configuration appears as in Figure 13-3.

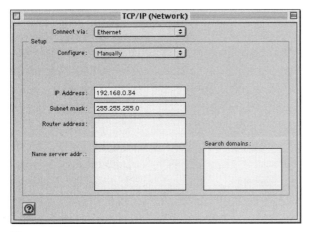

Figure 13-3.
Network configuration for TCP/IP.

6. Close the TCP/IP control panel and click Save when prompted.

Switching TCP/IP Configurations

You now have two TCP/IP settings. When you want to connect to the Internet using your Mac's modem, you'll need to designate as the default the TCP/IP that's configured for your ISP. To connect to the network again, you'll need to make the TCP/IP that's configured for your network the default. To select which configuration you want, follow these steps:

1. Open the TCP/IP control panel from the Control Panels list.

2. Choose Configurations from the File menu.

3. Select the configuration you want to use and click Make Active. The Configurations dialog box will close and the configuration you selected will be active.

Wireless Networking

Macintosh computers also have wireless Ethernet networking capability through Apple's AirPort wireless products. You can install a wireless AirPort network card into most Macs, including iBooks, iMacs, and PowerMacs.

Note

Chapter 5, "Installing Network Cards and Adapters," covers wireless networking on Windows computers.

AirPort-equipped Macs can communicate with each other without cables. You can even link AirPort-equipped Macs with a wired network using the AirPort Base Station. This device has a built-in 56-Kbps modem for Internet sharing and a port for connection to a wired Ethernet network. A program called AirPort Setup Assistant helps you install and configure the base station.

Because AirPort is compatible with the 802.11b wireless standard, you can network an AirPort-equipped Mac with a wireless PC network using 802.11b hardware.

To set up TCP/IP for wireless networking, follow the same steps described previously in "Configuring TCP/IP on the Mac," but select AirPort rather than Ethernet from the Connect Via list in the TCP/IP control panel. Then to connect to a Windows wireless network that uses an access point for communications, follow these steps:

1. Pull down the Apple menu on the Mac desktop and select AirPort.

2. In the AirPort dialog box, shown in Figure 13-4, select the access point from the Choose Network list in the AirPort Network section. The list shows all active 802.11b access points within range of the Mac's AirPort card.

Note

If you aren't using an access point, select Computer To Computer from the Choose Network list.

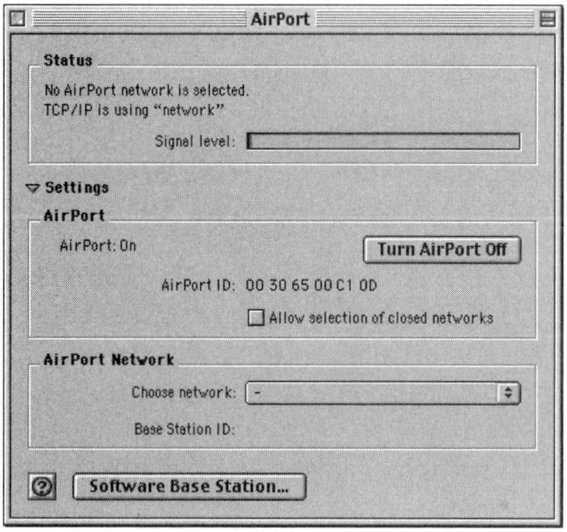

Figure 13-4.
Setting up a Mac for wireless networking.

3. If the access point uses the Wired Equivalent Privacy (WEP) security protocol for wireless LANs, a box will appear asking for the network password, as shown here.

4. Enter the WEP access code using hexadecimal characters in the format $*xxxxxxxx*, such as $F3F6F133AE, and click OK. The Status section of the AirPort dialog box, shown below, indicates that you're connected to the access point and indicates the relative strength of the signal.

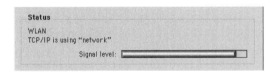

Installing DAVE

The next step is to install the DAVE software. Insert the DAVE CD, run the DAVE installer (Install DAVE), and follow the directions that appear on the screen:

1. After your Mac restarts, the DAVE Setup Assistant program begins. Click the right arrow at the bottom right of the window to move from page to page.

2. The next page asks whether you want to configure TCP/IP. Because you just configured it, select the option TCP/IP Is Already Configured, and then click the right arrow.

3. The next page asks for your name, organization, and license code provided on the DAVE license and registration form. Enter the information and click the right arrow.

4. The next page asks whether you're using Windows NT Server. Click No and then click the right arrow.

5. On the next page, enter a name that the Mac will have on the Windows network, called the NetBIOS name. The name can be up to 15 characters and must not already be used by another computer on the network. Enter the name and click the right arrow.

6. On the next page, specify the peer-to-peer workgroup being used by the network, as shown in Figure 13-5. The usual workgroup name is WORKGROUP, and it's located on the Identification tab of the Network icon in Control Panel on a Windows computer. DAVE displays WORKGROUP by default. Change the name as needed, then click the right arrow.

Figure 13-5.

Specify the network workgroup.

7. On the next page, enter a short description of your computer, such as Alan's Mac, then click the right arrow.

8. You're now asked whether you want to log on to the network at startup. Make your choice and click the right arrow.

9. The computer name, workgroup, and description appear. Click the right arrow if they're correct, or click the left arrow to make changes.

10. You're now asked whether you want to share your files on the network. Select I Want To Set Up DAVE To Share My Local Files, then click the right arrow to open the DAVE Sharing control panel, as shown in Figure 13-6.

Figure 13-6.
The DAVE Sharing control panel.

Note

You can later share files or turn sharing off using the DAVE Sharing control panel on the Apple menu.

11. Click New Share to see a list of resources on your Mac, as shown below.

12. Select a folder you want to share and click Choose to open the Password box.

13. Select whether you want Read/Write or Read-Only access, as shown here.

14. Enter a password if you want to use one.

15. Change the name in the Share As box if you want, then click OK to return to the Shared Resources dialog box. Repeat the steps to share any additional folders.

16. Select one of these options:

    • Log Sharing Activity creates a text file in the System folder that keeps track of who uses the shared folders.

    • Optimize For File Sharing or Optimize For User Applications specifies how the CPU allots resources to DAVE. (You should keep the default of File Sharing unless you have a reason to change this.)

17. Close the DAVE Sharing control panel to return to the DAVE Setup Assistant program, and then click the right arrow.

    You can always change the options or share other folders. Open the Apple menu, point to Control Panels, and click DAVE to open DAVE. Use the File Sharing option on the File menu if you no longer want to make your files available on the network.

Accessing the Mac from a PC

Accessing the shared files on your Mac from a Windows machine is easy. Open Network Neighborhood (or My Network Places in Microsoft Windows Millennium Edition [Me], Windows 2000, and Windows XP) to see an icon for your Mac, as shown on page 397.

Note

Remember, a computer's icon might take a few minutes to appear in Network Neighborhood or My Network Places. Rather than wait, however, you can use the Find or Search feature on the Start menu to locate a computer.

Double-click the icon to see the shared folders, as shown below, and open a folder to access its files. You can now copy files in either direction or open files that are on the Mac.

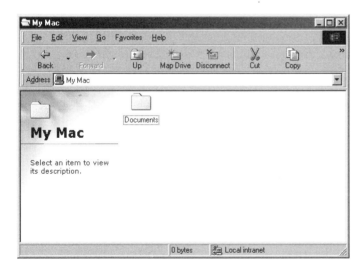

Note

After copying a folder from your Mac to the Windows computer, you might see some new folders on your Windows computer, such as Resource.frk and DesktopFolderDB. Don't delete these folders; you'll need them if you later decide to copy the original folder back to the Mac.

Accessing the PC from a Mac

You can also access shared folders on a Windows machine from the Mac. There are two ways to do it:

- Browse the network to locate the folder.

- Mount the Windows resource as an icon on the Mac desktop.

Browsing the Network

Browsing the network means to display each computer on the network, and then locate the disk and folders you want to access. To browse the network to access a folder, follow these steps:

1. Open the Apple menu and click DAVE. Then click the File menu, select Browse, and select Your Workgroup to see a list of computers on the network, as shown in Figure 13-7.

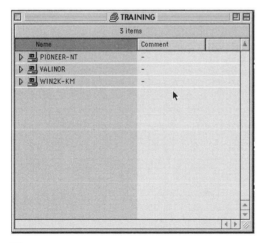

Figure 13-7.
Browsing the Windows network.

2. Click the down arrow next to a computer to display its shared resources, as shown below.

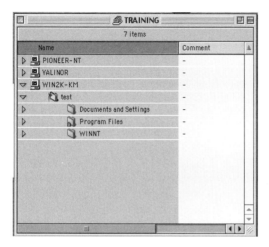

3. Double-click a folder to display its contents, as in Figure 13-8. You can now drag files from the list to your Mac desktop or a folder on your hard disk.

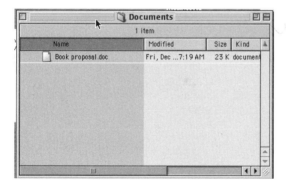

Figure 13-8.
The contents of a Windows folder.

Note

If you close the DAVE window, you can reopen it by choosing DAVE from the Application menu. If the browser window doesn't open when DAVE is shown on the Application menu, select Browse from the File menu and select one of the following options: Your Workgroup, Entire Network, or Location.

Mounting Resources

When you mount a resource, you place an icon for it on the Mac desktop. Mounting a disk drive on a Windows computer, for example, displays an icon for it on your Mac desktop so you can then access the disk drive by opening the icon, without needing to browse through the network to locate the resource.

You can mount a resource temporarily so it doesn't appear the next time you start your Mac, or you can mount the resource so it appears automatically each time you start your Mac and it's connected to the network.

To mount a shared drive from a Windows computer on your Mac desktop, follow these steps:

1. Open the Apple menu and click Chooser. An icon for DAVE Client appears in the Chooser window.

2. Click the DAVE Client icon in the Chooser window to display the network resources in the Select A Server window, as shown in Figure 13-9.

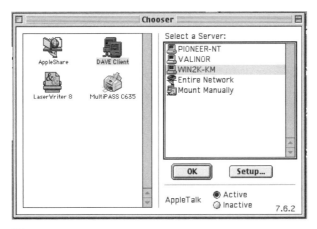

Figure 13-9.
The DAVE Client icon in the Chooser window.

3. Double-click the computer you want to mount to open its resource window, as shown in Figure 13-10.

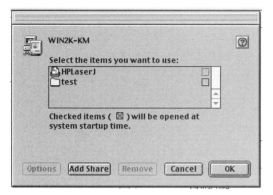

Figure 13-10.

Selecting the resource to mount.

4. Click the resource you want to mount.

5. Select the check box on the right for the resource if you want to mount it automatically when your Mac starts.

6. Click OK and then close the Chooser window. An icon for the resource appears on the Mac desktop, as shown below.

7. Double-click the icon to display its contents. You can now copy files between the two computers, just as you would between two Windows machines.

Communicating on the Network

DAVE includes a pop-up messaging feature that's compatible with the WinPopup program on Windows computers. Using DAVE and WinPopup, you can send and receive instant messages among network users.

Note

WinPopup must be running on the Windows computer. For a review of how to run WinPopup on Windows computers, see the section "Sending and Receiving Pop-Up Messages," in Chapter 9, "Learning to Share," on page 288.

Here's how to use WinPopup. First, set DAVE to accept WinPopup messages from Windows computers by following these steps:

1. Open the Apple menu and click DAVE to open the DAVE browser.

2. Open the Edit menu and choose Messaging Preferences to open this box.

3. Select Display Received Messages.

4. Select Beep When Message Received if you want to hear a sound when a new message is received.

5. Select Read Messages Aloud if you want the Mac voice feature to read the text of the message to you.

6. Click OK. An incoming message sent from a Windows computer appears, like this.

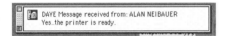

When you want to send a message from the Mac to a Windows computer running WinPopup, follow these steps:

1. Open the Apple menu and choose DAVE if it isn't already open.

2. Open the Access menu and choose New Message to open the window shown in Figure 13-11.

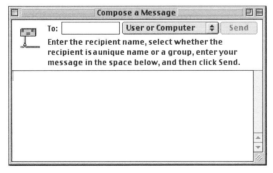

Figure 13-11.

Sending a message to another network user.

3. To send the message to a specific computer, select User Or Computer in the second pull-down list, then enter the user or computer name of the recipient in the To box. To send the message to everyone in the workgroup, select Workgroup in the list and enter the workgroup name if it doesn't automatically appear in the To box.

4. Enter the text of the message and click Send.

Sharing a Printer

Sharing printers across a Mac/Windows network is a little more complicated than sharing files. Using DAVE, you can share printers so long as all the printers use the PostScript method of printing. Printers designed for Macintosh systems are PostScript printers, so only PostScript printer drivers are provided with the Mac operating system.

To make a Mac printer available to Windows machines, follow these steps:

1. Open the Apple menu, point to Control Panels, and click DAVE to open DAVE.

2. Click File Sharing on the File menu.

3. You can drag a printer into the Shared Items list to share it, or you can click New Share to open the Choose Folders To Share dialog box.

4. Select the printer you want to share, and click OK. You can now access the printer from a Windows computer.

See Also

To use a network printer in Windows, see the section "Accessing a Shared Printer," in Chapter 10, "Printing Across the Network," on page 309.

Letting the Mac access a printer connected to a Windows computer isn't as straightforward as sharing a Mac printer with a Windows system. If the Windows computer uses a PostScript printer, you'll be able to access it from a Mac by following the instructions in the DAVE manual. You can also use a program or hardware device to share a Windows printer. Sharing a Windows printer on the network is explained in the section "Sharing a Windows Printer," later in this chapter.

A Windows-Based Solution

If your goal is to connect a Windows computer to a network that primarily consists of Macs, consider a Windows-based software solution. You can choose from two excellent programs: TSStalk from Thursby Software Systems, and PC MACLAN from Miramar Systems (*http://www.pcmaclan.com*). Because we looked at Thursby's DAVE program in the last section, we'll discuss using PC MACLAN for a Mac/Windows network here.

Preparing Your Macintosh

Before you can connect your Mac to a Windows network running PC MACLAN, you must set up your Mac for networking. If you have an AppleTalk network running between two or more Macs, the network is already set up. You just have to add the person who'll be networked on the Windows computer as a user and set his or her privileges.

If you already have this setup, you can skip ahead to the section "Configuring File Sharing," later in this chapter. If you don't already have networking set up on the Mac, your first step is to follow the directions in the section "Configuring TCP/IP on the Mac," earlier in this chapter, to assign your Mac an Internet Protocol (IP) address.

Setting Up AppleTalk

The next step is to set up AppleTalk on your Mac. AppleTalk is a popular protocol for all-Mac networks and the protocol used by the PC MACLAN program. Follow these steps on your Mac to set up AppleTalk:

1. Open the Apple menu and click Chooser to open the Chooser window, shown in Figure 13-12.

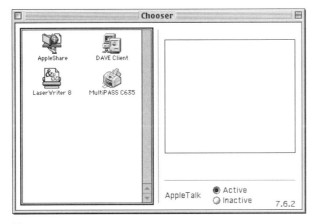

Figure 13-12.
Activate AppleShare in the Chooser window.

2. Click AppleShare.

3. Click the Active option if it isn't already selected.

4. Close the Chooser window.

5. Open the Apple menu, point to Control Panels, and click AppleTalk to open the AppleTalk control panel.

6. Make sure that the Connect Via option is set at Ethernet.

7. Close the AppleTalk control panel.

Configuring File Sharing

Now you must identify your Mac on the network, determine who can access it on the network, and specify which resources can be shared. Follow these steps:

1. Open the Apple menu, point to Control Panels, and click File Sharing to open the dialog box shown in Figure 13-13.

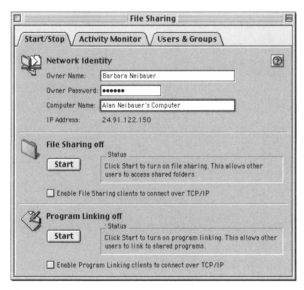

Figure 13-13.
File Sharing settings.

2. Click the Start/Stop tab if it isn't already displayed.

3. Enter your name as the owner of the computer, enter your password, and enter a name for your computer that will appear to Windows users.

4. Click Start in the File Sharing section.

5. Select Enable File Sharing Clients To Connect Over TCP/IP.

Note

The Enable File Sharing Clients To Connect Over TCP/IP check box is available only in version 9 and later of the Macintosh operating system.

6. Click the Users & Groups tab, shown in Figure 13-14.

Figure 13-14.

Creating a user account.

7. Click New User to open the New User dialog box.

8. Choose Identity in the Show list if it isn't already selected.

9. In the Name text box, enter the name of a Windows user who'll be sharing the Mac files.

10. In the Password text box, specify a password the user will have to enter to access the Mac. If you want, select Allow User To Change Password to let the user choose a new password.

11. Close the New User dialog box and then the File Sharing control panel.

12. Click the Hard Drive icon on the desktop.

13. Open the File menu, point to Get Info, and click Sharing to open the window shown in Figure 13-15.

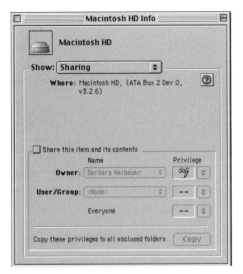

Figure 13-15.
Allowing your Mac hard disk to be shared on the network.

14. Select the check box labeled Share This Item And Its Contents.

15. If you want to assign privileges to everyone on the network, pull down the Privilege
     list next to Everyone and select the type of sharing allowed.

     The options are Read & Write, Read Only, Write Only, and None. You can
     also assign privileges to a specific user by choosing his or her name in the User/
     Group list and then setting privileges.

16. Close the window.

Using PC MACLAN in Windows

When you choose a Windows-based solution, you must perform two tasks on the
Windows computer:

- Configure the computer to communicate using the AppleTalk protocol.

- Configure the computer to be an AppleTalk file server so its files can be accessed by
  a Mac.

    When you install PC MACLAN, you perform both these tasks automatically. PC
MACLAN adds the AppleTalk protocol to the Windows Network icon in Control Panel
and binds it to your Ethernet network adapter. The installation program then restarts
your computer.

Note

If you see an AppleTalk error message when you restart your computer, click OK.

You can now access the shared drive on the Mac in almost the same way you can access files on any networked computer. Follow these steps:

1. Double-click Network Neighborhood on the Windows desktop. (Use My Network Places in Windows Me, Windows 2000, and Windows XP.) You should see an icon for the Mac computer, as shown below. If the icon doesn't appear in a few moments, double-click Entire Network and wait until the icon appears.

2. Double-click the icon for the Mac computer. The Enter Network Password dialog box appears, as shown below. You'll be asked for the user name and password that was specified for you as a Mac user.

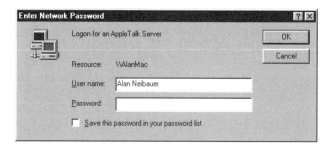

3. Enter your user name and password. (If you don't want to enter the password each time you connect, select the check box Save This Password In Your Password List.)

4. You'll now see an icon for the shared resource. Double-click the icon to open and access the folders and files being shared on the Mac, as shown in Figure 13-16.

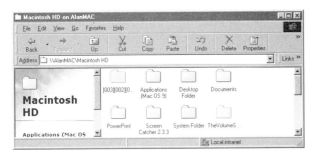

Figure 13-16.
Available folders and files on the shared Mac drive.

Setting the PC MACLAN File Server

PC MACLAN also lets a Mac user access files on the Windows computer. To provide this capability, you must enable the File Server function of PC MACLAN on your Windows computer and then designate which Mac users have access to the Windows resources.

On a Windows computer on which you installed PC MACLAN, follow these steps to enable the file server:

1. Click Start, point to Programs and then PC MACLAN, and click File Server to open the window shown here.

2. Click the Start Server button.

3. Click the Users & Groups Button to open the Users & Groups window.

4. Click New under Users to open the dialog box shown in Figure 13-17.

Figure 13-17.

Creating a new user account.

5. Enter the name of the user's Mac.

6. Click Set Password to open the Password dialog box.

7. Enter the user's password, press Tab, and retype the password.

8. Click OK to return to the User dialog box.

9. Click Admin, All Privileges, or both, and leave the Can Login box selected.

10. Click OK then click Done to return to the File Server window.

11. Click the Share Folders button to open the Share Folders dialog box shown in Figure 13-18.

Figure 13-18.

Select a resource to share with the Mac.

12. Select the drive you want to share or a specific folder within a drive.

13. Click the Share button to open the Shared Folder dialog box shown in Figure 13-19.

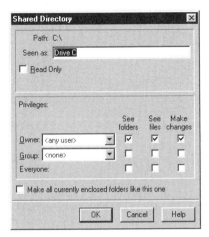

Figure 13-19.
Specifying share privileges.

14. Enter the name of the resource as it will appear on the Mac desktop.

15. Set the privileges for the Mac user.

   You can specify privileges for everyone or for a specific group or user. To allow everyone to access the files, select the options next to Everyone: See Folders, See Files, and Make Changes. To set privileges for a specific user, select his or her name in the Group list and then determine the type of access.

16. Select the Make All Currently Enclosed Folders Like This One check box to assign the same access to all folders.

17. Click OK. A message appears asking whether you want to change all the enclosed folders.

18. Click Yes, then click Done.

Connecting with the Mac

Your Windows computer is now ready to be accessed by the Mac. You can access the PC MACLAN file server as you would any Mac file server on the network, using the Chooser window.

   Follow these steps to access the PC MACLAN file server:

1. Open the Apple menu and click Chooser.

2. Click AppleShare to display a list of servers, as shown in Figure 13-20.

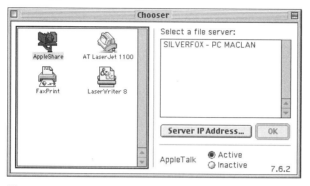

Figure 13-20.
Select the PC MACLAN file server in the Chooser window.

3. Click the PC MACLAN server name (it might take a moment for it to appear), and click OK to open this box.

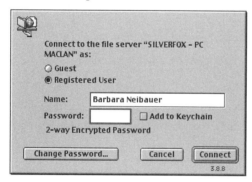

4. Click the Registered User option.

5. Enter your user name and password.

6. Click Connect to see a list of the resources that are shared by the PC MACLAN file server.

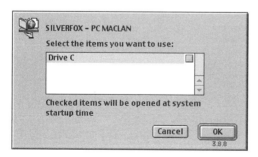

7. Click the resource to access.

8. Select the check box to the right of the resource to make it available whenever you start your Mac.

9. Click OK, then close the Chooser window.

10. Now you'll see an icon for the PC MACLAN resource on the Mac desktop, as shown below. Double-click the icon to access its folders and files.

Drive C

You can also access the Windows resource using the Network Browser. Choose Network Browser from the Apple menu, and click the arrow next to AppleTalk in the box that appears to list the PC MACLAN file server. Click the arrow next to the file server name to display its shared resources.

The PC MACLAN Print Server

If you have a PostScript printer connected to your Windows computer, you can provide access to it from the Mac. PC MACLAN includes a separate print server program for setting up your printer on the AppleTalk network.

1. Click Start, point to Programs and PC MACLAN, and then click Print Server to open the window shown in Figure 13-21.

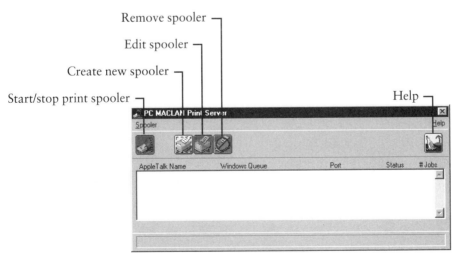

Figure 13-21.

Creating a print server on the Windows computer.

2. Click the Create New Spooler button to open the Spooler Configuration dialog box shown in Figure 13-22.

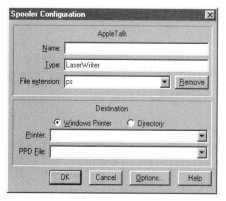

Figure 13-22.
Configuring a print spooler.

3. Enter a name to identify the printer.

4. Pull down the Printer list and choose the printer that's attached to your computer.

5. Pull down the PPD File list and select the appropriate PPD file. The PPD file contains the driver information required to use the printer.

6. Click OK.

     A Mac user can now select the printer in the Chooser window in the same way he or she would set up a printer attached to his or her own computer.

     Once PC MACLAN is set up, you can use the file server to send an instant message to a Macintosh computer. Here's how.

Note

PC MACLAN doesn't provide a mechanism for the Mac to send an instant message to a Windows computer.

1. Open the PC MACLAN file server.

2. Choose Connections from the Server menu.

3. Select the name of the person to whom you want to send a message.

4. Click Message.

5. Type the message and click Send. The message appears on the Mac desktop.

Sharing Files as a Web Server

If you don't want to purchase additional software, you can still share your Macintosh files by setting up the Web Sharing feature, which creates a Web server on the Macintosh and allows Windows users to access the Mac using their Web browser.

Note

The Web Sharing feature works both ways. If you set up a personal Web server on a Windows computer, you can access the Windows Web site from a Mac by pointing the browser to the IP address of the Windows machine.

To set up Web Sharing on your Mac, first verify that file sharing is enabled for the folder you want to use as your Web server location. This location contains the files you want to share with Windows users. The default folder for Web Sharing is Web Pages, but you can select any folder you want. Then follow these steps to set up Web Sharing on your Mac:

1. Open the Apple menu, point to Control Panels, and click Web Sharing to open the control panel shown in Figure 13-23.

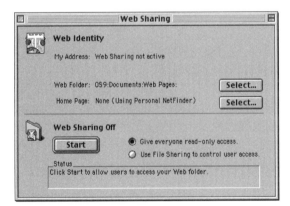

Figure 13-23.
Setting up Web Sharing.

2. Click Start to turn on Web Sharing.

    Your computer's address is shown at the My Address prompt when Web Sharing is active. Users will enter this address into their Web browser to access the Web Sharing folder.

3. To select another folder for the Web server location other than Web Pages, click the top Select button, choose the folder from the box that appears, and click Select.

4. If you want people to only read files but not change them, select Give Everyone Read-Only Access. If you want to provide Full access, select Use File Sharing to control user access, then create user accounts in the File Sharing control panel.

5. Close the Web Sharing control panel.

A person on a Windows computer can now start his or her Web browser and enter your computer's IP address to access the shared folder, as shown in Figure 13-24. If your Mac has the IP address of 192.168.0.15, for example, enter **http://192.168.0.15** in the browser's address box and press Enter. Others on the network can also use FTP to transfer files from the Mac to their Windows machine.

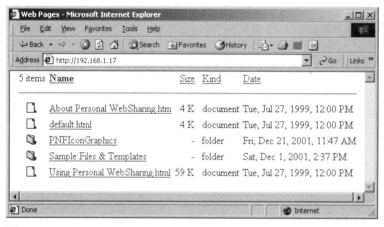

Figure 13-24.
A Mac folder shown in a browser window.

Sharing a Windows Printer

As mentioned earlier in the section "Sharing a Printer," the Macintosh computer is designed to be used with PostScript printers connected to the Mac's serial or USB port. If your network primarily consists of Windows computers, however, you probably have printers that aren't PostScript-compatible and that use a parallel printer port. Using a non-PostScript parallel port printer with a Mac requires additional software and hardware.

A company named Strydent (*http://www.strydent.com*) markets popular PowerPrint products that allow you to use a parallel printer with a Mac. The products include a set of Macintosh drivers for more than 1500 parallel printers and the hardware necessary to connect a parallel printer to your Mac. The drivers give your Mac the software capability to print documents and graphics on a Windows-compatible printer.

The PowerPrint Serial-to-Parallel kit includes a CD with the Mac printer drivers and a special cable that connects the printer's parallel port to the Macintosh serial port. The PowerPrint USB-to-Parallel kit includes the driver CD and a special cable that connects the Macintosh USB port to a parallel printer. Using either kit, you can connect the printer directly to your Mac.

PowerPrint for Networks is designed to share a Windows printer with the Mac and the Windows computers on the network. The product includes the driver CD as well as a network print server, such as those discussed in Chapter 10, "Printing Across the Network." You connect the print server to your network hub or switch and the parallel port of your printer to a parallel connection on the print server.

When you install the software on your Macintosh, choose the drivers for your Windows printer, as shown in Figure 13-25, and complete the installation process.

Figure 13-25.

Selecting a printer driver.

Now you'll see an icon for the printer in the Macintosh Chooser. Click the icon to see a listing for the print server in the Select A Printer list, as shown below.

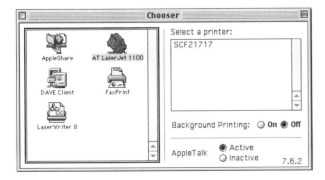

Select the print server and then close the Chooser to use the printer as the default. When you print a document, you'll see the Print dialog box shown here, although the options in the dialog box depend on your printer. Click Print to print your Mac document or graphic on the parallel printer attached to the network print server.

Note

The PowerPrint print server is compatible with the AppleTalk, TCP/IP, and NetBEUI protocols. The PowerPrint CD includes a program that installs a Windows printer driver using your choice of the TCP/IP and NetBEUI protocols so that you can access the printer server from all Windows applications.

Sharing an Internet Connection

Sharing a modem and Internet connection, as you learned in Chapter 11, "Going Online Through the Network," is a popular use for many home networks, and you can share the Internet with your Mac as well.

Sharing an Internet connection is actually more important when you add a Mac. Remember, with a Mac, you must choose to use TCP/IP for either the Internet or your network, but not both. So if you use TCP/IP to connect the Mac to your PC network, you can't use the Mac to connect to the Internet using its own modem through TCP/IP at the same time.

By letting the Mac share a connection on the Windows network, you can connect to the Internet and to the network at the same time. The Internet connection is made using TCP/IP on the PC that shares its modem, so the Mac can access the Internet and the network at the same time. How you set up the Mac to share an Internet connection depends on the type of software that the PC acting as the Internet server is using.

Windows Internet Connection Sharing

If you're using Microsoft Windows Internet Connection Sharing (ICS) on your PC, you must configure TCP/IP on the Mac to access it. In Chapter 11, "Going Online Through the Network," you learned how to configure a Windows computer to use ICS. If you used dynamic IP addressing, you ran a program installed on a floppy disk when you installed and configured ICS on a host computer. You can't run this program on a Mac because it's designed only for Windows. If you use static IP addresses, you also learned in Chapter 11 how to manually configure a Windows computer to use ICS.

To share the Internet account with a Mac, you must use static addressing on your network and manually configure the Mac's TCP/IP. Assuming that you have ICS installed on a PC and you're using static IP addresses, configure the Mac to access the Internet through the network by following these steps:

1. Open the Apple menu, point to Control Panels, and click TCP/IP to open the TCP/IP control panel.

2. If the network configuration isn't displayed, choose Configurations from the File menu, select the network configuration you want to use, and click Make Active. You will be returned to the TCP/IP control panel.

3. Be sure that TCP/IP is set up as explained earlier in the section "Configuring TCP/IP on the Mac." It should be set for Ethernet, with the appropriate IP address and subnet mask.

4. In the Router Address box of the TCP/IP control panel, enter the IP address of the PC acting as the Internet server.

5. In the Name Server box, enter the Domain Name Server (DNS) address that your ISP provided you. A sample of settings will appear, as shown in Figure 13-26.

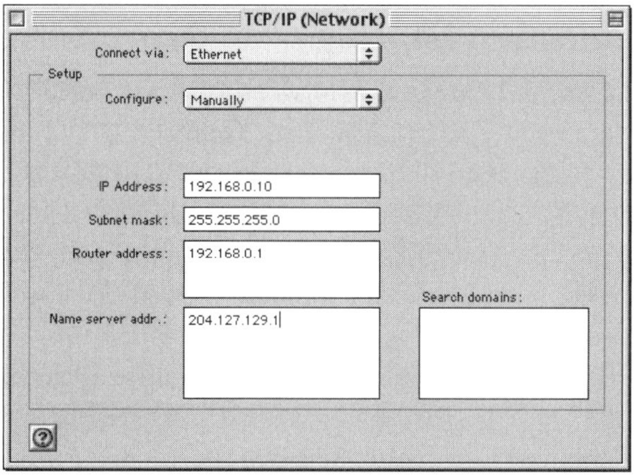

Figure 13-26.

A Mac set up to use Internet Connection Sharing on a PC network.

Now when you connect to the Internet using your Mac, it will access the modem and Internet connection of the ICS server computer on the network. If the ICS server isn't yet connected, it will dial the ISP and make the connection.

Note

As with a PC using ICS, you might get an error in your Mac browser when it first connects through the server. If an error message appears that the Web site cannot be opened, enter in the browser's address box the address of a site that you want to access and press Enter.

Using a Proxy Server

Some other Internet sharing software works using a proxy server. A proxy server looks for requests coming over the network to access an Internet site. It does so by watching a port—an electronic connection between the network computers. The server then gets the site using the modem and Internet account on the computer in which the proxy server is installed but sends it across the network to the computer that made the request.

If you're using proxy server software, you'll need to know the IP address of the server computer and the port to which the proxy server is connected. You'll get the IP address from the PC's Network icon in Control Panel and the port number from the proxy server's documentation.

When you have that information, start the Mac's Web browser but don't connect to the Internet. Open the browser's Preferences or Options dialog box, and set it to use a proxy server. Using Microsoft Internet Explorer for the Mac, for example, follow these steps:

1. Click Preferences on the browser menu bar and then select Proxies in the Network section to see the options in Figure 13-27.

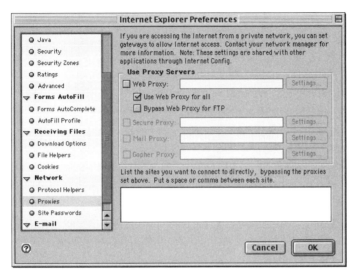

Figure 13-27.
Setting the Mac to access the Internet through a proxy server.

2. Select the Web Proxy check box, and then click Settings to display the options shown here.

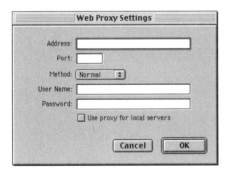

3. In the Address text box, following http://, enter the IP address of the PC being used as the Internet server.

4. Enter the proxy server port in the Port text box, then click OK.

Now when you connect to the Internet using the Mac, it'll send its request for a Web site to the computer containing the proxy server. The proxy server will access the modem and Internet connection on its computer and then send the retrieved site through the network to the browser on the Mac.

The Bottom Line

Windows and Mac computers have their own loyal groups who vigorously defend their systems as the better of the two. If you have at least one of each type of computer in your home, you can exploit the strengths of each.

Once you feel comfortable with the Windows or the Mac operating system, you can easily learn to operate the other. Although the inner workings of the systems are different, the user interfaces are similar. For example, Windows Control Panel contains icons for various features that you can customize, and the Mac Control Panels list on the Apple menu offers similar features. Windows has device drivers that must be loaded when your computer starts, and the Mac has extensions that are loaded at startup. Newer Windows and Mac computers both have USB ports, and now they can often share the same peripherals, such as Zip drives and scanners.

Because it's easy to use both Macs and Windows computers on the same network, don't be intimidated by the differences between them. Windows and Mac users can learn a lot from each other.

Chapter 14

Networking for Road Warriors

At some point, you'll probably hit the road for either business or pleasure. As you'll learn in this chapter, even when you're traveling, you can still communicate with the family back home on the home network and take advantage of all the benefits the network offers, such as sharing files and printing documents.

As countless computer-toting travelers—road warriors—already know, it's easy to stay in touch with a home computer from any place that's within reach of a telephone. In this chapter, you'll learn how to set up and use a process called *remote computing* to dial in to your home network to access its resources the same way you dial in to an Internet service provider (ISP) to access the Internet.

You'll also learn how to use Microsoft NetMeeting, Microsoft Windows XP Remote Assistance, and Microsoft Windows Messenger. All these programs let you chat with other people on remote computers over the Internet. NetMeeting and Windows Messenger even allow you to talk to and even see someone at a remote location, so long as each computer is equipped with a video camera (which can be inexpensive and easily added) and a microphone.

These programs not only allow you to hold long-distance meetings, but they also share applications across the Internet. NetMeeting and Remote Assistance, for example, let you take over another computer and actually operate it by remote control from your keyboard and screen, no matter where you are. In Windows Messenger, you can take control of a program running on the remote computer.

As you'll see later in this chapter, remote control and application sharing give you the opportunity to troubleshoot problems someone might be having with a computer on the network or even show someone how to perform a specific task on the computer.

Packing for the Road

Suppose you're on a trip away from home and you're relaxing in your hotel room going over the day's events. You'd like to dial in to your home computer to check e-mail messages from your family, send a file home, or perhaps print a note to your spouse on one of your home printers. At home, your modem is probably already plugged into the phone jack, so going online is simple. But when you're away from home, connecting to a phone line isn't always that easy. Even if your hotel room or a conference center has a standard, modular phone jack, the jack might not be in a location close enough to the spot at which you'd like to use your computer.

To avoid some potential hassles, you should start by packing a few essentials with your laptop:

- Two telephone extension cables, each 6 feet or longer
- A telephone cable coupler
- A two-to-one or three-to-one telephone adapter

The telephone cables, coupler, and adapter weigh practically nothing, and they take up little space in your computer case or briefcase, but they can be lifesavers when you want to connect to a home network or to the Internet. You can purchase all these items at a hardware store, your local Radio Shack, or even at your local "Nothing over $1" store. They'll allow you to reach a phone jack, even one that's in an out-of-the-way place.

The coupler lets you connect two lengths of telephone cable to lengthen your reach even farther. If a telephone is already connected to the phone jack, the two-to-one adapter lets you plug in both the phone and your modem.

Note

In a pinch, the adapter can also be used as a coupler—just plug both extension cables into the adapter and plug one end of the cable, rather than the adapter, into the jack.

Today, an increasing number of hotels are catering to travelers equipped with laptop computers. But not every hotel you stay in will be set up to facilitate remote computing.

The first hurdle you might encounter, especially if you're traveling abroad, is the lack of a standard RJ-11 modular phone jack in your room. This receptacle is the standard phone jack in North America. Even with the extra cables, couplers, and adapters that you've packed, you'll be stuck if there's no place to plug in your modem.

The second hurdle might be the phone line itself. The telephone lines in your home are regular analog lines. Your modem converts the digital information in your computer to analog signals that these regular phone lines can carry. But many hotels and offices have special digital telephone systems. In a digital system, voice and fax communications are transmitted through the system as digital information, so your analog modem won't work. What's worse is that if you connect your laptop to a digital network, the voltage from the digital lines might damage your laptop's modem permanently.

With a little preparation before your trip, however, you can overcome both of these hurdles. When you make hotel reservations, find out whether the hotel's telephone system is analog or digital. Even if it's digital, you might be able to request a room with an analog phone connection and an RJ-11 jack that you can use with your laptop.

You can also purchase an *acoustic coupler*, a device that fits over the telephone handset and connects to your modem. Instead of plugging directly into the phone system, you connect to the acoustic coupler, which sends and receives signals through the telephone handset. Another device that you can use with a digital system allows you to connect your modem to the jack into which the phone's handset is plugged. Both of these devices overcome the problems of not having access to a jack and to an analog phone system. These devices enable you to connect easily and safely to digital phone lines when you're on the road.

If you're traveling abroad, you can purchase jack adapters, which let you connect your modem to the type of jack used in the country you're visiting. To order the correct adapter, you'll have to determine which type of jack you'll be using, but most mail-order companies that specialize in remote-computing hardware, such as Hello Direct (*http://www.hello-direct.com*) and Road Warrior (*http://www.roadwarrior.com)*, can help you with that.

For maximum protection, you might consider buying a *line tester*, a device that indicates whether a line is analog or digital, and a *surge protector*, which safeguards a modem against power surges while you're connected. Road Warrior, for example, offers a product called the Modem Saver International. You plug this device into the phone jack before plugging in your modem. A green light indicates that the jack is safe to use; a red light indicates that it could damage your modem. A surge protector is also built into the Modem Saver International.

Dialing In to Your ISP

One other important item you should have for your trip is a local phone number for your ISP in the area in which you'll be staying. You've probably set up your computer to dial in to your ISP from home using the local number that's available where you live. You could use that same number when you travel, but you'd first have to perform two tasks:

- Adjust Microsoft Windows so that it dials the area code as well as the number.

- Take out a loan to pay the long-distance charges, especially at hotel rates.

Note

Some ISPs require that you install special software to connect to them. If that's the case with yours, you'll need to follow the instructions that came with the software to change the access number that your modem dials.

Using Broadband on the Road

If you connect to your ISP at home using a cable or digital subscriber line (DSL) modem, life gets complicated when you're on the road. You won't be able to take your broadband modem with you and just plug it in from your hotel room.

Some broadband ISPs offer an alternative dial-up number that you can use to browse the Internet and check your e-mail. In some cases, however, dial-up access costs extra and is charged to your account by the minute. You'll have to check with your ISP for a list of the charges and for local telephone numbers. You'll then need to set up a dial-up connection, as explained in the section "Creating an Additional Dial-Up Networking Connection," later in this chapter.

As an alternative, a growing number of hotels, airports, restaurants, and convention centers offer high-speed wireless Internet access for a fee. San Jose International Airport, Austin-Bergstrom International Airport, and Seattle-Tacoma International Airport, for example, provide high-speed 802.11b wireless Internet access using the Wayport service. All you need is a Wayport account and a laptop computer equipped with a Wi-Fi wireless network card to access the Internet from any Wayport-equipped location.

Some hotels, by the way, offer wired Wayport service for travelers with Ethernet network cards. Wayport and similar companies are making wireless and wired broadband Internet access readily available so business travelers can stay in touch with the office and home.

Fortunately, large, nationwide ISPs have local phone numbers in or near most major cities, so you should find out from your ISP ahead of time the local phone numbers for the areas in which you'll be staying. Call the ISP's support number and request the local access numbers, or connect online before you leave and look for the numbers on the ISP's Web site. When you arrive at your destination, you can change the phone number that your system dials to connect to the ISP. Be sure to make a note of the original number so you'll be able to restore it when you return home.

Tip

If you use a program such as Microsoft Outlook Express to check your e-mail, you'll need to change the connection it uses to dial in to your ISP to send and receive e-mail.

You can change the telephone number your computer dials by following these steps:

1. In Microsoft Windows 95 or Windows 98, double-click My Computer on the Windows desktop and then double-click the Dial-Up Networking icon. In Microsoft Windows Millennium Edition (Me), choose Settings from the Start menu and click Dial-Up Networking. In Microsoft Windows 2000, open Control Panel and then double-click Network And Dial-Up Connections. In Windows XP, click Start, click Connect To, and then click Show All Connections.

2. Right-click the connection you normally use and choose Properties from the shortcut menu. You'll see a connection dialog box, much like the one shown in Figure 14-1.

Figure 14-1.
Change your dial-up phone number to connect to your ISP from the road.

3. On the General tab, replace the existing area code and telephone number with the new numbers.

4. If you must dial 9 or some other number to get an outside line, add the number and a comma before the phone number, as in *9,5551212*. The comma causes the modem to pause after dialing the number 9 so the outside dial tone can be obtained.

5. Click OK.

Note

Remember to change the phone number again when you return home.

Creating an Additional Dial-Up Networking Connection

If you travel frequently to the same location, such as a branch office in a different city, changing and restoring the telephone number of your ISP can be an annoyance. Instead of changing the number in your dial-up connection, you can create a new connection that will have all the settings required to dial in to your ISP from the road. You can choose to use that connection when traveling and then switch back to the original when you get home.

Making a New Connection in Windows 95, Windows 98, or Windows Me

First, you need to check the existing settings, including the primary and secondary Domain Name System (DNS) numbers. If you're using Windows 2000 or Windows XP, see the section "Making Connections in Windows 2000 or Windows XP," later in this chapter. If you're using Windows 95, Windows 98, or Windows Me, follow these steps:

1. Double-click My Computer on the Windows desktop. In Windows Me, choose Settings from the Start menu, click Dial-Up Networking, and then go to step 3.

2. In the My Computer window, double-click the Dial-Up Networking icon.

3. Right-click the connection you use to dial in to your ISP, and then choose Properties.

4. Click the Server Types tab in Windows 95 and Windows 98 or the Networking tab in Windows Me.

5. Make a note of the settings, including the Type Of Dial-Up Server setting, and the check boxes that are selected in the Advanced Options and Allowed Network Protocols sections.

6. Click the TCP/IP Settings button.

7. In the TCP/IP Settings dialog box, write down any numbers that appear in the Primary DNS and Secondary DNS text boxes. Also make a note about the other settings in the box, although these are usually already set for you by default when you make a new connection.

8. Click Cancel to return to the Dial-Up Networking window, and click Cancel again to close the dialog box for the connection.

Now you can make a new connection by following these steps:

1. In the Dial-Up Networking window, double-click Make New Connection to open the Make New Connection dialog box.

2. Type a name for the connection, such as *Branch Office*.

3. If you have more than one modem, click the down arrow next to the Select A Device drop-down list and choose the modem you'll use to connect to the ISP.

4. Click Next.

5. Enter the ISP's local phone number at the remote location.

6. Click Next, and then click Finish.

While the Dial-Up Networking window is still open, you need to configure the connection for the proper protocols and server settings. Here's how to do it:

1. Right-click the connection you've just created, and choose Properties.

2. In the Connection To dialog box, click the Server Types tab in Windows 95 and Windows 98 or the Networking tab in Windows Me.

3. Set the options on the tab so they match the settings you noted earlier. Be sure to check that you've matched the Type Of Dial-Up Server, Advanced Options, and Allowed Network Protocols settings.

4. Click the TCP/IP Settings button.

5. In the TCP/IP Settings dialog box, enter the primary and secondary DNS numbers that you copied earlier. Also, look at the other settings to make sure they're the same as your main ISP connection.

6. Click OK to close the TCP/IP Settings dialog box.

7. Click OK to return to the Dial-Up Networking window.

Now when you're away from home and want to dial in to your ISP, you can choose the new connection you've made. When you want to connect to the Internet, you can open the Dial-Up Networking window and double-click the connection to dial in to your ISP. The first time you connect with the new connection, you'll have to enter your user name and password. Select the Save Password check box so Windows will remember the password for later connections. When you see a message reporting that the connection has been made, you can start your Web browser.

Making Connections in Windows 2000 or Windows XP

If you're using Windows 2000 or Windows XP, follow these steps to create an additional dial-up connection for your ISP:

1. In Windows 2000, open Control Panel and then double-click Network And Dial-Up Connections. In Windows XP, click Start, click Connect To, and then click Show All Connections.

2. Right-click the connection you use to dial in to your ISP, and then select Create Copy. This action makes a new copy of the connection icon.

3. Right-click the copy of the connection icon and choose Properties to open the connection's Properties dialog box.

4. In the Phone Number text box on the General tab, type the ISP's local phone number at the remote location. If you need to enter a new area code, select the Use Dialing Rules check box, and enter the area code in the Area Code text box.

5. Click OK.

Now when you're away from home and want to dial in to your ISP, you can choose the new connection you've made. When you want to connect to the Internet, you can open the Network And Dial-Up Connections window and double-click the connection to dial in to your ISP. The first time you use the new connection, you'll have to enter your user name and password. Select the Save Password check box so Windows will remember the password for later connections. When you see a message reporting that the connection has been made, you can start your Web browser.

Setting the Default Connection in Microsoft Internet Explorer 5

If you're using Internet Explorer 5, you can easily change the default connection. Just follow these steps:

1. Right-click the Internet Explorer icon on the desktop.

2. Choose Properties from the shortcut menu.

3. On the Connections tab of the Internet Options dialog box, click the connection you want to use and then click the Set Default button.

4. Click OK.

Now whenever you start your browser, it'll dial in to the ISP using the new connection. Using this technique means you'll need to change the connection again when you get home.

Connecting to Your Home Network

As long as you can connect your modem to a phone line, you can dial in to your home network to transfer files or print documents when you're away. But whether you want to connect to your home network to share or print files or just access your home computer to get messages, you must set up your home computer so that it will allow you to dial in from the road. You perform this task by installing Dial-Up Server, a Windows feature that sets up a computer so that its modem answers the phone when you call in from a remote location, such as from a hotel room when you're traveling with a laptop computer.

When you set up your computers for dial-up networking, you can choose to password-protect your system so that only authorized persons can access your files. Password protection is optional, but it's highly recommended.

See Also

You should also consider using password protection to restrict access to sensitive folders, as explained in the section "Sharing and Accessing Network Resources," in Chapter 9, "Learning to Share," on page 237.

Installing Dial-Up Server

Although it comes with Windows 98 and Windows Me, Dial-Up Server isn't installed by default. Installing Dial-Up Server, however, requires only a few simple steps.

Note

In Windows 95, Dial-Up Server is part of the add-on program called Microsoft Plus!

Preparing to Install Dial-Up Server

Your first step is to make sure that all three network protocols are installed and that your hard disk is shared. If you haven't performed these tasks already, go back to the sections "Installing Protocols" in Chapter 7, "Installing the Software," on page 171, and "Sharing and Accessing Network Resources," in Chapter 9, "Learning to Share," on page 237, and follow the instructions.

You'll need to install TCP/IP because Microsoft's Dial-Up Server software requires TCP/IP to connect to the remote computer. If your home network uses TCP/IP as its protocol, you can dial in to the dial-up server and access its files, but you won't be able to access the other computers on the network. To dial in to your dial-up server and access your entire home network, you must have installed either IPX/SPX or NetBEUI as a network protocol. In other words, you should install all three of the protocols—IPX/SPX, NetBEUI, and TCP/IP—on the computer you want to use as a dial-up server, but only IPX/SPX and NetBEUI on the other computers on the network.

Note

Windows XP doesn't support the NetBEUI protocol.

You also need to set the Primary Network Logon option to Windows Logon and enable file sharing through the dial-up adapter, which is usually a modem. If you just use your modem to connect to the Internet, file and printer sharing over the modem will be disabled, which helps prevent Internet hackers from accessing your files when you're connected to the Internet. To access your own files when you dial in to the network, however, you have to enable file sharing.

See Also

For more information on enabling file sharing and setting the primary Windows logon, see Chapter 9, "Learning to Share."

Installing the Dial-Up Server Software in Windows 95, Windows 98, or Windows Me

To install the Dial-Up Server software in Windows 95, Windows 98, or Windows Me, follow these steps:

1. On the Start menu, point to Settings, and then click Control Panel.

Note

If you're using Windows 95, you must first install the Windows add-on called Microsoft Plus! before you can set up and configure Dial-Up Server. If you run setup from the Microsoft Plus! CD, the Dial-Up Server will be installed as another connection in the Dial-Up Networking window. The Dial-Up Networking (DUN) 1.3 Performance and Security Update (available at *http://www.microsoft.com/ windows95/downloads*) also contains Dial-Up Server.

2. In Control Panel, double-click the Add/Remove Programs icon.

3. In the Add/Remove Programs Properties dialog box, click the Windows Setup tab.

4. In the list of components, click Communications, but be careful not to remove the check mark in the check box to its left.

5. Click Details.

6. In the Communications dialog box, select the Dial-Up Server check box, as shown in Figure 14-2.

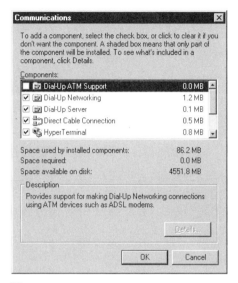

Figure 14-2.
If the component's check box is selected, the component, such as Dial-Up Server, is installed.

7. Click OK to close the Communications dialog box.

8. Click OK again to close the Add/Remove Programs Properties dialog box.

    At this point, you might need to insert the Windows CD. On some computers, the files that Windows needs are already stored on the hard disk. In either case, Dial-Up Server will be installed and you'll be ready for the next stage of the setup process.

Activating Dial-Up Server

Now that Dial-Up Server is installed, you have to activate it. This procedure sets up your computer to answer the telephone when it rings and establish the connection to the remote computer. Follow these steps to activate Dial-Up Server:

1. Double-click My Computer on the Windows desktop. (In Windows Me, choose Settings from the Start menu, click Dial-Up Networking, and then go to step 3.)

2. In the My Computer window, double-click the Dial-Up Networking icon.

3. From the Connections menu, choose Dial-Up Server to open the Dial-Up Server dialog box shown in Figure 14-3.

Figure 14-3.
The Dial-Up Server dialog box allows you to set up a modem to answer incoming calls.

If you have more than one modem, you'll see a tab for each modem in or connected to your computer. Click the tab for the modem you want to use to answer incoming calls.

4. Select Allow Caller Access.

5. To password-protect your system so that only authorized persons can connect to the network, click Change Password to open the Dial-Up Networking Password dialog box, shown below.

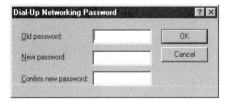

6. If you haven't yet set a password, leave the Old Password text box blank. Type your password in both the New Password and Confirm New Password text boxes, and click OK.

7. Click Apply. You'll see a new icon next to the clock on the right of the Windows taskbar, as shown below, indicating that Dial-Up Server is running.

Installing the Dial-Up Server Software in Windows 2000

If you're using Windows 2000, follow these steps to allow your computer to accept incoming calls:

1. Open Control Panel and double-click Network And Dial-Up Connections.

2. Double-click Make New Connection, and then click Next.

3. Click Accept Incoming Connections and then click Next to see a list of devices on your computer for accepting calls, as shown below.

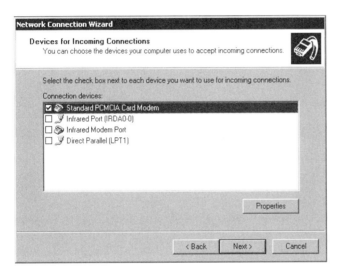

4. Select the check box for your modem and click Next.

5. Select the option Do Not Allow Virtual Private Connections and click Next. You'll see the Allowed Users list, shown below, detailing the users set up to access your computer.

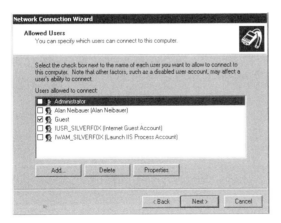

6. Select the check boxes for the users you'll allow to call in and click Next. (You can also use the dialog box to add other users, delete users, or change user properties.)

7. You'll see a list of networking components, such as Internet Protocol, File And Printer Sharing For Microsoft Networks, and Client For Microsoft Networks. Select the components you want to use for the dial-up server, and then click Next.

8. The name for the connection will be shown as Incoming Connections. Click Finish. You can now right-click the connection and choose Properties to adjust any server settings.

Installing the Dial-Up Server Software in Windows XP

If you're using Windows XP, follow these steps to allow your computer to accept incoming calls:

1. Open Control Panel and double-click Network Connections.

2. Click Create A New Connection, then click Next.

3. Click Set Up An Advanced Connection, then click Next.

4. Click Accept Incoming Connections, then click Next to see a list of devices on your computer for accepting calls.

5. Select the check box for your modem and click Next.

6. Select the Do Not Allow Virtual Private Connections option and click Next. You'll see the Users Allowed To Connect list showing all the users set up to access your computer.

7. Select the check boxes for the users you'll allow to call in, and click Next. (You can also use the dialog box to add other users, delete users, or change user properties.)

8. You'll see a list of networking components, such as Internet Protocol, File And Printer Sharing For Microsoft Networks, and Client For Microsoft Networks. Select the components you want to use for the dial-up server, and then click Next.

9. The name for the connection will be shown as Incoming Connections. Click Finish. You can now right-click the connection and choose Properties to adjust any server settings.

Preparing Your Windows 95, Windows 98, or Windows Me Laptop

Now you have to set up your laptop by creating a connection that'll call the number for your home network. If you're using Windows 2000 or Windows XP, see the section "Preparing Your Windows 2000 Laptop" or "Preparing Your Windows XP Laptop" later in this chapter. If you're using previous versions of Windows, follow these steps:

1. In Windows 95 or Windows 98, double-click My Computer on the Windows desktop. In Windows Me, choose Settings from the Start menu, click Dial-Up Networking, and then go to step 3.

2. In the My Computer window, double-click the Dial-Up Networking icon.

3. Double-click Make New Connection to open the Make New Connection dialog box, shown in Figure 14-4.

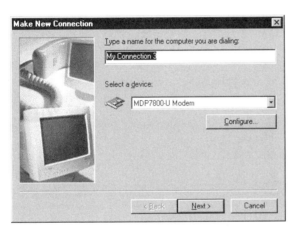

Figure 14-4.
The Make New Connection dialog box.

4. Type a name for your connection, such as *Road Warrior*.

5. If you have more than one modem, click the down arrow next to the Select A Device drop-down list, and choose the modem you'll use to connect to your computer.

6. Click Next to see the dialog box in Figure 14-5.

7. Type your computer's area code and telephone number.

8. Click Next, then click Finish.

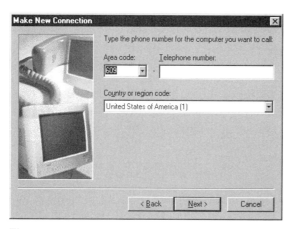

Figure 14-5.
Specify your computer's telephone number.

While the Dial-Up Networking window is still open, configure the connection for the proper protocol. Here's how to do it:

1. Right-click the connection you've created, and choose Properties.

2. In the Connection To dialog box, click the Server Types tab to see the options shown in Figure 14-6.

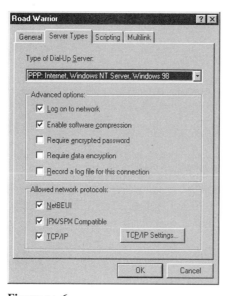

Figure 14-6.
Configure your dial-up connection from this set of options.

3. Make sure the Type Of Dial-Up Server option is set to PPP: Internet, Windows NT Server, Windows 98. If you're using Windows 95, make sure the option is set to PPP: Windows 95, Windows NT, Internet.

4. Select the Log On To Network check box.

5. Select all three protocols listed in the Allowed Network Protocols area of the dialog box: NetBEUI, IPX/SPX Compatible, and TCP/IP.

6. Click OK.

Note

You don't need to configure an IP address or set any other TCP/IP options.

Preparing Your Windows 2000 Laptop

If you're using Windows 2000 on your laptop, follow these steps to create a dial-up connection to use when you travel:

1. In Windows 2000, open Control Panel and double-click Network And Dial-Up Connections.

2. Double-click Make New Connection, then click Next to start the Network Connection Wizard, and click Next.

3. Select Dial-Up To Private Network, and click Next.

4. If you're asked to select a device, select the modem that you'll use to dial out.

5. Type the phone number of your home network, and click Next.

6. Select Only For Myself, and click Next.

7. Type the name of your dial-up connection, and click Finish.

8. In the Connect dialog box, click Cancel because you are not quite ready to dial in to the network.

While the Network Dial-Up Connections window is still open, configure the connection for the proper protocols. Here's how to do it:

1. Right-click the connection you've just created, and choose Properties.

2. In the Properties dialog box, click the Networking tab.

3. Make sure the Type Of Dial-Up Server I Am Calling option is set to PPP: Windows 95/98/NT 4/2000, Internet.

4. In the Components Checked Are Used By This Connection box, make sure that these protocols are present: Internet Protocol (TCP/IP), NetBEUI Protocol, and NWLink IPX/SPX/NetBIOS Compatible Transport Protocol. If all three are present, click OK.

If one or more of the three protocols aren't present, you'll need to install them. Continue with these steps:

1. Click Install.

2. Select Protocol, and click Add.

3. Select the protocol you want to install in the Select Network Protocol box, and click OK.

4. If you need to install another protocol, follow steps 1 through 3 again.

5. Once you've installed all the necessary protocols, click Close.

Preparing Your Windows XP Laptop

If you're using Windows XP on your laptop, follow these steps to create a dial-up connection to use when you travel:

1. Open Control Panel and double-click Network Connections.

2. Click Create A New Connection, then click Next.

3. Select Connect To The Network At My Workplace, and click Next.

4. Click Dial-Up Connection, and click Next.

5. If you're asked to select a device, select the modem that you'll use to dial out.

6. Type a name for the connection, then click Next.

7. Type the phone number of your home network, and click Next.

8. Click Finish. If the Connect box appears, click Cancel.

While the Network Connections window is still open, you need to configure the connection for the proper protocols. Here's how to do it:

1. Right-click the connection you've just created, and choose Properties.

2. In the Properties dialog box, click the Networking tab.

3. Make sure the Type Of Dial-Up Server I Am Calling option is set to PPP: Windows 95/98/NT 4/2000, Internet.

4. In the This Connection Uses The Following Items box, make sure that both of these protocols are present: Internet Protocol (TCP/IP) and NWLink IPX/SPX/NetBIOS Compatible Transport Protocol. If both are present, click OK.

If one or more of the protocols aren't present, you'll need to install them. Continue with these steps:

1. Click Install.

2. Select Protocol, and click Add.

3. Select the protocol you want to install in the Select Network Protocol box, and click OK.

4. If you need to install another protocol, follow steps 1 through 3 again.

5. Once you've installed all the necessary protocols, click Close.

Accessing a Home Computer Remotely

You're now ready to dial in to your computer from the road. Open the Dial-Up Networking window in Windows 95, Windows 98, and Windows Me, the Network And Dial-Up Connections window in Windows 2000, or the Network Connections window in Windows XP. Double-click the icon representing your connection to home. If you're asked, enter your user name and password. In Windows XP, you can also choose to save the password for just you, which is safer when you're on the road, or for all others who are using your computer. Click Connect (or Dial in Windows XP) to make the connection. Windows will dial in and make the connection to your computer. Enter your password if you're asked for it.

To access the files on a computer on your network, you must enter its name, as follows:

1. On the Start menu, click Run.

2. In the Run dialog box, type two backslashes followed by the name of the computer you're dialing in to, and then click OK. If the computer is named *adam*, for example, you'd enter **\\adam**, as shown below.

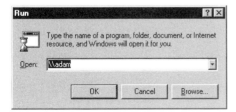

After you enter the computer name, you can access the computer just as if you were connected to the network at home. You'll see a window showing all the shared resources on the computer.

To access a file, double-click the shared drive and navigate to the file just as if you were using the My Computer window on your home computer. Copy and move files by dragging them between windows. For example, to get a copy of a file from your home computer onto your laptop, simply locate the file and drag it to your laptop's desktop.

Printing a document on a shared printer that's connected to the network is just as easy. Locate the document using My Computer or Windows Explorer on your laptop and drag it to the icon for the shared printer. The document will be waiting for you when you return home.

Keeping in Touch with Family

NetMeeting allows you to communicate with your family in a variety of ways when you're away from home. It's also a good way to keep in touch with other family members who are at remote locations.

Note

In Windows XP, you can also connect while on the road using Remote Assistance and Windows Messenger. Refer to the section "Communicating Remotely with Windows XP," later in this chapter.

Let's say you're on a business trip or your child is away at school. Instead of simply sending and receiving e-mail, you can use NetMeeting to talk to each other just as you would over the telephone. You can also send and receive files, work on programs together, and share drawings, as shown in Figure 14-7. If your computers are equipped with video cameras, you can even see each other as you're talking.

If you have version 4 or later of Internet Explorer, NetMeeting is already installed on your system. If NetMeeting isn't installed, you can download a free copy of it from the Microsoft Web site at this address: *http://www.microsoft.com/windows/netmeeting*.

The information in this chapter is based on NetMeeting 3, the version of the program that's installed with Internet Explorer 5 or later. If you have an earlier version of NetMeeting, you should download the newest version from the Microsoft Web site to obtain all the latest features.

Figure 14-7.
NetMeeting in action.

To start NetMeeting in Windows 95, Windows 98, or Windows Me, point to Programs on the Start menu, and then click Microsoft NetMeeting. The program might also be listed on the submenu that appears when you point to Internet Explorer on the Programs menu, or when you point to Accessories and then point to Internet Tools or Communications. In Windows 2000 or Windows XP, point to Accessories, point to Communications, and click Microsoft NetMeeting. In some cases, the Windows XP installation fails to place NetMeeting on the Communications menu. In that case, follow these steps to run NetMeeting:

1. Click Start on the Windows XP taskbar.

2. Click Run.

3. In the Run dialog box that appears, type **conf**, then press Enter.

The first time you run NetMeeting, you'll see a series of dialog boxes that help you set up the program on your system. Depending on your system's configuration and on the version of NetMeeting that you're using, the order and content of these dialog boxes might be somewhat different from the following description, which is based on Net-Meeting 3. Respond to the prompts in each dialog box, and then click Next to move to the next dialog box.

1. Click Next in the first dialog box, which explains the features available in NetMeeting.

2. In the next dialog box, enter your name, e-mail address, city, state, and country, and a brief comment about yourself that will identify you onscreen to other Net-Meeting users.

3. Click Next to continue.

4. In the next dialog box, shown in Figure 14-8, choose whether you want to log on to a directory server whenever NetMeeting starts, and select the default server.

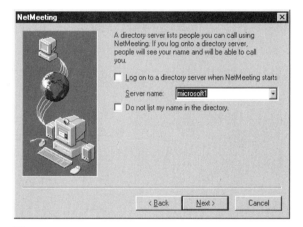

Figure 14-8.
This NetMeeting dialog box allows you to log on to a server.

A *directory server* lists people you can call and helps NetMeeting users find each other over the Internet. The server acts like a gigantic telephone switchboard, maintaining a directory of everyone who is logged on and ready to accept calls. The member of your family who you plan to contact over the Internet with NetMeeting should choose the same server.

Note

When you're home, you can also use NetMeeting directly over your home network as a family intercom. Because you don't need to log on to a server if you'll be using NetMeeting over your home network, don't choose to log on to a server when NetMeeting starts.

5. Click Next to continue.

6. If you have a video capture board installed in your computer, you'll see a dialog box that asks you to confirm its use. Click Next to continue.

7. If a dialog box appears asking for the speed of your connection, select the speed of your modem and click Next.

Now you're halfway there. Continue by following these steps:

8. To make NetMeeting easier to start, select both check boxes in the next dialog box to place shortcuts for NetMeeting both on your Windows desktop and on the Quick Launch toolbar, just to the right of the Start button, then click Next.

9. Click Next in the following window, when NetMeeting informs you that the Audio Tuning Wizard is about to help you tune your audio settings. It also instructs you to close all other programs that play or record sound.

    Now you might see a dialog box that asks you to select the devices that will record and play back sound on your system. Generally, your sound card performs both functions.

10. Select the sound card you have, and click Next.

11. Test the volume of your speakers by clicking the Test button in the dialog box shown in Figure 14-9 and by adjusting the slider to set a comfortable listening level. Click Stop to stop the sound, and then click Next.

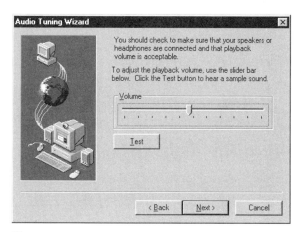

Figure 14-9.
Use the slider to adjust the sound volume.

12. To set the sensitivity of your microphone, speak into the microphone and watch the color bar that indicates the volume of your voice. Adjust the Record Volume slider so the bar reaches about the halfway mark, and click Next.

13. Click Finish when the Audio Tuning Wizard reports that you've successfully tuned your settings. When you click Finish, you'll see the NetMeeting window, shown in Figure 14-10.

Note

After you start NetMeeting, you can change all the setup options and fine-tune calling, audio, and video settings by choosing Options from the NetMeeting Tools menu.

Starting a Meeting

If NetMeeting is set to log on to a directory server automatically, it will dial in to your ISP each time it's started. If it doesn't dial automatically, choose Log On To from the Call menu, which is followed by the name of the directory server you are using.

To place a call, choose Directory from the Call menu to open a dialog box listing the people logged on to the server. If many people are logged on, the list might take a few moments to appear while their names are downloaded. Scroll through the list to locate the person you want to speak with and double-click that person's name.

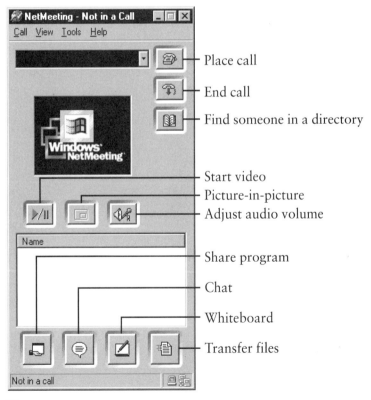

Figure 14-10.

The NetMeeting program allows you to call other network users.

Using NetMeeting on a Network

Although NetMeeting is initially set to work across the Internet, you can call someone on your home network by adjusting the program so that it places the call through the network instead of through the Internet.

Note

If your computer tries to dial in to the Internet when you're placing a network call, just close the Dial-Up Networking window to stop the call.

To adjust the NetMeeting program, follow these steps:

1. Find out the IP address or name of the network computer you want to dial. You must be using TCP/IP on the network to make NetMeeting calls across the network.

2. Click the Place Call button or choose New Call from the Call menu to see the Place A Call dialog box, as shown below.

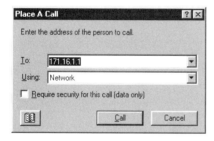

3. From the Using drop-down list, choose Network.

4. In the To box, enter the IP address or the name of the computer you're trying to reach, and then click Call.

   The person at the computer you're calling will hear a telephone ring sound, and a message box will open to ask whether the user wants to accept or ignore your call.

   If the person chooses to ignore the call, a message appears on your screen reporting that the other user didn't accept your call.

Note

NetMeeting might also display a message reporting that the person you've called is currently in another meeting and can't accept your call, or it might inform you that the person is in a meeting and ask whether you would like to join it.

When your call is accepted, the names of the people in the meeting are displayed in the NetMeeting window and you can start communicating. If each computer has a microphone and speakers, you can each speak into the microphone to talk to one another. If your computer is equipped with a camera, the person you're talking to will also be able to see you, as shown in Figure 14-11.

Figure 14-11.
You can see the people you're talking to using NetMeeting if you have additional equipment.

To end the meeting, click the End Call button or choose Hang Up from the Call menu.

Using the Microsoft Internet Directory

Rather than log on to a directory server, you can connect to the Microsoft Internet Directory and use MSN Messenger Service to connect to contacts who also have MSN Messenger Service accounts.

To use the Microsoft Internet Directory, you'll need to sign up for a free MSN Messenger Service account, which also signs you up for a free HotMail e-mail account and a Microsoft Passport. To do this, just follow these steps:

1. In NetMeeting, choose Options from the Tools menu to open the Options dialog box.

2. On the General tab of the dialog box, click the down arrow next to the Directory drop-down list, choose Microsoft Internet Directory from the list, and then click OK.

3. Select Log On To Microsoft Internet Directory from the Call menu. If that option is dimmed on the call menu, select Directory.

   If you already signed up for a MSN Messenger Service account, click Click Here to Log On to the MSN Messenger Service. Enter your sign-in name and password, and click OK. *To learn how to use the MSN Messenger Service, refer to the section "Windows Messenger," later in this chapter.*

4. If you have not yet signed up for a MSN Messenger Service account and .NET Password, a window appears asking whether you want to get a Passport account.

5. Click Next, and then click Get a Passport. Follow the prompts on the screen and enter the requested information to create the Hotmail e-mail account, and then click Sign Up.

6. Then you'll have to sign up for the .NET Password. Enter the information requested and click I Agree to accept the terms of the Passport.

7. Click Continue.

8. Enter your logon name and password, and then click Finish to return to the Microsoft Internet Directory and NetMeeting.

Chatting in NetMeeting

Even with the proper equipment, the audio quality of a NetMeeting call can be poor. Instead of actually speaking over the network, you might want to open a Chat window and type messages to the other participants in the meeting. Follow these steps to open a Chat window:

1. Click the Chat button or choose Chat from the Tools menu to open the Chat window. The Chat window also opens on the other participants' screens.

2. Read the chat messages as they appear in the large text box, as shown in Figure 14-12.

Figure 14-12.
With NetMeeting, you can create your own chat room on the network.

3. Type your messages in the Message text box and press Enter to transmit them.

4. If you want to send a private message to a particular chat participant, select the participant's name from the Send To drop-down list before clicking the Send Message button. To resume sending public messages to everyone in the chat, choose Everyone In Chat from the Send To drop-down list.

5. To exit the chat, close the Chat window or choose Exit from the File menu.

Using the Whiteboard

Sometimes you might need to communicate about something online that you can't easily express in words. Suppose, for example, that you want to communicate with a young member of your family by drawing pictures rather than writing in a Chat window. The solution in such situations is a handy NetMeeting feature called the whiteboard.

The *whiteboard* is a drawing window that you can share with everyone at the meeting. Whatever you draw on the whiteboard appears on the whiteboards of all the other participants. They, in turn, can use their whiteboards to add to your drawing, as long as you permit it. Figure 14-13 shows a NetMeeting whiteboard.

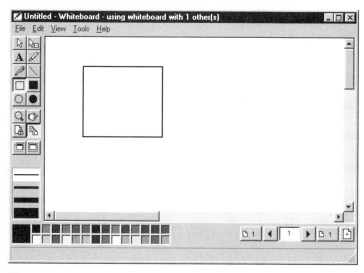

Figure 14-13.

The whiteboard feature in NetMeeting allows meeting participants to view and make changes to drawings.

To use the whiteboard, follow these steps:

1. Click the Whiteboard button or choose Whiteboard from the Tools menu.

2. Draw on the whiteboard using tools from the whiteboard tool palette, shown in Figure 14-14.

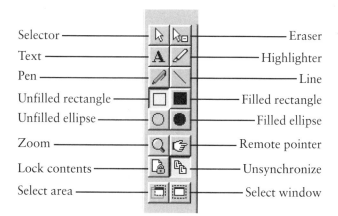

Figure 14-14.

The items in the whiteboard tool palette allow you to work on shared graphics and text.

The tool palette contains everything you need to create and edit drawings and text on the whiteboard. The same features are also available on the Tools menu.

Here's how to use the whiteboard tools:

- **Selector:** Click this tool on an object you want to select, choose Delete, Copy, or Cut from the Edit menu, or drag the selected object to move it on the screen.

- **Eraser:** Click this tool on an object you want to erase. You can also use it to drag a rectangle around an area. All objects that are even partially within the rectangle will be deleted.

- **Text:** Click this tool to use your keyboard to type on the whiteboard. Choose a color from the color palette, or click the Font Options button that appears when you select the tool to change the font, font size, and font style. The Colors and Font commands on the Options menu also allow you to change the color, size, and style of your text.

- **Highlighter:** Choose a line width and a color, and then drag this tool over the area you want to highlight.

- **Pen:** Click this tool and then drag it in the whiteboard area to draw freehand on the screen.

- **Line:** Click this tool to draw straight lines by dragging the mouse pointer from one point to the next. Select a line width and choose a color from the color palette shown in the Whiteboard window, as shown below. You can also use the Colors and Line Width commands on the Options menu.

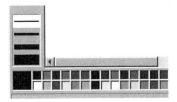

Note

You can use the Bring To Front or Send To Back commands on the Edit menu to change how objects overlap.

- **Rectangle:** Choose a line width and color from the palette, and then click the Unfilled Rectangle button and draw the outline of a rectangle by dragging, or click the Filled Rectangle button and draw a solid rectangle of the selected color.

- **Ellipse:** Click one of the two Ellipse buttons, then drag on the whiteboard to draw filled or unfilled circles or ellipses in the line width and color of your choice.

- **Zoom:** Click this tool, or use the Zoom command on the View menu, to switch between normal and enlarged views.

- **Remote Pointer:** Click this tool to display a pointer, and then move it to the area of the whiteboard you want others to look at.

- **Lock Contents:** Click this tool to prevent others from changing the whiteboard contents. Clear it to allow others to change the whiteboard.

- **Synchronize/Unsynchronize:** This tool lets you determine whether other whiteboard users can see the same pages you're viewing. To synchronize the pages, click the tool so that it appears engaged. To unsynchronize the pages, click the tool so that it appears released.

- **Select Area:** Click this tool to drag a rectangle over an area of the screen outside the whiteboard that you want to copy to the whiteboard.

- **Select Window:** This tool works in much the same way as the Windows clipboard. Click any window on your screen, even a partially obscured one, to copy the contents of the window to the whiteboard. The whiteboard will show the contents of the window inserted as a graphic.

Adding and Changing Whiteboard Pages

If a meeting you were conducting were held in person, you might use a flip chart to draw images and highlight important points. When you fill one page, just flip it over and start a fresh sheet. You can use the whiteboard in the same way, adding pages and changing them as needed.

Use the buttons at the lower-right corner of the whiteboard window, illustrated below, to insert a page and to switch from page to page.

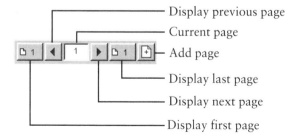

Display previous page
Current page
Add page
Display last page
Display next page
Display first page

Choose Clear Page from the Edit menu to erase the current page, or choose Delete Page from the Edit menu to delete the page. Erasing a page removes the page's contents on the screen of all NetMeeting participants but leaves the page in place. Deleting a page actually removes it from your whiteboard and from those of other participants as well.

Note

Normally, everyone in the meeting can see the same page that you have displayed on your screen. If you want to change pages without letting everyone see what you're doing, clear Synchronize on the View menu.

Saving and Printing the Whiteboard

When your meeting is over, you don't have to lose the contents of the whiteboard. While it's displayed, each participant in the meeting can print a copy of the whiteboard by choosing Print from the File menu. Each participant can also save the whiteboard by choosing Save from the File menu. Whiteboards are saved in a special format, with a .nmw extension. To reopen saved whiteboard files, choose Open from the File menu.

Note

Closing your own whiteboard doesn't close the whiteboards of other participants, who can continue to draw on theirs. If you open the whiteboard again, NetMeeting locates and displays the same whiteboard the other participants see in an updated version. If you try to close a whiteboard before saving it, NetMeeting asks whether you want to save it.

Working Together on Programs

In addition to sharing a drawing on the whiteboard, you might want meeting participants to share a program as well. When you share a program with others, the meeting participants can see the program, but they can't control it unless you specifically allow them to do so. The person running the program is called the *owner*, and only the owner has control over who can work with the program. Here's how to use NetMeeting to share a program:

1. Start the program you want to share, and then switch back to NetMeeting.

2. Click the Share Program button or choose Sharing from the Tools menu to see the Sharing dialog box in Figure 14-15.

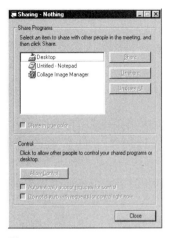

Figure 14-15.
The Sharing dialog box allows you to share programs with other meeting participants.

3. In the list of programs that are running, select the program you want to share, and then click Share. Other meeting participants will now be able to see exactly what you're doing with the shared program.

If you want to allow meeting participants to use the shared program, rather than just view it, click the Allow Control button in the Sharing dialog box. You'll be offered these two options:

- **Automatically Accept Requests For Control** lets a meeting participant use the program without your express permission.

- **Do Not Disturb With Requests For Control Right Now** prevents requests for sharing from appearing on your screen.

To gain control of a program, a meeting participant must double-click the program window on the screen. This action either gives the person control of the program or, if you haven't turned on automatic acceptance in the Sharing dialog box, displays a dialog box asking whether you want to reject or accept the request.

By clicking Accept, you transfer control of the program to the participant, and you'll no longer be able to use your pointer onscreen. To regain control over the program and your cursor, and to stop any participant who's currently working with the shared program, press Esc or click the mouse button. To stop sharing the program, click Unshare or Unshare All in the Sharing dialog box.

Sending and Receiving Files

While you're in a meeting, you can exchange files with other participants. Click the Transfer Files button or choose File Transfer from the Tools menu to view the File Transfer dialog box, shown below.

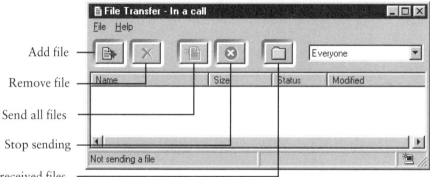

Add file
Remove file
Send all files
Stop sending
View received files

Click Add Files and, in the Choose Files To Send dialog box, select the files you want to transfer. Then click Send All to send the files to everyone or, from the drop-down list of meeting participants in the File Transfer dialog box, choose the participant to whom you want the files sent, and then click Send All.

When you receive a file from someone else, you'll see a dialog box, similar to the one shown below, giving you the option to close the dialog box, open the file, or delete the file.

Files that you receive are stored in the C:\Program Files\NetMeeting\Received Files folder. Click the View Received Files button—the one that shows an icon of a folder—to open that folder.

Controlling a Home Computer Remotely

NetMeeting includes a powerful feature that lets you actually control one of the other computers on the network. For example, suppose a family member is having trouble changing a setting in Control Panel or needs help performing a Windows task. You can take control of another person's computer from your own system and perform tasks as though you were sitting in front of the other computer.

To set up a computer to accept remote control, you have to use the Remote Desktop Sharing Wizard on that computer.

1. Start NetMeeting on the computer you want to control, and choose Remote Desktop Sharing from the Tools menu.

2. Click Next after reading the first Remote Desktop Sharing Wizard page.

3. In Windows 95, Windows 98, or Windows Me, enter a password of at least seven characters that will allow access from the controlling computer. To access a Windows 2000 or Windows XP computer, the user must log on with an account that has administrative privileges on the computer that's being remotely accessed. In such a case, just read the information shown by the wizard at this point, then click Next to proceed to step 5.

4. Reenter the password to confirm it, then click Next.

5. You can now choose to password-protect a screen saver as an extra security feature. Make your choice and click Next.

6. Click Finish.

7. Close NetMeeting. The Remote Desktop Sharing icon appears in the computer's system tray, to the left of the clock on the taskbar.

8. Right-click the Remote Desktop Sharing icon and select Activate Remote Desktop Sharing from the shortcut menu, as seen below.

9. Start NetMeeting on the computer that will be in control and call the computer you want to share.

10. In the Place A Call dialog box that appears, select the Require Security For This Call (Data Only) check box, then click Call. You'll be asked to enter the password.

11. Enter the password and click OK.

You'll see a window that contains the other computer's desktop, as shown in Figure 14-16. You can now control the remote computer as if you were sitting at its keyboard.

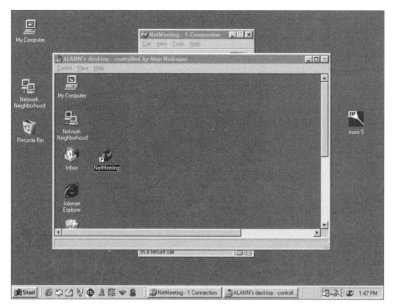

Figure 14-16.
With Remote Desktop Sharing, you can operate a remote computer from your own keyboard and screen.

12. To stop sharing, right-click the Remote Desktop Sharing icon on the desktop of the computer you're sharing, and select Exit.

Communicating Remotely with Windows XP

Windows XP offers three unique ways to communicate remotely: Remote Desktop Connection, Remote Assistance, and Windows Messenger.

- Remote Desktop Connection lets you take remote control of a Windows XP Professional computer, but not Windows XP Home Edition. For more information about this feature, refer to the help system in Windows XP Professional.

- Remote Assistance allows any two Windows XP computers (Home Edition or Professional) to chat, and it allows one computer to take control over the other.

- Windows Messenger lets you send and receive messages, transfer files, share a whiteboard, control programs, and see and talk to others.

When using Remote Assistance and Windows Messenger, all communication occurs over the Internet. You don't have to call long distance from a remote location. Instead, connect to the Internet using a local ISP telephone number, as explained in the section "Dialing In to Your ISP," earlier in this chapter.

Remote Assistance

Using Remote Assistance, one computer (we'll call it the *requester*) sends an e-mail message to another computer requesting assistance. The other computer (we'll call it the *assistant*) responds to the e-mail message by clicking a link in an attachment. The two computers are connected to each other over the Internet, they can send messages to each other, and the assistant can take control over the requester. So if you're on the road, either you or someone at home can initiate the connection to chat or transfer files.

The requester takes the following steps:

1. Select Start, select All Programs, and then select Remote Assistance to display the options in Figure 14-17.

2. Click Invite Someone To Help You.

3. Enter the e-mail address of the person you want to assist you. You can also sign in to Windows Messenger and send a request to a Windows Messenger contact.

4. Click Invite This Person.

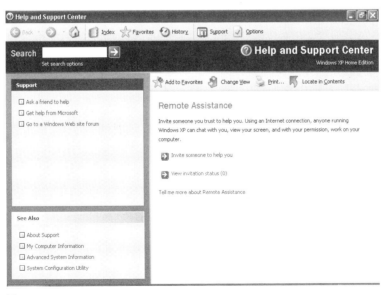

Figure 14-17.

Initiating a Remote Assistance request.

5. Enter a message to the person, then click Continue to see the options in Figure 14-18.

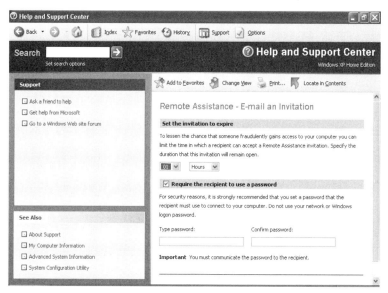

Figure 14-18.
Remote Assistance options.

6. Set an expiration date and a required password. The expiration date limits the amount of time in which the assistant can respond.

7. Click Send Invitation to see a box such as the one below.

8. Click Send.

The message is stored in the Outgoing folder of your e-mail application.

9. Go to your e-mail program and send the message.

The assistant takes the next steps:

1. After receiving an e-mail with an attachment, the assistant clicks the attachment. A drop-down menu appears with the options to open the attachment or save it, as shown below.

2. The assistant selects the option to open the attachment and is asked for your password, as shown below.

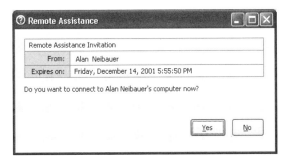

3. The assistant enters the password and clicks Yes to make the connection.

4. You (the requester) are asked whether you want to make the connection, as shown below. Click Yes.

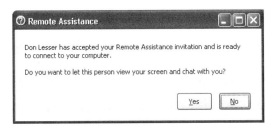

The requester now sees the options shown in Figure 14-19, and the assistant sees the requestor's screen. The assistant and requester can use text or voice chat, or transfer files.

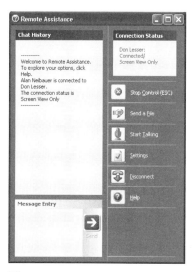

Figure 14-19.

A Remote Assistance connection.

Use the Message Entry section of the window to type messages and use the other options to transfer files or start a voice chat.

To remotely control the requester's computer, the assistant clicks the Take Control button on the toolbar. A message appears asking the requester whether he or she wants the assistant to take control, as seen below.

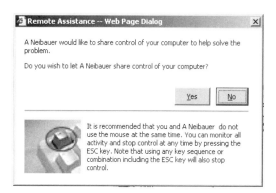

The assistant now works on the screen as if he or she were using the requester's computer, as shown in Figure 14-20.

To end the remote control, the requester clicks Stop Control or presses the Esc key. The assistant can click Release Control.

Figure 14-20.
The assistant can work with the requester's programs.

Windows Messenger

Windows Messenger is an immediate messenger program much like MSN Messenger and AOL Instant Messenger, but with added features. Using Windows Messenger, you can not only write back and forth, but you also have most of the capabilities provided by NetMeeting:

- Send and receive files.
- Use voice chat.
- Send and receive video, if the users are equipped with cameras.
- Share a graphic whiteboard.
- Share an application.
- Switch to Remote Assistance.

When you first start Messenger, you'll have the opportunity to sign up for a free Messenger account with Microsoft .NET Passport. *You'll find instructions for signing up for the account in the section "Using the Microsoft Internet Directory," earlier in the chapter.*

Once you create an account, start Messenger from the Windows XP Start menu. If you aren't signed in automatically, click the option Click Here To Sign In, enter your e-mail address and Messenger password, and click OK. You'll see the Windows Messenger window listing your name, as shown in Figure 14-21.

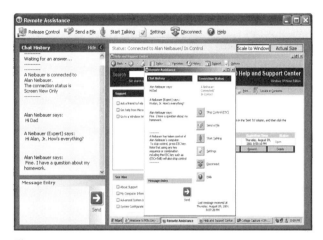

Figure 14-21.

Windows Messenger.

Click your name for options that report your status to others or to customize Messenger, as shown below.

Your first task should be to add contacts—other Windows Messenger users with whom you'd like to chat.

Click Add and then select to enter a contact by his or her e-mail address or sign-in name, or to search for a user currently signed in. If you choose to specify the user, enter his or her e-mail address and then click Next. If the e-mail address belongs to a person who doesn't have a .NET Passport account, you'll have the opportunity to send that person an e-mail message with an invitation to sign up for a free .NET Passport account.

Once you add a contact for a .NET Passport user, that person's e-mail address appears under the Online or Not Online sections to indicate his or her status, as shown in Figure 14-22.

Figure 14-22.

Windows Messenger with contacts listed.

To start chatting with an online contact, double-click that person's name to open the window shown in Figure 14-23. Type your message and click Send.

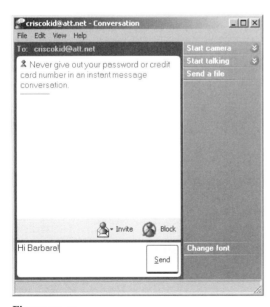

Figure 14-23.

The Windows Messenger chat window.

To take advantage of other features of Windows Messenger, use these techniques:

- To send a file, click Send A File, choose the file you want to transfer, and click Open. The contact will be asked whether he or she wants to accept or decline the transfer, as shown below.

> criscokid@att.net would like to send you the file "Document1.rtf" (1 Kb). Transfer time is less than 1 minute with a 28.8 modem. Do you want to <u>Accept</u> (Alt+T) or <u>Decline</u> (Alt+D) the invitation?

- To start a voice chat, click Start Talking.

- To send and receive live video, click Start Camera. The other person will be asked to accept the use of cameras before seeing your picture, as shown in Figure 14-24.

Note

If you're using the audio or video features for the first time, the Audio And Video Tuning Wizard begins. This wizard works in the same way as the Audio And Video Tuning Wizard for NetMeeting, described in the section "Keeping in Touch with Family," earlier in this chapter.

Figure 14-24.
Using video in Windows Messenger.

- To invite another contact into the conversation, click Invite, select To Join This Conversation, and select another online contact.

- To share a whiteboard, click Invite and select To Start Whiteboard. The other contact or contacts will receive a message with the options Accept and Decline. If they choose Accept, a whiteboard window appears, on which all users can draw. The whiteboard is similar to the NetMeeting whiteboard.

- To share an application, click Invite, and select To Start Application Sharing to open the window shown in Figure 14-25. Choose the currently running application that you want to share, and click Share. To allow the other user to actually run the shared application, click Allow Control.

The person who wants to take control of the application selects Request Control from the Control menu. The person sharing the application can then accept or decline the request, unless he or she selected Automatically Accept Requests For Control from the Sharing window. To avoid requests, select Do Not Disturb With Requests For Control Right Now.

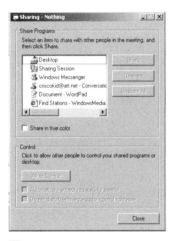

Figure 14-25.
Select an application to share.

Voice over IP (VoIP)

When you're on the road, making long-distance telephone calls home can get expensive. As an alternative, you can take advantage of Voice over IP (VoIP). With VoIP, you connect to the Internet over a local dial-up number and then make long-distance calls at little or no cost to you.

Using VoIP, you can use your computer's microphone and speakers as you would a telephone. You can find some popular VoIP services at *http://www.dialpad.com*, *http://www.net2phone.com*, and *http://www.deltathree.com*. With Dialpad, you don't need to download special software. Just log on to your account, click Make A Call, and then use the window that appears, as shown in Figure 14-26.

Net2Phone and Deltathree supply their own software that you download for free and install on your computer.

Depending on your computer and the speed of your Internet connection, however, the sound quality of VoIP calls might not be as clear as calls placed over a regular telephone line. You might experience delays (the time it takes for what is said to be heard by the other party), some loss of words, and static. To increase the quality of VoIP communications, you can purchase an add-on that plugs into your laptop. The hardware takes the place of your built-in sound card and reduces the burden on your computer's processor, resulting in higher quality sound. The Internet Phone Card from QuickNet (*http://www.quicknet.net*) is one example.

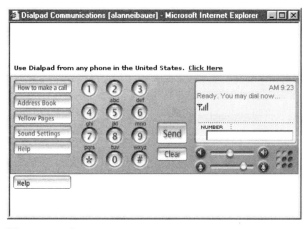

Figure 14-26.
Making telephone calls over the Internet with Dialpad.

You can also purchase the QuickNet Smart Cable that lets you plug an ordinary telephone into the card so you don't have to use the computer's microphone and speakers to make the call. In fact, once you log on to your account, just pick up the telephone and dial the call as you would normally.

You can use the QuickNet card to make free calls over Dialpad, Net2Phone, and Deltathree, but for even better voice quality, you can get an account through *http:// www.microtelco.com*. Microtelco channels your calls to the least expensive VoIP provider that offers the best connection quality. Although the calls are not free, calls within the United States cost between three and five cents per minute. International costs are slightly more.

The Bottom Line

Dialing in from the road, remotely controlling a computer, and seeing the folks you're talking to over the Internet—it all seems like something out of the future, but these options are available today. In the next chapter, you'll learn which other futuristic features are available right now or are soon headed your way.

Chapter 15

Your Future Home Network

In previous chapters, you learned how to set up a home network using the latest available technologies: Ethernet networks, wireless systems, as well as phone-line and power-line networks. Although computers and their peripherals are constantly changing, the technologies and techniques described in this book will see your home network well into the future.

In this chapter, however, we'll take a look at some emerging and alternative technologies and see what the future might hold for you and your home. A wired home, as you'll learn, will no longer be one that simply has a computer network.

Universal Plug and Play

In an effort to standardize the way various electronic devices communicate with each other, Microsoft and more than 350 other companies have developed Universal Plug and Play (UPP).

Don't confuse UPP with *device plug and play,* which is supported by newer versions of Windows. With device plug and play, your computer recognizes when a new peripheral is attached and automatically loads, or looks for, the necessary supporting drivers. UPP extends this concept even further, to all types of electronic devices, including home automation, audio and video, communications, home appliances, and security. UPP devices can communicate using the standard Internet Protocol (IP) protocol regardless of the medium: Ethernet, wireless, phone line, power line, low voltage line, infrared, or IEEE 1394.

The UPP standard is designed for zero configuration. Just plug in a UPP device, and your computer and other UPP devices on the network automatically recognize its presence and its capabilities. For example, the UPP gateway mentioned in Chapter 11, "Going Online Through the Network," is automatically detected and used for Internet sharing with NAT Transversal.

Although the initial UPP products include computer peripherals, such as printers, scanners, and audio devices, such companies as General Electric and Maytag have already joined Microsoft to develop smart home appliances based on UPP technology. The concepts proposed by General Electric, for example, include a microwave oven that would read a frozen dinner's Universal Product Code (UPC), display its nutrition information, and begin cooking it automatically.

To take the ultimate example, suppose you had a complete UPP home. From any wireless computer in the house, you could check to see whether your wash was done, whether coffee was made, or whether dinner in the oven has reached the proper cooking temperature. Install a bar code reader in your refrigerator, and you could take an inventory and automatically reorder groceries from your local store. You can program your UPP alarm clock so when it goes off in the morning, it would also turn on your coffee pot, turn up the heat, and display your day's appointments on your computer screen.

Sunbeam Corporation and its Thalia Products division have announced a series of future products that will use the UPP protocol, including the HomeHelper Kitchen Console, the HandHelper Personal Digital Assistant, and the TimeHelper Alarm Clock. Each of these products will be designed to control the company's smart products: a coffee maker, electric blanket, smoke detector, mixer, bathroom scale, and blood pressure monitor. If you forgot to put water in the coffee maker, for example, the coffee maker will send a message to one of the controlling devices, such as the TimeHelper Alarm Clock, which will then alert you to the problem.

The Everyday Web

Microsoft, along with hardware manufacturers, is working toward the vision of the Everyday Web. The *Everyday Web* means that Web access and e-mail will be made available inexpensively to everyone in the household, at any time, and from any place.

The Internet in Your Hand

With the Everyday Web, you could take a small, handheld device on a shopping or business trip so you could stay in touch with the family, and wireless devices could provide connectivity from any location. The Palm Pilot personal digital assistant

(PDA), for example, already provides connectivity to the Internet and e-mail. Another such device available today is the Pocket PC, a handheld computer that offers the familiar Windows interface, as shown in Figure 15-1.

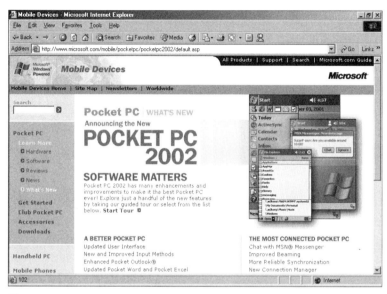

Figure 15-1.

The Pocket PC 2002 Windows interface.

The Pocket PC includes specially designed applications, including the following:

- **Pocket Outlook** for sending and receiving e-mail, scheduling appointments, managing contacts, and organizing tasks

- **Contacts** for storing and finding addresses, telephone numbers, and other personal contact information

- **Tasks** for managing your to-do list

- **Pocket Word** for creating and editing documents

- **Pocket Excel** for creating and editing spreadsheets

- **Pocket Internet Explorer** for browsing the Internet

- **Terminal Services Client** for connecting to a Windows 2000 or Windows XP server

- **File Explorer** for managing files

Pocket PC–compatible devices are manufactured by a number of companies, including Audiovox, Compaq, Intermec, Toshiba, Casio, Hewlett-Packard, and Symbol.

In addition, a growing number of *smart phones* combine a mobile telephone with Internet and e-mail connectivity, and personal information management (PIM) features such as a personal calendar, address book, planner, and notepad.

Microsoft and other companies are now developing smart phones that offer voice and wireless data capabilities in one device, including e-mail and Web-browsing capabilities. Mitsubishi Wireless Communications, for example, will offer the Trium G520 and GT550 browser phones. These telephones provide wireless Internet access and e-mail using Microsoft Mobile Explorer software.

Note

Many pagers are now capable of sending and receiving text e-mail messages.

Other companies also plan to offer a variety of smart-phone products. For example, the Motorola Accompli 009 Personal Interactive Communicator is a telephone that also includes a small color screen and keyboard. Weighing just over 6 ounces, and measuring about 3 inches by 4 inches, the device supports a number of applications, such as word processing, as well as e-mail. The Ericsson Smartphone R380e is shaped like a mobile phone, but it includes a small monochrome touch screen for selecting options and entering PIM information.

Note

Many smart phones support the General Packet Radio Service (GPRS), a service that allows information to be sent and received over the mobile phone network worldwide.

The Latest Internet Devices

The Internet is also becoming more accessible and convenient in the home with products such as the MSN Companion, MSN TV, and Ultimate TV. Linked to the Web through the MSN Internet service, the MSN Companion is a small, inexpensive plug-and-play Internet device, shown in Figure 15-2.

The MSN Companion provides Internet access and e-mail without the user having to worry about configuration, ISPs, operating systems, or other hardware and software issues. Setting up an MSN Companion is as easy as plugging in the power cord and phone line, or connecting the device to a broadband cable or digital subscriber line (DSL) modem or home network.

Figure 15-2.

The MSN Companion.

Because of the MSN Companion's low cost, a family could easily have them located throughout the house—in the kitchen, family room, or den, and in all the bedrooms. You can have up to nine users on an MSN Companion. Each user has private e-mail, an instant messenger buddy list, a chat identity, and a personalized home page. The MSN Companion even automatically checks for e-mail messages and displays a blinking light notifying you that e-mail is waiting.

MSN TV (formerly WebTV) integrates the Internet directly into your television through a dial-up connection with the MSN Internet service. The Classic MSN TV system offers Internet, e-mail, online chatting, and instant messaging. The Plus Receiver model also provides Web picture-in-picture so you can simultaneously watch television and browse the Internet, receive-e-mail, or view TV listings.

Ultimate TV combines broadband Internet access for Web surfing and e-mail with DIRECTV satellite technology. The system allows you to record up to 35 hours of television in digital quality, and you can even record two live shows at the same time.

The future of convenient computing and Internet access, however, might be more like the Tablet PC, shown in Figure 15-3. Using a special pen for direct input, the Tablet PC recognizes handwriting and lets you create and edit documents.

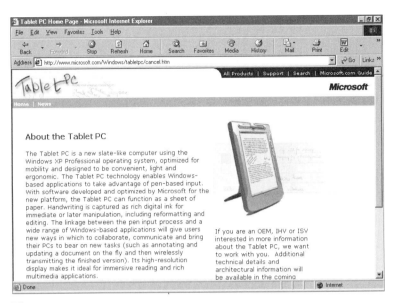

Figure 15-3.
The Tablet PC.

The Tablet PC is actually a full Windows computer, capable of running Windows software, such as Microsoft Office, and of supporting 802.11, Bluetooth, and other wireless standards. Stand it up on a desk, or pack it away in your briefcase, for computing power and Internet communications anywhere.

Some futurists, however, believe that the natural extension of Internet devices such as the Tablet PC, Ultimate TV, and smart phones might be a single device that would serve all your personal communications needs. Today's home has at least six devices that provide communications and entertainment: a telephone, a computer, a television (along with VCR and DVD player), a radio, an stereo, and an alarm system. All these devices might someday converge into a single communications and entertainment machine some futurists generically call a *teledevice*. (Another name is *convergence appliance.*) The teledevice will connect you to the Internet, serve as a video-phone and answering machine, and bring movies, information, and music into every room of your home. It'll be integrated into every major appliance in the home, including a home control and security system, and even your refrigerator and coffee maker. You'll use the same display screen to watch movies, to surf the Internet, check dinner, and to see your friends and relatives as you speak with them.

The teledevice jibes with Microsoft chairman Bill Gates's vision. In a 1997 speech, Gates described a future in which "the boundary between what is a TV and what is a PC will be completely blurred" and "Americans will live a Web lifestyle." If this dream is realized, you'll be able to get your entertainment and communications needs through one device. You'll no longer need a television to watch entertainment programs and movies, a VCR to watch videos, and a computer to run programs, send and receive e-mail, and surf the Internet. One device might serve all these functions.

In a "Web lifestyle," getting information online and communicating through e-mail will become a standard fact of life. Just as most people consider the telephone a basic necessity today, the teledevice might well become a ubiquitous household fixture.

Currency and charge cards might eventually be replaced completely by smart cards that automatically debit your accounts for purchases and identify your personal needs. When you come home, you'll swipe your smart card through the reader on the teledevice to automatically get your e-mail and other messages, update your bank accounts and portfolio, get the latest headline news that matches your interests, and set the temperature for your personal comfort level. You can see examples of personalized news, investment information, and retailing on the Internet. Amazon.com, for example, can track your interests and buying habits and use that information to recommend new books as they are published.

Smart-card technology promises to extend this personalization into many other areas of your life. In fact, some of the technology is already available. Microsoft's Smart Card for Windows provides a smart-card interface for the Windows environment. You can use it, for example, to authorize logon to a PC or to a computer network.

In addition, the smart card might play an important role in providing security and privacy in the future. With computers and communications equipment becoming a major source of information and interaction, the need for personal security is growing. The most obvious use for smart card security is in financial transactions, such as performing credit and debit operations to purchase products and services. Smart card interfaces can be built into home computers, point-of-purchase terminals, and even wireless telephones to acquire authorization and record transactions.

Some experts, however, believe that the concept of the teledevice as described above has its disadvantages. Centralizing a large number of functions into one device is convenient only so long as that device works—if it fails, then you lose all the associated functions, which could spell disaster. An alternative might be to integrate your house's systems with a teledevice, but also have the systems maintain the ability to function on their own. That way, should the teledevice fail, the individual systems would still work.

Universal Connectivity

In Chapter 14, "Networking for Road Warriors," you learned how to connect to your home network and to the Internet when traveling, and about broadband access being made available in hotels, airports, and convention centers. The Wayport service mentioned in Chapter 14, however, is just one example of a broadband service that is available today. Some other companies that provide wireless or wired broadband access from hotels include the following:

- **Ardent Communications** *(http://ardentcomm.com/index3.html)*
- **LodgeNet Entertainment** *(http://lodgenet.com/guests/index.html)*
- **OnCommand** *(http://www.ocv.com)*
- **STSN** *(http://www.stsn.com)*

  Hotels and convention centers offer Internet access in four general ways:

- **Television-based**: A keyboard is connected to a set-top box that interfaces with the television as the monitor, much like the MSN TV service. Users can browse the Internet and send and receive e-mail through a Web-based service.

- **Hotel-provided computers**: Some hotels provide rental computers and printers that have broadband Internet access.

- **Direct broadband wireless**: This type of access is provided by a Wi-Fi network, so users need their own computer with a Wi-Fi-compatible network card.

- **Direct broadband wired**: This type of access is provided by Ethernet jacks in the hotel room, linked to the facility's network and broadband service, so users need their own computer with an Ethernet adaptor.

The ultimate in universal access, however, might be even closer that you think: You might actually be able to wear your computer and access the Internet from virtually anywhere. Research is being conducted into wearable computers and peripheral devices that are sewn directly into clothing or incorporated into eyeglasses or jewelry.

The Massachusetts Institute of Technology (MIT), for example, has a number of projects underway to study wearable computers. The MIT Memory Glasses project, for instance, is investigating the use of eyeglasses as a short-term-memory aid that can also alert the wearer about appointments and other important information. The glasses would be able to record visual activity for short-term storage and playback.

The MIThrill project, on the other hand, is looking at embedding computer technology into clothing, known as body bus technology. Articles of MIThrill clothing would be able to interface with universal serial bus (USB) and other devices. You can find out more about these and other projects in this program by visiting *http://www.media.mit.edu/ wearables*.

All this technology will be possible because of advances in hardware and home wiring. In the future, homebuilders will probably routinely install Ethernet, coaxial cable, or fiberoptic cable in all new houses. The home network you're setting up now is just the beginning. You'll have a jump on the future by planning for the complete wired home today.

The Bottom Line

Creating a home computer network is easy and inexpensive if you follow the guidelines in this book. But a home computer network is just the beginning. Technology is changing the way we interact with each other and interact with machines. It is changing the way we buy goods and services, the way we are entertained and educated, and the way we must prepare for the future.

Glossary

Numbers and Symbols

2-to-1 switch A device that enables you to connect one computer to two printers, or one printer to two computers.

10Base-2 An Ethernet standard for communicating data using thin Ethernet coaxial cable at speeds up to 10 megabits per second (Mbps). Also known as thinnet.

10Base-5 An Ethernet standard for communicating data using thick Ethernet coaxial cable at speeds up to 10 megabits per second (Mbps). Also known as thicknet.

10Base-F An Ethernet standard for communicating data using fiberoptic cable at speeds up to 10 megabits per second (Mbps).

10Base-T An Ethernet standard for communicating data using unshielded twisted-pair cable at speeds up to 10 megabits per second (Mbps).

10 Gigabit Ethernet An Ethernet standard for communicating data at speeds up to 10,000 megabits per second (Mbps).

100Base-T An Ethernet standard for communicating data using twisted-pair cable at speeds up to 100 megabits per second (Mbps). Also known as Fast Ethernet.

802.11 A family of standards for wireless networks: 802.11 up to 2-megabits per second (Mbps) transmission in the 2.4-gigahertz (GHz) band; 802.11a up to 54 Mbps in the 5-GHz band; 802.11b (also called WiFi) up to 11 Mbps in the 2.4-GHz band; and 802.11g above 20 Mbps in the 2.4-GHz band.

A

access point A device for linking wireless computers to an Ethernet network.

acoustic coupler A device in which a telephone handset is placed to connect a computer to the Internet.

active hub An Ethernet network hub that includes built-in error correction and other management features.

ad hoc network A wireless network in which computers communicate directly with each other without a central hub.

adapter address A unique number assigned by the manufacturer to every Ethernet adapter. Also called the Media Access Control (MAC) address.

adapter A connector that enables two devices to work together.

address A unique identification assigned to a network device. The address can be the hardware address of a network device, or the Internet address used by the Transmission Control Protocol/Internet Protocol (TCP/IP) protocol.

AppleShare A networking system used by Apple Computer devices.

AppleTalk A communication standard for AppleShare networks.

B

backing up The process of making a copy of important computer files for safekeeping.

backup job In Microsoft Backup, the description of the files you want to copy.

bandwidth A network's capacity to transmit and receive data.

barrel connector A device that joins two coaxial cables.

bayonet Neill-Concelman *See* BNC connector.

bidirectional A two-way connection, such as a printer cable that allows communications between the computer and printer.

bit A binary digit, either a one or a zero.

bits per second (bps) A measurement of the rate at which data is transferred.

Bluetooth A short-range wireless networking protocol.

BNC connector Short for barrel node connector, British Naval Connector, or bayonet Neill-Concelman; a type of connector used with coaxial cables for the 10Base-2 Ethernet system.

bps *See* bits per second (bps).

bridge A device or software application that connects two local area networks, whether similar or dissimilar, such as an Ethernet network and a wireless network.

British Naval Connector *See* BNC connector.

broadband router A device that connects multiple computers to a high-speed Internet service.

broadband A network that can accommodate multiple and independent carriers on one cable. The term has come to mean high-speed Internet service using cable or DSL modems.

browse master The computer that keeps track of every shared resource on a peer-to-peer network.

browsing the network Displaying the names of computers on the network to locate shared resources.

buffer An area of memory in a computer, printer, or peripheral device that temporarily stores information as it's being transmitted from one device to another. Typically, a buffer accepts computer data at a rate that is too fast for a printer, hard disk, or other device to accommodate.

bus A central circuit that connects multiple devices.

byte Eight binary digits, or bits, that represent a character.

C

cache A high-speed area of memory or space on a disk that stores information for quick retrieval at a later time. Internet browsers use cache to store recently viewed Web pages.

Category 5 (Cat 5) Refers to a measurement system for the quality of network cable. Category 2 (Cat 2) is the minimum for use with alarm systems and telephone lines. Category 3 (Cat 3) and Category 4 (Cat 4) can be used for 10-megabit-per-second (Mbps) computer networks, but Cat 5 or enhanced Category 5 (Cat 5e) is recommended for Ethernet networks. Category 6 (Cat 6) and Category 7 (Cat 7) are designed for high-speed networks that must span long distances.

CD-RW A compact disk that can be recorded on and erased multiple times.

Centronics port A standard interface for connecting printers to a computer. Also known as a parallel port and printer port.

channel A path for transmitting and receiving data.

client A computer that requests services from a network server or network software.

client/server network A network in which a central server stores data and performs operations that are requested by clients.

coaxial cable A type of cable that contains a solid wire core surrounded by insulation, which is surrounded by a braided wire shield.

communications port An interface for sending and receiving data serially between a computer and other device. Also known as a COM port or a serial port.

convergence appliance A device that combines many communications functions, such as Internet access, telephony, television, and other entertainment functions. Also known as a teledevice.

cookie Information given to a Web browser by a Web server, and stored on your disk.

crimper A tool that presses together a connector and wire, making a tight electrical connection.

crossover cable A twisted-pair cable designed to connect two computers directly, rather than through a hub.

crosstalk The unwanted transfer of data between adjacent circuits.

D

demilitarized zone (DMZ)   *See* perimeter network.

device driver   Software that enables a device to interact with an operating system.

device plug and play   The capability of the computer operating system to sense that a peripheral has been attached and to configure it automatically.

DHCP   *See* Dynamic Host Configuration Protocol (DHCP).

DHCP server   The device that assigns a dynamic Internet Protocol (IP) address to other devices on a network.

digital subscriber line (DSL)   A high-speed communications technology using regular telephone lines.

direct cable connection   The process of networking two computers through a single cable connected between them.

direct sequence spread spectrum (DSSS)   A method of wireless communications in which the signal is encoded with extra redundant bits of information that the receiving device can decode to help correct errors.

directory server   In Microsoft NetMeeting, a computer server that lists people you can call and helps NetMeeting users find each other over the Internet.

DMZ   *See* perimeter network.

DNS   *See* Domain Name System (DNS).

Domain Name System (DNS)   A database of Web and Internet Protocol (IP) addresses for the Internet.

DSL   *See* digital subscriber line (DSL).

DSSS   *See* direct sequence spread spectrum (DSSS).

dynamic addressing   The process of assigning a temporary network address to a device as it's needed.

Dynamic Host Configuration Protocol (DHCP)   The process by which a device assigns a dynamic IP address to other devices on a network.

E

Ethernet address   *See* Media Access Control (MAC) address.

Ethernet   A standard for transmitting and receiving information over a network using coaxial cable or twisted-pair wires.

F

FD   *See* frequency-division multiplexing (FDM).

FHSS   *See* frequency-hopping spread spectrum (FHSS).

fiberoptic cable   Network cable that uses a bundle of glass threads to carry data.

File Transfer Protocol (FTP)   The protocol used on the Internet for sending and receiving files.

firewall   A software program or hardware device that prevents unauthorized users from accessing certain ports or files on a computer or network.

FireWire   A name trademarked by Apple Computer to refer to the IEEE 1394 high-performance serial bus.

firmware   Software that determines how a device operates and whose routines are recorded in a device's read-only memory.

frequency-division multiplexing (FDM)   The technique of using different frequencies to carry multiple streams of information over a single telephone cable.

frequency-hopping spread spectrum (FHSS)   A method of wireless communications in which the system switches, or hops, between several different frequencies for a specific amount of time.

FTP   *See* File Transfer Protocol (FTP).

full access   Granting a network user the permission to both read and write data to a shared folder on your computer.

G

gateway   A device that connects two or more networks.

H

host   A computer that provides services to another computer.

HTTP   *See* Hypertext Transfer Protocol (HTTP).

hub   A common connection point for network devices.

Hypertext Transfer Protocol (HTTP)   The protocol used by the World Wide Web to determine how data is formatted and transmitted.

I

ICS   *See* Internet Connection Sharing (ICS).

IEEE 1284–compliant   A printer cable that meets industry quality standards for bidirectional communications.

IMAP   *See* Internet Message Access Protocol (IMAP).

Industry Standard Architecture (ISA)   An early computer bus system for connecting modems, video displays, and other devices to the computer.

infrared port   A device that allows the communications of data by infrared light waves.

infrastructure   A wireless network in which computers communicate through a central wireless access point.

input/output (I/O) address   The location in your computer's memory in which the signals from the device are stored. No two devices can have the same I/O address or their signals will conflict.

intelligent hub   A hub that allows a network administrator to monitor traffic and configure each port independently.

Internet   A collection of computers, networks, and gateways connected through the Transmission Control Protocol/Internet Protocol (TCP/IP) protocol.

Internet Connection Sharing (ICS)   The technique of allowing multiple computers to share one computer's Internet connection.

Internet Message Access Protocol (IMAP)   An e-mail system in which messages are stored on the e-mail server rather than downloaded to a client computer.

Internet Protocol (IP)   A standard for transmitting data on a network or over the Internet in packets of information.

Internet Protocol (IP) address   The Internet address assigned to a network device using the Transmission Control Protocol/Internet Protocol (TCP/IP) protocol. Every device connected to the Internet or to a network must have a unique numeric IP address. The domain name server translates between a device's IP address (such as 204.22.55.32) and its domain name (as in www.microsoft.com).

Internet service provider (ISP)   A company that provides Internet access.

interoperability   The capability of devices from different vendors to work together.

interrupt request (IRQ)   A signal to a computer from a hardware device indicating that it's requesting some service from the computer. Each request is carried along a circuit called an IRQ line.

intranet   A collection of computers, networks, and gateways within an organization that use the Transmission Control Protocol/Internet Protocol (TCP/IP) protocol and World Wide Web technology for sharing information.

I/O address   *See* input/output (I/O) address.

IP   *See* Internet Protocol (IP).

IP address   *See* Internet Protocol (IP) address.

IRQ   *See* interrupt request (IRQ).

ISA   *See* Industry Standard Architecture (ISA).

ISP   *See* Internet service provider (ISP).

J

jumper   A device that lets you select which electrical circuit should be closed. Jumpers are commonly used to configure Industry Standard Architecture (ISA) cards.

K

KB   *See* kilobyte (KB).

Kbps   *See* kilobits per second (Kbps).

kilobits per second (Kbps)   A measurement of the rate at which data is transferred, in this case 1024 bits per second.

kilobyte (KB)   A unit of measure for computer data in which 1 kilobyte equals 1024 bytes.

L

LAN   *See* Local area network (LAN).

local area network (LAN)   A computer network used within a relatively small area, such as in a home, office, or building, that enables users to share information and printers.

LocalTalk   An Apple computer network system using shielded twisted-pair cables.

M

MAC address   *See* Media Access Control (MAC) address.

mandatory profile   A user's profile created by the network administrator that the user can't change.

mapping   The process of creating a logical connection between two devices.

MB   *See* megabyte (MB).

Mbps   *See* megabits per second (Mbps).

Media Access Control (MAC) address   A unique numeric address assigned to every network device.

megabits per second (Mbps)   A measurement of the rate at which data is transferred, in this case, 1,048,576 bits per second

megabyte (MB)   A unit of measure for computer data in which 1 megabyte equals 1,048,576 bytes.

modem   A device that converts digital computer data for transmission and reception across regular telephone lines. The name is derived from the process of modulation (converting digital to analog for transmission) and demodulation (converting analog back to digital data when it's received).

modem server   A device that converts an external modem into a LAN modem that can be shared by all network users.

mount   The process of making available a disk drive located in another computer.

MS-DOS   Developed by Microsoft, a disk operating system that preceded Windows and which does not use a graphical interface.

N

NAT   *See* network address translation (NAT).

NetBEUI   *See* NetBIOS Enhanced User Interface (NetBEUI).

NetBIOS Enhanced User Interface (NetBEUI)   A simple network protocol for small networks.

network adapter   A device that connects a computer to the network.

network address translation (NAT)   The process by which a router shares a single IP address with computers on a network.

network client   The software that determines how users gain access to the network.

network driver   The software that allows Windows to access your network interface hardware.

network interface card (NIC)   A circuit board inserted into a computer that lets it connect to a network.

network service   A network setting that determines which computer resources you will allow others to share.

networking   The process of linking computers to share resources.

NIC   *See* network interface card (NIC).

NT file system (NTFS)   An advanced file system used with Microsoft Windows NT, Windows 2000, and Windows XP operating systems.

NTFS   *See* NT file system (NTFS).

O

owner   The person running a program that is shared by others in NetMeeting.

P

parallel port   The computer connection used for most printers.

passive hub   A network hub that provides no monitoring, control, or error-correction capabilities.

passphrase   A series of alphanumeric characters used for encrypting a wireless transmission.

patch cable   A length of cable with connectors on each end.

path   The specification of the disk drive and directories and folders in which a file is located.

PCI   *See* Peripheral Component Interconnect (PCI).

PCMCIA   *See* Personal Computer Memory Card International Association (PCMCIA).

peer   A computer on the network having the same rights and privileges as all other computers.

peer-to-peer network   A network in which data sharing occurs directly between computers, with no central server to control communications and other services.

perimeter network   A security network at the boundary between a local area network (LAN) and the Internet. Also called a demilitarized zone (DMZ).

Peripheral Component Interconnect (PCI)
A bus system for connecting modems, video displays, and other devices to the computer.

Personal Computer Memory Card International Association (PCMCIA)   An organization that developed the standard for credit card–sized devices that plug into laptop computers, called PCMCIA cards, or just PC cards.

plug and play   The capability of the computer operating system to sense when a peripheral has been attached.

plug-and-play compatible   Devices that can be recognized by the operating system.

Point-to-Point Protocol (PPP)   The protocol used to make a Transmission Control Protocol/Internet Protocol (TCP/IP) connection over regular telephone lines.

Point-to-Point Protocol Over Ethernet (PPPoE)
The protocol that uses Point-to-Point Protocol (PPP) over a digital subscriber line (DSL) or cable modem.

POP   *See* Post Office Protocol (POP).

port   A hardware device that provides a channel of communication between the computer and a peripheral device.

Post Office Protocol (POP)   An e-mail system in which messages are downloaded from the server to the user's computer.

PPP   *See* Point-to-Point Protocol (PPP).

PPPoE   *See* Point-to-Point Protocol Over Ethernet (PPPoE).

print server   A device or software that connects a printer directly to a network, enabling all network computers to access the printer.

profile   A record of a user's settings.

protocol   A formal set of rules that determine how network devices can communicate. A protocol specifies the format of data, the timing, and the method by which transmissions are checked for errors.

proxy server   A hardware device or software used to forward Internet data between devices and the Internet, also used to share a single Internet account among multiple users.

punchdown tool   A special tool that presses wires into place to make a firm electrical connection.

R

read-only rights   Rights that grant a network user the permission only to read the data in a shared folder, not to modify it.

Registered Jack-45 (RJ-45)   An eight-wire connector used for Ethernet networks.

remote computer   A computer on the network other than the one you're using.

repeater   A device that regenerates a network signal to extend the distance between networked computers.

residential gateway   A device that allows multiple computers in a home network to access the same Internet connection.

restore   The process of retrieving a backup copy of a file.

RJ-45   *See* Registered Jack-45 (RJ-45).

roaming profile   The creation of a user's profile that allows a user to log on to the computer remotely and download the profile information from the server to the remote computer.

router   A hardware device that connects two or more networks, used to share a single Internet account among multiple users.

S

secure network   A network in which others are prevented from accessing information during transmission.

server   A network computer that performs central services to a network, responding to requests for services by client computers.

Service Set Identifier (SSID)   The name assigned to a wireless network, and used to designate which network accepts wireless transmissions.

shared resources   The collection of files, folders, disks, printers, and peripheral devices that are shared among network users. Also called just a *share*.

share name   The name assigned to a shared resource, such as a folder, disk, or printer.

sharing   Allowing a computer, printer, or other device to be used by more than one person.

shareware   Software that is distributed on an honor system, in which users can freely obtain and use a program, but are requested to pay a fee for its continued use.

shielded twisted pair (STP)   Network cable that has a layer of woven copper and foil around the wires within the plastic sheath to shield them from extraneous electrical signals.

Simple Mail Transfer Protocol (SMTP)   A Transmission Control Protocol/Internet Protocol (TCP/IP) protocol for sending e-mail messages.

SMTP   Simple Mail Transfer Protocol (SMTP).

spread spectrum   A wireless communications technology that breaks the wireless signal into small pieces.

SSID   *See* Service Set Identifier (SSID).

stackable hub   A hub that uses a special high-speed bus to carry network signals from one hub to another.

static addressing   The process of assigning a fixed network address to a computer or other device.

STP   *See* shielded twisted pair (STP).

stripper   A tool for removing the insulation from wires.

subnet mask   A network address that determines to what Internet Protocol (IP) address a subnet belongs.

subnet   A portion of a network that shares a common address component.

surge protector   A device that prevents fluctuations in electricity from damaging electronic equipment.

suspend state   A condition in which information about all open programs are saved on the hard disk before a computer turns off automatically.

switch   A common connection point for network devices that can select the proper path for data between devices.

switching hub   A hublike device that forwards packets of information between computers.

T

TCP/IP   *See* Transmission Control Protocol/Internet Protocol (TCP/IP).

thick Ethernet coaxial cable   Round coaxial RG-8 cable with a solid insulated wire at its core and a layer of braided metal under its external jacket. Its name derives from the fact that it's thicker than thin Ethernet coaxial cable. Also called 10Base-5 or thicknet.

thin Ethernet coaxial cable   Round coaxial cable with a solid insulated wire at its core and a layer of braided metal under its external sheath, but thinner than standard coaxial cable used for televisions. Also known as 10Base-2 or thinnet.

transceiver   A device that both transmits and receives signals.

transformer   A device that transfers electric current from one circuit or set of circuits to another.

Transmission Control Protocol/Internet Protocol (TCP/IP) A suite of protocols for communicating data.

Trojan horse A destructive computer program that masquerades as a harmless application.

twisted pair Two insulated wires twisted around each other, typically with four pairs of wires grouped together in a single cable. Also known as 10Base-T cable.

U

UNC *See* Universal Naming Convention (UNC).

Uniform Resource Locator (URL) The address of a document on the Internet. A URL contains two parts: the protocol to use to access the document, such as Hypertext Transfer Protocol (HTTP) or File Transfer Protocol (FTP) and the Internet Protocol (IP) address or domain name of the computer on which the document is stored.

Universal Naming Convention (UNC) The format for designating a location on a local area network (LAN).

universal serial bus (USB) A 12-megabit-per-second (Mbps) external bus standard.

unshielded twisted pair (UTP) A network cable that contains four pairs of loosely intertwined wire.

uplink port A special port on a hub or switch that is designed for connection directly to another hub or switch.

URL *See* Uniform Resource Locator (URL).

USB *See* Universal serial bus (USB).

USB hub A device that provides multiple USB connections.

user account The term applied to user profiles in Microsoft Windows XP.

UTP *See* unshielded twisted pair (UTP).

V

virtual private network (VPN) A secure network connection over the Internet between computers in two locations.

VPN *See* virtual private network (VPN).

W

WAN *See* wide area network (WAN).

WEP *See* Wired Equivalent Privacy (WEP).

WEP key *See* Wired Equivalent Privacy (WEP) key.

whiteboard A window on the screen in which users can write and draw.

wide area network (WAN) Two or more connected LANs in separate locations.

Wi-Fi *See* 802.11.

Wired Equivalent Privacy (WEP) A protocol used for wireless networks to provide the same level of security as that of a wired LAN.

Wired Equivalent Privacy (WEP) key A password used to encrypt and decrypt data transmitted over a wireless network.

Wireless Fidelity (Wi-Fi) *See* 802.11.

wireless LAN (WLAN) A local area network (LAN) in which data is transmitted through a radio connection.

wiring closet A central location in which all network, communications, and video cables converge.

wizard A program that performs a complex operation through a series of easy-to-use dialog boxes.

WLAN *See* Wireless LAN (WLAN).

workgroup Two or more individual computers on a network that share files, printers, and other resources.

workstation An individual computer connected to a network.

World Wide Web (WWW) A collection of files interconnected by a system of hypertext documents stored on multiple servers and accessed by a Web browser.

WWW *See* World Wide Web (WWW).

X

xDSL A term that refers collectively to all variations of digital subscriber line (DSL) technologies.

Index

Alan Neibauer

Alan Neibauer has written several best-selling computer books, including *Running Microsoft Outlook 2000* and *Small Business Solutions for Networking*. With a master's degree from the Wharton School, he has helped organizations of all sizes network their business information systems. Neibauer also served as chairperson of an innovative computer MIS program at the college level.

The manuscript for this book was prepared and galleyed using Microsoft Word 2000. Pages were composed by nSight, Inc. (nSightWorks.com) using Adobe PageMaker 6.52 for Windows, with text in AGaramond and display type in Garamond Condensed. Composed pages were delivered to the printer as electronic prepress files.

Cover Designer/Art Director: Patricia Bradbury

Cover Illustrator: Todd Daman Design

Interior Graphic Designer: James D. Kramer

Illustrator: Joel Panchot

Project Manager: Susan H. McClung

Copy Editor: Chrisa Hotchkiss

Technical Editors: Don Lesser, Margaret Lampron, Janet Lowry

Principal Compositor: Mary Beth McDaniel, Joanna Zito

Principal Proofreader: Jan Cocker, Rebecca Merz

Indexer: Jack Lewis

Work smarter—
conquer your
software *from the inside out!*

Hey, you know your way around a desktop. Now dig into Office XP applications and the Windows XP operating system and *really* put your PC to work! These supremely organized software reference titles pack hundreds of timesaving solutions, troubleshooting tips and tricks, and handy workarounds in a concise, fast-answer format. They're all muscle and no fluff. All this comprehensive information goes deep into the nooks and crannies of each Office application and Windows XP feature. And every *Inside Out* includes a CD-ROM full of handy tools and utilities, sample files, links to related sites, and other help. Discover the best and fastest ways to perform everyday tasks, and challenge yourself to new levels of software mastery!

MICROSOFT WINDOWS® XP INSIDE OUT
ISBN 0-7356-1382-6

MICROSOFT® OFFICE XP INSIDE OUT
ISBN 0-7356-1277-3

MICROSOFT WORD VERSION 2002 INSIDE OUT
ISBN 0-7356-1278-1

MICROSOFT EXCEL VERSION 2002 INSIDE OUT
ISBN 0-7356-1281-1

MICROSOFT OUTLOOK® VERSION 2002 INSIDE OUT
ISBN 0-7356-1282-X

MICROSOFT ACCESS VERSION 2002 INSIDE OUT
ISBN 0-7356-1283-8

MICROSOFT FRONTPAGE® VERSION 2002 INSIDE OUT
ISBN 0-7356-1284-6

MICROSOFT VISIO® VERSION 2002 INSIDE OUT
ISBN 0-7356-1285-4

Microsoft Press® products are available worldwide wherever quality computer books are sold. For more information, contact your book or computer retailer, software reseller, or local Microsoft® Sales Office, or visit our Web site at microsoft.com/mspress. To locate your nearest source for Microsoft Press products, or to order directly, call 1-800-MSPRESS in the United States (in Canada, call 1-800-268-2222).

Prices and availability dates are subject to change.

Microsoft

microsoft.com/mspress

Target your problem and
fix it yourself—
fast!

When you're stuck with a computer problem, you need answers right now. *Troubleshooting* books can help. They'll guide you to the source of the problem and show you how to solve it right away. Get ready solutions with clear, step-by-step instructions. Go to quick-access charts with *Top 20 Problems* and *Prevention Tips*. Find even more solutions with *Quick Fixes* and handy *Tips.* Walk through the remedy with plenty of screen shots. Find what you need with the extensive, easy-reference index. Get the answers you need to get back to business fast with *Troubleshooting* books.

Troubleshooting Microsoft® Office XP
ISBN 0-7356-1491-1

Troubleshooting Microsoft® Access Databases
(Covers Access 97 and Access 2000)
ISBN 0-7356-1160-2

Troubleshooting Microsoft® Access 2002
ISBN 0-7356-1488-1

Troubleshooting Microsoft Excel Spreadsheets
(Covers Excel 97 and Excel 2000)
ISBN 0-7356-1161-0

Troubleshooting Microsoft Excel 2002
ISBN 0-7356-1493-8

Troubleshooting Microsoft® Outlook®
(Covers Microsoft Outlook 2000 and Outlook Express)
ISBN 0-7356-1162-9

Troubleshooting Microsoft Outlook 2002
(Covers Microsoft Outlook 2002 and Outlook Express)
ISBN 0-7356-1487-3

Troubleshooting Your Web Page
(Covers Microsoft FrontPage® 2000)
ISBN 0-7356-1164-5

Troubleshooting Microsoft FrontPage 2002
ISBN 0-7356-1489-X

Troubleshooting Microsoft Windows®
(Covers Windows Me, Windows 98, and Windows 95)
ISBN 0-7356-1166-1

Troubleshooting Microsoft Windows 200 Professional
ISBN 0-7356-1165-3

Troubleshooting Microsoft Windows XP
ISBN 0-7356-1492-X

Troubleshooting Your PC
ISBN 0-7356-1163-7

Microsoft Press® products are available worldwide wherever quality computer books are sold. For more information, contact your book or computer retailer, software reseller, or local Microsoft Sales Office, or visit our Web site at microsoft.com/mspress. To locate your nearest source for Microsoft Press products, or to order directly, call 1-800-MSPRESS in the U.S. (in Canada, call 1-800-268-2222).

Prices and availability dates are subject to change.

Microsoft
microsoft.com/mspress

Tune in and turn on to the *ultimate digital media experience!*

U.S.A. $29.99
Canada $43.99
ISBN: 0-7356-1455-5

Listen to Internet radio. Watch breaking news over broadband. Build your own music and video playlists. With the MICROSOFT® WINDOWS MEDIA® PLAYER FOR WINDOWS® XP HANDBOOK, you control the air-waves! Personalize the way you see, hear, and experience digital media with this all-in-one kit of tools and how-tos from the Microsoft Windows Media team. You get everything you need to bring cutting-edge music and video everywhere your PC, laptop, or portable device goes!

Microsoft Press® products are available worldwide wherever quality computer books are sold. For more information, contact your book or computer retailer, software reseller, or local Microsoft® Sales Office, or visit our Web site at microsoft.com/mspress. To locate your nearest source for Microsoft Press products, or to order directly, call 1-800-MSPRESS in the United States (in Canada, call 1-800-268-2222).

Prices and availability dates are subject to change.

microsoft.com/mspress

Get a **Free**
e-mail newsletter, updates,
special offers, links to related books,
and more when you

register on line!

Register your Microsoft Press® title on our Web site and you'll get
a FREE subscription to our e-mail newsletter, *Microsoft Press
Book Connections.* You'll find out about newly released and upcoming
books and learning tools, online events, software downloads, special
offers and coupons for Microsoft Press customers, and information
about major Microsoft® product releases. You can also read useful
additional information about all the titles we publish, such as detailed book descriptions, tables of contents and indexes, sample
chapters, links to related books and book series, author biographies,
and reviews by other customers.

Registration is easy. Just visit this Web page and fill in your information:

http://www.microsoft.com/mspress/register

Microsoft

Proof of Purchase

Use this page as proof of purchase if participating in a promotion or rebate offer on
this title. Proof of purchase must be used in conjunction with other proof(s) of
payment such as your dated sales receipt—see offer details.

This Wired Home: The Microsoft® Guide to Home Networking, Third Edition

0-7356-1494-6

CUSTOMER NAME

Microsoft Press, PO Box 97017, Redmond, WA 98073-9830